Pestilence and Persistence

Pestilence and Persistence

Yosemite Indian Demography and Culture in Colonial California

Kathleen L. Hull

UNIVERSITY OF CALIFORNIA PRESS
Berkeley   •   Los Angeles   •   London

University of California Press, one of the
most distinguished university presses in the
United States, enriches lives around the world
by advancing scholarship in the humanities,
social sciences, and natural sciences. Its activities
are supported by the UC Press Foundation and
by philanthropic contributions from individuals
and institutions. For more information, visit
www.ucpress.edu.

University of California Press
Berkeley and Los Angeles, California

University of California Press, Ltd.
London, England

© 2009 by The Regents of the University of
California

Library of Congress Cataloging-in-Publication Data

Hull, Kathleen L. (Kathleen Louann), 1959–.
    Pestilence and persistence : Yosemite Indian
demography and culture in colonial California /
Kathleen L. Hull.
        p.   cm.
    Includes bibliographical references and index.
    ISBN 978-0-520-25847-1 (cloth : alk. paper)
    1. Miwok Indians—Colonization.   2. Miwok
Indians—Diseases.   3. Miwok Indians— History.
4. Indians of North America—First contact with
Europeans—California—Yosemite Valley.
5. Epidemics— California—Yosemite Valley—
History.   6. Communicable diseases—California—
Yosemite Valley—History.   7. Indians of North
America—History—Colonial period, ca. 1600–
1775.   8. United States—History—Colonial
period, ca. 1600– 1775.   9. Yosemite Valley
(Calif.)—History.   10. Yosemite Valley (Calif.)—
Antiquities.   I. Title.

E99.M69H85 2009

304.6'2089974133—dc22   2009011533

Manufactured in the United States of America

18 17 16 15 14 13 12 11 10 09
10 9 8 7 6 5 4 3 2 1

This book is printed on Cascades Enviro 100, a
100% postconsumer waste, recycled, de-inked fiber.
FSC recycled certified and processed chlorine free. It
is acid free, Ecologo certified, and manufactured by
BioGas energy.

*To the memory of those who did not survive
and the descendants of those who did.*

Contents

List of Illustrations	ix
List of Tables	xi
Acknowledgments	xiii
1. Disentangling Colonial Encounters	1
2. Multiple Perspectives on a Critical Time	31
3. Colonial Encounters in Yosemite Valley	53
4. The People of Awahnee	79
5. Peopling the Past	115
6. A Tradition of Survival: Archaeological Evidence for Awahnichi Depopulation	135
7. Daily Practices in a Changing World	156
8. Hol'-low and He-le'-jah: Cultural Continuity and Change	181
9. The Colonial Experience: Epidemic Disease and Cultural Outcomes Elsewhere in North America	220
10. Culture, History, and Colonialism	283
Appendix: Population Proxy Data	301
Notes	309
References	321
Index	353

Illustrations

FIGURES

1. View of Yosemite Valley from Inspiration Point, circa 1859   56
2. View of a deserted Yosemite Indian village, circa 1873   75
3. Typical projectile points of the Yosemite region   85
4. Conical bark house in Yosemite Valley, circa 1880s   101
5. Bedrock mortars   108
6. Scatterplot and nonlinear regression of debitage and subsite frequency data   132
7. Diachronic trends in debitage and calibrated subsite frequency data as a percentage of maximum population   137
8. Diachronic trends in population growth rates per 50-year increment based on the debitage population proxy   138
9. Relationship between total fertility rate (TFR) and life expectancy at birth (e_0) in historical and modern nonindustrial populations, including Yosemite Indians   145
10. Comparison of flaked stone tool assemblages from the hearth areas at Hol'-low and He-le'-jah   194
11. Serrate Desert Side-Notched projectile points from He-le'-jah   202
12. Subsite temporal components based on obsidian hydration dates   211
13. Comparison of fire-scar frequency and intermediate-age conifer-stand start dates   215

MAPS

1. Russian and Spanish colonial interests in California circa 1815 in relation to Yosemite Valley — 17
2. Cultural and natural locales of significance to Mariposa Battalion activities (1851–1852) in the Yosemite region — 37
3. Native Californian ethnolinguistic areas — 66
4. Location of obsidian quarry sources and primary trans-Sierra trade routes of the Yosemite region — 88
5. Isopleth maps of faunal remains, beads, edge-modified flake tools, and projectile points at Hol'-low — 195
6. Isopleth maps of faunal remains, beads, edge-modified flake tools, and projectile points at He-le'-jah — 196
7. Ten case-study areas of interior native peoples with possible precontact infiltration of Old World fatal disease — 223
8. Iroquoian case-study area — 225
9. Mid-Atlantic Piedmont case-study area — 232
10. Upper Creek, Choctaw, and Natchez case-study areas — 240
11. Caddoan case-study area — 255
12. Eastern Prairies case-study area — 263
13. Middle Missouri case-study area — 267
14. Southwest case-study area — 276

Tables

1. Chronological sequence for the Yosemite region — 84
2. Frequency of flaked stone tool types at Hol'-low and He-le'-jah — 184
3. Proportional representation of debitage by technological type and reduction stage at Hol'-low and He-le'-jah — 185
4. Frequency of use-wear on edge-modified flake (EMF) tools at Hol'-low and He-le'-jah — 187
5. Types of faunal remains recovered at Hol'-low and He-le'-jah — 190
6. Proportional representation of obsidian source materials in debitage samples from Hol'-low and He-le'-jah — 205
A-1. Proxy population data — 302

Acknowledgments

I have had the great good fortune to travel, live, and work in the Yosemite region for more than half my life. The well-known natural landscape and more isolated mountain retreats are incomparable, and the opportunity to explore the cultural dimensions of Yosemite spanning thousands of years provides boundless inspiration. This book began with my dissertation research at the University of California, Berkeley—a fortuitous intersection of interests and intellect both at Berkeley and in the years leading up to my time there. I am especially indebted to Kent Lightfoot, M. Steven Shackley, Eugene Hammel, and Frank Bayham for their support and guidance, and this research also benefited from conversations with Patrick Kirch during my graduate studies.

Financial support for my dissertation work was provided by the Lowie/Olsen Fund of the Department of Anthropology at UC Berkeley, a Stahl Grant of the UC Berkeley Archaeological Research Facility, a UC Berkeley Vice Chancellor for Research Fund Grant, and a grant from the James A. Bennyhoff Memorial Fund of the Society for California Archaeology. This latter grant also provided the obsidian studies services of Richard Hughes and Tom Origer, and additional analyses were undertaken by Eric Wohlgemuth of Far Western Anthropological Research Group, Christopher O'Brien and Jason Wiersema of California State University, Chico, and Margaret Newman of the University of Calgary. Likewise, equipment support was provided by Elena Nilsson and Michael S. Kelly of URS Corporation (formerly Dames & Moore Inc.). Expansion of this work for the current book was made possible by the generous support of a Richard Carley Hunt Fellowship from the Wenner-Gren Foundation. Donn Grenda and Christopher Doolittle supported my leave of absence from Statistical Research Inc. to undertake the work under the fellowship.

The Yosemite research was undertaken in consultation with, and with the permission of, the American Indian Council of Mariposa County Inc. (AICMC) and the National Park Service (NPS). The collaboration with both the AICMC and NPS was fundamental to the success of this project. I am particularly indebted Laura Kirn, Roger Kelly, Greg Greenway, Dave Forgang, Barbara Beroza, Craig Bates, Jim Snyder, Sonny Montague, Scott Jackson, and Linn Gassaway of the NPS, as well as Jay Johnson, Bill Leonard, Dawn Briese, and Chris Brochini of the AICMC. These individuals shared their insights on various aspects of Yosemite research over many years. As the scope of this book grew beyond Yosemite, various other scholars also generously shared their work with me, including William Green, Kurt Jordan, and Ann Ramenofsky.

Kathleen Pierson and Michael K. Lerch both read and commented on an earlier draft of the entire book manuscript, displaying dedication and commitment one rarely expects even from the best of friends. The manuscript also benefited substantially from comments of two anonymous reviewers acting on behalf of the University of California Press. At the University of California Press, Blake Edgar was a calm and consistent guide throughout the entire process, as was his assistant Matthew Winfield. Suzanne Knott and Julie Van Pelt handled the copyediting, and their efforts were much appreciated. All maps and several figures were prepared for publication by Kat and Landis Bennett of 360Geographics. Assistance with use of historical images was provided by Susan Snyder of the Bancroft Library, University of California, Berkeley, and Tammy Carter of the Center for Creative Photography, University of Arizona.

In this endeavor, as in all aspects of my life, I have enjoyed the support of family, colleagues, and friends. My parents introduced me to Yosemite at a very early age, and over the past thirty years, I have also explored much of the Yosemite backcountry with my brother. He has patiently endured my obsession with obsidian flakes found on remote trails during our trips. In addition to the colleagues and friends noted above, I have enjoyed several remarkable friendships during this process and beyond, including the support of John Douglass, Mark Hale, Jill Onken, and Barb Voss. I hope I have returned, and will continue to return, the favor to them and to all whom I have the good fortune to know.

CHAPTER 1

Disentangling Colonial Encounters

Survival is a simple concept and a complex act. Day-to-day decisions that affect such endurance draw on the past through experience and look to the future for vindication. But they are executed in a present often fraught with fear and uncertainty. Our lives are dominated by the iterative performance of tasks that provide for our nourishment and protect us from multiple threats to health and happiness. This daily demonstration of purpose and resolve addresses both the mundane and the extraordinary. And in the latter case, the effort to survive requires not only recognizing new enemies but also finding the means to withstand their varied assaults. Some adversaries are overt and make no attempt to hide their intent to control the resources, minds, and bodies of others by coercion or force. Whether they invade in large numbers or small, their will to prevail is fostered by a belief in their right to proceed and is empowered by technology equal to or better than that which they face. Other enemies are more insidious, creeping unseen into communities that awake to the smell of death and the trauma of loss. Such subtle destruction is wrought not at the hands of men with weapons but, rather, by microscopic biological warriors that invade human tissues and organs. In the wake of devastation, these two aggressive forces test both the fortitude of those assaulted and their commitment to their way of life. Survivors are sometimes stronger and often wiser for enduring the experience, but a high price is paid for such wisdom. And the value of the lesson is fully realized only if the knowledge is incorporated into the practices of daily life and if the experience is passed on to future generations through text, story, song, and tradition.

Yosemite Indian history resounds with such experience, and their story of survival provides a lesson to us all. Like other native people throughout North America, the Yosemite Indians faced aggression on both of these fronts in colonial encounters with European people in the late eighteenth and early nineteenth centuries. The first adversary was fatal disease that was inadvertently introduced from a distant colonial outpost. The second was physical incursion into their traditional territory in the central Sierra Nevada of California by men determined to usurp their ancestral claim to the land and its resources. Yosemite Indian population was severely reduced—and their resolve was repeatedly tested—by both of these foes. But they survived these assaults and maintained their traditional ways, as revealed in native oral history, written historical accounts, and archaeological evidence of past lives and people.

Their particular story—encompassing the dual forces of disease and violence—is a microcosm of the process of European colonialism in the Americas, Australia, and the Pacific Islands in the four centuries following Columbus's landfall in the Caribbean in 1492. Colonialism, in this sense, extends well beyond a simple reference to colonies linked to a distant homeland or to the practices and characteristics of colonists in such settings (Gosden 2004). Rather, it both embraces and symbolizes a systematic global process that refers especially to the spread of European empires, economies, culture, values, diseases, and material goods since the late fifteenth century. *Colonialism* is a politically charged term, as well as a social process that left a devastating legacy for indigenous people around the world. One need only undertake a cursory review of history to realize that the outcome of colonialism in other places and times was often quite different than that of Yosemite Indians. Many other indigenous peoples did not endure in the face of enemies intent on their disenfranchisement or destruction. Either they did not survive as communities, or they lost their connection to their land and traditions in the wake of one or more colonial assaults. In light of these various histories, we are left to ponder why outcomes were so different when the colonial assaults appear much the same. We are challenged to disentangle the dual assaults of colonialism and understand each in much greater detail to find the answers we seek. And given the relevance of this colonial heritage to past peoples and to modern life, research regarding the role that introduced infectious diseases played in both the process and outcome of colonialism for people such as the Yosemite Indians takes on special significance.

Scholarly deliberation on the biological assault of colonialism has focused on three issues: the timing, the magnitude, and the cultural consequences of fatal epidemics. With respect to timing, cultural anthropologists, anthropological archaeologists, historians, and demographers continue to debate whether introduced infectious diseases spread throughout the Americas relatively quickly after the Columbian landfall and preceded face-to-face encounters between colonists and indigenous people or whether the process unfolded later and much more slowly, encompassing multiple direct introductions with more geographically limited impact in any one case. For early pandemic spread, introduced Old World diseases would have been transmitted unwittingly by native intermediaries through a sequence of contacts such as existing trade relationships or flight in the wake of disease outbreaks. Assessment of the magnitude of resulting mortality has drawn on evidence from these disciplines as well as the contributions of epidemiologists. These latter researchers have addressed not only the mechanisms, parameters, and possibilities for the spread of various pathogens in diverse physical and cultural settings, but they have also estimated the potential severity of population loss due to various contagions. Although these studies suggest potentially significant depopulation with exposure to a particular fatal pathogen, such theoretical possibilities must still be assessed with real-world data for specific indigenous groups to determine the magnitude of depopulation in each case. In addition, only oral history and archaeology can provide specific data about demographic consequences if introduced disease preceded direct encounters with colonists and reveal if populations rebounded relatively quickly after this assault. Since cultural consequences are intimately linked to both timing and magnitude of population decline, the causal relationship between demographic collapse and cultural change is sometimes tenuous and contentious as well. In this case, anthropologists, archaeologists, indigenous scholars, and historians have all brought their particular knowledge to bear in an effort to determine cultural outcomes for various native groups, including consequences for sociopolitical systems, rules of kinship and affinity, marriage practices, household organization of labor, and settlement patterns.

Given the debate and uncertainly on key issues of timing, magnitude, and cultural consequences of depopulation, the Yosemite Indian story stands as an important example of native experience in the face of colonial-era assaults. While their traditional organization as a small-scale, nonagricultural, and residentially mobile population was far from unique, these characteristics set them apart from nearly all other native groups that have been subject to archaeological assessment of colonial-era depopulation in North America. Thus, the persistence of Yosemite Indians informs our understanding of both native history and culture in North American colonial encounters. Their experience and actions expand our view and thereby help to clarify and define the process of European colonialism itself, as models of colonialism variously ascribe a central role to introduced disease or stress intentionality, colonial power, and native resistance. Preserved in words and objects, the Yosemite Indian story encompasses all of these phenomena and reveals the mechanisms of European colonialism from a native perspective. In so doing, their story underscores the significance of both intentional and unintentional acts and the consequences to indigenous experience and survival in such circumstances.

THE CULTURAL LANDSCAPE OF COLONIAL NORTH AMERICA

Beginning in the 1500s, the native people of North America were forced to contend with introduced disease or violence, or both, during encounters with European explorers, missionaries, settlers, trappers, and traders. This drama played out over the next 350 years—a general period referred to herein as the colonial era[1]—as successive waves of intruders and their biological agents swept across different regions of the continent. The reasons that Spanish, English, French, and other Old World colonists came to the Americas were diverse. Some sought to save indigenous souls and exploited native labor to build and maintain ambitious mission systems. Others searched for gold or acquired furs destined for Europe, often trading with native people to procure these goods. Still others established agrarian communities and carved out fields, pastures, and homesteads within traditional Indian territories in the quest for self-sufficiency in the New World. These and other efforts sometimes depended upon the labor of enslaved Africans, who were themselves colonists of a sort. European colonists' relationships with native people varied greatly, depending on the purpose of their enterprise, their need for native labor or partners, their continued connection to their homeland, and their short- or long-term intentions in

North America. These factors, in part, also determined the extent to which their activities affected native life and culture and the nature and pace of such impact.

The Indian people who were parties to these encounters were similarly diverse, and their experience and traditions constituted the complementary component contributing to the process and outcome of colonial encounters. Language, religion, customs, and social structure differed significantly between these groups, as did their interaction with and response to the invasion of Old World people and disease. In the Southeast and middle Mississippi River valley, multiple chiefdoms were forged around monumental civic-ceremonial centers that were interconnected by long-distance exchange networks that dealt in symbolic items and exotic materials available only to elite individuals. The tiered settlement structure of these hierarchical societies also included lesser towns and community centers, satellite villages, and farmsteads. An agricultural economy based on maize and other cultivated plants supported priests, chiefs, lesser political officials, craft specialists, and commoners, who together constituted populations numbering in the thousands. In the northeastern forests, midwestern plains and prairies, and southwestern deserts and mesas, groups were generally organized as tribes, with relatively little differentiation in the status of individuals other than by age and gender. Multiple kin groups were represented within communities, and authority beyond such groups was often temporary or situational, specific to a task requiring community coordination. These tribes often occupied fortified or otherwise defensible villages comprised of hundreds and sometimes even thousands of individuals. Like the chiefdoms of the Southeast, tribal groups generally engaged in farming, and maize was a major component of their diet. Similar communities were present along the northwest coast of North America, although here, autonomous groups were smaller, numbering only in the hundreds, and individuals relied on abundant wild food resources for their subsistence. Salmon was particularly important in the diet, and rights to rich fishing locales along major rivers were held by specific kin groups. Through such control, some lineages acquired more resources and prestige than others, but no central authority existed beyond each village. Elsewhere in the West and in the Far North, native groups were organized into bands. These small, kin-based communities made their living from hunting and gathering wild resources from the land and, in some areas, harvesting marine mammals, fish, and shellfish from the adjoining coastal waters. Such foodstuffs were distributed unevenly across the landscape, however, and it was not unusual for households or groups to relocate during the course of a year to take advantage of resources available in various environmental zones during different seasons or to follow migrating animals.

Within this varied landscape of colonizers and native people, the intent of European invaders was diverse but unambiguous. Whether seeking to exploit people or to obtain resources, the goals and actions of specific intruders are revealed in official documents, mercantile records, and personal journals of the time. But the response of native people to such intentional encroachment or aggression—and the role of introduced infectious disease in colonial encounters—is often more difficult to discern. Historical documents either do not address the native side of the encounter, or else they only present events involving indigenous people from the perspective of colonists. There is often no indication of how these processes played out, what the motivations and efforts of native people were in this dynamic setting, or how daily lives of Indian people were affected. One shortcoming of documentary records is especially glaring: there is no account of the colonizers' influence on Indian people prior to their physical presence within a native territory, particularly with respect to the demographic and cultural impacts of European diseases that may have preceded actual occupation (see Milner et al. 2001). Thus, only a very general, incomplete, and possibly inaccurate picture of colonial encounters and their effects on native people can be drawn from written records. To complete this portrait, these data must be augmented by native oral histories and by information derived from archaeological investigations of Indian life and death.

DEBATING THE COURSE AND IMPACT OF INFECTIOUS DISEASE IN COLONIAL ENCOUNTERS

In broad brush, both anthropological and historical studies acknowledge the potentially profound effect of disease-induced population loss on Native American cultures during the colonial era (e.g., Alchon 2003; Brose et al. 2001; Cook 1976; Crosby 1986; Dobyns 1983; Fitzhugh 1985; Larsen 1991; McNeill 1976; Phillips 1993; Ramenofsky 1987; Ramenofsky et al. 2003; Smith 1987; D.H. Thomas 1989, 1990, 1991; Wolf 1982; see also Diamond 1997; Mann 2005). It is clear that some native groups suffered a staggering number of fatalities from a variety of infectious diseases to which they lacked biological immunity. In North

America, this impact began as early as the 1520s in the Southeast and was initiated no more than a century or two later in the Southwest, Northeast, and upper Midwest (Dobyns 1983). Brought from the Old World, these foreign killers may have been introduced and reintroduced among native people over successive generations. Diseases such as smallpox, measles, influenza, typhus, scarlet fever, and whooping cough were endemic to Old World populations (Bianchine and Russo 1995; Ramenofsky 1993; Ramenofsky et al. 2003). Therefore, in European communities, if no new genetic strains of pathogens developed, each outbreak resulted in the death of only a few particularly vulnerable individuals relative to overall population size. In contrast, mortality in previously unexposed Indian populations reached epidemic proportions and could exceed 90 percent for some pathogens, since contraction of the disease (i.e., morbidity) was as high as 100 percent (see Bianchine and Russo 1995; Dobyns 1983; Ramenofsky 1987; Stearn and Stearn 1945).[2] Such disease struck down not just the very young and old but also men and women in the prime of life.

These statistics on morbidity and mortality derive primarily from epidemiological studies of both contemporary and historic populations around the world (see Ramenofsky 1987); thus, this research serves to augment the broad view of historical and anthropological studies of colonial-era introduced disease within Native American groups. Epidemiologists have also considered the nature of pathogens typically introduced to the New World (e.g., viral, bacterial, or protozoal) and their transmission (e.g., airborne or vector organism) to estimate both the potential speed with which a contagion could have spread and the subsequent persistence of a pathogen within a population after introduction. Population characteristics of the host community, including genetic diversity, existing disease load (e.g., endemic diseases), nutrition, population size and density, and geographic or social isolation, affect both of these facets of epidemic disease.[3] For example, epidemics are more likely in large populations that contain a sufficient number of susceptible individuals to sustain the outbreak, while less sanitary conditions typical of crowded living conditions also facilitate the spread of infectious airborne diseases.[4] Since these and other factors related to specific pathogens introduced as part of the "Columbian exchange" have been discussed at length elsewhere (e.g., Alchon 2003; Bianchine and Russo 1995; Ramenofsky 1987, 1993, 1996; Ramenofsky et al. 2003), these data are not reiterated here. Still, it must be emphasized that while epidemiological studies are consistent with the broad picture of disease-induced native depopulation developed from historical and anthropological data, they also suggest complexity and the subtle interplay of multiple factors, including the potential for different strains of the same pathogen within the Americas. Thus, the specific pathogen responsible for any given colonial-era epidemic should be determined, if possible, since this had consequences for exposure to, duration of, and morbidity and morality deriving from a disease event.

Such epidemiological complexities contribute to the fact that, in detail, the picture of the spread and impact of colonial-era disease among native people becomes much less clear and more contentious, fueling the debate among anthropologists, archaeologists, and historical demographers about just how significant disease-induced depopulation was to the colonial experience of specific native groups (e.g., Brose 2001; Dobyns 1983, 1991; Milner et al. 2001; Thornton 1987, 1997, 2000; Ubelaker 1992, 2000). Especially contentious is the timing of epidemics in various regions and, by extension, the potential size of native populations prior to direct encounters with colonists (e.g., Henige 1998).[5] Ethnohistorian Henry Dobyns (1966, 1983, 1991) has been most vocal in arguing that massive population decline resulted from the introduction of pathogens in widespread areas of North America prior to direct contact between native and nonnative people. Some Indian people may have contracted European disease directly from interactions with colonists, but many epidemics likely resulted from the subsequent passage of nonnative pathogens from one native group to another along traditional trade routes or via native people fleeing devastation.[6] Epidemiological studies confirm this possibility, although the nature of the pathogen involved made specific diseases more or less likely to be transmitted over long distances (see Ramenofsky 1987, 1996; Ramenofsky et al. 2003) and thus disposed to precede face-to-face encounters between colonists and Indians.[7]

This pandemic perspective follows the work of physiologist and historical demographer Sherburne Cook, who was one of the first scholars to suggest significant loss of life in California due to native interactions with Ibero- and Anglo-Americans. Cook (e.g., 1976) sought to quantify such losses and examine the multiple factors, from disease to violence, that contributed to such decline. His study did not significantly alter the quantitative estimates of California native population at European contact presented earlier by anthropologist Alfred Kroeber (1925, 1934, 1939), but Cook's work was a departure from the dominant view that

Indian people—and therefore Indian culture—had not suffered significant change during the colonial era. Dobyns's (1983, 1991) perspective of catastrophic depopulation prior to direct contact with nonnative peoples took Cook's notion even further (see also Crosby 1986; Preston 1996; Ramenofsky 1987) and provided quantitative estimates of pre-contact population size well in excess of those proposed by any other researcher (Dobyns 1966, 1983).[8]

Because this catastrophic view relies implicitly or explicitly on a relatively "disease-free" native world or "virgin soil" spread of introduced disease (Crosby 1986) without subsequent significant population rebound, other researchers have been somewhat skeptical of this argument. Computer simulations of demographic outcomes in such situations suggest that even significantly affected populations could have rallied back after population decline from epidemic disease (e.g., Thornton et al. 1991), and a few archaeological and ethnohistoric studies also support this conclusion (e.g., Galloway 2006:16). Many bioarchaeologists also point to evidence for the prior existence of deadly diseases among native populations (e.g., Baker and Kealhofer 1996; Larsen and Milner 1994; Ubelaker 2000; Verano and Ubelaker 1992; see also Cook and Lovell 1991), thereby refuting the "Garden of Eden" characterization sometimes applied to precolonial settings, particularly in reference to California (see Denevan 1992; Preston 1996, 1997). Such endemic diseases and potentially fatal maladies include tuberculosis, hepatitis, fungal infections, gastrointestinal parasites, congenital abnormalities, and treponemal diseases such as syphilis and yaws, as well as other ailments sometimes exacerbated by seasonal malnutrition or traumatic injury (Ubelaker 2000). Archaeological data also indicate that late-precontact cultural changes sometimes attributed to European disease actually predate the potential introduction of nonnative pathogens, so epidemics are neither represented by nor implicated in apparent social upheaval in these areas (e.g., Brose 2001; Fitzgerald 2001; Snow 2001). Other archaeologists note that the timing of depopulation, if evident, varied greatly. Also, this observation is inconsistent with a more uniform spread of introduced disease across the landscape necessary to support the catastrophic view of widespread demographic consequences. Finally, epidemiological data indicate that differential native settlement aggregation or dispersal could significantly affect the spread of disease, even in virgin soil conditions (see Cook and Lovell 1991; Erlandson and Bartoy 1995:156; Johnson and Lehmann 1996; Milner et al. 2001; Snow and Lanphear 1988). For example, pathogens would be more likely to spread through the dense populations of chiefdoms than between small, mobile bands of hunter-gatherers (but see Thornton 2000:18; Ramenofsky 1990:41). Researchers argue that such differences would have effectively halted the early, widespread dispersal of Old World diseases throughout North America prior to direct transmittal by colonists. Together, these data suggest that native demographic change due to introduced European disease during the colonial era—and the consequent culture change—might not have been as severe and unidirectional as implied by Dobyns. Instead, scholars opposed to the catastrophic view of depopulation significantly preceding face-to-face encounters contend that other factors resulting from nonnative presence or pressure, such as intergroup aggression or starvation, contributed to native population decline during this time (see Alchon 2003; Cook 1976; Hickerson 1997; Ramenofsky 1987).

THREE SCENARIOS OF DEPOPULATION

Thus, three alternate scenarios regarding the timing, magnitude, and cultural consequences of native depopulation during the colonial era emerge from a review of existing archaeological, ethnohistoric, and epidemiological literature. The first scenario—based largely on ethnohistoric and epidemiological data—is that colonial-era population collapse was early, unique, and devastating (Dobyns 1983). Depopulation preceded direct contact with nonnative people in many areas, and population declines were both severe and sustained. Significant cultural changes would have been the inevitable consequence of such population collapse, including language extinctions, loss of traditional knowledge, changes in material culture, shifts in ritual as elder cohorts were lost to European disease, collapse of complex social structure, and changes in settlement patterns, at a very early time in colonial settings (Dobyns 1983, 1991; Dunnell 1991; Ramenofsky 1987, 1991; Smith 1987). Even if groups had been previously exposed to fatal diseases endemic to North America, scholars contend that these pathogens created no demographic crises comparable to that experienced at contact with nonnative diseases. In addition, the repeated exposure to different Old World pathogens, or second waves of the same disease after immune individuals were no longer present in the population, kept groups from rebounding to any significant extent.

A second view—uncommon in the archaeological literature but suggested by demographic simulations and some ethnohistoric accounts—

also holds that colonial-era population decline due to nonnative disease was indeed catastrophic and likely preceded face-to-face contact. But this event was not necessarily unique nor did it inevitably result in significant culture change due to depopulation alone. Over the long term, various large- or small-scale oscillations in population size, growth rates, or other demographic characteristics probably occurred within native communities. Colonial-era depopulation was only one, and not necessarily the most significant, of such shifts. Due to likely histories of population fluctuation in small-scale societies in particular, hunter-gatherers and perhaps even some horticultural peoples would have had adaptable cultural systems that could weather short-term changes and manifest long-term cultural continuity in the wake of colonial-era depopulation (Rubertone 2000:435). Native communities may also have had enough time to rebound from significant population loss from introduced disease (if not suffering subsequent epidemics of different pathogens), thereby allowing reestablishment of groups at predisease size (Thornton 2000:19; Thornton et al. 1991; see also Galloway 1994). This process may have been facilitated, in part, by the incorporation of survivors from neighboring groups (e.g., Bradley 2001; Snow 2001).

The third scenario—inspired primarily by extant archaeological data from selected regions—suggests that contact-era demographic collapse from introduced disease was neither that significant nor that early (e.g., Baker and Kealhofer 1996; Snow 1995, 2001; Thornton 2000). As a result, any apparent culture change during the colonial era was not due to demographic change alone nor was it the most significant factor. Instead, proponents contend that significant depopulation among native groups occurred later in time and resulted from a host of factors, including deliberate genocide of native people and potential escalated warfare between Indian groups under conditions of contact stress (Cook 1976; Jackson and Castillo 1995; Phillips et al. 1951). Colonial-era culture change simply reflects greater interaction with nonnative people rather than response to disease-induced depopulation.

Although defining distinct processes and outcomes of European colonialism for native people, this tripartite categorization should not be taken to imply that only one of these views applies to North America as a whole or even to a particular region to the exclusion of other scenarios. Instead, the data amassed thus far make it clear that different scenarios probably apply to different areas—or even to the same native group—during the colonial period. Such coincident or serial transformations are especially true with respect to the second scenario, since what it describes entailed no long-term demographic or cultural consequences. Where this process occurred, there might not be any subsequent demographic and cultural shifts, or later population decline and culture change may have resulted from other causes consistent with the third scenario. The process of colonial-era depopulation and repopulation would be evident during a brief interval of a few generations and thus might be difficult to recognize in archaeological data and be unrecorded in native oral history.

Each scenario has important implications for anthropological and historical understanding of intentional versus unintentional consequences of colonial encounters for native experience, response, and survival in North America. In fact, if devastating Old World disease significantly preceded direct interaction and involvement of Indians with nonnative people and enterprises during the colonial era as suggested in the first two scenarios, the very notion of "colonialism" in such circumstances may be called into question or may require a broader definition than that generally implied by use of this term (cf. Gosden 2004; Silliman 2005; Stein 2005; see also Alexander 1998). From an anthropological perspective, such demographic change prior to face-to-face encounters may not differ markedly from other cases of population decline in the precolonial world—for example, loss of life due to natural disaster. And coincident culture change may not be distinguishable as a "colonial" process from dynamics set off by incursion of Indian people into a new region in the precolonial past, regardless of their intent with respect to the resident population. Is "colonialism" a proper representation of similar processes simply because they occurred during the colonial era and were initiated—albeit sometimes at significant distance—by a European presence? Can later engagements between colonists and native people in more traditional colonial settings such as missions, ranchos, and trading posts be understood without first understanding these early seeds of the colonial process? Analysis of the effect of colonial encounters on Native Americans, particularly in the short term, is hampered by the potential inability to disentangle depopulation due to introduced disease from the physical incursion of nonnative people so that the consequences of each can be separately understood. It is often difficult to determine whether the "colonizers" at a given time were European people, their ideas and goods, or simply their pathogens. As noted by Gosden (2004:123), however, the precedence of infectious disease in many colonial encounters in the Americas, Australia, and the Pacific Islands effectively *permitted* colonialism as we generally conceive of it today—that is, the taking of territory perceived as *terra nullius* (empty land) by European invaders.

ESTABLISHING EVIDENCE FOR COLONIAL-ERA DEPOPULATION

Determining which of the three scenarios of colonial-era depopulation and culture change applies to a particular native group—and thus disentangling the two major forces of European colonialism in the New World—relies on native oral history, historical accounts, or archaeological investigations. In many regions, however, these records have thus far proven equivocal about whether introduced disease preceded direct interaction between native and nonnative people or if the dual colonial enemies arrived in tandem to claim their victims and their spoils. This ambiguity exists, in part, because precontact and colonial-era demographic trends are rarely well defined (Dean et al. 1994; Ramenofsky 1987; see also Petersen 1975; Plog and Hantman 1990; Schacht 1981). For example, historical records often do not provide quantitative data on native population size before and after encounters, and studies in various areas have demonstrated the difficulty of establishing demographic profiles—even for the historic era—with archaeological data (e.g., Perttula 1991; Ramenofsky 1987; Walker et al. 1989).

The archaeological difficulties are partly a function of temporal control (see Milner et al. 2001), because focus on specific decades within the colonial period calls for very fine-grained chronologies. This generally precludes the use of techniques such as radiocarbon dating that have inherent statistical error ranges (cf. Campbell 1990; Green 1993). Instead, colonial-era chronologies for Indian sites often rely on the qualitative or quantitative incorporation of European goods into native material culture, with these observations sometimes augmented by additional traits such as local native ceramics (e.g., Arkush 1995; Brose et al. 2001; Ramenofsky 1987; Smith 1987; Snow 1996). The frequency and diversity of nonnative items—including glass, copper, and brass beads, other metal ornaments, and various metal tools—are generally assumed to increase through time. But different archaeological data-collection strategies, variation in site function and duration of occupation, material preferences, differential native access to goods within or between groups due to social or geographic factors, or the presence of heirlooms could significantly distort interpretations based on these methods. In addition, this approach may be tautological if data are subsequently applied to the issue of consequent culture change. Using these methods, examination of population size is limited to the immediate contact era, with population estimates spanning at most two to three centuries (e.g., Ramenofsky 1987). Such short-term population profiles preclude the possibility of recognizing whether colonial-era decline was simply a function of stochastic fluctuation common to some human populations over the long term or whether decline was related to colonial encounters (cf. Kulisheck 2005).

There are also difficulties resulting from sampling biases. Archaeological estimates of colonial-era population size have traditionally relied on existing settlement information, but these data were often not originally collected for demographic purposes. For example, the sample may tend to overrepresent late sites, larger deposits, locales with architecture or other more visible elements, or sites in certain regions subject to more intensive archaeological reconnaissance. Since site frequency or habitation space are often used as proxies for population size, estimates of the number of individuals for a given region may be statistically indefensible if drawn from samples that are neither spatially nor temporally representative. Demographic results are often ambiguous and interpretations may be subject to wide latitude based on the proclivities of the investigator (cf. Ramenofsky 1987; Snow 1995, 2001; see also Galloway 1994; Henige 1998). In the absence of reliable demographic data, catastrophic depopulation is sometimes simply assumed to have taken place during the colonial era when early, significant culture change is evident in the archaeological record (Perttula 1992; Smith 1987). Presumed cultural consequences of depopulation are analyzed without developing direct evidence for population collapse.

Only rarely have archaeological and ethnohistoric evidence for both colonial-era demographic and cultural changes been developed together in a systematic or quantitative fashion. Nor have such characteristics of Indian groups generally been examined over a longer time span to allow examination of colonial-era native experiences within the broader context of long-term group history (cf. Brose et al. 2001; Palkovich 1996). Thus, it is often unclear how dramatic the population loss was, what the timing of population decline and subsequent culture change were, what constituted short- or long-term change in various situations, and whether such impacts occurred within communities previously exhibiting long-term continuity and population stability (see Baker and

Kealhofer [eds.] 1996; Verano and Ubelaker 1992). In other words, was colonial-era population decline and consequent culture change relatively unique and traumatic, or was it part of a preexisting pattern of change and accommodation that developed over hundreds or thousands of years? These questions probe at the very heart of when and whether—or which aspects of—colonial encounters were significant to the culture history of a particular native group.

In the absence of rigorous and complementary analyses, arguments regarding the timing and magnitude of depopulation based on archaeological data—particularly prior to face-to-face contact and historical recording—are frequently speculative. Such studies also often reach disparate conclusions for various areas. This suggests either that data or methods are insufficient or that significantly different processes were occurring in different regions and among different groups. With such ambiguous historical or archaeological records and associated methodological challenges, it is difficult to assess the specific relationship between demographic impacts, on the one hand, and culture change, on the other. It is impossible to know how the process of colonial encounters unfolded, including sequence and timing. What factors pertained to specific areas? Why were certain native groups able to persist? Would the progress or outcome of the encounter have been different in the short term or the long term given a different scenario?

The stories that emerge from this era—partially rendered through archaeology, native oral history, and historical documents—suggest a complicated mosaic response to colonial challenges and equally diverse outcomes. Such different processes and results seem reasonable, given the diversity of Indian groups, colonizers, and intentional and unintentional factors contributing to encounters (see also Stein [ed.] 2005). But a more detailed, contextual analysis is necessary to bring texture, meaning, and understanding to the native experience in any given area and to provide a perspective that is missing from written records. Only in rare cases did native people, culture, identity, and homeland remain relatively intact. Instead, the power of the dual forces of colonialism initially undermined one or more of these qualities, altering native life swiftly, dramatically, and often irrevocably. In such circumstances, facing the subsequent onslaught of nonnative people onto native lands was overwhelming and, often, the final blow to traditional life.

COLONIAL ENCOUNTERS IN CALIFORNIA

Whether gauged by the spread of nonnative disease or physical incursion of colonists, historical records indicate that California was one of the last regions of North America touched by European colonialism. Still, the processes that played out between colonists and native people in this region were similar to those that had unfolded in portions of the East, Midwest, and Southwest during the previous two centuries. Initial contact between a few native and nonnative people in California likely occurred in the mid-to-late 1500s (Costello and Hornbeck 1989; Engstrand 1997; Erlandson and Bartoy 1995), but sustained nonnative influence and colonization did not begin until the mid-1700s. From that time forward, the history of native and nonnative interaction proceeded from an initial environment of coexistence to ultimate near exclusion of Indian peoples after the annexation of California by the United States in 1846 and the initiation of the Gold Rush in 1848.

In this region of the Far West, colonialism came in two primary forms. Spanish missions were widely scattered on the Central and Southern California coastal plain and adjoining oak-covered ranges, and the Russian mercantile operation at Colony Ross was located just 75 kilometers northwest of the northernmost mission on the fog-drenched, forested coast of what is now Sonoma County (see map 1). At Fort Ross, a multiethnic community of Russian, Creole (individuals of both Russian and native descent), native Alaskan, and Kashaya Pomo people was established to undertake and support the procurement of pelts from fur-bearing marine mammals for overseas trade. Native Alaskan men were employed as hunters, using their traditional boats and weapons. Russians and Creoles served as administrators who oversaw hunting and other commercial and agrarian activities necessary to support this enterprise. Both Pomo and neighboring Miwok men and women from nearby Indian villages were employed as laborers, particularly on a seasonal basis. Finally, local Kashaya women often married native Alaskan men who settled at the fort, founding households in the native neighborhood adjacent to the stockade. Established in 1812 and maintained until 1841, this Russian colonial operation eventually grew to include three ranches, one port, and an outlying island hunting station in addition to the original administrative center (Lightfoot 2005).[9]

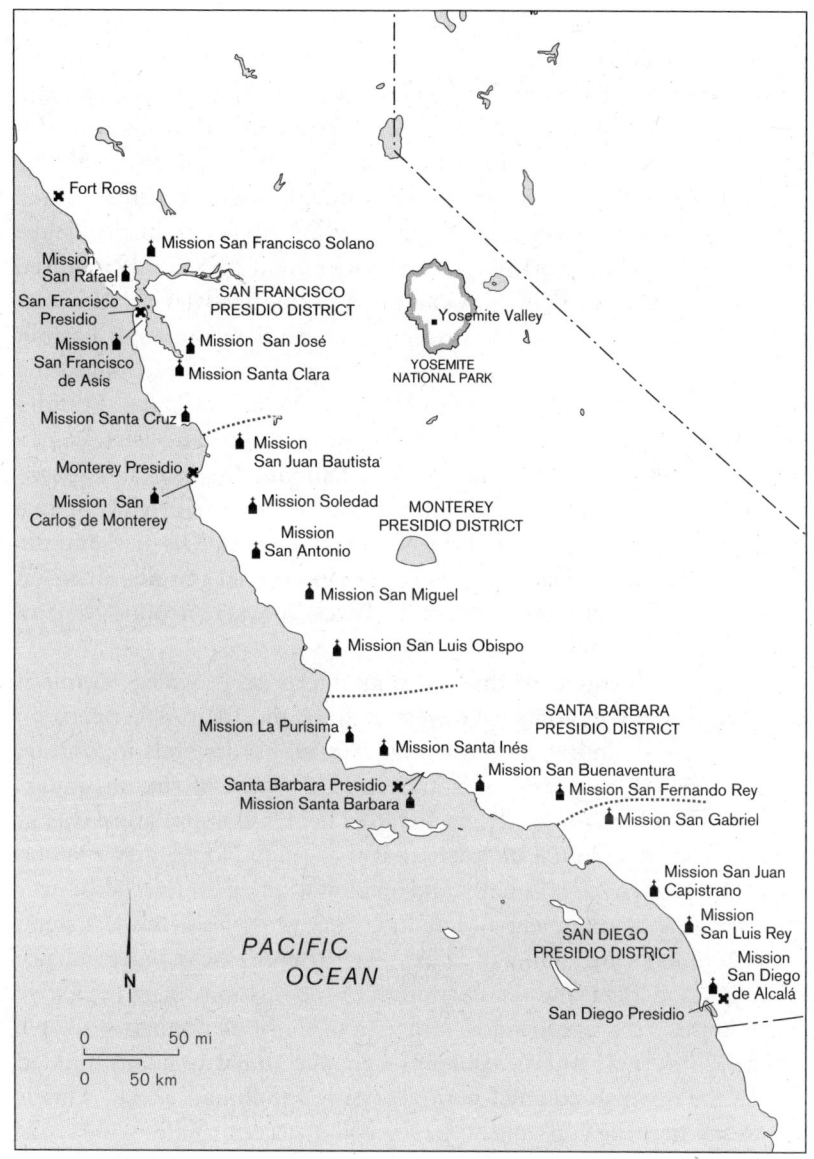

MAP 1. Russian and Spanish colonial interests in California circa 1815 in relation to Yosemite Valley (after Lightfoot 2005: map 2).

The twenty-one Spanish missions—four with associated military presidios and several others with nearby small, secular pueblos—were located from San Diego de Alcalá in the south to San Francisco Solano at Sonoma in the north. The latter was the final mission in the system of outposts that were constructed between 1769 and 1823. Native people from multiple local groups were brought to the missions—often by force—to receive religious indoctrination, to labor in the fields, and to serve in the workshops to produce food and goods required for the community. This life contrasted dramatically with their traditional beliefs and practices as hunters, gatherers, and fisherfolk living in relatively small communities. Yuman- and Takic-speaking peoples comprised the native populations of the San Diego Presidio District; the missions within the Santa Barbara Presidio District primarily encompassed Chumash people; Salinan, Esselen, and speakers of southern Costanoan languages constituted the original native population for the missions of the Monterey Presidio District; and the missions within the San Francisco Presidio District initially drew on the additional local Costanoan and Miwok speakers around the San Francisco Bay.

The religious intent of this colonial enterprise provided an initial experience in direct contact between natives and Ibero-Americans on the West Coast similar to that of the Spanish borderlands in Florida, Texas, New Mexico, and Arizona. Since the goal of the missionaries was not to destroy or displace native peoples, assimilation was at the forefront of colonial interaction at that time. Non-Indian mission populations were very small, and exploitation of native labor was critical to the development and maintenance of the missions (Hurtado 1988; Milliken 1995; Silliman 2001). Even after Mexican independence from Spain in 1821 and secularization of the missions in 1834, native populations were significantly larger than those of nonnative people in Alta California, and the economic reliance on native labor initiated during the Spanish colonial period persisted (Silliman 2004). This is not to say that the consequences of missionization or later secularization were not severe for native peoples (see Cook 1976; Jackson and Castillo 1995) but rather were similar to the Russian colonial objectives at Colony Ross—the intent was not destruction or annihilation of the Indians. Still, the missions were centers for the introduction and spread of European diseases among the native population, and loss of life from epidemics within the Spanish mission system is well documented (Walker and Johnson 1992, 2003; Milliken 1995).

Given the geography of Spanish and Russian infiltration, local manifestations of contact and colonialism during this period varied greatly throughout California, both in timing and impact on native peoples. Coastal groups from San Diego to Sonoma experienced mission life directly, albeit sequentially over the sixty-five-year period from mission development to secularization. Adjacent inland groups likely had delayed direct interaction or simply took advantage of opportunities created by the Spanish or Russians at a distance (see Phillips 1993). In the Sierra Nevada and far Northern California, however, there was no direct contact with either the Spanish (and later Mexican) or Russian colonists during the colonial period. Still, native oral tradition and archaeological evidence indicate that the colonial drama of native California during this time was not limited to the missions, coast, or even a larger area also encompassing adjoining inland valleys. Despite the relative isolation of native people in the interior from initial nonnative incursion into California, the force and momentum of colonial activity on the coast ultimately led to developments farther inland that served to initiate a new chapter in the cultural history of these native groups.

Historical records and anthropological data indicate that Indian people throughout much of California felt the weight of the Spanish occupation in particular, whether they had direct interaction with these intruders or not. By their very presence, the Spanish changed the cultural landscape of the region, creating challenges and opportunities not only for Indian people brought to the missions but also for native people beyond the immediate reach of the religious and associated military operations (see also Milner et al. 2001:16). In the interior valleys, foothills, and mountains, traditional trading partners were lost as families were removed to the missions or people perished from epidemic disease. These same dislocations or fatal encounters provided access to new territory and resources by those households or communities that remained. Groups as yet untouched negotiated or clashed with those closer to the expanding grasp of the Spanish who sought refuge in more distant tracts of land to the east. Escape of mission neophytes was also common, and many individuals fled to the temporary safety of marshlands in the Central Valley or strongholds in the Sierra Nevada, where they sought to avoid recapture (Castillo 1989; Hurtado 1988:32; Milliken 1995; Phillips 1993). Unfortunately, such flight likely led to the spread of nonnative diseases to these distant places and peoples.

UNDERSTANDING INDIGENOUS COLONIAL EXPERIENCES: THE YOSEMITE INDIAN STORY

Living a traditional life within their ancestral homeland in the central Sierra Nevada, the Indian people of Yosemite Valley were one such group that faced the dual assaults of colonialism after the establishment of European enterprises and, finally, the invasion of nonnative people into their traditional territory during the Gold Rush. The distance of Yosemite Indians from the closest Spanish outposts situated around San Francisco Bay—more than 250 kilometers to the west—was not enough to keep them safe from deadly disease that originated in these or other Spanish colonial communities and spread inland via native people. Yosemite Indian oral tradition indicates that their population declined significantly and abruptly after the introduction of a fatal disease, forcing survivors to make choices that would decide their fate as a people. And their remote valley—although a potent ally in their fight against a militia intent on removing them from the Sierra Nevada in the early 1850s—ultimately proved an insufficient defense against those determined to take their land, consume their game, and extract gold from the streambeds of the adjacent foothills. But Yosemite Indian history and culture also show that these people had remembered and internalized the lessons of hardship and survival of past generations, dating back to a time before Spanish, Russian, and American penetration into California. Thus, despite setbacks and tragedy resulting from the dual assaults of colonial encounters, this memory helped contribute to the maintenance of traditional life, culture, and identity in their territory well after nonnative people were also occupying this land.

The story of Yosemite Indian population collapse due to the introduction of European disease during the colonial era, yet their subsequent cultural endurance, provides a compelling picture of people who survived in the face of enormous difficulties and swiftly changing circumstances. The details, characters, and timing are specific to Yosemite, but this story of introduced disease at the forefront of colonial encounters is not unique. The process documented by Yosemite Indian oral tradition and regional archaeology is consistent with that posited in the second scenario of colonial-era depopulation—early, severe population decline preceding face-to-face encounters with colonists but no consequent cultural disintegration. The fact that nonnative disease evidently spread to and through small hunter-gatherer populations in California is especially interesting, as this pattern is not predicted based on epidemiology.

Instead, epidemiological data suggest that large, sedentary populations are more vulnerable to infectious pathogens such as those known to have been introduced into the Americas from the Old World.

In light of these factors, this presents an excellent case for analyzing the dual threats of colonial encounters separately and understanding what these processes might look like in other regions of North America that lack such unambiguous historical and, perhaps, archaeological records. This scenario of discrete colonial-era assaults is particularly challenging from an interpretive standpoint, however, exactly because the anticipated impacts of "colonialism" may be invisible in the archaeological record for all but the briefest time. By definition, populations partially or completely rebounded and culture may not have changed irrevocably. Thus, it is important to consider archaeological evidence of the process unfolding and, perhaps, reversing. This also allows us to critically assess which is most plausible: the catastrophic view of disease-induced demographic and cultural change posited for widespread areas of North America, or the contrary perspective of no significant demographic and cultural impacts in the early colonial era.

The colonial era was clearly a time of turmoil and change for native people in North America—perhaps more so than at any other time in the history of most of the groups affected. Certainly, some had previously faced fatal disease, natural disasters, or other challenges to their way of life, including hostility and aggression from neighboring groups. But the invasion of traditional territories by European interlopers or their lethal biological agents—or both—was a widespread phenomenon that ultimately extended across the entire continent and changed the course of history and the daily life of native people throughout North America. Many Indian people were forced to relocate, while others aggregated into communities with neighboring groups or altered their social organization to cope with change and remain in their homeland (see Brose et al. 2001). At the same time, however, some groups were able to maintain their culture, identity, and traditional residence against incredible odds despite short-term changes necessary for their survival—first, perhaps, in the face of catastrophic depopulation and later after direct incursion of nonnative people. Anthropological analysis of these disparate outcomes of colonial encounters entails seeking answers to two key questions: What role did introduced disease play in the initial colonial experience of native groups in North America? And what practices or circumstances allowed some native cultures to endure throughout this period and prevail in the maintenance of their identity and customs, while others did not? In other words, why did groups such as the Yosemite Indians survive to tell the tale?

In initially considering these questions, it is tempting to reduce such an analysis to anthropological generalities—to make claims, for example, that resilience is rooted in broad economic distinctions such as the inherent cultural and geographic flexibility of residentially mobile hunter-gatherers versus sedentary horticultural people. Or to pose an anthropological argument centering on the social complexity of the native group involved and, thus, on the potential vulnerability of chiefdoms or states to collapse given the hierarchy of such society and the specialization in roles that allowed these systems to function. In contrast, bands or tribes might remain relatively unscathed. Or we might look for answers in the dichotomy between the colonizer and colonized, focusing on the power of the participants. Such disparities include the superior weapons technology of the foreigners; the support of a larger economic system, complex political structure, and substantial population beyond the shores of North America; and the debilitating effects of epidemic diseases that preceded or accompanied encounters. But review of the cases for which there is sufficient archaeological and archival documentation suggests that an understanding of cultural survival or decline cannot be found by limiting discussion to such simplistic or generalizing dichotomies.

An alternate approach might be to highlight the historical rather than anthropological aspects of the encounter. Instead of considering groups cast as stereotypes or archetypes of social and cultural forms, the focus would be on individuals and the particular context in which the events unfolded. Such an analysis would consider the specific antagonists involved—the central figures, both native and nonnative, who were jockeying for power or serving their personal or group interests in interaction with the other. Specific native leaders or priests might be significant in guiding survivors back from the brink of collapse brought on by disease-induced depopulation or dislocation from traditional territories and resources. This analytical approach would be facilitated by access to ethnohistoric accounts and native oral history instead of emphasizing or relying on archaeological data. Or we might look to the specific history of the people and groups involved, placing the event of depopulation or the process of colonial encounters more generally in longer-term perspective of action and experience. Such analysis would include assessment of existing conditions of population health as well as the previous experience of native communities with demographic crises. This approach—suited to archaeological study with or without complementary archival sources—fosters an assessment of past knowledge and an appreciation for lessons learned. Such study provides context for understanding decisions made by individuals during this time of swiftly changing conditions.

In fact, the Yosemite Indian experience suggests that the answer to the question of cultural persistence or change through the colonial era may lie in both culture and history—in the convergence of circumstance, the specific personalities involved, and the traditional beliefs, practices, and embodiment of knowledge in daily life that provided for native cultural survival up to that time (see Stein 2005). The outcome of specific colonial encounters was the result of choices made by those who participated or survived, exercised within the context of both their own personal experience and the experiences of their ancestors that were preserved in oral tradition. Yosemite Indians, as native people elsewhere in North America, were individuals making decisions in the most trying of circumstances. These decisions would affect them as individuals and as a group in the short term or the long run, or both. But the choices they made and the options they perceived were those dictated by both culture and history.

With culture and history so irrevocably intertwined in creating the experience and defining the outcome of colonial-era encounters, anthropological analysis must bring together both of these elements to understand the significance of introduced disease or violence, or both, to the process of colonialism. The essential bond of meaning, practice, people, place, and circumstance require an "event-centered" approach to study—a historical anthropology that acknowledges momentaneous cause but views cultural consequences as the intersection of long-term structure (i.e., culture) and short-term event (i.e., history) (e.g., Ohnuki-Tierney 1990:10; Sahlins 1981). Such methodological commission represents an intellectual move away from the distant roots of anthropology born in era in which "history" was decisively placed within the domain of literate societies and all others were consigned to a timeless "prehistory" (Conn 2004), an imagined past before engagement with Europeans that lacked change, transformative events, and individual agency (Ohnuki-Tierney 1990:3). In contrast, contemporary historical anthropology acknowledges that culture is constantly changing, or has the capacity to change at any time, due to both internal and external factors. Therefore, anthropologists are observers and recorders of serial manifestations of culture in a dynamic world (Biersack 1991), much like other witnesses to contemporary and past human action. The historical anthropological charge, however, is not to simply report *what* happened but rather to examine the *how* and *why* of any event and its cultural consequences for the people involved (Ohnuki-Tierney 1990:6–7). In addition, such assessment must consider whether evident change in the short term represents a deep structural shift or simply surficial change in practice but enduring understanding of meaning (Ohnuki-Tierney 1990:7). To facilitate this analytical task, short-term events must be placed in long-term context (Biersack 1991).

The methodological demands and interpretive goals of historical anthropology are met by drawing on multiple sources of data that encompass both of these temporal scales (Washburn and Trigger 1996: 62). Encompassing native oral history and material culture accessible through archaeology, as well as nonnative historical narratives and ethnographic accounts that include both written documents and visual images, analysis treats each as a different "historical" record of the conditions and practices of both the observer and the observed.[10] Since every record brings a unique voice and perspective, each also generates specific challenges and opportunities for a holistic analysis of phenomena, process, and outcome. Analysis requires the critical appraisal of the particular contribution of each record, including understanding the context of production (which, in archaeology, encompasses both the formation of the archaeological record itself by cultural and natural processes [Schiffer 1976] as well as the archaeological interpretation of this material record), the goals and proclivities of the author or voice, and the intended audience (Biersack 1991:20; Galloway 1991, 2006; Ohnuki-Tierney 1990:4). These facets reveal the inherent strengths and prospective weaknesses of each record, including the types of biases common to each type of informant and the data on which they may rely. Woven together, these diverse sources and the different perspectives offered by each create a single picture—in this case, a view of the timing, magnitude, and cultural consequences of colonial-era disease-induced depopulation.

With the mandate and methods of historical anthropology as a guide, the first step in analysis of the Yosemite Indian experience is study of what is already known, or can be further gleaned, from sources regarding the introduction of nonnative disease and subsequent depopulation. That is, we must define what we know of the "event." Critical examination of existing sources is also fundamental in the second step, which entails exhaustive compilation of all existing data on native life prior to and following the infiltration of nonnative fatal disease into the central Sierra Nevada. That is, we must define "structure" both prior to and after the event. Although detailed in terms of the number of sources and use of such source material, analysis in both of these steps serves primarily as an outline, a starting point of what we know of the event and native culture at the time and, perhaps, an initial index to changes that might be attributable to the catastrophic depopulation. It is only after these first two steps have been completed that can we can move on to a closer examination of the timing, magnitude, and cultural consequences through further archaeological study. Such additional analysis fills in critical and substantive detail on each of these three elements of colonial-era depopulation as only archaeology can.

For this final step as well as the two preceding, the research strategy assumes no continuity in either cultural identity or practice but rather recognizes that these are two among many issues that must be critically assessed in review of the documentary, oral, and artifactual records. Thus, this undertaking contrasts with other anthropological and archaeological approaches to colonial-era culture change such as acculturation studies and the direct historical approach (Cusick 1998b). In the latter case, the intent was to trace the cultural evolution of a specific ethnic group back in time by starting with study of village sites attributable to the group based on historical records. Archaeologists assumed ethnic continuity and sought to document the broad scope of material change from the distant past until initial contact with European colonists (Ramenofsky 1990). Acculturation studies, on the other hand, traced cultural change forward since initial contact, assuming discontinuity, but analysis was often limited to identifying the incorporation of new, or the loss of old, material traditions (Cusick 1998a). Neither of these approaches drew on multiple sources in a critical way, problematized the process of colonialism itself, considered the how and why of cultural change during the colonial era with an eye to native agency and event, or brought together both the short term and long term in analysis and explanation.

MEMORY IN WORDS AND OBJECTS

The story of the timing, magnitude, and cultural consequences of colonial-era catastrophic depopulation among the Indian people of Yosemite Valley is chronicled in this book by bringing together native oral tradition, ethnohistoric accounts, historical images on film or canvas, later ethnographic data, and archaeological information that extends well beyond the span of the colonial era. This approach is not unique. Many scholars have recognized the value of working between documents and the archaeological record in assessment of colonial encounters (e.g., Deagan and Scardaville 1985; Galloway 2006; Heizer 1941; Kirch and Green 2001; Lightfoot 1995:199, 2005; Silliman 2005; Voss 2002) and incorporating native oral tradition into long-term archaeological analysis (Anyon et al. 1996; Echo-Hawk 2000; Mason 2000, 2006; Vansina 1985). This strategy inherently promotes a change in temporal focus, as one moves from the event of depopulation and possible culture change in the colonial era to the broader multigenerational view of demography and culture. Likewise, such a perspective encompasses changes in spatial scale, moving from the single occupational episode or community to the region and beyond. This "multiscalar" approach (e.g., Lightfoot 1995; Tringham 1991; see also Palkovich 1996) establishes the essential long-term demographic perspective on native population decline and allows both demographic and cultural change to be considered together.

Before we can undertake this venture, however, it is first necessary to consider the various voices that contribute to this endeavor. Chapter 2 introduces the leaders, miners, journalists, innkeepers, artists, naturalists, and anthropologists who produced the records upon which much of this study relies. The potential biases of each type of record are considered—and, in some cases, the biases and background of a particular witness are analyzed—while this discussion also explores the context of production that may have influenced how native people and culture were perceived. Such analysis applies to oral and documentary, as well as archaeological, sources and reveals the strengths and weaknesses that must be taken into account in using such records.

With this critical examination of sources in place, this journey in historical anthropology begins in chapter 3 with history. The chapter details the sequence of events leading up to the ultimate incursion of nonnative people into Yosemite Valley; the actions of Chief Tenaya, Maj. James Savage, and other Indian and non-Indian people in this region at that time; and the story of colonial-era native population collapse and cultural response occurring more than a half a century earlier. This poignant history is revealed first through accounts from the Gold Rush era, when Yosemite Indians were living in a world of growing violence and desperation. Encounters between Indians and miners were common, and both parties were increasingly agitated by the presence of the other. But as we will see, this was the second, rather than the first, colonial assault on the native people of the region. Native oral tradition speaks of the earlier time—not many decades prior to contact with nonnative people—and provides our first glimpse of depopulation and whispers of the voices of Yosemite Indian ancestors. These recollections are brief but also infused with emotion, humanity, and resilience. Family genealogy, dendrochronology, and additional historical evidence both support and augment this tale. Particularly important, these data establish the timing of population decline—the first critical issue that must be addressed—while also providing a key clue regarding the magnitude of depopulation. This chronicle also sets the stage for subsequent analysis, placing Yosemite Indian experience in the theater of colonial California and later developments and identifying recurrent themes in Yosemite Indian actions during colonial encounters that have deep roots in native history.

Next, a blending of historical and anthropological voices provides a review of Yosemite Indian culture during the millennia before and the few decades after the introduction of nonnative disease. Based on extant records, chapter 4 provides the broad panorama of life prior to the infiltration of deadly pathogens as well as a more detailed scene of daily life afterward. This picture of native life at and after contact with nonnative disease begins with a view of the more distant past as revealed through archaeology. These data depict major long-term patterns of Indian subsistence, settlement, technology, and exchange spanning more than five thousand years, and native oral tradition hints at specific events within this span. In contrast, much of what we know about the everyday practices and worldview of these people in the wake of disease has heretofore been derived from historical accounts, including observations by miners, innkeepers, and travelers. Some of these men and women came to know the Indian people and their customs intimately through the life they shared together away from the formalities—and, sometimes, the prejudices—of city life. Later, anthropologists and other academics recorded what they learned of traditional ways from Yosemite Indians and related groups of the adjoining foothills through interviews and observation. Together, these ethnohistoric, ethnographic, and archaeological observations provide a picture of daily life that contributes to further archaeological examination of cultural change or continuity that resulted from colonial encounters. These records also reveal practices significant to cultural survival.

The faces and personalities of history fade as we prepare to consider the archaeological evidence for colonial-era depopulation in Yosemite.

In response to the evident shortcomings of much previous archaeological research on the topic of disease-induced native demographic and cultural change, chapter 5 details how the analysis of Yosemite Indian colonial-era cultural history was structured from the outset as a demographic study. Data were gathered with the specific aim of deriving a view of changes in population size in both the colonial era and precontact times, with temporal resolution commensurate to the task at hand. More general discussion also considers mechanisms of demographic change such as migration, fertility, and mortality that might be revealed by archaeological data and contrasts the methods of demographic archaeology and historical demography for examination of such demographic phenomena in the colonial era.

The methods of science rather than the voices of the participants continue the Yosemite Indian story in a quantitative rather than qualitative fashion in chapter 6. This element is not a timeless history, but is fixed to a particular place and time, firmly anchored to the experience of a few generations of Indian people and their immediate descendants. Information on relative population size and other demographic parameters provide a picture of the consequences of introduced infectious disease, the cultural milieu of decision making by individuals under these circumstances, and the demographic mechanisms potentially contributing to evident population rebound. These data reveal a deeper history of demographic change that is also recorded in native oral tradition and may provide clues to the choices made by Yosemite Indians during the colonial era in the face of depopulation.

In chapter 7, historical records, native oral history, and previous archaeological studies from throughout North America serve to outline the range of possible cultural consequences for native people in the aftermath of disease-induced population collapse. As this discussion reveals, this experience could have touched native lives in many ways and at scales ranging from the individual to community. The assault of the unknown enemy also disrupted the practices of people and the networks of relationships both local and distant. Some consequences may have resulted from decisions made by survivors, although such agency was often exercised in an environment of few options. Other outcomes are simply accidental—the result of stochastic processes that reflect fate and circumstance rather than choice and action. Thus, these data highlight the diverse venues for archaeological inquiry into the cultural consequences of catastrophic depopulation.

This canvass of the broad contours of population-related cultural consequences is used in chapter 8 to assess evidence for consequent Yosemite Indian culture change or continuity revealed by archaeological data. In this case, it is the daily practices of the people evident at pre- and postdisease occupation sites that are of interest. This assessment avoids a focus on the incorporation of nonnative goods, which has been a common element in many previous studies of colonial encounters in California (e.g., Arkush 1995; Bamforth 1993; Costello 1989; Deetz 1963; Farnsworth 1989, 1992). Rather, the context of use and meaning of objects of both native and nonnative manufacture are considered through a spatial and material approach. Such a strategy is especially suited to an area where nonnative items were either not present or were rare, even well after the Spanish colonial presence in California. Cultural change is viewed from the scale of household to the village and region, with site-specific archaeological data expressly collected with this research goal in mind. Ethnographic and ethnohistoric observations complement this analysis and begin to bring history back into the foreground of this historical anthropology once again.

With the Yosemite Indian story of introduced disease, depopulation, and cultural persistence thus established, the focus shifts in chapter 9 to compare this history with that of other native people elsewhere in North America. With the three alternate scenarios of the timing, magnitude, and cultural consequences of depopulation in mind, ten studies representing a broad geographic cross-section of North America are considered. In other areas, the circumstances were quite different than in Yosemite Valley, as native groups were organized differently, had other customs, or lived in a very different environment. In addition, these other peoples had their own distinct histories, and they also experienced colonial encounters differently either because of the colonizer's intent or because the timing and types of introduced disease were different. What happened elsewhere? What light does the Yosemite Indian example of early depopulation—but cultural persistence—shed on patterns evident in archaeological data from other areas? What anthropological or historical similarities and differences can be drawn between various cases? Several previous archaeological studies have considered the apparent cultural consequences of colonial encounters in California and elsewhere, but the specific role of population collapse to such changes has rarely been assessed.

This journey concludes in chapter 10 with a return to the larger debate on the timing, magnitude, and cultural consequences of colonial-era native depopulation and an assessment of the dual assaults of

European colonialism in regional and continental perspective. Did widespread pandemics precede face-to-face encounters and irreparably alter indigenous lifeways prior to European contact? Or is it possible that precontact Old World disease infiltrated other areas, but populations either recovered or demographic decline alone did not result in significant culture change? What generalizations, if any, can be made about native experience, choice, and outcome in colonial encounters in North America? It has been argued that infectious disease was the most potent weapon in the arsenal of European colonialism, even though this assault may have preceded colonists' physical presence and served their aims without ever being intentionally deployed (but see Stearn and Stearn 1945). The devastation of introduced disease and creation of a "widowed landscape" (Dobyns 1983; Jennings 1976) left large tracts of land "empty" for settlement and exploitation or, at least, reduced and weakened native populations enough to permit colonial expansion and domination in a relatively short time (see Gosden 2004). But the Yosemite Indian case suggests that epidemic disease on its own—although devastating—was not sufficient to lead to the permanent abandonment of regions and collapse of many native societies in North America. Given distance from invaders and time to recover from the demographic shock through short-term changes that facilitated their survival, Yosemite Indians were able to rebuild their traditional lives with continuity in tradition, story, and song. This also appears to be the case for some other groups in North America. Such communities were not the same people in some ways—as indicated by the emergence of Yosemite Indians in both name and action after the impact of introduced disease—nor would we expect them to be after the trauma of death and the struggle for survival in the face of continued assaults. But their story indicates that the culture and history of any native group during the colonial era was intimately linked to the vision and resilience of individuals who survived and to their commitment to the way of life they had previously known.

CHAPTER 2

Multiple Perspectives on a Critical Time

What are the specific sources of data that are available and have been brought to bear on the case of Yosemite Indian colonial-era depopulation and concomitant cultural consequences? Who are the voices, what are the biases, and what was the motivation for production of these records? In this case, we are fortunate to have diverse lines of evidence and, for the most part, multiple contributions within each class of record. Oral history, historical narratives, personal memoirs, ethnographic accounts, and archaeological data all contribute to this analysis, while a substantial visual record of Yosemite Valley—and sometimes of Yosemite native people—was also produced after 1859. Certainly, one of the great strengths of the Yosemite Indian colonial story is the availability of such diverse and substantial evidence of native history and culture. And nearly all of these records are specific to the Yosemite region and the native people of Yosemite Valley rather than to a broader cultural group or geographic area, which is especially unusual for a study of this kind (Galloway 2006:34–35).

NATIVE VOICES

Oral history constitutes a small but extremely important source in this study. There is just one voice—that of Chief Tenaya,[1] aged leader of the Yosemite Indians at the time nonnative people first entered Yosemite Valley. His narrative was recorded by Lafayette Houghton Bunnell, one of the members of the Mariposa Battalion, the volunteer militia formed in 1851 to remove Yosemite Indians from their traditional homeland. Bunnell questioned Tenaya directly about many things and, with the aid of a native interpreter, elicited a brief account of the recent history of the Yosemite people that described the introduction of nonnative disease and decisions made by survivors in the aftermath of subsequent depopulation. It was in this testimony that this study found inspiration, although Tenaya's voice is also heard in additional short vignettes recorded by Bunnell that reveal the character of the man and tell us something of his community. Bunnell did not pen a direct translation of Tenaya's words,[2] but what he recounts speaks of known people, places, and personal experience rather than drawing on a mythic past that incorporates nonhuman characters and other worlds (Nabokov 1996:12). Thus, Tenaya's account appears as an unequivocal source that requires no literary translation. What his history does share with other forms of native oral tradition, however, is a lack of reference to a specific time or year (Nabokov 1996:3; see also Mason 2006; Vansina 1985).

Bunnell's (1990) rendering of Tenaya reveals a judicious man prone to passionate oration or measured silence, as circumstance required. Tenaya's history of the Yosemite people seems to have been offered in private conversation only at the prompting of Bunnell, rather than in a more public forum, and the author was very clear in his confidence in and respect for Tenaya's version of events. Bunnell (1990:65) stated emphatically that readers should "give credit to Ten-ie-ya's own history of his tribe" rather than relying on stories conveyed by other authors who had no direct interaction with Yosemite native people. Furthermore, Bunnell's representation of the story is likely accurate, as his accounts of some of Tenaya's public exchanges with members of the corps are verified by other records of the Mariposa Battalion (e.g., Hutchings 1856; see also Boling 1851; Crampton 1957). Those details of Tenaya's oral history that are subject to verification based on historical events, including Tenaya's place of leadership within his community, further support this story. Likewise, other particulars of this tale examined as part of the current study are supported by multiple additional sources. Thus, we can have confidence in this record.

NARRATIVES OF THE GOLD RUSH ERA

Historical narratives, memoirs, and prose of nonnative people that further develop the story of the colonial-era native experience and depict the daily life of Yosemite Indians were produced by a diverse cast of characters over a period of approximately fifty years beginning in 1856. Most are eyewitness accounts, and two among these are especially important, as their observations date to the early 1850s, at or within months of the initial nonnative incursion into Yosemite Valley. The first is the account of Lafayette Bunnell noted above (Bunnell 1990). It is significant not only because of Bunnell's intimate conversations with Chief Tenaya over a series of weeks but also because this history encompasses firsthand observation of Indian life in Yosemite Valley literally at the moment of contact (although Yosemite people had already been exposed to nonnative people and culture outside of Yosemite Valley for at least one generation by 1851). Only twenty-seven years old at the time the Mariposa Battalion entered Yosemite Valley, Bunnell had spent much of his youth on the frontier in Michigan. His brother was an Indian trader there, and young Bunnell was fascinated by the customs of the Chippewa and other Indians who came to deal at the post. Before he was a teenager, he was already a student of the native languages he heard spoken, and he noted that "subsequent attempts to civilize me . . . failed to entirely eradicate" his fascination with, appreciation for, and knowledge of, native cultures that initially developed during these formative years (Bunnell 1990:35). As he grew, Bunnell began training in medicine under the tutelage of his physician-father and later, when he moved away from the family home, he worked as an apprentice to another doctor. The lure of gold brought him to California in his midtwenties, however, and it was only after his return to the Midwest more than a decade later that he was awarded an honorary medical degree and practiced as a physician (Johnston 1990; Kelly 1921). Still, during his time with the Mariposa Battalion from its formation in January of 1851 to disbandment in July of 1851, his medical experience was called for on more than one occasion (e.g., Bunnell 1990:121, 140), and his comrades often chided "Doc" for his exuberant appreciation of nature and his captivation with Indian language and customs that harkened back to his youth.

Due to his experience and education, Bunnell's (1990) history of the Mariposa Battalion, published nearly thirty years after the events occurred,[3] is a relatively thorough and sometimes sympathetic portrait of the Indian people he met and the native life he witnessed.[4] For Bunnell, the scene was both inevitable and tragic, as he watched the volunteers torch the native acorn caches and burn houses to starve out those Indians who did not surrender. He recognized the "natural right of the Indian to their inheritance" (i.e., the land; Bunnell 1990:35; see also Bunnell 1990:213, 243, 256), and he clearly had contempt for those among his company or in the mining community at large who aimed to take "justice" into their own hands when it came to dealing with Indians (Bunnell 1990:140, 150). And unlike the narratives of many of his contemporaries, Bunnell's writing is relatively free of derogatory remarks when describing native people and customs. In fact, his account reveals recurring tolerance of, and even respect for, Tenaya (Bunnell 1990:156ff, 170ff, 214). Any incendiary rhetoric regarding Yosemite Indians is limited to his discussion of the violence that precipitated the "Mariposa Indian War." Still, Bunnell was clearly ambivalent in his affinity and concern for native people, as he also expressed scorn for those Americans predisposed to afford native people too much charity or grace (Bunnell 1990:117, 209). In this, Bunnell was consistent with many historical narrators of the nineteenth century, who grappled with their sense of justice and dissatisfaction when it came both Indian people and Indian policy (Washburn and Trigger 1996:82).

As narrative history (mixed with personal memoir), Bunnell's treatment of native people followed a major literary theme of the era—the trope of the "Vanishing American." Indians were familiar characters in the literature of the nineteenth century; the acute national awareness of native people did not fade from public consciousness until the 1890s. While so-called Indian wars unfolded in the West, romantic notions of the "noble savage" born in eighteenth-century France (Dibbie 1982; Washburn and Trigger 1996:72) intertwined with the stark reality of demographic and cultural decimation to forge this common story, best exemplified by James Fennimore Cooper's *The Last of the Mohicans* (Dibbie 1982). Thus, by the mid-1800s when Bunnell first encountered the Yosemite people, the "Vanishing Indian" was a recognizable character that had been embraced in American literature and culture for nearly half a century. The "inevitable" disappearance of Yosemite Indians from the "sublime" landscape of their traditional homeland was a theme to which he returned again and again in his narrative (e.g., Bunnell 1990:62, 72, 198, 213, 214). Moreover, Bunnell's decision to relate Chief Tenaya's story of population decline before the arrival of the Mariposa Battalion—which was absent from his much more brief 1859 account of the "discovery" of Yosemite Valley—and his own assessment of continued native decline afterward underscore this narrative tradition. Unlike the romanticism of Cooper's native characters, however, Bunnell did not extol the virtues of the "noble savage," using the phrase instead only in derision (Bunnell 1990:90, 193, 197, 198). Still, some of his rhetoric mirrors the discourse of the age, which attributed the "fall" of virtuous natives to vices acquired from the white "civilization" (e.g., Bunnell 1990:17; see Dibbie 1982). He discharged his own potential complicity in this decline by recounting precontact native population collapse and noting relatively few native men killed by the militia (and these always under conditions that Bunnell condemned), while locating the decline of the Yosemite instead at their own feet due to their resistance to white authority (Bunnell 1990:198) and placing the ultimate demise of Tenaya a few years later in the hands of Mono Indians rather than whites (Bunnell 1990:265).

Literary analyses of Bunnell's account of the Mariposa Battalion have recognized his dependence upon the trope of the Vanishing American (Mazel 2000; Solnit 1994), but have focused on this text primarily as an example of literary environmentalism, a treatise largely dedicated to expounding the virtues of wilderness and nature. Certainly, the landscape of Yosemite is a dominant presence in the narrative that, arguably, justified Bunnell's historical recounting of the Mariposa Battalion's activities. But even as this recent scholarship has focused on the tension between aesthetic appreciation of nature and Bunnell's apparent callousness to the endeavor in which he was a participant—that is, a history that is a harsh blend of violence and romance unusual in literature of the environment—Bunnell's juxtaposition of his enthusiasm for nature (in which he probably would have included native people, given the intellectual temperament of the times) with some of the unconscionable actions of his compatriots could also be taken as an important parallel theme given his affinity for native people and ambivalence to Indian policy born of years on the frontier.

While Bunnell's choice to record Yosemite native history is laudable—although perhaps colored by his reliance on the notion of the "inevitable disappearance" of native people—the importance of his narrative is more than a simple record of people, place, and event. In Bunnell we are fortunate to have had a very keen observer of indigenous culture and an individual who had personal experience with native people. Thus, Bunnell's observations and text at times approach ethnography, especially in his examination of native material culture such as architecture and tools, familial relationships and social organization, and customs such as mourning and mortuary practices. As noted above, Bunnell provided a glimpse of native life at the exact moment of contact with nonnative people in Yosemite Valley, even if we must acknowledge that Yosemite Indians were already dealing with the impact of gold miners and the consequences of introduced European disease at that time. Bunnell not only recounted Tenaya's words and placed this story of disease-induced depopulation within the broader scope of American history via the idea of the Vanishing American, he also brought the much more mundane into view. This dispassionate contribution to knowledge and even his responsibility to native people are things he seemed to recognize. That is, Bunnell saw himself in part as an ethnographer. For example, he referred to Tenaya as "an object of study" (Bunnell 1990:214) and identified an old native woman discovered in Yosemite Valley as an "ethnological curiosity" (Bunnell 1990:74). More generally, he pled that "before it be too late, a careful and full collection of vocabularies . . . should be worked by the Smithsonian Institute or ethnological societies" for all native groups (Bunnell 1990:191), and he pondered intellectual terrain common to the emerging discipline of anthropology, including the "origin of the races" (Bunnell 1990:52). Because Bunnell wrote at a time when anthropology and history were both only just coming into their own as professional disciplines, it is inappropriate to restrict the contribution of his account in the current study of Yosemite Indian depopulation and consequent cultural change to just one sphere of knowledge. Bunnell's telling is equally important as a record of native culture and practice within just a few decades of population decimation due to European diseases.

The same can be said of the second major historical eyewitness account of native people of the Yosemite region during the early 1850s. This memoir was written by Jean-Nicolas Perlot (1985), a Belgian argonaut who worked the streams to the west of Yosemite Valley in the months and years immediately following the formation of Mariposa Battalion in 1851. Born in 1823, Perlot was nearly the same age as Bunnell when he came to California in 1850 to escape difficult economic conditions in France and seek his fortune in the goldfields. He, too, based his operations in the Mariposa area (see map 2), but came to the region after treaties had been negotiated with several native groups of the Sierra foothills[5] and only months before the Mariposa Battalion made the second, and last, of their unsuccessful attempts to permanently remove Yosemite Indians to the Fresno River reservation. One of five children, Perlot had been raised by pious working-class parents who had been successful enough in business to see that their children received a formal education (Lamar 1985:xvi). After leaving his family to work in Paris in 1845, Perlot continued his studies by drawing on

Multiple Perspectives on a Critical Time

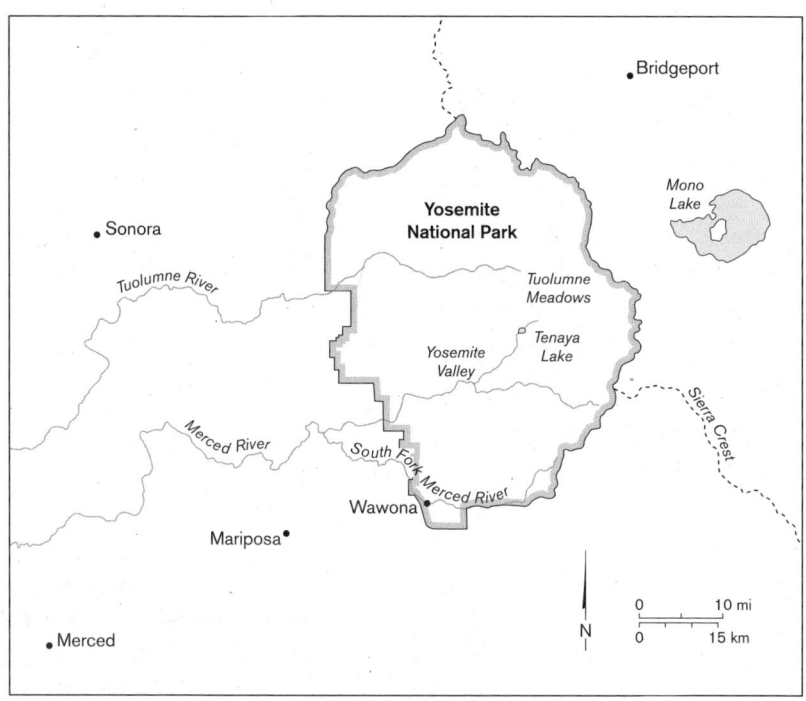

MAP 2. Cultural and natural locales of significance to Mariposa Battalion activities (1851–1852) in the Yosemite region.

his own financial resources, and he took a particular interest in mathematics and engineering (Lamar 1985:xvii). These skills ultimately led him to become a significant figure in the construction of the northern road into Yosemite Valley in the mid-1850s, after the local gold deposits had largely played out. But unlike Bunnell, Perlot sought no personal recognition or aggrandizement through his association with Yosemite. Instead, he described his memoir, comprised of stories recorded in his journals and published in 1879, as a tale "quite simply that of a man at grips with the difficulties of life who finally manages to surmount them; it can interest some friends, not the public" (Perlot 1985:xi). Thus, the account of his mining adventures and interactions with native people along the Merced River—written in French, composed strictly for the enjoyment of family and friends, and seeking only limited publication—remained unknown to the literary world for nearly a century (Lamar 1985).[6]

Although Perlot lacked previous experience with native people and the intellectual call that prompted Bunnell to elicit specific information from Tenaya, he was nonetheless fascinated by and had a quick appreciation for the native people of the Yosemite region. Both his words and actions—including interceding with local officials on behalf of native people of the Merced canyon country to allow movement free from physical threat (Perlot 1985:223–228)—indicate Perlot's compassion for the native people with whom he interacted over a number of years. As a foreigner, Perlot was untainted by the prejudices and negative images of native people that prevailed in the United States at the time (Lamar 1985:xxv; Solnit 1994:280). Therefore, his perceptions and narrative were unencumbered by the tropes of the Vanishing Indian, manifest destiny, and the triumph of civilization over wilderness. Instead, we find a detailed, charitable portrait of native individuals and daily life and intimate insights into the struggles of these people in a landscape overrun by often hostile Euro-American invaders. Solnit (1994:282) noted that Perlot's understanding of native people "is a remarkable assessment for its time, making them out to be neither Diggers nor noble savages," and she further concluded that "no other nineteenth century outsider wrote about the [Yosemite Indians] with the camaraderie and respect he did" (Solnit 1994:284). Whereas Bunnell provides precontact history related to the first assault of colonialism and a rather detached ethnographic view of native life at the time of contact, Perlot's account explores the practices, needs, motivations, and relations of Indian people during the second assault of colonialism. In this, he treated his "subjects" much as he did himself—as individuals coping with, and presumably overcoming, life's difficulties. Perlot's continued interaction with indigenous people over a number of years also provides a diachronic view of some changes that occurred in native life at that time. These facets of Perlot's memoir blend history and anthropology together, while also distinguishing his "ethnography" from the formal work of anthropologists in region several decades later.

TRAVELERS, NATURALISTS, AND INNKEEPERS

Less substantial secondary historical narratives and, especially, brief firsthand personal accounts of Yosemite Indian life, culture, and language during the mid- to late 1800s are available in the writings of early nonnative residents of, or visitors to, Yosemite Valley. Geared toward the general public, either in the form of memoirs or prose responding directly to the growing interest in and reputation of the incomparable natural landscape, these records were usually written by self-styled—and often self-published—authors within what might be broadly termed natural history or travel literature. Journalistic tendencies are evident in the work of James Hutchings, an entrepreneur who actively endeavored to promote California as a destination for travel or settlement and later became one of the early innkeepers in Yosemite Valley. Like thousands of other men, the Englishman Hutchings came to California during the Gold Rush and was initially successful in the diggings. His success was short-lived, however, and he determined that his fortune was better made elsewhere. Taking an early interest in Yosemite after he learned of its scenic grandeur, he traveled there in 1855 to develop material for the inaugural issue of *Hutchings' California Magazine*. He followed this initial visit with several others in subsequent years and eventually took up permanent residence in Yosemite Valley in 1864, three years after the final edition of the magazine was published. The lead article in the first issue of his magazine was a history of "Yo-ham-i-te" Valley, including a brief summary of the activities of the Mariposa Battalion (Hutchings 1856). This was a secondhand account of these matters, however, and differs in significant respects from the version penned later by Lafayette Bunnell. In fact, Hutchings's article may have prompted Bunnell's (1859) initial rejoinder and later book-length treatment on the subject. Although Hutchings's piece lacks detail on Yosemite Indian history prior to the arrival of the Mariposa Battalion, this and some of his later writings regarding Yosemite natural history make reference to and provide additional insight into the recent history and culture of local native people (e.g., Hutchings 1888). These records are generally impartial, likely reflecting his warm familiarity with Yosemite Indians given his daily contact with and employment of native people in his role as innkeeper of the Upper Hotel (Russell 1992:57).

Sporadic accounts pertaining to Yosemite Indians continued to appear during the late 1800s and into the early 1900s. These included notes on Indian names for topographic features, such as those recorded by Whitney (1869), and brief observations hidden within personal memoirs otherwise focused on other subjects. The most well-known author in the latter genre is naturalist John Muir, who sometimes made brief note of Indian trails, camps, material culture, activities, and foods (e.g., Muir 1894, 1911, 1912). More typical of this genre are accounts such as that of Constance Gordon-Cumming (1886), a Scottish artist with the means to travel the world and the inclination to record what she witnessed on her journeys. Like other artists and photographers of the day, Gordon-Cumming made brief mention of native life and also made Yosemite native people the subject of a few of her artistic endeavors. Two literary figures of this period, however, are notable exceptions to the "one hit wonders" common at the time. The first is Stephen Powers, a journalist and author educated at the University of Michigan, and the second is Galen Clark, the longtime guardian of Yosemite. Shortly after graduation from Michigan, the twenty-three-year-old Powers became a Civil War correspondent and later worked as a writer for the *New York Times* and other newspapers. He arrived in San Francisco in 1869 at the end of a cross-country journey and, after publishing a book recounting the adventures of his continental trek, turned his professional attention to the native people of California. During 1871 and 1872, he traveled throughout the northern and central portions of the state to gather material for a series of articles on the "habits, customs, legends, geographical boundaries, religious ideas, etc." of California Indians for the *Overland Monthly* and *Atlantic* (Heizer 1976). Eventually revised, compiled, and published by the U.S. government as *Tribes of California* in 1877, this volume included one chapter dealing exclusively with Yosemite native place names, village locations, and myths, while another chapter considered Miwok people of the central Sierra Nevada more generally.[7]

While Powers was largely neutral in his portrayal and discussion of Yosemite Indians, his treatment of other groups was significantly less sympathetic and his language much harsher than that of Bunnell. This, despite the conclusion of at least one commentator that Powers maintained genuine favor for California native people (Heizer 1976:4). Thus, Powers's negative judgments and tone might simply reflect the time in which he was writing, as the twenty years since Bunnell's observation of Yosemite Indians had been particularly difficult for the native people as a result of their dire economic circumstances and ever-expanding American settlement. Powers's account was a faithful, if somewhat jaded, record of what he observed or was able to elicit from native informants, although he chose to focus his efforts only on those people and customs he felt most closely represented traditional (i.e., precolonial) life. Anthropologist Alfred Kroeber subsequently recognized Powers's work as the first systematic attempt at California Indian ethnology, despite his lack of professional training and the "looseness of his data and method" (Kroeber 1925:ix). Thus, in style and content, Powers' work falls somewhere between the Yosemite natural history and travel literature typical of the late 1800s and the institutionally based anthropological research initiated in the region in the early 1900s.

This same literary territory is represented by Galen Clark's major contribution to the current study. Clark followed the lure of gold to California from New York in 1853 at the relatively mature age of thirty-nine, and he worked as a miner and surveyor in the Mariposa area until health problems led him to give up this life (Clark 1907:xii). Thus, in 1857, having discovered the beauty of Yosemite Valley for himself just two years earlier, Clark chose to establish a way station for Yosemite travelers along the South Fork of the Merced River in Wawona (see map 2). With the creation of the state reserve encompassing Yosemite Valley and the Mariposa Grove of Big Trees in 1864, Clark's duties expanded to serve as "Guardian of the Valley," a responsibility he shouldered until the early 1890s. Although he produced brief annual reports for the government as part of his caretaking duties, Clark was inclined to leave literary efforts to the likes of fellow Yosemite resident James Hutchings. In fact, it was only at the prompting of some associates that he finally produced the most readily available of his writings, a slight book on Yosemite Indians self-published in 1907. Based on his years of interaction and experience with local native people, Clark's *Indians of the Yosemite Valley and Vicinity* is best considered a concise ethnography, although like Powers he lacked any formal training in anthropology. Clark (1907:1) himself describes his literary effort as an attempt to satisfy the curiosity of Yosemite visitors rather than filling any intellectual niche.

Notably absent from Clark's account is any invective or judgment regarding the people and customs he described. Instead, it appears that the venerable guardian of Yosemite's natural wonders also saw the protection of Yosemite Indians as part of this charge. This is suggested, for example, by his admonishment to tourists to "treat the Indians with courtesy and consideration," including paying Indian people for their services as subjects of photography (Clark 1907:104). Clark (1907:1) also decried the fact that native "tribal relations were ruthlessly broken up by the sudden advent of the white population of gold miners . . . and subsequent war," and headings such as "Hardship and Suffering" in the chapter titled "Effects of the War" leave little doubt where his sentiments lay. Clark drew on Bunnell for his section on Yosemite Indian history, but in the remainder of the volume he relied on his own knowledge and relationships with native people. As noted in the introduction by W. W. Foote, a prominent San Francisco citizen and former senatorial candidate, "Mr. Clark has told the story of these people from their own standpoint, and with a sympathetic understanding of their character" (Clark 1907:x).

ANTHROPOLOGICAL PERSPECTIVES

Clark's book appeared at a time when institutionally based anthropologists were just beginning to turn their attention to California Indian people, but unlike *Indians of the Yosemite Valley and Vicinity*, publications resulting from such disciplinary studies were produced for an audience of other professionals rather than for the edification of the general public. As the preceding discussion suggests, description of Yosemite native peoples and cultures had, up until that time, been spread across various literary genres, open to whomever had an interest and inclination to record what they observed. This was true elsewhere in the United States during the nineteenth century as well, but as disciplinary walls were constructed around the previously commingled pursuits of history and anthropology in the early to mid-1800s, definition and acceptance of what constituted true ethnology became much more rigid (Conn 2004). Professional anthropological practice crystallized first in museums and later in university departments, as anthropologists sought to establish a systematic approach to the collection of objects, traditions, language, and even people as representative of regional cultures. In fact, such practices arose in tandem with the trope of the Vanishing American so prevalent in other literary genres of the time and was pursued with the specific intent to preserve what was viewed as destined to be lost. That is, just like the romantic authors of the age, intellectuals feared the eminent demise of traditional native cultures, although they saw their work as undertaking science rather than constructing narrative (Conn 2004).

What distinguished ethnographic literature from historical fiction and prose was the reliance on "memory culture" and construction of the so-called ethnographic present. Professional practice called for retrodicting native culture back to a time before presumed "contamination" of traditional lifeways due to interaction with Euro-Americans, with such influences largely seen as nonnative "vices" that had corrupted the "noble savage." Therefore, ethnological methods required asking elder informants to remember back to their youth or to draw on stories and memories of their parents or grandparents to reveal traditional customs, unlike other nonfiction writers of the time who simply wrote about what they directly observed. The resulting depiction is a "composite description of the probable baseline behavior of people, one in which time is loosely held constant and which is drawn from diverse [informants]" (Burton 1988:424). In their literature, anthropologists attempted to create a timeless view of indigenous cultures that lacked history, consistent with the prevailing view that relatively little cultural change had occurred within native communities prior to the arrival of European colonists. As discussed by Hastrup (1990:45), the ethnographic present thus served as "a literary device, and as such it needs to be questioned along with other conventions of representation" (see also Burton 1988:422). She argues that it "came to represent the reality of the other *society*" (Hastrup 1990:50, emphasis original), instead of being more accurately acknowledged as representing the field methods of anthropologists who produced it.

Such was the professional context and established practice prevailing when several scholars first undertook ethnological fieldwork within the native households and villages of Yosemite Valley and elsewhere in the central Sierra Nevada in the early 1900s. The first of these scholars was actually not an anthropologist by training but rather C. Hart Merriam, a Yale-educated biologist and Columbia-educated physician from a wealthy New York family. Although he served as head of the Division of Economic Ornithology and Mammalogy within the U.S. Department of Agriculture beginning in the mid-1880s, Merriam also maintained a keen interest in native people and some of his ethnographic fieldwork was funded privately by railroad tycoon E. H. Harriman (Kroeber 1955). Merriam first collected information from the native people of Yosemite in 1898, when he was in his midforties, but continued his work sporadically until the early 1920s (Bates 1993). He interviewed individuals living in Yosemite Valley, visited families in the lower reaches of the Merced River watershed, and had a clear rapport with and respect for the native people with whom he worked. He noted that "they (both men and women) often tell me that I am not like other white folks—meaning of course the kind they usually come in contact with. Thank God I'm not" (Clark 1902:210, cited in Bates 1993:10). Significantly, Merriam was able to understand and perhaps converse in the Miwok language, and sought to also learn the personal background of his many informants (Bates 1993:10–11). During his lifetime, Merriam wrote several papers on ethnogeography, language, myths, and other aspects of Miwok culture, including an informative article on the location of native village sites within Yosemite Valley. After his death in 1942, some of Merriam's original ethnographic notes and maps were variously accessioned by the Bancroft Library at the University of California, Berkeley, and the Library of Congress. Materials at the former institution were subsequently prepared and published posthumously in the 1970s.

In contrast to Merriam, Samuel A. Barrett came to the Yosemite region relatively early in his career as an anthropologist. He studied under the direction of Alfred Kroeber and earned the first Ph.D. from the newly formed department of anthropology at the University of California, Berkeley, in 1908. While a still a graduate student, Barrett conducted his fieldwork among the Me'-wuk (especially those living north of Yosemite) for a few months in 1906 (Bates 1993). Following graduation, he left California to accept a position as curator at the Milwaukee Public Museum, but Barrett maintained his research interest in California native people throughout his life and even undertook the production of ethnographic films of California Indians shortly before his death in the 1960s. Unlike Barrett, Edward W. Gifford received no formal training in anthropology nor any education beyond his high-school diploma. Instead, nearly a decade of museum and field experience as an ornithologist at the California Academy of Sciences in San Francisco in the early 1900s eventually brought him to the anthropology museum at the University of California, Berkeley, in 1912. In this position, he undertook ethnographic fieldwork under the direction of Kroeber, and his success as an anthropologist led to his advancement both within the museum and as an instructor within the anthropology department (Foster 1960). Although Gifford became well known for his work in the Pacific Islands later in his career, his early anthropological fieldwork was with California Indians, especially Sierra Me'-wuk peoples.[8] Gifford began his fieldwork in the Sierra Nevada in 1913 and continued this effort into the 1920s (Bates 1993:11). Thus, he had a much more enduring and prolonged relationship with native people of the region than Barrett, although he never undertook work within Yosemite itself. The ethnographic studies of both Barrett and Gifford were primarily published by the University of California in an anthropological monograph series, although some of Gifford's work remained unpublished (Bates 1993:11). These publications included treatises on myths, geography, language, and religion, but the most substantial ethnography they produced was a coauthored volume published in 1933, which stands as the only comprehensive primary ethnography of the Indians of the Yosemite region.

These three scholars all shared an affinity for native people that was necessary for successful work and, like Perlot, Hutchings, Clark, and others who lived and worked with Yosemite native people, the extended fieldwork in which they engaged allowed them to "develop sympathy for those they studied . . . [and led] them to portray Indians as something other than obstacles to white progress" much like other early anthropologists (Conn 2004:24). These records are especially important, however, because of the thorough and systematic methods used. On the other hand, it is now clear that the records of these and other ethnographers likely reveal as much, if not more, of postcolonial culture than they do of an earlier time, despite their desire to capture a pristine view of native culture unaffected by nonnative interaction. The potential for introduced disease and significant cultural consequences preceding face-to-face encounters, in particular, was not even conceived of by these researchers. Thus, a shadow is cast over the presumed clarity of the ethnographic present, since the baseline was often set no earlier than the Gold Rush.

Still, such concerns do not require that the data compiled by these early ethnographers be ignored, especially since direct contact with nonnative people had occurred only sixty to seventy-five years earlier. Elder Yosemite informants were not expected to reconstitute native life much beyond their own experience, and there is evidence that Gifford, at least, was able to retrodict native culture based not only on memory but also by drawing inferences from Miwok terminology that revealed archaic institutions and practices. Therefore, it is simply necessary to see such sources for the record they are rather than the record they were intended to be. That is, they are accounts of native culture, albeit ones that were, by the methods used, decoupled from time and thus of less direct utility in a historical anthropological study than observations and practices that can be linked to a particular date. Instead of "baseline ethnography" (Burton 1988:424) of a primordial past, the work of Barrett, Gifford, Merriam, and even Clark is a composite of Yosemite Indian culture representing or spanning some unknown period of time—presumably at least the lifetime of the informant(s), even if that "informant" was the conveyed memory of individuals no longer living at the time the interview took place.

It is possible to be torn between two analytical extremes as we struggle to determine exactly what period, if any, these records actually represent. At one extreme, we might conclude that the ethnography of "memory culture" is simply a precontact figment of the imagination with no analytical merit (e.g., Dunnell 1991). Less pessimistically, we might conclude that each record either accurately represents the postcontact life in the mid-1800s or is some reasonably accurate picture of precontact life, although not necessarily dating back to before the infiltration of nonnative disease. Since the Gold Rush records of Bunnell and Perlot clearly reveal that many traditional practices (and presumably traditional beliefs) were maintained well past the introduction of disease and even beyond the physical incursion into and occupation of Yosemite Valley by nonnative people, there is no reason for extreme pessimism in this case. In fact, we are fortunate in the Yosemite case, because we have the additional historical observations of several individuals who were not burdened with or hampered by the dictates of a disciplinary science that constrained both what was asked of native people and how the data were presented. Instead, these records reflect what was actually observed. Thus, while it is difficult to place ethnographic observations of anthropologists in time relative to either the introduction of nonnative disease or the incursion of nonnative people given the methodological approach employed, these records can be assessed and utilized in light of ethnohistoric evidence, oral tradition, and archaeological data.[9]

ARCHAEOLOGICAL EVIDENCE

Authors of archaeological investigations are relative latecomers to the historical anthropological narrative of Yosemite Indians. Such work was initiated by graduate students of the University of California, Berkeley, in the early 1950s and continues to be carried out to this day by government employees and contractors under the auspices of the National Park Service. By the time archaeological investigations were underway in the Yosemite area, anthropologists no longer maintained a belief in static native cultures that had stymied the work of an earlier generation of archaeologists and ethnographers. The development of radiocarbon dating in 1948 provided a scientific method with which to demonstrate the time depth of native occupation in North America, and decades of archaeological research in Central California had established a relative chronology based on artifact assemblages, especially from burial lots. Archaeologists working in Yosemite in the 1950s and

1960s followed this lead, focusing on the construction of cultural chronology based on diagnostic artifacts recovered through stratigraphic excavations of habitation sites. The size and form of projectile points was central to this effort, although types of milling implements, varieties of stone used to manufacture flaked and ground-stone tools, and presence or absence of some types of flaked stone or bone tools also contributed to chronology building. Broad periods spanning centuries or millennia were outlined, with rough estimates for the age of period transitions proposed based on comparison with the Central California sequence (Bennyhoff 1956).

By the 1980s, government archaeologists undertaking projects for cultural resource compliance were moving away from a focus on chronology. Their work became more firmly rooted in the contemporary concerns of processual archaeology, including reconstructing practices of subsistence, settlement, technology, and exchange. The potential significance of history, contingency, and the individual was ignored in favor of cultural causation originating in interacting systems of technology and environment. While the ultimate goal of processual archaeology was to establish broad generalizations of culture, much of the archaeological work in Yosemite maintained a concern with local culture history and tracing diachronic trends within broad research domains. Given that compliance motivated investigations, excavation at any given site tended to be limited, with a series of dispersed 1-by-1-meter excavation units rather than broad areal exposures. In addition, much more data were derived for more-developed areas of Yosemite National Park, such as Yosemite Valley and Wawona, than for higher-elevation zones (see Hull and Moratto 1999).

Results of archaeological investigations since the initiation of work in the 1950s have been presented in technical reports intended strictly for a professional disciplinary audience and park managers. Only limited report publication by the National Park Service has been undertaken to support the dissemination of information. An important contribution of contemporary work, however, was a major synthesis of archaeological investigations undertaken in Yosemite National Park since 1980 (Hull and Moratto 1999). This document reviewed the state of knowledge within a series of research domains and also included a thorough assessment of the regional chronology (Moratto 1999). Periods defined for the archaeological record of the nineteenth and early twentieth century are based on historical records and temporally diagnostic artifacts of Euro-American manufacture. Conversely, that portion of the chronology predating A.D. 1800 is based on

- calibrated radiocarbon dates from intact cultural features or deposits;
- the presence of temporally diagnostic artifacts such as projectile points, which have age ranges known from their association with radiocarbon dates in the Sierra Nevada and western Great Basin;
- stratigraphic observations; and
- obsidian hydration data used for either relative or absolute dating of flaked stone artifacts.

The widespread application of obsidian hydration analysis in studies undertaken since the early 1980s has proven to be a particularly effective tool for archaeological research in the Yosemite area, as radiocarbon-dateable features are rare and obsidian is abundant. This technique measures the depth of molecular water penetration into the surface of an artifact, as this depth increases with increasing age of the artifact. When used as an absolute dating technique for obsidian from the Casa Diablo quarry source, raw obsidian hydration measurements are converted to calibrated radiocarbon years based on a source-specific, temperature-dependent rate formula (Hull 2001b). It has been demonstrated repeatedly that empirically based methods such as this avoid substantial errors and problems common to rates based on hydration induced in a laboratory (e.g., Hull 2001b; Rogers 2006). Relative dating with raw obsidian hydration measurements for Casa Diablo or other types of obsidian found in the region is possible when artifacts are recovered from similar environmental contexts and are of the same geological source material.

Studies over the past twenty-five years have revealed many challenges in dealing with the archaeological record of Yosemite (Hull and Moratto 1999). The poor preservation of organic materials is particularly acute due to acidic and abrasive soils, and this results in a paucity of information regarding health, diet, and some forms of material culture such as baskets and architecture. Especially important to the current study is the lack of information on endemic disease and even general maladies in precolonial times that might manifest themselves in human skeletal or fecal remains. The paucity of organic material also makes the routine application of radiocarbon dating impossible.

The archaeological record is necessarily biased toward stone tools and manufacturing debris, rather than representing the full suite of items and features produced and used by native people. Excavations and attendant analyses have also demonstrated complex occupational histories for individual habitation and use locales. And teasing apart such complexity is made more difficult by cultural and natural site formation processes such as artifact scavenging and bioturbation due to rodent activity. Such factors result in the disturbance of features such as hearths as well as potential mixing of cultural materials from more than one occupational episode. Finally, continuing debate and discussion regarding the utility of obsidian hydration dating, the method most often relied upon to date artifacts and sites in the Sierra Nevada, has necessitated continued critical assessment of how this technique should be used in Yosemite. A complete review of the literature on this topic is beyond the scope of the current discussion, but it is worth noting that the empirical approach now commonly employed for the development of obsidian hydration rates for geological source materials used by Yosemite Indians has proven to be much more robust than methods based on induced-hydration studies (Hull 2001b; Rogers 2006). Moreover, continued testing and refinement of these methods provides confidence in the regional chronology based on obsidian hydration dates.

BRINGING THE RECORDS TOGETHER

As this review indicates, there is a diversity of sources and voices that facilitate historical anthropological study of the timing, magnitude, and cultural consequences of colonial-era disease-induced depopulation within Yosemite Valley. In that, we have met the first of two challenges in any study of this kind—the quantity of material available (Galloway 2006:33). The remaining challenge is that of bias—especially the personal, political, cultural, or religious perspectives potentially clouding an author's understanding of what was being observed or that person's ability to accurately represent such observations in writing (Galloway 2006:36–38). In the Yosemite corpus, such bias is most evident in the historical narratives and travel literature of the mid- to late 1800s. Prejudices common to the time are evident in the choice of language and the abhorrence of some native practices. This is especially true with respect to perceived uncleanliness of person and home as well as disapproval of the strenuous work required of native women, which was often compared unfavorably to the activities of native men by contemporary observers. Both of these judgments derive from contrast with the genteel life of men and women in the well-heeled society to which the authors belonged, as nearly all were white males who benefited from a formal education and a comfortable life. Significantly, such opinions are most common to those observers whose time among Yosemite Indians was relatively brief rather than prolonged. Still, such biases seem rather insignificant given what we know of the observers, as most demonstrate enduring interest in native people and culture and, by the standards of the day, were relatively sympathetic and careful observers.

The record of Yosemite Indians produced in mid- to late nineteenth century also represents a fortuitous intersection of people, events, and a social and intellectual climate at a time when ethnography was beginning to emerge. The developments of the science of ethnology and the constitution of anthropology as a discipline at this same time likely brought less passion and prejudice to these accounts than may have been typical of previous centuries (see Washburn and Trigger 1996). In addition, all of these accounts were written at a time when native people and cultures were presumed to be quickly disappearing. Individuals drawn to Yosemite at this critical time often felt an underlying, or even overt, sense of responsibility to make a record of native culture and language, and this sense of urgency led in part to the abundance of records we now enjoy.

On a more general level, the ethnohistoric sources available for Yosemite share a problem common to all such records, regardless of the time or place in which they were collected. As noted by Galloway (2006:12), there is a tendency for documentary evidence to be well understood in terms of time but to exhibit less clarity with respect to place. Conversely, archaeology often suffers from the reverse, with place firmly established and time more loosely defined. Oral history may be difficult to affix in either time or place. These are fundamental issues that make specific records more or less suited to analysis at a particular temporal or spatial scale. The relative recency of the colonial encounter, availability of eyewitness records that date to the very moment of physical invasion of the Yosemite homeland by nonnative people, and the abundance of primary material for Yosemite may compensate for some of these problems. In addition, the latter factor may address biases specific to certain types of records, since there is often the opportunity to examine multiple sources on any given issue and to check one record against another. For example, the atemporal ethnographic present of anthropologists may be juxtaposed with the observations of native life and culture in historical narratives and personal memoirs that are firmly fixed in time. Such interrogation helps clarify the period actually represented in ethnography. Similarly, archaeological data provide an alternate source with which to assess the events or practices revealed in historical accounts, thereby contributing to assessment of timing, change, or continuity. Finally, use of multiple dating methods such as obsidian hydration dating, radiocarbon assays, and temporally diagnostic artifacts can provide greater confidence in archaeological chronology.

Among the many strengths of the Yosemite historical records is the significant time that nonnative observers actually spent with Yosemite Indian people, the efforts they made to learn about history and culture, and equitable relationships of trust and mutual understanding that often developed between Indian and nonnative interlocutors. And with respect to archaeology, a similar enduring commitment to archaeological study of native people and lifeways has been demonstrated, with each new project building upon the last (Hull and Moratto 1999). With these strengths in mind, the ability of the Yosemite Indian case to contribute to the debate on the significance of native depopulation and to inform on the broader process of colonial encounters in North America is clear. Three factors stand out as especially important. First, the facts and timing of demographic collapse are established by multiple lines of nonarchaeological evidence. Both ethnohistoric data and tree-ring dating reveal temporary exile from Yosemite Valley in the face of disease-induced population loss. Native oral history also suggests the potential for significant culture change in the short term—and perhaps even the long term—as native peoples initially relocated, intermarried with neighboring peoples, and then reestablished settlement a generation later. Therefore, both depopulation and consequent culture change can be further assessed with independent, archaeological data rather than relying solely on archaeology to prove that such change occurred. Second, these diverse records indicate that epidemic disease preceded nonnative encroachment into this region by at least fifty years. Given the temporal gap between population collapse and direct contact with nonnative peoples—and the fact that the Indian inhabitants of Yosemite Valley were physically isolated from the direct effects of missionization and later secular developments in Mexican California—the potential exists to examine culture change resulting from population decline without the likely confounding influence of change prompted by native participation in colonial enterprises and institutions. This is exactly the social context that would prevail elsewhere in North America in cases where introduced disease significantly preceded face-to-face encounters with nonnative people. Finally, temporal control of archaeological data from the Yosemite area is possible through obsidian hydration dating of flaked stone artifacts (Hull 2001b). Unlike colonial-era research relying on chronologies based on the incorporation of nonnative goods, use of this temporal technique in a large-scale regional approach fosters a long-term view that facilitates a historical anthropological understanding of the issue of colonial encounters (see also Kulisheck 2005:9). With these strengths in mind, we can now turn to what these records reveal.

CHAPTER 3

Colonial Encounters in Yosemite Valley

In March of 1851, the Mariposa Battalion entered Yosemite Valley intent on removing the Indian people living there. For months before, small parties of Indians had been raiding miners' camps in the foothills to the west, stealing provisions, gear, horses, and mules. In late 1850, however, an encounter at a trading post on the Fresno River had left three white men dead (Bunnell 1990:9). Within days, additional violence farther south confirmed recent threats that the Indian people of the mountains would join together in a concerted effort to remove the miners from their territory (Bunnell 1990:6, 12). These native people were being slowly starved to death by the loss of game taken by the miners and the inability to access the oaks that provided their staple acorns (Clark 1907:7; Perlot 1985:126, 128, 223). But the men working the gold-bearing placer deposits of the central Sierra Nevada foothills had no concern for the plight of the nearby native families. Organized response by the mining community was deemed necessary to put an end to the escalating Indian menace.

Support for a militia was sought from California governor John McDougal. By January of 1851, more than two hundred volunteers had mustered to form three companies of the Mariposa Battalion. The men selected James D. Savage as their leader, with John Boling,[1] William Dill, and John J. Kuykendall serving as the company captains (Bunnell 1990:15–16, 20). Savage was the proprietor of the Fresno River trading establishment at which the original incident occurred. Earlier in

1850, he had been forced to abandon another trading post he operated at the confluence of the south fork and main Merced rivers due to Indian aggression (Bunnell 1990:3, 39). This, despite the fact that, in the custom of the region, Savage had married several Indian wives to establish and solidify his relationship with local native groups (Bunnell 1990:3; Russell 1992:21). The battalion volunteers were convinced that some of the native people responsible for the recent offenses were the "Yosemite"—Indians known to live in the rugged country to the east and to inhabit a mysterious valley that had heretofore only been seen by non-Indian people from a distance. When Savage's militia entered Yosemite Valley in the waning light of that March day, they were the first nonnative people to do so. This action heralded the end, rather than the beginning, of colonial history for the Yosemite Indians.

SUBJUGATION AND DEFIANCE

Two companies of the battalion had traveled on horseback for several days from the plains below the mining town of Mariposa in the Sierra Nevada foothills, some 250 kilometers east of San Francisco (see map 2). Riding east over Chowchilla Mountain and into the Wawona basin, they continued downriver to an encampment of Nutchu[2] on the South Fork of the Merced River known to Major Savage (Bunnell 1990:41–43; Crampton 1957:46). Taken by surprise, the Indian families and their leader, Ponwatchee, did not resist capture. They agreed that they would go peacefully to the reservation on the Fresno River, and they burned their village as a sign of their commitment to this path (Bunnell 1990:46). At the request of Savage, Indian messengers were sent to the two other nearby bands to ask them to surrender as well. Pohonichi villagers living on the divide to the north conceded within hours (see Crampton 1957:47–48), but only the aged chief of the Yosemite came to the battalion camp to hear what Savage proposed (Bunnell 1990:48). Chief Tenaya listened as Savage told him the battalion would wage war on his people if they did not come to the reservation and make peace with the U.S. Indian commissioners who were charged with negotiating treaties. Tenaya was unmoved and saw no reason for the Yosemite to leave their home if they consented to cease provoking miners through theft or violence. Still, after further interchange facilitated by hand gestures and a mission Indian translator who had once lived in the mountains, Tenaya agreed to return with his people. He set off to bring them back to the battalion camp, but when he returned the next day he was alone. Tenaya claimed that the Yosemite were delayed by the deep, fresh snow. Days passed, and still the Indian people did not arrive (Bunnell 1990:50). At last, Savage lost patience and decided that the battalion must seek out the Yosemite in their valley home.

Given the anticipated rough travel ahead, a smaller force was deemed sufficient for the final leg of the journey into Yosemite Valley. Footraces decided who among the company of 105 men would march on and who would stay behind at the river camp to guard the captives already gathered there (Bunnell 1990:51). With Tenaya as guide, Savage and 57 company men began the trek on horseback through the snow over the ridge between the south fork and main Merced rivers (Crampton 1957:48). Hours later—and still many miles from their destination—the battalion was met by a group of 72 native men, women, and children (Bunnell 1990:54; cf. Crampton 1957:48; Hutchings1856:4). These, Tenaya claimed, were the only people who were willing to make peace with the U.S. government. He said the remainder were households headed by men of other bands who had Yosemite wives. These men and their families had gone north or east, refusing to be confined to a reservation in the San Joaquin Valley and be at the mercy of both Indian and white enemies. But Savage was not convinced. He believed that more Indian people must still be hiding, and he determined to continue on to Yosemite Valley to capture all who remained. As Tenaya turned to follow his people on the trail heading south, the battalion continued north, traveling the path in the snow left by the retreating families.

At last emerging from the forest above the cliffs that formed the southwestern precipice of the valley of the Yosemite, near what is now known as Inspiration Point, the company beheld the sheer granite walls that extended nearly 600 meters down to the valley floor (figure 1). Light and shadow played off the rocks, and white clouds perched on distant peaks and domes. Creeks rushed over the cliffs nearby, forming majestic waterfalls that plunged to the talus slopes below. These rocky inclines were obscured in the misty spray of the crashing water and the groves of oak, pine, and cedar that fringed the valley margins. Farther from the valley walls, the trees gave way to verdant meadows still laced with snow, and the creeks emerged from the forest to join the meandering river that bisected the valley from east to west. Intent on their mission and fatigued from many hours on the trail, few in the company stopped to marvel at the breathtaking landscape. Instead, the horses and their weary riders picked their way, single file, through the snow and rocks, descending as a brittle thread to the valley floor. They

FIGURE 1. View of Yosemite Valley from Inspiration Point. (*General View of the Great Yo-Semite Valley, Mariposa County, California,* circa 1859, lithograph by Thomas A. Ayres. Robert B. Honeyman Jr. Collection of Early Californian and Western American Pictorial Material, BANC PIC 1963.002:0001–1886. Courtesy of the Bancroft Library, University of California, Berkeley.)

made camp that night at the foot of their trail at the western end of the valley, near Bridalveil Meadow (Bunnell 1990:58).

The next day, the battalion forded and reforded the frigid Merced River several times as they followed Indian trails up the valley. The company made their way 9.5 kilometers upriver to the confluence with what is now known as Tenaya Creek, near the eastern end of the valley. At this location and elsewhere along the way, the interlopers saw the abandoned dwellings, acorn caches, and sweathouses of the Indians. Fires still smouldering in the hearths—and houses full of tools, baskets, and other belongings—attested to the fact that many of these places had been left in haste only hours before (Bunnell 1990:73–74). Native oral tradition indicates that adults may also have left children hidden nearby in the rocks, to be rescued after the troops had passed (Bibby 2005:176). As the militia broke into smaller groups to continue their hunt in the rugged upper canyons on foot, the men saw footprints of the retreating Yosemite. The fresh tracks headed into the rocks or up to narrow, forested ledges that bisected the cliff walls. The only Indian discovered, however, was an elderly woman found sitting stolidly by a dying fire in a rockshelter below the Royal Arches (Bunnell 1990:74). She was too old to follow her people in either escape or surrender, and the battalion left her behind as well. Frustrated in their quest to find more captives, the men were ordered to set fire to the houses and food caches they found, with the goal of starving out anyone who might attempt to return. Low on provisions themselves, the company headed out of Yosemite Valley the following morning and rejoined their comrades on the South Fork of the Merced River that afternoon.

Approximately 350 Yosemite, Nutchu, and Pohonichi were gathered there, and the Indians began the march toward the Fresno River reservation, carrying what property they had saved before their villages were burned. The journey was slow, however, as the native men, women, and children were on foot and they had to acquire and prepare food along the trail to augment the acorn meal they still possessed. Their guard grew ever more restless and tired with each passing day, as battalion provisions continued to dwindle and the men refused to eat native foods—other than pine nuts—that were offered to them. Finally, after several days' march, the company and their captives had succeeded in traversing nearly all of the 80 kilometers from their rendezvous point to the awaiting Indian commissioners.

They made camp just hours from their destination, and all but ten of the hungry company went ahead to partake of a full meal at the commissary. Major Savage reasoned that Captain Boling and the small squad left behind were a sufficient guard, since the Indians had proven complacent. Savage believed these people were eager to reach their destination and receive the gifts that had been promised to them on their arrival. Before daybreak the following morning, however, all but one of the captives had fled while their guards slept. They had been alarmed by warnings of Indian messengers from the south, who had come through the camp the night before. The captives feared they would be ambushed once they reached the plains. Boling and his men were unable to track their former charges into the nearby brushy sanctuaries where they sought safe haven. Within a few days, however, many of the wary fugitives came to the reservation, persuaded to do so by Bautista, an Indian intermediary from the Mariposa area who followed them to their hiding places (Bibby 2005:165). But the Yosemite remained hidden. As before, only Chief Tenaya ventured down to the reservation to determine if his people should follow. He was offended by the conditions and behavior that he observed there (Bunnell 1990:97) and left without speaking to the commissioners. He took his people back to their Yosemite Valley home.

Pursuit of the Yosemite by the battalion was delayed while the militia concentrated their immediate efforts on rounding up Indians inhabiting the canyons of the upper San Joaquin River. But the refusal of Tenaya to meet with the commissioners and make peace was not forgotten. As the high waters of spring runoff began to subside in May, the battalion undertook a second military mission to Yosemite Valley, this time led by the somewhat humbled Captain Boling. Although they succeeded in capturing five young Indian scouts soon after their arrival in the valley, the talus and cliffs once again proved a powerful ally of the Indians. Two of the captives were sent out to take a message to Chief Tenaya to come down from his rocky fortress, and another hostage escaped not long thereafter. Unscrupulous guards allowed the two remaining men to break free of their bonds, believing that both could be shot with impunity when they attempted to flee. Only one—Tenaya's youngest son—was killed.[3] Within hours, the grief-stricken father found himself the latest captive, after being cornered on a ledge by Indian scouts attached to the company (Bunnell 1990:150–152).

Still, the chief refused to capitulate and, despite daily searches in and around the valley in the weeks that followed, no other Yosemite or signs of them were observed. Tenaya claimed all of his people had escaped to the eastern side of the Sierra. As spring turned to summer, the company decided to extend their search efforts farther to the east, following the receding snowline. At last, with the aid of Ponwatchee and several Nutchu guides, the battalion found their quarry camped on the frozen shore of Pywiack—Lake of the Shining Rocks—a high-country gem now known as Tenaya Lake (Kuykendall 1921:13; Russell 1992:39). The circuitous route the company had taken to the lake bypassed the village scouts who had kept watch on the battalion's movements from the valley rim ever since Tenaya's capture. Thirty-five men, women, and children—most of whom were apparently relatives of the chief—surrendered and were marched down to the Fresno River reservation with their leader (Bunnell 1990:203–209). A report from Captain Boling (1851), however, indicates that some additional Yosemite Indians may have previously sought refuge in the Merced River canyon with another group under the leadership of Cypriano (cf. Perlot 1985:182). This time, Tenaya agreed to stay on the reservation, although he did not sign a treaty or otherwise cede Yosemite Indian rights to their homeland. Previously feared and esteemed for his resistance, however, Tenaya's apparent defeat led to derision by the other Indian people living there (Bunnell 1990:246). He was also dissatisfied with the food and conditions at the reservation. After only one month, Tenaya applied for permission to return to Yosemite Valley temporarily to live off the land of his forefathers and escape the heat of the plains (Johnston 1995:9). The agent-in-charge granted his request, but Tenaya and the other Yosemite Indians who followed him would never return to the reservation again.

The Yosemite were pursued just one more time, after eight miners who entered the valley in May of 1852 were attacked and two were killed (Bunnell 1990:246–247; Johnston 1995:11; Perlot 1985:138). A regular U.S. Army company under the command of Lt. Tredwell Moore and guided by James Savage was dispatched to seek out the perpetrators and round up all others of their band (Johnston 1995:12; Perlot 1985:139). Savage returned to the San Joaquin Valley after leading the company as far as the divide between the south fork and main Merced rivers, but the company continued their search of the surrounding region, including Yosemite Valley. Many abandoned villages were found, but only one occupied encampment was discovered. Six Indian men—allegedly wearing garments of the dead men, or at least in possession of some of their belongings—were summarily executed by Moore's command, and the fifteen women and children of the group were taken prisoner (Johnston 1995:13, 22). The remainder of the Yosemite Indians, who had abandoned other villages prior to Moore's arrival, escaped across the Sierra since the snow was not deep that year (Bunnell 1990:249).

Although the company attempted to overtake them, the Yosemite found refuge with Paiute people at Mono Lake and remained there undetected by the military. Tenaya and his people were granted access to land by their hosts and stayed for more than a year (Bunnell 1990: 265). They returned to their valley in the late summer of 1853, but Tenaya and many of the young men of his band were killed shortly thereafter, as a result of a dispute with their former hosts over the theft of horses.[4] At the same time, many of the women and children were taken as "slaves" by the Mono Paiute back to the eastern side of Sierra (Bunnell 1990:265–266). The remaining members of the Yosemite tribe suffered through conflicts with neighboring native groups (e.g., Perlot 1985:220–223; Powers 1976:365) and miners on the Merced River (Bunnell 1990:266–271) during the next few years. They remained in Yosemite Valley and the adjoining Merced River canyon after 1853, however, unmolested by organized military action or the threat of removal.

In his travels, Belgian miner Jean-Nicolas Perlot visited one cluster of three villages on the divide north of the main Merced River between the south fork and Yosemite Valley in 1854. He described an active encampment of approximately 250 people (Perlot 1985:190). His physical description of the landscape and his routes of travel suggest that this settlement was located near Big Meadow, approximately 15 kilometers west of Yosemite Valley (see Bates and Lee 1990:29). At this settlement, he spoke to a chief with at least two adult sons who had been born at an unidentified mission. Although Perlot identified this group as Yosemite, the chief's reference to a treaty—a copy of which was kept by his eldest son, Scipiano (Perlot 1985:180, 223)—indicates that at least some of these people were not associated with Tenaya's original group, since Tenaya never entered into any written agreement with the U.S. government.[5] Conversely, Boling's (1851) mention of Yosemite Indians going "down to Cypriano's people" indicates the likely presence of some former members of Tenaya's band within this group. Three years later, Perlot noted that this village had been abandoned in favor of a new location in the same valley at or near Big Meadow, although only about one hundred villagers lived at the new site (Perlot 1985:296).

THE UNSEEN ENEMY: A BLACK SICKNESS IN YOSEMITE

Lafayette Bunnell's account of the Mariposa Battalion reveals—albeit briefly—the spirit and wisdom of Chief Tenaya and his Yosemite people in persisting in these threatening times. Their history was one of setbacks and triumphs, as Tenaya built his community of survivors and "outlaws" (Bunnell 1990:64) in the decades leading up to the Gold Rush. Their place in Yosemite Valley was hard-won—though not necessarily through battles with traditional enemies. It was little wonder, then, that they resisted the battalion's repeated attempts to remove them to the plains of the San Joaquin Valley.

Tenaya stated that his valley home was called Awahnee by his people and that the Indians living there in past generations were known as the Awahnichi,[6] the people of Awahnee (Bunnell 1990:64). Unlike the small band of less than one hundred individuals that remained with Tenaya on that snowy March day in 1851, the Awahnichi had once been a large and prosperous group. They lived comfortably off the game, fish, acorns, pine nuts, and other plants that were abundant in their territory. Despite the protection afforded them by their bountiful mountain enclave, however, the Awahnichi were not free from conflicts with their neighbors, nor were they safe from other threats to their livelihood and happiness. Bunnell (1990:64–65) recounted:

> I afterwards learned the traditional history of Ten-ie-ya's ancestors. His statement was to the effect that the Ah-wah-ne-chees had many years ago been a large tribe, and lived in territory now claimed by him and his people. That by wars, and a fatal black-sickness (probably smallpox or measles), nearly all had been destroyed. The survivors of the band fled from the valley and joined other tribes. For years afterward, the country was uninhabited; but few of the ... tribe ever visited it, and from a superstitious fear, it was avoided.

The Awahnichi sought refuge with neighboring groups. Tenaya's father went east to Mono Lake at that time and there met the Mono Paiute woman who gave birth to his son. Born on the eastern side of the Sierra and living there in his youth, Tenaya was prompted to return to Yosemite Valley as a young man by an aged Awahnichi "medicine man" who had been his father's trusted friend. Subduing the fear that likely derived from the mystery of disease rather than from the threats of human enemies, Tenaya returned to reclaim the territory his father's people had temporarily vacated the generation before (Bunnell 1990:65, 70–71, 264).

Tenaya's old friend continued to advise the young leader in their ancestral home, and the chief noted that shortly before his death, the medicine man,

> as if endowed with prophetic wisdom, ... assured Ten-ie-ya that while he retained possession of Ah-wah-ne his band would increase in numbers and become powerful. That if he befriended those who sought his protection, no other tribe would come to the valley to make war upon him, or attempt to drive him from it, and if [Tenaya] obeyed his counsels he would put a spell upon it that would hold it sacred for him and his people alone; none other would ever dare to make it their home. He then cautioned the young chief against the horsemen of the lowlands (the Spanish residents), and declared that, should they enter Ah-wah-ne, his tribe would soon be scattered and destroyed, or his people be taken captive, and he himself be the last chief in Ah-wah-ne. (Bunnell 1990:71)

Tenaya followed the old wise man's guidance, and the chief "was joined by the descendants from the Ah-wah-ne-chees, and by others who had fled from their own tribes to avoid summary Indian justice" (Bunnell 1990:71). Bunnell concluded that Tenaya "thus became the founder of the new tribe or band, which has since been called the 'Yosemite'" (Bunnell 1990:65). Some of those who sought refuge may have fled from the missions, since Bunnell (1990:156, 176) remarked on Tenaya's understanding of Spanish in addition to his command of multiple Indian languages (Bunnell 1990:66, 260). Tenaya likely learned Spanish from Indians who had interacted with Spaniards or Mexicans themselves, rather than his own engagement with colonists on the coast or in the interior. The Yosemite didn't live an isolated existence in terms of knowing and understanding the changing world beyond their Sierra enclave. This knowledge was likely brought home to them through mission refugees and others they welcomed into their band (see also Bunnell 1990:13, 46).

The exact timing of the "black sickness" in Yosemite remains uncertain, but this deadly epidemic clearly preceded nonnative incursion into the region, as revealed by the subsequent admonition of the medicine man to keep white strangers from ever entering their valley home. Still, tension with neighboring native groups at that time—indicated by the reference to "wars"[7]—may reflect growing pressure on the Awahnichi exerted by the colonial presence to the west. Bunnell (1990:65) lamented that he "was unable to fix upon any definite date at which the Ah-wah-ne-chees . . . [temporarily abandoned the valley], but from the fact that some of the Yosemite claimed to be direct descendants [of people who had survived the black sickness], the time could not have been as long as would be inferred from their description." Fortunately, it is possible to estimate the time of this event based on family history, physical evidence for temporary abandonment of Yosemite Valley, and records of historical epidemics and other introduced disease events in colonial California.

The first approach is to consider Tenaya's age and, therefore, the approximate year of his birth. Some, if not all, of Tenaya's offspring were adults when the battalion entered Yosemite Valley. This is indicated by the capture of three of these young men and his son-in-law during the second battalion foray (Bunnell 1990:135). The chief's granddaughter, Maria Lebrado Ydrte (To-too-yah), was born in the 1840s (Bates and Lee 1990:191; see also Bates and Wells 1981:5) and was old enough at the time of the initial battalion entry to clearly recall physical details of Maj. James Savage, who died in 1852 (Russell 1992:25; Taylor 1932). These observations suggest that Tenaya—described as gray-haired by Captain Boling (Kuykendall 1921:11)—was at least in his fifties when Bunnell recorded his statements in 1851. Hutchings

(1856:6) cites another battalion member who claimed that Tenaya (referred to as "Je-ne-a-eh") was "about sixty-five or seventy years of age." An age for Tenaya much in excess of fifty-five to sixty years old seems unlikely, however, as the "old chief" mentioned in Bunnell's account stands in contrast to the "extremely old" woman discovered by the Mariposa Battalion alone in the rockshelter at the eastern end of the valley during their initial visit (Bunnell 1990:74–75). That is, there were individuals alive who were older—even significantly older— than Tenaya. When asked about her apparent remarkable antiquity, the chief replied that "when he was a boy, it was a favorite *tradition* of the *old* members of his band, that when she was a child, the peaks of the Sierra were but little hills" (Bunnell 1990:75, emphasis original). Presumably based on the assessment of his comrades who had seen the woman themselves, battalion member Robert Eccleston recorded in his diary that this woman was more than one hundred years old (Crampton 1957:49).

In an era when expectation of life at birth for nonnative populations in North America was only approximately forty years of age (Haines 2000: table 8.2), there is no reason to believe that native people enjoyed significantly longer life and, in fact, may have rarely survived beyond age fifty (Thornton 2000:15; Ubelaker 2000:80). So Tenaya may have been considered "old" in the eyes of the young Bunnell by simply meeting, rather than exceeding, this life expectancy. The very old woman was clearly an anomaly, worthy of comment even by her contemporaries, but Tenaya was not identified as of especially great age relative to other native or nonnative men. And given that the woman was considered old even when Tenaya was young, Tenaya cannot have been more than about sixty years of age in 1851, Hutchings's account notwithstanding. Bunnell (1990:176) also noted that the chief had "agility beyond his years," and this good physical condition is consistent with an approximate age in his fifties or sixties. If this estimate of Tenaya's age in 1851 is correct, he was born between 1790 and 1800 (cf. Reynolds 1959:168). This sets self-imposed exile from Awahnee due to the black sickness sometime around the turn of the nineteenth century or perhaps as much as a decade earlier, since there is no indication how many years elapsed between his father's exodus and Tenaya's birth. His return to Yosemite Valley as a young man must have occurred between circa 1805 and 1820 (cf. Reynolds 1959:168, 191, 216).

Additional data bearing on and confirming this approximate timing of the epidemic is provided by dendrochronology of stands of trees in

Yosemite Valley. The steep-walled valley is essentially a giant trough, with groves of trees on the rocky talus slopes encircling the central meadows like bathtub rings. Dendrochronological study of the growth rings in the trees of the mixed-conifer stands and oak groves within the valley (Reynolds 1959: 173, 197) revealed that initial growth of "old-growth" conifer groves encircling the higher valley margin above the oaks and meadows generally predated 1760. "Young-growth" conifers of the valley bottom, on the other hand, invaded the meadows and flourished only after the substantial displacement of Indians by Anglo-Americans between 1860 and 1875. Initial growth of the so-called intermediate-age groves of conifers, which engulfed the older oak groves between the rings of young- and old-growth conifers, dated to between 1785 and 1810 (Reynolds 1959:196, 204). Reynolds (1959) concluded that these intermediate groves represent a period of encroachment of conifers upon the oaks, which had been previously favored by native burning. Such intentional burning of trees and undergrowth served a number of purposes, including enhancing growth of plants used for food, medicine, and basket-making materials (M.K. Anderson 2005:136). Thus, the time between the termination of expansion of the intermediate growth (i.e., circa 1810) and beginning of the young growth (i.e., circa 1860) spans the period when native people returned to the valley from their self-imposed exile and burning practices commenced once again. Significantly, Bunnell (1990:220) may have observed the results of the temporary cessation of aboriginal burning in Yosemite Valley during the previous generation without realizing the cause, as he noted that the "larger trees, pines, firs, etc. are of smaller growth than are usually found on the mountain slopes and tables." These data, then, place the temporary abandonment reported by Tenaya around 1790, with return sometime after 1805, at the earliest (see Reynolds 1959:196–197, 216).

Both the estimates of Tenaya's year of birth based on historical data and the tree-ring dating for temporary abandonment of Yosemite Valley are consistent. These data suggest pathogen infiltration and native relocation sometime between circa 1785 and 1800. Introduced Old World disease struck in Awahnee at a time when California Indian interaction with foreigners was still primarily limited to Spanish missionaries and military personnel on the coast and in adjoining valleys. The closest missions were those established in the San Francisco Bay area at San Francisco in 1776, in Santa Clara in 1777, and at San Jose in 1797. The greater bay area Ibero-American community also included a military presidio at San Francisco and a secular pueblo at San Jose. Most of the neophytes at these three missions were initially drawn from the immediate local populations of Costanoan (Ohlone) and Bay Miwok peoples (Milliken 1995). As the reach of the bay area missions extended, however, Coast Miwok residing in areas to the north of San Francisco Bay were brought into the system, as were some Patwin, Plains Miwok, and Yokuts people to the northeast, east, and southeast, respectively (map 3).[8] Resistance and desertion by neophytes—prompted by mistreatment, burdensome restrictions on personal freedom, or fear of disease—was not uncommon. Thus, this early date for Yosemite Indian depopulation around the end of the eighteenth century suggests that the black sickness was introduced inadvertently to this population by a mission neophyte or an Indian of the San Joaquin Valley fleeing the Spanish. It is also possible that an Indian of the Central Valley involved in trade or other interaction with both colonial and inland native groups may have been the disease vector.

Historical data on California epidemics are equivocal with respect to refining the date for the onset of fatal introduced European disease in Yosemite Valley, and Bunnell's parenthetical notation of smallpox or measles in his account of the black sickness is particularly problematic. No colonial outbreak of either of these diseases was recorded during the apparent period of infection in Yosemite Valley. It is important to recognize, however, that a nonnative disease reaching epidemic proportions in this inland region need not have resulted from a coeval epidemic elsewhere in colonial California. This is especially true if the culprit was smallpox, given the communicability of this particular disease for weeks, months, and even years in a dried state (Ramenofsky 1987). The singularity of an inland epidemic might also have resulted if the introduced disease originated as a "second wave" infection within a mission community that already had a significant number of immune individuals. In this case, a pathogen that would have had devastating consequences in a nonimmune population like the Awahnichi would have resulted in relatively few deaths within the original immune population. Thus, it may have gone unrecorded by the missionaries. In fact, the Yosemite case could indicate that there were many such "unrecorded" epidemics in the hinterlands of colonial California—or in North America as a whole, for that matter—due to these or other factors. Unknown and unrecorded, that is, except by the native people who survived.

Numerous episodes of nonnative disease were documented in the missions in the decades around 1800. Smallpox was largely unknown

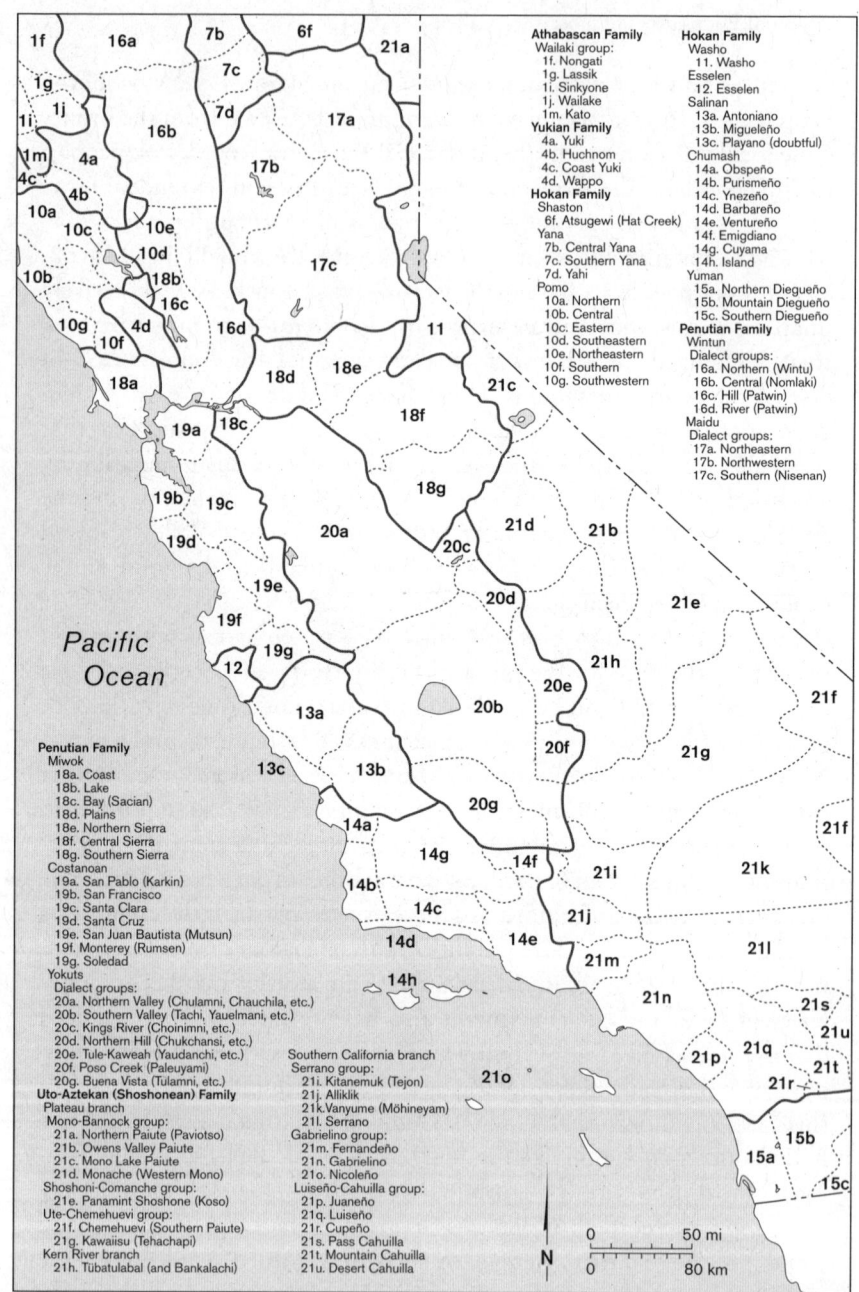

MAP 3. Native Californian ethnolinguistic areas as recognized by Heizer and Whipple (1971) (adapted from Lightfoot 2005: map 5).

in California until a major outbreak in 1828 (Cook 1939; cf. Milliken 1995:91), but there may have been potential earlier exposure to this disease in Southern California in 1781 (Cook 1939:154). There is no written evidence or native oral history to indicate that smallpox penetrated inland native populations at that time. Similarly, measles may have made a relatively late appearance in California in 1827 (Cook 1939:185), although Milliken (1995:194) identified an earlier major measles epidemic that spread northward through the missions beginning in June of 1805, and Preston (2002:79) concluded that at least some coastal people had been exposed to measles even earlier. By March of 1806, measles began penetrating the missions of the San Francisco Bay area. Significantly, Milliken (1995:194) noted that the "east-to-west movement of the epidemic suggests that it reached the bay area missions via tribal populations in the San Joaquin Valley." If this was the case, then spread to native people of the central and southern Sierra Nevada seems equally likely, particularly since historical trade relationships between Indians of the Sierra Nevada and the southern missions are indicated by both documentary and archaeological evidence (see Arkush 1993; Clark 1907:23; Heizer 1941). The timing of this epidemic is inconsistent with the above-cited physical evidence for abandonment of Yosemite Valley, however, so measles may not be the "black sickness." Unfortunately, it is unknown whether Bunnell received some information from Tenaya that specifically led to the conclusion of smallpox or measles—for example, mention of pustules or a rash—or if Bunnell was simply speculating when writing his memoir many years later. Both of these Old World diseases were highly visible in coastal California and the northern Plains just twenty years prior to the Mariposa Battalion's entry into Yosemite Valley, and this may have prompted Bunnell to suggest such pathogens among the Awahnichi.

If we discount Bunnell's "diagnosis," other possible sources of the black sickness can be considered. Two other epidemics occurred in the missions within the span of interest, both of unknown cause (Cook 1976). Milliken (1995:67) suggests that the 1777 event at Mission San Francisco was due to water contamination, and Cook (1976:18) speculates that the 1802 epidemic was a respiratory ailment. This undetermined pathogen appears to have spread north from Santa Barbara in the spring of 1801 to arrive at Mission San Francisco and Mission Santa

Clara in August of 1802 (Milliken 1995:173–174). The symptoms of the disease were sufficiently broad to encompass several potential Old World pathogens, although pneumonia, diphtheria, and scarlet fever have been suggested (Milliken 1995:174). Other infectious disease episodes, apparently not severe enough within the missions themselves to warrant designation as epidemics, also occurred during this time. For example, an outbreak of smallpox or some other nonnative disease swept through Mission Santa Clara and Mission San Francisco in 1785 (Milliken 1995:91), and a possible typhus outbreak occurred at Mission San Francisco in 1795 (Milliken 1995:138). The timing indicates that any one of these events between 1777 and 1802 could have been source for the pathogen in Yosemite, although those indirectly transmitted through agents such as lice and fleas (e.g., typhus) seem less likely. Several Old World diseases, including certain types of pneumonia and smallpox, can result in tissue necrosis that blackens the skin and thus might lead to the term *black sickness*. On the other hand, *black* may simply have been a euphemism for *fatal*.

Given so many episodes of suffering related to introduced disease around the period of interest and the likelihood of other unrecorded nonnative disease events in the interior, it is difficult to know which of these recorded epidemics—or some other unrecorded episode of introduced disease—is actually the black sickness described by Tenaya. But one thing is certain—the dendrochronological, genealogical, and ethnohistoric information all contradict the often-cited conclusion that Tenaya's statements refer to the well-documented disease "pandemic" of the early 1830s in California's Central Valley (e.g., Mundy and Hull 1988:12). The epidemic that swept through the region in 1833 was malaria (Cook 1955, 1978:92), introduced by Hudson's Bay trappers working their way down the Sacramento Valley. The symptoms of this disease are inconsistent with Bunnell's assessment of smallpox or measles, and the timing is much too late. A smallpox epidemic also occurred at about the same time as the malaria epidemic in California, but the effects of this disease were largely confined to the southern North Coast Ranges (Cook 1939, 1978:92).

BETWEEN COLONIAL ENCOUNTERS

Regardless of the exact timing of the colonial-era epidemic among the Awahnichi, the presence of nonnative infectious diseases in California between 1777 and 1833 doubtless contributed to significant changes in the demographic constitution of Yosemite Indians throughout this period. As noted above, many accounts indicate that people fled to the Sierra Nevada from the disease-ridden areas of the coast and San Joaquin Valley (Bates and Lee 1990:25; Hurtado 1988:47). And those people who survived may have remained in the mountains. Tenaya's personal history also indicates intermarriage of Awahnichi and Paiute prior to invasion by the Mariposa Battalion (see also Bunnell 1990:53–54, 64), and Savage noted that Tenaya spoke a "Paiute jargon" (Bunnell 1990:63, 156, 193; Perlot 1985:166). In fact, several languages were evidently spoken by the chief and his followers (Bunnell 1990:66, 179–180). Additionally, Bunnell (1990:64, italics original) recorded that "it was traditionary with the other Indians, that the band to which the name Yosemite had been given, had originally been formed and was then composed of outlaws or refugees from other tribes. That nearly all were descendants of the neighboring tribes on both sides of the 'Kay-o-pha,' or *Skye Mountains;* the 'High Sierras.'" Thus, by the late 1800s, if not earlier, Yosemite Indians included a mixture of Miwok, Paiute, Yokuts, and Western Mono people (Bates and Lee 1990:32).

The cosmopolitan nature of the band following the epidemic circa 1790 to 1800 may have contributed to their decision to identify themselves as "Yosemite" rather than "Awahnichi" upon their return to Awahnee. Bunnell (1990:65) observed that "from my knowledge of Indian customs, I am aware that it is not uncommon for them to change the names of persons or localities after some remarkable event in the history of either. It would not, therefore, appear strange that Ten-ie-ya should have adopted another name for his band." The substantial population decline, self-imposed exile, and subsequent return would certainly seem sufficient to prompt such a change. The word *Yosemite* itself—more properly pronounced "ūzūmati" or "ūhūmati" in the Miwok language (Barrett 1908:343; Kroeber 1921:59; see also Broadbent 1964:302; Bunnell 1990:63; cf. Bates and Lee 1990:19)—means "grizzly bear," a predator common in this region at the time. Tenaya stated "that his tribe had adopted the name because those who had bestowed it were afraid of the 'the Grizzlies' and feared his band" (Bunnell 1990:64).

By the time the descendants of the Awahnichi returned to their ancestral homeland sometime between circa 1805 and 1820, the Spanish and, later, Mexican presence was increasing in the Central Valley. The allusion by the old medicine man to the horsemen on the plains indicates that this warning and Tenaya's return to Awahnee likely occurred during a time when forays into the foothills by nonnative people were becoming more common. In the years following the turn of the nineteenth century, the escape of mission neophytes led to punitive expeditions of Spanish military, missionaries, and neophyte detachments farther inland from the coast. Gabriel Moraga led one such campaign into the San Joaquin Valley in 1806, and his traverse of some drainages in the Sierra foothills brought him closer to Yosemite than any other Spanish expedition. It was during this trek that he named the Merced River (Rio de Nuestra Senora de las Merced) and the area of Las Mariposas west of Yosemite Valley that later became the mining center for this region. Moraga returned to the Central Valley and Sierra foothills two years later, traversing some of the same territory on the lower Merced River at the edge of the San Joaquin Valley but primarily exploring areas farther to the north (Cutter 1957). Such inland forays to recapture runaways and acquire new converts were especially crucial as neophytes were lost to diseases at an alarming rate, neophyte birth rates slowed, and missions struggled to maintain sufficient populations for labor and production (e.g., Cook 1976; Milliken 1995).

The earliest direct nonnative incursion into the Yosemite area, however, did not occur until 1833. In that year, the expedition of Joseph Walker crossed the Sierra into the San Joaquin Valley from a camp somewhere near present-day Walker Lake in western Nevada. On their journey, they saw stunning waterfalls dropping over "mile-high" cliffs while following a route along a ridge between two major drainages. Many scholars believe this description refers to Yosemite Valley and the divide between the Tuolumne and Merced rivers (Russell 1992:6–7), but others are somewhat skeptical of a Walker party overview of the valley. For example, Johnston (1990:x) concluded that the description in the lone published account of the trip recorded in the diary of Zenas Leonard (1978) is too simple for such an expansive and impressive landscape. Bunnell (1990:34) also cites later conversations with Walker himself in which he denied seeing the valley. And Tenaya claimed that a party of white men preceding the Mariposa Battalion (perhaps Walker) was guided north of Yosemite Valley so as to avoid their observation of it (Bunnell 1990:70). It may be that the travelers saw Hetch Hetchy Valley instead. Regardless, Leonard (1978) makes no mention of encountering or seeing native people during the trans-Sierra trek.

The presence of American and Canadian trappers and explorers in interior California had been increasing ever since Jedediah Smith's first entry into the region in 1827. But these men did not establish permanent residence. Instead, nonnative occupation of the interior began with the establishment of ranchos, which were large tracts of land granted to individuals by the Spanish and Mexican governments for agriculture and livestock production. More than eight hundred such claims were established throughout California, although only a handful of these awards date to the Spanish period. Most were granted later by the Mexican government after 1830. Las Mariposas rancho was closest to Yosemite Valley, and this parcel of approximately 18,000 hectares extended east from the San Joaquin River in the Central Valley into the Sierra foothills. It was granted to Juan Alvarado in 1844 but was purchased by John C. Fremont in 1847. Surrounding ranchos in the eastern portion of the Central Valley included Panoche de San Juan y de los Carrisolitos, awarded to Julian Ursua in 1844, and Del Campo de los Franceses (French Camp), awarded to William Gulnac that same year and purchased by Charles Weber in 1847. The latter rancho was named for camps of French-Canadian trappers, who frequented the area beginning in 1832. The rather late entry of Mexican ranchos of the Sierra foothills into the economic picture of colonial California—and their swift demise with the initiation of the Gold Rush—meant that these institutions had relatively little direct impact on native people of the inland area, unlike on those of the Coast Ranges. Elsewhere, local Indians were drawn into the ranchos voluntarily or by force as a ready source of manual labor (Silliman 2005).

Despite their physical isolation from nonnative residents, however, Yosemite Indians were becoming more economically involved with nonnative people during the colonial period. In particular, horse thievery had become a profitable activity for native people across the San Joaquin Valley, apparently by providing an alternate source of meat in the diet and by serving as a trading commodity (see Phillips 1993). Foothill and mountain Indians would venture to the southern Coast Ranges, stealthily round up horses, and then drive them back across the San Joaquin Valley and into the Sierra for slaughter or elsewhere to exchange with Santa Fe traders and mountain men. The native people of the central and southern Sierra participated in this profitable endeavor when the opportunity presented itself (Hurtado 1988; Phillips 1993; see also Broadbent 1964:176; Bunnell 1990:21, 39, 49, 77, 197). Farther north, Sierra groups may have occasionally shifted to paid labor at Sutter's Fort near present-day Sacramento or at ranchos elsewhere in the Central Valley after secularization of the missions (Hurtado 1988). In this respect, the Indians of the western Sierra Nevada were particularly adaptable—moving from various traditional and nontraditional economic pursuits and from accommodation and resistance prior to the Gold Rush. This flexibility evidently served to enhance their survival in these changing times (Hurtado 1988:214).

As long as nonnative populations in California remained small and primarily confined to the coast, stasis in Indian-white relations prevailed for inland people. The relationship between nonnative people and Indians characteristic of the Spanish and Mexican periods only changed after the discovery of gold in the Sierra Nevada foothills and the resulting influx of miners into the new U.S. territory in 1848. Prior to the Gold Rush, foothill and mountain areas had been of little interest to newcomers, and native people occupying these territories had been beyond the direct influence of the missions or ranchos. Some had chosen to work at ranchos, but the boom in non-Indian population provided alternate sources of labor and undermined such mutualistic economic relationships. And unlike the Spanish and Mexicans before them, the majority of the gold seekers had no intention of staying on in California after striking it rich. Therefore, they had no interest in establishing or maintaining relationships with Indians. Physical conflicts between natives and nonnatives escalated, as land in the gold-bearing districts of the far north and interior of California became desirable. Relative isolation changed swiftly with the mining frenzy and resulted in particularly bloody encounters in areas such as the Trinity River in northwestern California, where the influence of nonnative people had been negligible before. Conflicts may have been less broadly punitive in the south-central Sierra Nevada, however, given the tradition of accommodation among the native people, who had some experience with nonnative peoples in the past (Hurtado 1988:123; cf. Castillo 1978:105). Still, violent encounters did occur, and opportunistic and organized actions such as that of the Mariposa Battalion were not uncommon against Sierra native peoples.

Miners flooded into the gold-bearing districts in the foothills west of Yosemite Valley after 1848, and Savage's original trading post was established at the confluence of the south fork and main Merced rivers just 22 kilometers west of Yosemite Valley in 1849 (Farquhar 1965:71). This year also witnessed the next documented nonnative observation of Yosemite Valley, as two American men employed at the trading post viewed the valley while lost on a hunting expedition (Greene 1987:xxxv; Farquhar 1965:74). Similar to the Walker party's experience, they did not enter the valley, nor is there any record of them observing or encountering native people living there. They did, however, follow an established Indian trail on their return to the trading post.

Bunnell's (1990) account includes information on camp locations, village features, and Indian routes of travel in Yosemite Valley at that time. As other members of the Mariposa Battalion party set fire to the vacated houses and deserted acorn stores, Bunnell (1990:76–77) examined the items left behind by the dispossessed native residents. He observed numerous and varied traditional Indian tools and households items as well as horse remains: "Among the relics of stolen property were many things recognizable by our 'boys,' while applying the torch and giving all to flames. A comrade discovered a bridle and part of a riata or rope which was stolen from him with the mule *while waiting for the commissioners to inquire into the cause of the war with the Indians!*" (Bunnell 1990:77, emphasis original). Bunnell (1990:79) added that "in their camps were found articles from the miners' camps, and from the unguarded 'ranchman.' There was no lack of evidence that the Indians who had deserted their villages or wigwams [in advance of the Mariposa Battalion], were truly entitled to the *soubriquet* of 'the Grizzlies,' 'the lawless.'" These observations of stolen goods highlight the vicious cycle in which the Yosemite found themselves: deprived of access to land for subsistence by the invading miners, they resorted to theft of livestock as a source of meat. This in turn prompted retaliation and further encroachment upon the native lands. Some Indians even turned to mining themselves to acquire gold for their own economic needs. It is known that Savage employed Nutchu and other Indians in an operation on the South Fork of the Merced River prior to his retreat from this region and before formation of the Mariposa Battalion (Bunnell 1990:2–3). And Perlot (1985:181, 218) observed Indians mining along the south fork in 1854 (see also Powers 1976:353).

AFTER THE GOLD RUSH

Due to the stories of the magnificent valley provided by the Mariposa Battalion and those visitors who followed shortly thereafter, homesteading and the development of tourism grew rapidly in Yosemite Valley and Wawona beginning in the late 1850s. As placer deposits were exhausted to the west and miners moved onto other regions, the Indians remained in their traditional or adopted territory in the Merced River region and found sources of income within the nonnative economy. Early tourists sought native people as guides to Yosemite Valley and, later, native men and women provided essential labor for the hotels that were quickly established beginning in 1856 (Bates and Lee 1990:29; Johnston 1995:32; Russell 1992:54). Indian men hunted and fished to supply hotel dining rooms and also worked as wranglers, trackers, laborers, or at other jobs. Indian women worked as laundresses and domestic help (Clark 1907:71) but also had an economic role through the production of baskets for sale to American and European tourists and collectors (see also Clark 1907:69). It is clear from historical photographs and written accounts that basket making continued to be important in the daily life of Yosemite Indians well into the twentieth century, regardless of the external economic opportunities associated with weaving.

Both Bunnell (1990:52) and Perlot (1985:72, 235) observed Indians still sparely clothed in traditional dress in the early 1850s (cf. Bunnell 1990:97), but by the mid- to late 1850s Yosemite Indians had taken to wearing castoff or purchased American-made clothes at least in part due to pressure from the growing non-Indian population (Bates and Lee 1990:29; Gordon-Cumming 1886:134; Hutchings 1888:23; Perlot 1985:261). Bates and Lee (1990:30) indicate that "metal implements became commonplace and newly introduced food such as bread and tortillas fast became staples," although Hutchings (1888:424) noted relative self-sufficiency with respect to foodstuffs and material goods during the mid- to late 1800s and Clark (1907:29) observed that "older Indians still cling to their old customs and manner of living." Despite the adoption of nonnative dress, incorporation of nontraditional manufactured goods, and increasing involvement in the nonnative economy after the Gold Rush, however, the 1860 census data suggest that Indian family life in the Sierra Nevada may have endured much as it had prior to contact (Hurtado 1988). This is in marked contrast to the experience of Indians who lived in many other regions of California.

The census statistics reveal that many of the Indians in the south-central Sierra continued to live in traditional families, maintaining separate residences from non-Indians (Hurtado 1988:205–206). In fact, separate native villages appear to have been the norm throughout the late 1800s and even into the 1900s in Yosemite Valley and Wawona (see Bates and Lee 1990:33; Hutchings 1888; Merriam 1917). In contrast, many Indians who survived on the Southern California coast lived as isolated domestic workers in nonnative households. And to the north in the Sacramento Valley, native laborers at ranches were often housed in single-sex dormitories under the direct control of the white landhold-

FIGURE 2. View of a deserted Yosemite Indian village with Upper Yosemite Fall in the background. (*The Deserted Village,* circa 1873, photograph by Eadweard Muybridge. Lone Mountain College Collection of Stereographs by Eadweard Muybridge, BANC PIC 1971.055. Courtesy of the Bancroft Library, University of California, Berkeley.)

ers. This suggests that the Yosemite Indian pattern of flexibility and adaptation, as well as their relative isolation from the growing nonnative population in California and access to land, provided for the maintenance of the family before, during, and after the Gold Rush. To a certain extent, other traditional practices also continued long after many other California Indian societies had been radically altered by nonnative contact and domination.

One of the more specific accounts of villages during this period is that of journalist Stephen Powers, who visited Yosemite Valley in the early 1870s. He recorded the Indian names and general location of nine villages previously occupied in the eastern portion of the valley, and noted "there were formerly others extending as far down as Bridal-Veil Fall, which were destroyed in wars that occurred before the whites came" (Powers 1976:365). Similarly, naturalist and avocational ethnographer C. Hart Merriam visited Yosemite Valley several times between 1900 and 1920 and recorded recollections of Indians who were still living in the region and had been in the valley in the late 1800s. One particularly significant report provides the names and locational information for thirty-seven village or camp sites in Yosemite Valley, one additional site west of the valley at Cascades, and fifteen other residential sites located downstream along the Merced River (Merriam 1917). Some of these villages were also recorded by Powers. Of particular note, Merriam (1917:202) observed that "at least six [sites in Yosemite Valley] were occupied as late as 1898." Four villages—Hoo-ke'-hahtch'-ke, Wah-ho'-gah, Soo-sem'-moo-lah, and Hah-ki-ah—are denoted as "inhabited up to about twenty years ago" (i.e., circa 1897), while three others—Loi'-ah, Hoo'-koo-me'-ko-tah, and Koom-i-ne or Kom-i-ne—were "occupied during my earlier visits" (i.e., in the early 1900s; Merriam 1917). Indian settlements in Yosemite Valley were generally unobtrusive and were often simply unseen by tourists (figure 2). This may reflect the marginalization of village locations in the face of expanding nonnative activities, including grazing of livestock (Bates and Lee 1990).

THE CHANGING CULTURAL LANDSCAPE
OF THE YOSEMITE PEOPLE

This is the story of colonial encounters with nonnative disease and human aggression in the Yosemite region revealed by oral and written historical accounts. These sources also provide a glimpse of important threads that weave through a much longer history of the Awahnichi and their descendants. Such themes include population decline and survival, connection to place, maintenance of both family life and community identity, and flexibility and resilience in the face of challenges to their way of life. Their colonial-era history reveals that Yosemite Indians were exposed to fatal infectious disease in the late 1700s or early 1800s (Bunnell 1990:64; see also Perlot 1985:220–223; Powers 1976:365) and that the consequences of this encounter shaped much of their subsequent history. Although the exact timing and the specific pathogen remain unknown, native oral history, dendrochronology, and ethnohistoric evidence of depopulation are unequivocal. Likewise, the high mortality associated with this event and Bunnell's reference to nonnative pathogens identify the agent as something other than endemic disease. Infiltration of fatal Old World disease clearly predated direct contact with nonnative people, and sources unambiguously document an "unrecorded" epidemic that may have affected people in an even wider region. For example, Bunnell (1990:88) observed abundant bedrock mortars between the Merced and Fresno rivers in 1851 that "had been formed and used by past generations [to pound acorn].... as there was no indications of recent uses having been made of them. From their numbers it was believed that the Indians had once been much more numerous than at that date."

The process of nonnative disease preceding face-to-face colonial encounters is consistent with the hypothesis of early, catastrophic population decline posited for North America by Dobyns (1983). In fact, no known direct contact with nonnative people within the Yosemite region occurred until more than fifty years after initial exposure to introduced disease, although there may have been interaction with foreigners in the San Joaquin Valley by at least the 1830s due to horse-thieving activities (Phillips 1993). Demographic changes, including population declines and augmentation of the population by nonlocal Indians, occurred within the group after circa 1810, as continued nonnative impingement on traditional lands to the west and additional epidemics prompted some people of other groups to seek refuge in the Sierra Nevada. Yosemite Indians acknowledged their connection to previous generations of Awahnee residents but also recognized their new identity and community under the direction of a charismatic leader, Tenaya.

The lag time between depopulation and direct contact with nonnative people indicates that the potential cultural consequences of depopulation can be studied in this case without the confounding effect of direct native involvement with colonists or colonial institutions. Even with this distance, change is suggested within and between native communities beyond the direct influence of Spanish colonial enterprises. Intergroup conflicts, such as the wars mentioned by Tenaya, may have been prompted by increasing colonial pressure from the west (Bunnell 1990:64; see also Perlot 1985:220–223; Powers 1976:365). Some of these native interactions likely built on previous tensions or alliances between groups and were further exacerbated during the Gold Rush when direct contact between native and nonnative people in the Yosemite region finally took place. Shifting relations and loyalties between groups may also be indicated by the collusion of Ponwatchee and the Nutchu with the Mariposa Battalion in the capture of the Yosemite. The derision of Tenaya by other Indians at the Fresno River reservation after his temporary removal from Yosemite Valley in 1851 may relate to previous enmity and opportunism in this new social environment. And the Yosemite dispute with the Mono Paiute over the theft of horses that had been previously stolen from the whites demonstrates how the presence of nonnative people affected native relationships at that time. Native groups and individuals were ready to face challenges and exploit opportunities with both native and nonnative people resulting from the changing cultural landscape in California.

The burgeoning nonnative population and interracial hostilities in the south-central Sierra Nevada during the Gold Rush also had significant impacts on mortality, health, resource procurement, and traditional economic practices of Yosemite Indians. The tradition of flexibility and accommodation of the Indian people of the south-central Sierra, however, assisted in providing for their survival in the face of these enormous changes. This cultural resilience contrasts with the devastating consequences of military action against groups in far Northern California who chose large-scale armed resistance, and with the breakdown of many Indian communities in coastal Southern California with social isolation in nonnative households. In the latter half of the 1800s, the development of tourism provided new economic opportunities for Yosemite Indians, often at jobs utilizing traditional skills of guiding, hunting, fishing, and basket making. Therefore, incorporation of native labor into the growing tourist industry was a natural and relatively rapid process, mirroring the early reliance on native labor that had been fundamental to nonnative occupation on the California coastal frontier one hundred years before.

CHAPTER 4

The People of Awahnee

Although the dominant narrative of Indian life in colonial California is one of dispossession, exploitation, and death, of equal truth is a remarkable story of strength and cultural survival. Faced with successive waves of missionaries, military, merchants, ranchers, mountain men, and miners—as well as the deadly diseases that accompanied these intruders—many California Indian people, customs, and traditions endured. And groups such as the Yosemite maintained ties to the territories of their ancestors despite repeated attempts to dislodge them from the places that both provided for their livelihood and served to reinforce their cultural identity. More than 150 years after statehood and the Gold Rush brought an end to the colonial era, this persistence is preserved in the bewildering mosaic of traditional Indian languages and cultures first glimpsed by Spanish colonists and later described by ethnographers in the late 1800s and early 1900s.

Who were the people of Awahnee? What were their particular traditions and practices both before and after the arrival of fatal foreign diseases? In order to consider how Yosemite Indian culture changed in both the short term and long term in the face of disease-induced depopulation, we must first address these basic questions with existing anthropological information that complements the profile of Yosemite Indian colonial history. Archaeological evidence and native oral tradition offer general insights into broad cultural trends and specific events from the distant past until about A.D. 1800. Our knowledge of everyday life is clear again after 1850, given the benefit of written accounts and systematic ethnographic studies. Ethnographic and ethnohistoric data provide a comprehensive picture of daily life and culture during the mid- to late 1800s that is much more detailed than that for earlier periods. Together, these records indicate occupation of Yosemite Valley by native people for thousands of years, with both change and continuity in native culture over the millennia preceding the colonial period as well as in the years following the Gold Rush. These records lay the groundwork for subsequent archaeological assessment of the specific consequences of either introduced nonnative disease or later physical incursion for Yosemite Indian identity and cultural practices during the colonial era. In addition, they begin to reveal how the outcome of colonial encounters in this region resulted from both history and culture.

RECORDS OF YOSEMITE INDIAN CULTURE

Systematic archaeological investigations within Yosemite Valley and the greater Yosemite region have been ongoing since the 1950s (Hull and Moratto 1999), and researchers have documented a long history of use by Indian people spanning several millennia. Broad changes in technology, subsistence, settlement, and exchange are indicated over this time, but the archaeological record is not as detailed as the ethnographic and ethnohistoric records due in part to the poor preservation of organic remains such as animal bone and vegetal materials. As a result, relatively little specific information can be gleaned about topics such as native diet or use of objects that are prominent in the ethnographic record, such as basketry and bows. Conversely, archaeology and native oral history serve as a counterpoint to ethnographic and ethnohistoric observations, since it is unclear how well these relatively recent observations reflect deeper time. This is especially true given the probability of native culture change in the face of disease-induced depopulation and other colonial influences. Thus, extant archaeological data serve to establish a general picture of native life prior to colonial influences, while also documenting the cultural trajectory leading up to the assaults of nonnative disease and people.

Written records of the traditional language, culture, and social organization of the Indian people of Yosemite Valley after the infiltration of Euro-Americans into the region are found in various forms. The earliest glimpses are those that local miners and settlers chronicled in journals and letters. Anecdotal references and even quite detailed accounts began in the 1850s with the keen observations of men such as Lafayette Bunnell and Jean-Nicolas Perlot. Bunnell's participation in the military action of the Mariposa Battalion and his interest in Indian culture and language resulted in a relatively detailed portrait of Yosemite Indian life between 1851 and 1853. Similarly, Perlot worked and lived along the streams of the south-central Sierra Nevada between 1851 and 1857. Not long after his entry into the lower Merced River canyon, he began encountering small parties of Indians, mostly men. As he and his cohorts worked the tributaries of the Merced and the Merced River itself, Perlot developed relationships with some of the native people in the area, which provided him with unusual access to their lives.

Other observations continued with the records of Yosemite residents and travelers dating as far back as the late 1850s and early 1860s. Prominent innkeepers such as Galen Clark and James Hutchings often queried their native neighbors and employees during the late 1800s regarding traditional Indian culture and legends. And visitors' accounts of this period provide sometimes brief but important information on the daily life of Indian people (e.g., Gordon-Cumming 1886; Muir 1894; Powers 1976). The record of Yosemite Indian people and culture at that time also benefits from a uniquely rich and detailed visual archive. Some of the most prominent and talented landscape artists of the day recorded both natural and cultural features of the region. Drawn to Yosemite Valley and the Mariposa Grove of Big Trees by the spectacular scenery, photographers such as Carleton Watkins, Eadweard Muybridge, J.P. Soule, J.J. Reilly, C.L. Weed, George Fiske, and Isaiah West Taber produced stereographs and large-format images of native people, camps, and material culture. Likewise, sketch artists and painters including T.M. Ayres, Albert Bierstadt, Washington F. Friend, Constance Gordon-Cumming, Thomas Hill, Raymond Dabb Yelland, Chris Jorgensen, and William Keith created both broad landscapes and careful studies of native subjects. Although some of the canvases these artists produced were perhaps somewhat fanciful, the accuracy of others is verified by comparison of scenes with those depicted in contemporary photographs.

Formal anthropological studies in the Yosemite region began around the turn of the twentieth century and were especially prevalent between

1900 and 1920. This work included notes on material culture, social structure, language, and myths, with additional detailed linguistic studies undertaken in the 1950s and 1960s. More recent anthropological work has included native oral history and focused studies on various aspects of Yosemite Indian material culture (e.g., Bates 1993; Bates and Lee 1990; Bates and Wells 1981; Bibby 1994, 2005). The most readily available sources of ethnographic information are papers that synthesize observations of various scholars and native groups within the broader ethnolinguistic groupings of "Miwok" or "Sierra Miwok" (e.g., Kroeber 1925; Levy 1978). Some of the richness of the record and potential uniqueness of the Yosemite people is masked in such general ethnographies, however, while the reliance on "memory culture" disconnects these data from a specific period of time. This is especially problematic because the current analysis seeks to understand the very colonial history that ethnographers tried so hard to avoid—in this case, a cultural history of Yosemite Indians that included the incorporation of individuals from other groups into the band following the "black sickness" and attendant processes that may have resulted in language, cultural practices, and traditions unique to this area.

In order to maintain focus on the specific cultural history and practices of Yosemite Indians, ethnographic observations available in historical narratives, memoirs, and other Yosemite literature from the mid- to late 1800s are given equal, if not greater, weight than data collected in the greater region somewhat later by professional ethnographers. Reliance on Bunnell (1990) and Perlot (1985), in particular, is justified given their direct observation of Yosemite Indian lifeways at or within only a few months or years of nonnative incursion into Yosemite Valley. Their chronicles are primary records of a specific, brief period, and Bunnell appears to have conceived of himself as an ethnologist to a certain extent. These records are also extremely important because the data were obtained almost entirely through observation rather than query—that is, the authors were not constructing an "ethnographic present" of traits in a timeless past but were observing practices in a current world of cultural challenges. For these reasons, general ethnography serves more to reinforce and fill out the picture of native life during the Gold Rush initially developed from the ethnohistoric sources rather than the other way around. In this sense, the ethnohistoric sources are used to place the ethnographic present of anthropologists within a known history rather than allowing these observations to languish in an imagined "prehistory" (Conn 2004).

TRACES IN THE DISTANT PAST

While the ethnographic record reveals a full suite of cultural practices for native people of the Yosemite area, primary cultural patterns considered in regional archaeological studies have been limited to exchange, flaked and ground-stone tool technology, settlement, and subsistence (Hull and Moratto 1999). Lithic technology has received significant attention, since stone artifacts and manufacturing debris (i.e., debitage) dominate the archaeological record. Detailed analysis of tool and flake attributes reveals manufacturing strategies and patterns of tool use. Selective obsidian hydration sampling of lithic technological types has been employed to explore changes in technology through time, artifact reuse, biface caches, raw material scavenging, and bipolar reduction—using percussion to split a core or biface while placed on an anvil—that suggests exhaustive use of lithic materials. Studies of exchange have been undertaken using geochemical analysis of obsidian tools and debitage, since obsidian accounts for nearly all of the stone used by the native people of this area. Geochemical signatures of artifacts are linked to geological sources in eastern California, western Nevada and, to a much lesser extent, the southern North Coast Ranges north of San Francisco Bay, indicating the origin of raw material and objects acquired directly or through trade. Settlement analysis draws on site constituents and environmental data to reveal patterns of land use through time. Such study relies primarily on artifacts, as features such as structures and hearths are rare in the Yosemite region. The paucity of such features may be due to disturbance of deposits by burrowing rodents or the ephemeral nature of these constituents, as suggested by ethnographic data. Finally, diet has been studied through analysis of faunal and macrobotanical remains as well as organic residues on stone tools. Unfortunately, poor preservation of organic materials has necessitated qualitative rather than quantitative assessment of subsistence practices. These cultural trends are reviewed here within temporal periods that encompass more than 5,500 years of Indian habitation in the Yosemite region (see table 1).

The most detailed archaeological information is available for the three periods of the Late Prehistoric (1200 B.C.–A.D. 1800), whereas data are currently much more limited for periods both preceding and following this era. Cultural traits and practices of people inhabiting Yosemite Valley during periods prior to the Late Prehistoric are especially vague. In fact, many of the potential periods of use remain to be documented

TABLE 1.
Chronological Sequence for the Yosemite Region

Period	Dates	Complex/Phase
Historic 4	cal A.D. 1945–	
Historic 3	cal A.D. 1891–1944	
Historic 2	cal A.D. 1864–1890	Rancheria
Historic 1	cal A.D. 1848–1863	Tenaya
Protohistoric	cal A.D. 1800–1847	Yosemite
Late Prehistoric 3	cal A.D. 1350–1800	Mariposa
Late Prehistoric 2	cal A.D. 650–1350	Tamarack?
Late Prehistoric 1	cal 1200 B.C.–A.D. 650	Crane Flat
Intermediate Prehistoric 2	cal 3500–1200 B.C.	Merced, Wawona, and others
Intermediate Prehistoric 1	cal 6000–3500 B.C.	?
Early Prehistoric 4	cal 7500–6000 B.C.	El Portal
Early Prehistoric 3	cal 8500–7500 B.C.	?
Early Prehistoric 2	cal 9500–8500 B.C.	?
Early Prehistoric 1	cal > 9500 B.C.	?

SOURCE: Moratto (1999).

archaeologically and date ranges are uncertain. This is particularly true with respect to the Early Prehistoric, as the existence of such use is merely speculative and relies on data from farther north in the Sierra Nevada (Moratto 1999). Occupation during the Early Prehistoric periods, if present, would be represented by use of large, stemmed spear points and a settlement system based on frequent residential moves. The evidence available for the Intermediate Prehistoric periods indicates use of heavy side-notched and shouldered dart points, millingstones, handstones, and various flake and core tools. This suggests technology similar to that of the subsequent Late Prehistoric 1 period, although much of the data for the Intermediate Prehistoric 1 period derives from sites in the Merced River canyon rather than from higher-elevation zones such as Yosemite Valley. Similar to later times, use of eastern California obsidians was dominant in both the Early and Intermediate Prehistoric periods, but use of nonobsidian toolstone, including basalt and chert, was somewhat more common than during the Late Prehistoric period. Moratto (1999) concluded that residential mobility was also somewhat greater during both the Early and Intermediate Prehistoric periods compared to later in time, and population size increased through time. As noted above, however, such conclusions for the Early Prehistoric

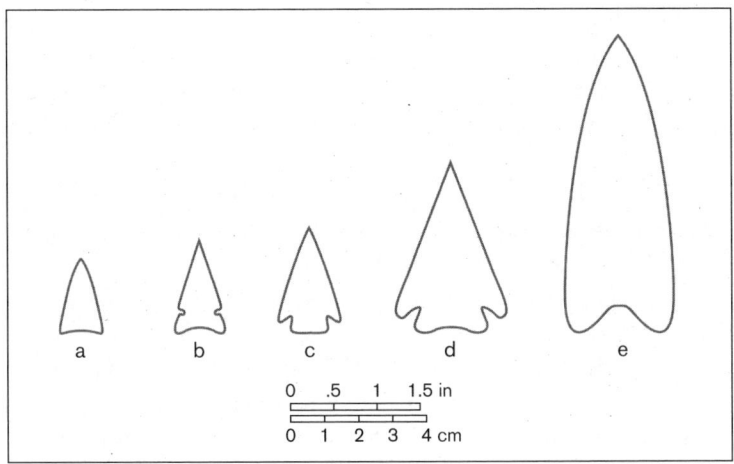

FIGURE 3. Typical projectile points of the Yosemite region: (a) Cottonwood Triangular; (b) Desert Side-Notched; (c) Rose Spring Corner-Notched; (d) Elko Corner-Notched; and (e) Sierra Concave Base.

period are not necessarily indicated by archaeological data specific to the Yosemite region.

Cultural patterns become much clearer during the Late Prehistoric 1 period (1200 B.C.–A.D. 650). Manufacture of Elko Corner-Notched, Sierra Concave Base, and various contracting-stem projectile points (see figure 3) was typical of this time and indicates the use of the atlatl and dart rather than the bow and arrow. Other traits included use of expedient flake tools, cobble choppers, *Haliotis* and *Olivella* shell beads, and portable millingstones and handstones to process vegetal material (Moratto 1999:187–188). Given the unsuitability of such implements for milling acorns, the presence of millingstones and handstones suggests reliance on small seeds in the diet. Obsidian was the dominant material used for flaked stone tools, and lithic technological studies at the eastern Sierra quarries, in Yosemite, and at other western Sierra sites have demonstrated that biface reduction was the most common strategy for tool manufacture at that time (Hull 2007). In particular, large flake blanks were prepared into bifacial or unifacial forms at the quarry or elsewhere east of the Sierra crest. These partially reduced forms were then transported west for further reduction into bifacial tools or used as cores for smaller flake production. In some cases, large bifacial cores or preforms were cached in areas such as Tuolumne Meadows for later use or exchange (Hull and Roper 1999; Humphreys

1994). This emphasis on biface production and transport was likely related to the significant trans-Sierra trade at that time. Obsidian tools were traded west in exchange for marine shell beads and ornaments, some of which were destined for consumers as far away as the eastern Great Basin. In fact, this period encompasses the apogee of long-distance trade between California and the Great Basin. The constituents of Late Prehistoric 1 sites suggest that both residential bases—villages and camps—and task-specific locales were used. Residential sites were located along major watercourses, and processing locales were present elsewhere. This pattern indicates a logistically organized settlement strategy, with relatively few residential moves during a year or from year to year. Moratto (1999) concluded that occupation in the Merced River watershed during the Late Prehistoric 1 period represents ancestral Yokuts Indians, since the assemblage traits are similar to coeval records elsewhere in the Sierra foothills from the Cosumnes to the Chowchilla rivers.

The material record of the Late Prehistoric 2 period (A.D. 650–1350) indicates some of the same practices and technology as the Late Prehistoric 1 period, but also distinct differences. One significant change is the inferred adoption of the bow and arrow, as projectile points are smaller than those found in earlier deposits. For example, Rose Spring Corner-Notched arrow points were first used at that time and were the dominant type, although larger Sierra Concave Base knives or dart points were also used. Bedrock mortars and cobble pestles, typical of milling of acorns rather than seeds, also appear during this period, although the date of their introduction remains unclear. Triangular drills and oval scrapers were utilized (Bennyhoff 1956), and shell ornaments were available, including shell rings likely acquired through trade with the people living on the south-central California coast. The most distinctive feature of Indian life during the Late Prehistoric 2 period, however, was a settlement pattern that differed from both earlier and later periods. During the Late Prehistoric 2, residential camps were small and were occupied relatively briefly. This pattern indicates a residentially mobile settlement strategy of relatively frequent moves during the course of a year. Some scholars have suggested that this ephemeral settlement system reflects initial migration of Me'-wuk into the region, perhaps in response to deteriorating environmental conditions in the foothills. Physical evidence of interpersonal violence in the Chowchilla River drainage southwest of Yosemite Valley, such as projectile points embedded in human bone, attests that this was a time of conflict and stress. The coincident adoption of bedrock-mortar technology and the inferred importance of acorns—despite the significant investment of time and energy necessary to process acorn flour—suggests one response to prevailing environmental conditions and the need to use resources more intensively. People relied on obsidian for flaked stone tools, just as they did earlier in time.

Finally, the Late Prehistoric 3 period (A.D. 1350–1800) is characterized by the use of bedrock mortars and milling slicks (i.e., bedrock surfaces on which vegetal material was milled in a back-and-forth motion), cobble pestles, expedient cutting and scraping tools fashioned on flakes, drills with long bits, steatite vessels, steatite disk beads, and *Olivella* and clam shell beads. While most mortars likely relate to acorn processing, complementary geographic distributions of deep mortars and milling slicks in the Merced and Tuolumne river watersheds suggest that one or the other of these technologies was favored for small seed processing in particular areas. This may reflect distinctions between Me'-wuk and non-Me'-wuk groups. Use of the bow and arrow is inferred based on the presence of small, lightweight, triangular projectile points of types common in the Great Basin (i.e., Desert Side-Notched, Cottonwood Triangular), as well as small corner-notched arrow points that first appear somewhat earlier in time (i.e., Rose Spring Corner-Notched). The persistence of Rose Spring points in some areas but not in others during this period may relate to geographic trends in arrow-point preference that also encompass two subtypes of Desert Side-Notched points (Hull 2001a). Obsidian was the dominant lithic material used at that time, and geochemical studies indicate that a variety of geologic materials were accessed either directly or through trade. The only source unique to this period is Mono Craters (see map 4), which was formed by volcanic activity circa A.D. 1325 to 1365 (Sieh and Bursik 1986). Red pictographs are present at a few sites dating to the Late Prehistoric 3 period, but they are rare. In fact, pictographs may relate to seasonal or permanent occupation of certain areas of the Merced and Tuolumne river drainages by Paiute people, since such imagery is more common in the western Great Basin.

The climate during the Late Prehistoric 3 period was variable in both the short and long term but was generally similar to that of today. Pollen stratigraphic studies of noncultural deposits in Yosemite Valley dating to this time, however, indicate significant vegetation change that may have facilitated the shift to greater emphasis on acorns in the diet and also may have supported higher native populations in the area. Charcoal frequencies in these deposits indicate that a major fire swept through the

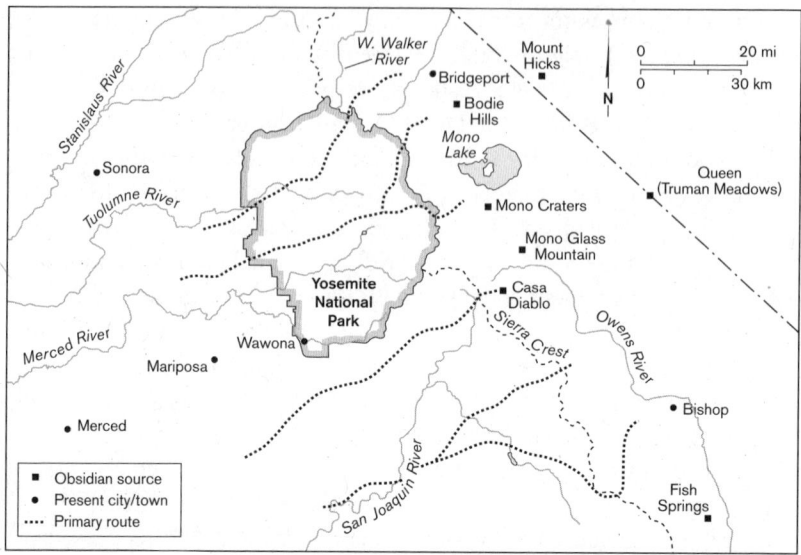

MAP 4. Location of obsidian quarry sources and primary trans-Sierra trade routes of the Yosemite region.

valley around A.D. 1300. This conflagration decreased the abundance of pine and other conifers and promoted the subsequent growth of oaks. Somewhat elevated charcoal frequencies in post- versus prefire deposits indicate that continued periodic burning of the vegetation by Indians maintained this biotic community (Anderson and Carpenter 1991), consistent with practices documented in the ethnographic record. Similar to the Late Prehistoric 1 period, people also practiced a logistically oriented settlement strategy. The focus of habitation in a few large sites has been taken as evidence for a large population (Moratto 1999:193), although this may simply represent the aggregation of the existing population into a few villages rather than population growth. Since the material culture of Indian people during the Late Prehistoric 3 period was so similar to that noted in the ethnographic record, archaeologists have concluded that this period relates to occupation by the "late prehistoric Sierra Miwok, albeit with contributions by such neighboring peoples as the Paiute and Western Mono" (Moratto 1999:191).

In addition to the cultural traits specific to just one period within the Late Prehistoric, there are also general patterns that transcend the entire span from 1200 B.C. to A.D. 1800. For example, people produced bifacial tools and expedient flake tools from biface thinning or core reduction flakes throughout the Late Prehistoric. And the projectile points used or produced were of types common in the Great Basin rather than contemporaneous types typical of Central or Northern California. The paucity of cores suggests that many items were brought to Yosemite Valley in partially reduced or finished form or that cores were thoroughly reduced. There is also evidence for acquisition of obsidian from nonquarry sites in various forms, such as scavenging flakes or tools from habitation sites on the western side of the Sierra. This scavenging is evidenced by disparate obsidian hydration rims on worked and unworked surfaces of the same artifact. Thorough use of lithic material for flaked stone tools was accomplished through bipolar reduction of complete or fragmentary bifaces to produce usable flakes. For example, Sierra Concave Base points were scavenged by people during the Late Prehistoric 3 period and broken as bipolar cores to produce usable flakes for other tasks or tools.

Geochemical studies of obsidian artifacts and debitage indicate that people living in the Merced River watershed primarily used Casa Diablo obsidian, whereas Bodie Hills obsidian was accessed by people living in areas to the north. Both of these materials, as well as some less-common obsidian source materials—including Queen (Truman Meadows), Mono Glass Mountain, Mount Hicks, and Fish Springs—were introduced into the region as exotic materials from quarry areas east of the Sierra Nevada (see map 4). Obsidian from quarry areas in the mountain ranges north of San Francisco Bay was obtained only rarely. These geographic trends also pertained farther south along the western slope of the Sierra, with the prevalence of Casa Diablo obsidian even more pronounced in the San Joaquin River watershed (e.g., Goldberg and Skinner 1990:182). Three distinct geochemical types within the Casa Diablo source have also been recognized (Hughes 1994), and the northernmost subtype, Lookout Mountain, dominates the Casa Diablo sample in Yosemite Valley. Despite significant distance from geologic sources, obsidian constituted 97 to 100 percent of the flaked stone material used by Indian people in the region during the Late Prehistoric.

Understanding native subsistence in the Yosemite area during the Late Prehistoric period, as well as earlier in time, is more difficult due to poor preservation of organic materials. Still, general statements about use of plants and animals are possible. Faunal analyses suggest the exploitation of deer, bear, elk, sheep, and canids (e.g., dog, coyote) by the residents of Yosemite Valley, although some of these species did not occur locally. For example, elk was procured in the Central Valley and bighorn sheep were available near the Sierra crest. Little insight can be offered with regard to the relative importance of various faunal species in the diet or changes through time, as samples are very small and highly fragmented. Organic residue analysis of tools indicates geographic trends in animal use in the Merced and Tuolumne watersheds similar to those revealed by faunal assemblages. Macrobotanical studies suggest that Indian people used pine *(Pinus* sp.), oak *(Quercus kelloggii),* manzanita *(Arctostaphylos patula),* legumes, cinquefoil *(Potentilla* sp.), sedge *(Cyperus* sp.), and bedstraw *(Galium* sp.), although the presence of all of these taxa in archaeological deposits may not be related only to subsistence.

Taken together, regional archaeological data indicate broad changes in material culture and settlement over more than six millennia and cultural similarities to people inhabiting areas to both the east and west. For example, projectile-point styles are typical of the Great Basin, but use of bedrock mortars and inferred reliance on acorns during the Late Prehistoric 3 period is a trait common to Central California. Archaeologists have speculated about the cultural affiliation of native people living in the Yosemite region, but all agree that the Me'-wuk were firmly established by at least A.D. 1350. With the exception of rock-art production and use of milling slicks, all of the observations for the Late Prehistoric 3 period are consistent with the material culture and practices noted by ethnographers and other observers of Yosemite Indian life after 1850. Therefore, it is likely that many of the additional facets of daily life and material culture noted after the Gold Rush also pertained to the Late Prehistoric 3 period, although this has been assumed rather than demonstrated by regional archaeologists.

Despite nearly fifty years of archaeological research in Yosemite, the cultural affiliation of archaeological materials identified in Yosemite is perhaps best summarized by Bennyhoff (1956:57–58), who was responsible for the initial work in this region. He concluded that

> if nothing but the artifacts were considered one would suggest a closer affiliation of Southern Miwok with Paiute rather than with Plains Miwok. The abundance of Southern Miwok myths dealing with the local landscape suggests that this group had long occupied the Yosemite Valley. One might speculate that sites of the [Late Prehistoric 2 period] represent the arrival of the Central and Southern Miwok in the Yosemite region after these groups had already acquired such Sierran traits as the bedrock mortar and cobble pestle. . . . Sites of the later [Late Prehistoric 3 period] probably represent Central and Southern Miwok occupation after these groups were well established in their Sierran environment, while the

arrow points suggest influence from their eastern Shoshonean neighbors. The [Late Prehistoric 1 period] very likely represents pre-Miwok occupation; perhaps the strongest affiliation of this early period is with the Southern California desert, though relationships will probably appear in the Southern San Joaquin Valley when more is known about this latter area.

Moratto (1984) considered the entry into and spread of various ethnolinguistic groups within California based on both archaeological and linguistic data, and he reached much the same conclusion as Bennyhoff (1956) for occupation in Yosemite region by the late 1700s.[1] With Miwok affiliation with the Awahnichi thus determined through regional archaeology, we can proceed to consider what we know of native life and culture in Yosemite after the "black sickness" struck.

LANGUAGE AND GEOGRAPHY

Rather than referring to a tribal or other political affiliation, the broad ethnolinguistic category of Miwok—and the specific dialectal variations thereof—simply means "people." The Miwokan language is one of two subfamilies within the Utian language family, which is, in turn, one division within the posited Penutian language stock (Shipley 1978:89). There are also distinctions within the broad Miwokan group that reflect geographically more specific divisions (see map 3). The Western Miwok peoples to the north of San Francisco Bay define two of these divisions, and the remaining three groups of Eastern Miwok encompass the Bay Miwok of the inland valleys of the Coast Ranges in the Mount Diablo area, the Plains Miwok of the San Joaquin River delta, and the Sierra Miwok of the western slope of the Sierra Nevada (Levy 1978; Shipley 1978). Merriam (1907:338) referred to the Bay and Plains divisions collectively as Mew'-ko and the Sierra division as Me'-wuk. Thus, *Me'-wuk* is used here when discussing Sierra peoples, and *Miwok* is used when non-Sierra Miwok-speaking peoples, all Miwok-speaking peoples, or the language subfamily are discussed.

The Sierra Miwok language group is subdivided into three languages. The Northern Sierra Miwok region encompassed the Cosumnes and Mokelumne river drainages, speakers of Central Sierra Miwok dialects resided in the Stanislaus and Tuolumne river drainages, and the Southern Sierra Miwok region encompassed the Merced and Chowchilla river drainages above the San Joaquin Valley floor (Barrett 1908; Levy 1978; Merriam 1907). People who lived in the Merced River watershed spoke one dialect within the Southern Sierra Miwok language, and a second dialect was centered farther west and south on Mariposa Creek and in the Chowchilla River drainage (Barrett 1908:354; Broadbent 1964:2; Levy 1978:398; Shipley 1978:89). The use of the -*tcī* suffix for the Awahnichi, Pohonichi, and other Southern Sierra Me'-wuk groups to indicate territorial affiliation is unique to this region and may be related to the use of this form among the neighboring Yokuts to identify tribal groups (see Barrett 1908:343).

Bunnell (1990:66) observed that "the dialect of the Yosemites was a composite of that of almost every tribe around them and even words of Spanish derivation were discovered in their conversation." This might account for the fact that Me'-wuk from the Mariposa area had difficulty understanding the speech of Yosemite Indians (Broadbent 1964:3). In addition, Southern Me'-wuk claimed they did not readily understand the language of Central and Northern Sierra Me'-wuk (Broadbent 1964:2), despite the fact that multilingualism likely prevailed here and elsewhere in native California (Shipley 1978:81). Such linguistic skill would have facilitated communication between various Miwok and non-Miwok peoples, especially within a linguistically diverse area such as eastern California. Bunnell's (1990:179) account confirms this ability with respect to Chief Tenaya, who he observed "was reputed to be quite a linguist, speaking, besides his native Ah-wah-ne-chee, the Paiute, and other dialects."

Lexicostatistical techniques for establishing the timing of language divergence remain controversial,[2] but such analyses suggest that the Western and Eastern Miwok languages split approximately 2,500 years ago and that Sierra Miwok separated from Plains Miwok about 2,000 years ago. Finally, the three Sierra Miwok languages diverged from each other approximately 800 years ago (Levy 1978:398). Similar techniques for assessing the time of linguistic divergence form the basis for the further hypothesis that "the ancestors of the Miwok have been resident in the Central California delta region for a long period of time, [while] the occupation of the Sierra Nevada and its foothills is probably a much more recent event" (Levy 1978:398). That is, the ancestral homeland of Miwok-speaking peoples within California may have been in the Central Valley rather than in the mountains.

This geographic origin in the Central Valley is also hinted at by various Me'-wuk legends, which—in addition to their contribution to linguistic studies—are valuable sources of information on native life, history, and cosmology (see Broadbent 1964; Freeland and Broadbent

1960). Fortunately, there is a substantial body of such tales collected among the Yosemite Indians (Barrett 1919; Broadbent 1964; Clark 1907; Hutchings 1888; Kroeber 1907; Latta 1999; Merriam 1910; Powers 1976). These myths make reference to traditional characters such as Coyote *(ahē'lī)*, Condor *(mo'llok)*, and Falcon *(we'kwek)* and also describe the origin of people and the formation of the landscape within Yosemite Valley. One legend refers to a hill in the vicinity of Mount Diablo (near present-day Concord, 215 kilometers west of Yosemite) that was "the center of various important events in Miwok mythology" (Barrett 1919:6). This supports the contention that the Me'-wuk had a Central Valley origin (Levy 1978:398). The same conclusion is suggested by Clark's (1907:64) observation that the Yosemite Indians had "a vague, indistinct belief or tradition that their original ancestors, in the long forgotten past, dwelt in a better and much more desirable country than this, in the . . . distant West, and that by some misfortune or calamity they were separated from that happy land, and became wanderers in this part of the world." One origin myth indicates six successive peoplings of the earth (Barrett 1919), although this is a composite of distinct myths (see Barrett 1919:2, footnote). This tale describes how the original people were destroyed by a cannibal giant. Subsequent peoplings brought about the transformation of animal-people into the forms of creatures we see today, and the final episode created the people *(Me'-wuk)* of today. This last portion of the tale appears elsewhere in a generally similar form as a separate myth (e.g., Powers 1976:358).

The Yosemite Indian connection to Awahnee is underscored by local geographic references in their legends and Indian names for both rock formations and hydrologic features in the valley (Bunnell 1990; see also Whitney 1869). The domes and cliffs were often named for mythic figures or animals, while the terms for lakes, rivers, and waterfalls were generally descriptive. For example, the section of the Merced River encompassing Vernal Fall is *Yan-o-pah* (water cloud), and the portion encompassing Nevada Fall is *Yo-wy-we-ack* (twisting rock) (Bunnell 1990:183). In contrast, tales describe the formation of El Capitan *(Tutankanula)*, Half Dome *(Tisiack)*, North Dome *(Tecoya)*, and Sentinel Rock *(Loya)*, among other features (Barrett 1919). Such landforms are often linked through myths to daily practices such as acorn preparation and storage (see Bunnell 1990:193; Ortiz 1991), and they sometimes figure prominently in legends that record events such as the introduction of basket making or the onset of drought (see Clark 1907:85; Powers 1976:368). These legends and place names indicate the intimacy of Yosemite Indians with the environment and their connection to Awahnee for many generations.

GROUP AND HOUSEHOLD STRUCTURE

Although the Miwok peoples of the western Sierra Nevada, Sierra foothills, and Central Valley delta area "spoke a common language, [they] were not in any sense a single people, but rather a number of separate and politically independent nations that happened to share a common language and common cultural background" (Levy 1978:398). Levy (1978:410) refers to these groups as "tribelets," following Kroeber (1962). The exact number and configuration of such separate "nations" is unclear, but these "independent autonomous political units" were patrilineal joint families, or *nena*, that took their individual appellations from a place name (Gifford 1926b; cf. Dick-Bissonnette 1998:51). For example, the Awahnichi made their home in and took their name from Awahnee, their name for Yosemite Valley (see Bates and Lee 1990:19; Broadbent 1964; Bunnell 1990:64; Powers 1976:349, 361). Similarly, the Pohonichi took their name from Pohono, which referred to the Bridalveil Creek watershed directly south of Yosemite Valley (Bunnell 1990:188). Therefore, each lineage identified with a distinct locale, consisted of several settlements or habitation sites, and held a small territory in common for use by the members of the lineage who worked cooperatively for political, social, and economic purposes (Clark 1907:22; Barrett 1908:344; Gifford 1926b; Levy 1978:411). Whitney (1869:15) observed that "the families of the tribe had each its special 'reservation' or tract set apart for its use, each of these, of course, having it distinct appellation. . . . [but] these names . . . have already almost passed into oblivion." Gifford (1926b:91) also noted that "the bulk of the country, however, was unclaimed by the *nena* and was regarded as 'no-man's-land,' or more correctly 'every-man's land,' upon which people from any *nena* might seek vegetable foods and hunt animals" (see also Clark 1907:22, 33). Since the Awahnichi name is consistent with the practice recorded by ethnographers, this may indicate that such territorial settlement practices existed prior to the infiltration of nonnative disease.

Nearest tribelet "neighbors" may have lived several days' walk from each other (Perlot 1985:183), and ethnohistoric accounts suggest occasional tension and violence between Yosemite Indians and neighboring groups. Causes for war included acquisition of women, retaliation for hunting or fishing trespasses, or threats to sovereignty by outsiders (Bunnell 1990:259; Hutchings 1888:433; Perlot 1985:220; see also Crampton 1957:48). Such conflicts may have been inflamed or prolonged, in part, by the desire of young men to gain social status through the demonstration of valor in war (Bunnell 1990:259). Disputes with Paiute people living in Hetch Hetchy Valley on the Tuolumne River are specifically identified in ethnohistoric records, and additional conflicts with other people in the Tuolumne watershed are also possible (Hoffman 1868; Perlot 1985:222). It is clear, however, that native groups of the Sierra were also capable of forging alliances—sometimes solidified through strategic marriage (Bunnell 1990:260; see also Perlot 1985:232)—to facilitate amicable relations or to combat common enemies. For example, the initiation of the "Mariposa Indian War" in 1850 against the miners is one such cause that brought Indian people together. Hosted festivals with dancing and exchange of gifts were a "friendly gathering . . . for the purpose of cementing and perpetuating the bonds of family and tribal union more closely; and at the same time to orally transmit to posterity the noble deeds and valorous actions of their ancestors" (Hutchings 1888:430).

The "chief" resided at the primary settlement of each tribelet, which was also the location of the assembly house *(hange'-e)*. This structure—also known as a round house—functioned as a meeting place for ceremonies and social events that were sponsored by the chief, and it was considered to be the personal property of that officeholder (see Merriam 1917:205). The chief served as the sole legal and political authority and also managed the natural resources and acted as an advisor and arbitrator.[3] The office generally passed down from father to son (Powers 1976:352; see also Bunnell 1990:260), so the death of both Tenaya and his sons during the Gold Rush would have necessitated a change in leadership among the Yosemite if this form of organization was common at the time. Perlot (1985:188) met a chief on the Merced River in 1854 who may have assumed this role. In keeping with tradition, this aged chief—José—was destined to pass this responsibility on to his oldest son, Scipiano (Perlot 1985:182). Bunnell (1990: 261) also specifically mentions a patriarchal "government" for the Yosemite people.[4] Given their duties, chiefs were supplied with meat by hunters in their service and enjoyed somewhat greater wealth or possessions than other tribelet members (Levy 1978:410). "Speakers" served as "subchiefs" in the smaller satellite settlements of the tribelet, transmitting edicts of the chief and organizing the acquisition of food and materials for ceremonies at the hamlet level. Speakerships were elected rather than hereditary (Levy 1978:410).

Gifford (1926b, 1944) recognized the kin-based political structure of Me'-wuk tribelets primarily through the terms used by individuals to identify themselves rather than through observation of existing organization at the time of his fieldwork in the early 1900s. In fact, he suggested that this political and social organization was altered by the incursion of nonnative people into the area:

> Even before the coming of the Americans to Sierra Miwok territory in 1848 there had already been considerable pressure from the Spaniards and Mexicans resulting in the abandonment of certain of the *nena* which lay in the lowest hills close to the San Joaquin Valley. This seems to have been the beginning of the process of amalgamation of the *nena* into villages. . . . The Caucasian invaders drove the people from their ancestral *nena* sites to take refuge with other Miwok in less disturbed places and thus true village life arose and new territorial ties were created. (Gifford 1926b:391)

Colonial and Gold Rush–era pressures were probably most intense within the Northern and Central Sierra Me'-wuk regions in which Gifford worked, but such amalgamation may have been the case in the Merced River region as well. Consistent with Gifford's thesis, ethnohistoric and ethnographic records for the Yosemite area suggest that after the introduction of infectious disease and pressure of nonnative presence in the Central Valley native occupants of Yosemite Valley included descendants of various Me'-wuk tribelets and even some non-Miwok peoples (e.g., Bunnell 1990). Archaeological evidence for villages dating to the late precontact period farther south on the Chowchilla River, however, is contrary to the contention that village life was strictly a colonial or post–Gold Rush era phenomenon (Moratto 1972:188). It is unclear how offices such as "chief" or "speaker" were manifest—and potentially differed—in pre- and postvillage life.

The population size of tribelets varied, but some estimates for Yosemite Indians are available. Tenaya's band numbered as many as 200 individuals, including Tuolumne Me'-wuk and Mono Paiute people who fled Yosemite Valley prior to the arrival of the Mariposa Battalion (Bunnell 1990:54; see also Bates and Lee 1990:27). Perlot's (1985:190, 296) somewhat later record clearly indicates large village populations on the order of 100 to 250 individuals. James Savage judged a total of 4,800 Indians lived in the Merced River watershed at the time of the Gold Rush, including 600 Yosemite, 200 Nutchu, and 400 Pohonichi (Elliot 1882:181). Powers (1976:365) concluded there was a total native population of 450 people for Yosemite Valley in the 1870s, but this appears to be based on an estimate of 50 people for each of the nine villages he recorded rather than direct observation of the population. Finally, Hutchings (1888:59) posited 1,000 Awahnichi (i.e., prior to the colonial period) and 500 Yosemite Indians in 1851 (Hutchings 1888:421; see also Hutchings 1856:4), although these figures may simply be rough approximations for the purposes of his discussions. In fact, none of these population figures for Yosemite native people are based on careful enumeration or census.

Beyond the political organization embodied in a tribelet, each lineage also belonged to one of two moieties—social subdivisions that further served to organize social life among and between tribelet members. Each lineage was either of the land or water moiety and also had "representative animal members" (Levy 1978:411). Among the Southern Sierra Me'-wuk, blue jay and grizzly bear signified the land moiety, and coyote represented the water moiety (Merriam 1917:204). Within Yosemite Valley, settlements to the north and south of the Merced River were identified with the land and water moieties, respectively (Merriam 1917). People's names also made reference to the moiety to which they belonged, although the connection might draw on metaphor or hidden meaning rather than an overt link (Kroeber 1925). For example, the Indian name of Maria Lebrado Ydrte meant "foaming water" (Taylor 1932), and this suggests association with the water moiety. But there may be a connection to land in this name that is not immediately obvious to an outsider. Data from the Central Sierra Me'-wuk suggest that moiety membership brought with it certain ceremonial responsibilities, including participation in funeral and puberty rites for members of the opposite moiety. Individuals were also expected to marry outside of their moiety, although these rules "were not rigidly adhered to even before the coming of the whites" (Gifford 1926a:141; see also Kroeber 1925:456; Perlot 1985:230, 232). About 75 percent of the Central Sierra Me'-wuk marriages recorded by Gifford (1926a) were exogamous.

Polygyny was practiced, at least in part in response to the death of a husband or married sister (Bunnell 1990:89; Clark 1907:52; Hutchings 1888:433; Perlot 1985:232–234). In these two cases, a woman would marry her former husband's brother or her sister's husband, respectively (see Powers 1976:356). Perlot (1985:234) suggested that it was difficult for a man to obtain his first wife because the woman would have to conduct all of the household work herself, whereas multiple wives could share such tasks. This consideration may have been particularly important given the reliance on women's labor in maintenance of the household and the relatively rigid roles of men and women in society. For example, Bunnell (1990:211) noted the outrage that resulted among both Yosemite Indian men and women when Capt. John Boling insisted that the men carry some of the household supplies during the second withdrawal of the Indians to the Fresno River reservation. Several observers commented on the drudgery and significant burden of women's work relative to that performed by men (Bunnell 1990:49; Hutchings 1888:424; Muir 1894; Perlot 1985:234), although this bias might be a function of the visibility of women in camps whereas men undertook many of their tasks (e.g., hunting) in other locations. Although Hutchings (1888:433) suggested a chief might have as many as seven wives, a man rarely had more than three wives and "even has to be a chief to have three" (Perlot 1985:234).

When a man had multiple wives, each woman had children of her own (Perlot 1985:192, 233). But native tradition cautioned men against having too many wives, as "the more you have, the fewer children they will have and the less happy you will be" (Perlot 1985:234). Marriage might occur for any woman after puberty as long as her intended spouse was older than her (Perlot 1985:230), and marriage was often approached as a business arrangement (Bunnell 1990:260; Clark 1907:52). The prospective groom also gave gifts to the bride's father in exchange for the right to marry his daughter (Hutchings 1888:431). A marriage could not be dissolved by divorce (Perlot 1985:233). Patrilocality was the rule prior to the advent of village life (cf. Dick-Bissonnette 1998), so a bride relocated to the home of her husband, presumably in another local territory (Perlot 1985:232). Tenaya himself had at least one Paiute spouse among his four wives (Bunnell 1990:89, 135; Taylor 1932). It is interesting to note, however, that some men of other groups were residing with their Yosemite wives in Awahnee in 1851. This may reflect the breakdown of patrilocality somewhat in the face of nonnative incursion into the Sierra foothills.

FROM CAMPS TO VILLAGES

Given this social structure, traditional tribelet settlements of the post–Gold Rush era, if not earlier, consisted of males of the lineage, the females who married in, children, and any yet unmarried female offspring. It is difficult to determine the population of an individual settlement prior to the change to village life after the disruption caused by nonnative actions, but it is apparent that size would have varied as a function of the number of male descendants and surviving offspring, as well as fission or fusion of settlements within the tribelet territory. Lt. Tredwell Moore's capture of a village with 6 men and 15 women and children in 1852 suggests a settlement population of approximately 20 to 25 people (see also Levy 1978:410). This figure is also consistent with Perlot's (1985:80) observation of a group of 18 persons in the foothills moving from one settlement to another. Bunnell (1990:209), on the other hand, noted that "nearly all" of the 35 Yosemite Indians captured by the Mariposa Battalion in May of 1851 "were in some way a part of the family of the old patriarch, Ten-ie-ya." This suggests a slightly larger kin-group size (see also Clark 1907:21), although some "kin" ties might have simply reflected membership in the same moiety (see Broadbent 1964:155), or this larger size may have been due to the fact that Tenaya had multiple wives.

Perlot's (1985:190) account of a settlement with more than 200 individuals almost certainly reflects the post–Gold Rush village life discussed by Gifford (1926b; see also Hutchings 1888:367), but it is evident that the total population recorded by Bunnell only a few years earlier was probably not occupying a single village. Upon entry into Yosemite Valley in March of 1851, the Mariposa Battalion observed at least one large village, three smaller villages, and an unspecified number of additional small clusters of dwellings that had been recently used (see Bunnell 1880: map, 1990:73–75). Much later, Merriam (1917) recorded the location of "village" and smaller "camp" sites in Yosemite Valley, and he noted apparent occupation of multiple sites at any given time (see also Powers 1976:365). The data suggest that population size of any given settlement was likely flexible, at least on a seasonal basis. For example, most ethnographers indicate that the Me'-wuk moved and likely dispersed during the summer months to access seasonally available resources in higher elevations (Barrett and Gifford 1933:134; Hutchings 1888:422). Villages in lower-elevation areas were generally along river courses, whereas summer settlements at higher elevations were "habitually on the ridges, not in the canyons" (Barrett and Gifford 1933:135). Bunnell (1990:55) observed a somewhat broader pattern of summer land use, however, stating that people "were scattered in bands on the sunny slopes of the ridges, and in the mountain glens" at certain times of the year. In the higher elevations, a stream or spring provided water for the camp inhabitants (Barrett and Gifford 1933:135). In this, the documentary sources are consistent with the archaeological evidence for a logistical settlement strategy, although none specifically mention task-specific locales as part of this regime (but see Clark 1907:36), nor do they indicate how frequently residences were relocated during a season.

Given what is known of native trails in the region (e.g., Bunnell 1990; Muir 1894), Yosemite Indians likely summered upriver in Little Yosemite Valley, in the Tuolumne Meadows area, or on the divide between the Tuolumne and Merced rivers north of Yosemite Valley. Fall may have been spent in Yosemite Valley itself, while people may have wintered in Yosemite Valley, downriver in El Portal, or along Bull Creek east of Coulterville (Bates and Lee 1990; Merriam 1917:202, 208; Perlot 1985). Ethnohistoric information is ambiguous regarding whether or not Yosemite Valley was occupied in the winter, although snowpack, acorn harvest, physical threats of miners, and employment opportunities likely influenced decisions of families from year to year. Yosemite Indians were clearly living in Yosemite Valley during the winter of 1851, and Muir (1912) in 1873 also noted that a portion of population remained in Yosemite Valley, even as others wintered at Bull Creek.

Merriam (n.d.) recorded multiple constituents of a typical Me'-wuk village. These included dwellings *(oo-moo'-chah)*, an assembly house *(hange'-e)*, a village "plaza," one or more sweathouses *(chap-poo')* and menstrual huts, arbor shades *(sal'-lah)*, bedrock mortars, scaffolds for drying acorns or meat *(he-wa'-ah)*, hearths, separate areas set aside for cooking acorns or manufacturing flaked stone tools, and a cremation area *(yu'-lah)*. This suggests an internal structure to each village and segregation of activities that may also have applied to previllage life. In the case of polygyny, each wife maintained a separate house within a village (Perlot 1985:234). In addition, structures for storage of foodstuffs were associated with residential sites. Historical photographs and ethnohistoric accounts suggest that these structures were not located within villages but were located relatively close by (cf. Powers 1976:351). For example, Bunnell (1990:73) observed that "not far from the camp, upon posts, rocks, and in trees, was a large cache of acorns and other provisions" (see also Hutchings 1888:422).

General ethnographic records indicate that various house types were used by the Me'-wuk. These differences were due, at least in part, to different needs in seasonal environments (Barrett and Gifford 1933: 198). The conical bark house *(o'-chum)* is generally depicted as the typical structure in the midelevation areas such as Yosemite Valley (figure 4; see Bates 1993; Clark 1907:24; Gordon-Cumming 1886:136; Powers

The People of Awahnee

FIGURE 4. Conical bark house in Yosemite Valley. (*Indian—Wigwam*, circa 1880s, photograph by George Fiske. Collection Center for Creative Photography, University of Arizona.)

1976:350), where year-round habitation sometimes occurred and large bark slabs would have been available for construction. Barrett and Gifford (1933:199) suggested that no framework was used to support these dwellings, but other researchers indicate that the foundation of such a structure was made of poles lashed together with grapevines (Bates 1993:13). This construction is also confirmed by some historical photographs. Overlapping bark slabs were then laid against the framework, leaving an opening on one side for entrance and egress. Dwellings varied from approximately 2.5 to 4.5 meters in diameter (Barrett and Gifford 1933:199) and accommodated "a family of a half-dozen persons, with all their household property, dogs included" (Clark 1907:24). Clark (1907:26) described the bedding and blankets of animal skins within a house, and Bunnell (1990:76) commented on the "useful and ornamental" domestic property he observed therein. Historical photographs and paintings, however, suggest that many household items were kept outside rather than inside the dwelling (see Bates and Lee 1990: plates 32, 33, 44, and 45). Conversely, Clark (1907:26) stated that "during the warm summer season [Yosemite Indians] generally lived outside in brush arbors and used their *o'-chums* as storage places." A central hearth may have been present in the house for additional warmth and cooking during the winter (Gordon-Cumming 1886:137), although

Powers (1976:350) noted a hearth in front of the house. Such extramural hearth placement is also evident in many historical photographs.

Some scholars contend that the cedarbark structure was not traditional (e.g., Bates 1993; see also Bibby 2005:162), since early historic photographs sometimes depict smaller, domed brush shelters such as those known in lower-elevation areas (Barrett and Gifford 1933:198). Bates (1993:13) suggested these brush dwellings would have been used in Yosemite Valley prior to nonnative incursion, since large cedar-bark slabs would only have been readily available after the advent of logging in the 1870s. Unfortunately, ethnohistoric information is somewhat vague on this point, since details of dwelling construction are not provided. Bunnell (1990:46) referred to "bark huts" at the Nutchu encampment in the Wawona area and "wigwams" in Yosemite Valley in the early spring. At about the same time of year in the Merced River canyon, Perlot (1985:188) noted "three villages, whose huts, scattered as if at random, resembled enormous beehives." This "beehive" caricature might indicate domed brush or earthen shelters for the houses themselves or could simply refer to the level of activity within the villages in general. Perlot (1985:189) also made reference to the people returning to their work after his arrival in the village and "constructing, with split osiers and with the bark of certain trees, the huts, winnowing-baskets, and sort of panniers which served them as vessels." This may indicate use of bark for house construction in the 1850s.

Given the lack of direct archaeological evidence pertaining to habitation structures, it is difficult to know to what extent these anecdotal descriptions or the photographic evidence cited by Bates (1993) reflect the full range of house types either prior to or after the Gold Rush. For example, Gordon-Cumming (1886:245) noted that a newly arrived group of Mono Paiute had only constructed brush shelters rather than more-substantial bark houses. It is also unclear if seasonal differences in housing are documented in these records, and whether it is appropriate to assume that photographs taken in the 1860s are any more representative of precontact native life than photographs from the 1870s. Since all photographs postdate cultural disruption, considerations such as the threat of displacement may have factored into decisions regarding investment in house construction in the 1850s and 1860s relative to later times (Bibby 2005:162). If this were the case, then greater stability in Yosemite Indian life after 1860 might account for the apparent trend from brush to bark shelters recorded in photographs, and this may represent a return to a preferred house type.

Other traditional structures built by the Me'-wuk included the assembly house and sweathouse. Bunnell (1990) did not mention any of the former in Yosemite Valley, although Merriam (1917:205) reported the location of one present in the late 1800s. In contrast, sweathouses were numerous (Bunnell 1990:78) and were located adjacent to the river near villages. Barrett and Gifford (1933:200–206) provided details of construction for both types of structures, and Bunnell (1990:78) also described the sweathouses he observed in Yosemite Valley (see also Gordon-Cumming 1886:247). Assembly houses were semisubterranean structures with four large central posts and eight peripheral posts supporting beams of a conical roof (see also Moratto 1972:196). Constructed over a 1- to 1.5-meter-deep pit measuring 13 to 17 meters in diameter, the superstructure was in turn covered with brush and earth. An entrance was maintained on one side and a smoke hole was present in the center. Sweathouses were also conical or domed structures covered with brush and earth over a pit, although in this case structures only measured 0.5 to 1 meter deep and 2 to 5 meters in diameter. Up to six persons could be accommodated inside. Bunnell (1990:78) noted that sweathouses were one of the "conveniences of a permanent Indian encampment . . . used as a luxury, as a curative for disease, and as a convenience for cleansing the skin." Sweating was also required prior to hunting for deer (see Barrett and Gifford 1933:178, 205–206; Clark 1907:35). Bunnell (1990:78) went on to describe how "hot stones are taken in, the aperture is closed until suffocation would seem impending, when they crawl out . . . and with a shout spring like acrobats into the cold waters of the stream" (see also Gordon-Cumming 1886:247). Conversely, Barrett and Gifford (1933:205) suggested that a fire was tended inside the sweathouse, with a small hole at the top of the structure to allow the smoke to escape. This construction is also confirmed by historical photographs from the 1870s.

SPIRITUAL LIFE AND CEREMONY

The assembly house served as the location for many ceremonies, particularly the more elaborate rituals that tended to take place at the primary tribelet village and that often involved invitations to neighboring groups (Levy 1978:412). Based primarily on work among the Central Sierra Me'-wuk, Gifford (1955) recognized two general types of ceremonies. "Sacred" ceremonies required ritual costume and adherence to strictures on handling such regalia. "Profane" ceremonies lacked such elaboration and primarily served as entertainment rather than a religious purpose. These various ceremonies were practiced to maintain balance within the world, to give thanks for different resources, and to summon prosperity and health (Bates and Lee 1990:22; Gifford 1955; Perlot 1985:170).

Ceremonies also accompanied the death of an individual. The funeral rite included cremation of the tightly bound body of the deceased (Bunnell 1990:49, 79, 151; Clark 1907:50, 59; Hutchings 1888:434–437; Perlot 1985:131, 218; Powers 1976:356) and a subsequent mourning ceremony held several months to a year after the death (Gifford 1955; Powers 1976:353, 355). Personal property of the deceased was burned at the time of death or during the annual mourning ceremony, even when groups were often in very destitute circumstances after the Gold Rush (Clark 1907:63–64). Cremation and mourning rituals were clearly recognized as important to Yosemite Indians, since Captain Boling permitted Chief Tenaya to retrieve the body of his youngest son for proper funerary treatment, even in the midst of the ongoing standoff between the military and the Indians (Bunnell 1990:151). Female family members of the deceased cut or singed off their long hair as a sign of mourning (Hutchings 1888:437), and the pulverized charred bone and ash of the deceased was mixed with pine pitch and spread on the face of mourning female family members for up to a year (Bunnell 1990:79; Hutchings 1888:437).

Shamanism encompassed a variety of types and forms, with the craft inherited patrilineally. Levy (1978:412) further noted that shamanistic skill "emanated from a combination of instruction by an older shaman and acquisition of supernatural power" through dreams and vision quests. Spirit doctors and sucking shamans undertook curative functions and acquired their power through dreaming (see also Bunnell 1990:260; Clark 1907:58). Disease objects, identified through the assistance of guardian spirits, were sucked from the patient's body (Hutchings 1888:433; Perlot 1985:189; Powers 1976:354). Clark (1907:56–57) suggested that failure to cure disease could cause people to think that the shaman was "under the control of some evil spirit," and therefore they might kill the doctor (see also Hutchings 1888:433). Herb doctors focused on less serious diseases, using medicinal plants to treat ailments such as heartburn, swelling, warts, colds, rheumatism, pneumonia, pox, measles, and venereal disease (Barrett and Gifford 1933:165ff; Bunnell 1990:90, 198). At least sixty-seven plants were used in this way by the Me'-wuk, with medicinal qualities gained through chewing, inhaling smoke, imbibing steeped drinks, or external applications (Barrett and Gifford 1933:16; see also Bunnell 1990:79). Certain other specialists included deer, bear, rattlesnake, and weather shamans, who served to foretell or prompt certain events or to undertake specific performances (see Levy 1978:412). Such activities were often directed toward improving hunting and gathering success (see Powers 1976:354–355).

Objects and features of the natural world were imbued with "innumerable spiritual occupants, possessed of supernatural or spiritual powers, none of which are believed by them to equal the power of the Great Spirit whose home is in the West" (Bunnell 1990:195). This Great Spirit—Nang-wa[5]—was a benevolent deity giving order to the universe (Clark 1907:65; Perlot 1985:229). Perlot (1985:229) observed that there was no formal religious worship of this god, but rather obedience and conduct that "the old teach the young [and that] constitute his civil code and penal code." Failure to adhere to standards of behavior would offend the deity and result in temporary exile or, in the case of murder, death. Perlot recognized Yosemite Indian religion as a direct relationship between the individual and Nang-wa "without any intermediary. . . . a theocracy without priests." But the influence of Christianity was also evident among Sierra groups—perhaps including Yosemite Indians—by 1851 as well, since Bunnell (1990:260) observed that

> with their mythology and traditions, [there] would occasionally appear expressions evidently derived from the teachings of Christianity, the origin of which, no doubt, might have been traced to the old Missions. The fugitive converts from those Missions being the means of engrafting the Catholic element on to the original belief of the mountain tribes. Their recitations were a peculiar mixture, but they vehemently claimed them as original, and as revealed to them by the Great Spirit, through his mediums or prophets (their "medicine men"), in visions and trances. These "mediums," in their character of priests, are held in great veneration.

It may be significant that Perlot (1985:166, 188) likened some gestures of greeting used by Chief José and his people to those of Catholic priests, since the chief once lived at a mission and his two sons were born there (Perlot 1985:182).

FEEDING THE FAMILY

The diet of Yosemite Indians and other Me'-wuk groups consisted of a variety of game and fish as well as seeds, nuts, fruits, bulbs, greens, and insects (see Barrett and Gifford 1933; Clark 1907:31; Bunnell 1880; Gordon-Cumming 1886; Hutchings 1888; Muir 1894, 1912). Fish and game were acquired using a variety of techniques and implements, whereas plants were gathered by women who employed a somewhat more generalized toolkit consisting of a digging stick, seed beater, and burden basket (see Muir 1894; Perlot 1985:169). Hunting and fishing were the province of men (Gordon-Cumming 1886; Hutchings 1888; Perlot 1985), and men were also responsible for the manufacture of their equipment for such tasks (Perlot 1985:189, 234). Deer were hunted either individually via ambush or stalking, or communally through drives (Barrett and Gifford 1933:178–179; Bunnell 1990:77, 121; Clark 1907:31–32; Powers 1976:364). In the latter case, long nets or brush fences were used to entrap deer or to funnel animals into corrals. Large animals were generally pursued by groups of hunters, sometimes with the aid of dogs (Bunnell 1990:159). Hunters might be concealed in pits or blinds when working together, and deer-head decoys or masks were used by lone hunters (Barrett and Gifford 1933:179; Perlot 1985:260). Perlot (1985) generally observed hunting or fishing parties of three to four men, although such groups may have in part been a response to the physical threats of miners common at the time.

Once game was trapped or confronted, bows and arrows usually served to dispatch the animals, including deer, bear, antelope, and elk. The latter two species were only accessible through travel to the foothills or plains (Barrett and Gifford 1933:182). Horses were also available in the Central Valley after Spanish incursion into California and by others in the foothills after the Gold Rush (Bunnell 1990; Perlot 1985:129). Horses and mules were driven into Yosemite Valley and prevented from escaping by "poles, brush and loose rock" placed across the entrance trail (Bunnell 1990:86). Thus "corralled," these animals could be dispatched for meat as needed. Bows measured 1.2 meters long, and arrows were 0.6 meters in length (Perlot 1985:72, 80). Smaller game, including squirrels and birds, were taken with arrows, snares, or deadfall traps. Clubs were also sometimes employed, particularly in communal rabbit drives. Fishing for trout and lampreys was accomplished with spears, nets, and traps or by stupefying fish with plant extracts (Bunnell 1990:165; Clark 1907:37; Perlot 1985). Weirs were also sometimes constructed (Clark 1907:37); angling was introduced after the Gold Rush (Hutchings 1888:366). Bunnell (1990:77) observed that "fish spears were but a single tine of bone, with a cord attached near the centre, that when the spear, loosely placed in the socket in the pole, was pulled out by the struggles of the fish, the tine and cord would hold securely as though held by a barbed hook." These spears were approximately 4 meters long (Perlot 1985:72).

For large game, much of the processing and cooking of the meat occurred at camp rather than at the kill site (see Barrett and Gifford 1933:181). Deer viscera, however, were apparently removed and consumed in the field (Gordon-Cumming 1886:138). Animals taken communally were divided among the multiple hunters, whereas meat from game taken by an individual was shared with the hunter's relatives. Bunnell (1990:92) noted that bones were "cracked and picked" during consumption, suggesting marrow extraction in addition to consumption of the meat (see also Muir 1894). Some meat was dried for later use (Barrett and Gifford 1933:140; Bunnell 1990:29; Clark 1907:36; Gordon-Cumming 1886:138; Perlot 1985:220). Small game and fish were prepared by cooking and, on occasion, by pulverizing in mortars for consumption by elderly people (Barrett and Gifford 1933:139; Clark 1907:38).

Black-oak acorns were the prominent vegetal foodstuff gathered (Bunnell 1990:198, 252; Clark 1907; Hutchings 1888:359; Powers 1976:351) and remain important in Yosemite Indian life today (see Ortiz 1991). Gathering occurred as acorns fell to the ground in the fall, and large conical burden baskets were used for collection (Bunnell 1990; Perlot 1985; Powers 1976:351). Subsequent preparation was an involved process of shelling the acorns, winnowing in baskets, pounding in bedrock mortars with cobble pestles to make flour (see figure 5), and leaching the flour to remove bitter tannins prior to cooking (Barrett and Gifford 1933; Bunnell 1990:88–89; Clark 1907:41–43; Gordon-Cumming 1886:140; Hutchings 1888:425–426; Ortiz 1988, 1991). Mortars of particular depths were preferred for various steps within the milling process (see Ortiz 1991), and deep mortars may have been abandoned for acorn preparation in favor of new, shallow mortars more suited to the task (see Barrett and Gifford 1933:208). The resulting flour was generally mixed with water—and, perhaps, with edible greens, seeds, and insects (Hutchings 1888:427, 429; Perlot 1985:194)—to produce a soup, mush, or "biscuit" mixture that was boiled by placing hot stones into a cooking basket (Bunnell 1990:88; Gordon-Cumming 1886:140; Hutchings 1888:427; Perlot 1985:194). A looped stick was used to stir the mixture and to move the stones to prevent burning (Barrett and Gifford 1933:146; Ortiz 1991). With the loss of access to oak groves in the foothills during the Gold Rush, use of acorns may have declined

FIGURE 5. Bedrock mortars. (Photograph by Kathleen L. Hull.)

somewhat. Scipiano declared that his people "were forced to seek their winter provisions [i.e., nut stores] among the Monos" on the east side of the Sierra (Perlot 1985:223). This likely refers to the collection of pinyon pine nuts in place of acorns, and 40 bushels or more of such nuts might be collected and stored per household (see Gordon-Cumming 1886:143).

Granaries *(chuk-a)* were constructed for storage of acorns, pine nuts, and other foods. Bunnell (1990:77) estimated that 400 to 600 bushels of acorns were in storage at the time the Mariposa Battalion entered Yosemite Valley in March of 1851. Bunnell (1990:75) noted that "*cachés* were principally of acorns although many contained bay (California laurel) [*Umbellularia californica*], Piñon pine (Digger pine) [bull pine, *P. sabiniana*], and chinquapin [*Castanopsis* sp.] nuts, grass seeds, wild rye or oats (scorched) [perhaps *Avena barbata*, a nonnative plant evidently borrowed from the Spanish; see Barrett and Gifford 1933:152], dried worms, scorched grasshoppers and what proved to be the dried larvae of insects, which I was afterward told were gathered from the waters of the lakes in and east of the Sierra Nevada." These granaries were constructed of several vertical poles set into the ground and smaller vertical poles lashed together with grapevines. A lining of twigs, brush, and grass was placed within the smaller poles to form the elevated storage receptacle for the foodstuffs. Granaries were up to 4 meters high and 3 meters in diameter (Gordon-Cumming 1886:139; Hutchings 1888:422).

As these passages suggest, and Barrett and Gifford (1933) confirm, numerous plants were exploited for food, with various plant elements collected (see also Bunnell 1990:89, 188, 220; Clark 1907:48; Gordon-Cumming 1886:138; Muir 1894, 1912; Perlot 1985:169). These included greens, bulbs, corms, tubers, roots, seeds, and nuts. Plants were consumed raw, boiled, steamed, parched, or pulverized, as appropriate. Agriculture was not practiced except for the apparent minimal cultivation of tobacco (*Nicotiana* sp.; Barrett and Gifford 1933:140), but certain horticultural practices such as burning, thinning, coppicing, and pruning of individual plants were utilized to enhance harvests or specific qualities of selected plants (see M.K. Anderson 1993, 2005). Such techniques may have been particularly important with respect to nonfood plants such as basketry materials, since plant-management techniques provided for straighter shoots and higher-quality working material. More general seasonal burning of larger areas (as opposed to individual plants) was used to enhance the growth of certain vegetal species and to inhibit the spread of others (Gordon-Cumming 1886:242; Hutchings 1888:189; Muir 1894, 1911). Fires may have been set annually in Yosemite Valley for this purpose (Clark 1894, cited in M.K. Anderson 2005:157). Fire was also sometimes used to drive insects such as grasshoppers into collection pits (Hutchings 1888:429).

THE MATERIAL NECESSITIES AND COMFORTS OF LIFE

Vegetal materials, stone, bone, and other animal products served as raw materials for a myriad of manufactured implements and personal adornment. Bunnell (1990:76–77; see also Hutchings 1888; Perlot 1985) observed sinew and milkweed cordage, bone fish spears, antler hammers and punches, sling stones, rabbitskin and squirrelskin blankets, obsidian, pumice, salt, musical instruments such as wooden drums and reed flutes, and ornaments of bone, bird bills, claws, and feathers. Baskets were the most conspicuous items in the native household, however, as Bunnell (1990:76) noted:

> Their supplies of furniture of all kinds, excepting baskets, were meagre enough. These baskets were quite numerous, and were of various pat-

terns and for different uses. The large ones were made either of bark, roots of the Tamarack or Cedar, Willow or Tule. Those made for gathering and transporting food supplies were of large size and round form, with a sharp apex, into which, when inverted and placed upon the back, everything centers. This form of basket enables the carrier to keep their balance while passing over seemingly impassable rocks, and along the verge of dangerous precipices. Other baskets found served as water buckets. Others again of various sizes were used as cups and soup bowls; and still another kind, made of a tough, wiry grass, closely woven and cemented, was used for kettles for boiling food.

Although the plant species identified by Bunnell are likely not entirely accurate, various plant materials were used for basketry (Barrett and Gifford 1933; see also Bates and Lee 1990), and baskets were employed for a variety of tasks, since ceramics were not produced. Foundation materials included willow *(Salix* sp.), buckbrush *(Ceanothus cuneatus)*, deerbrush *(C. intergerrimus)*, and sourberry *(Rhus trilobata)*. Sewing materials included willow, big-leaf maple *(Acer macrophyllum)*, redbud *(Cercis occidentalis)*, and bracken fern *(Pteridium aquilinum)*. Basket making was the responsibility of women (Clark 1907:67; Gordon-Cumming 1886:137; Perlot 1985:234). Twined basketry served as winnowing trays, seed beaters, burden baskets, and cradles, whereas coiled baskets were used primarily for cooking, eating, and storage (Barrett and Gifford 1933; Bates and Lee 1990). Bone awls were used in the construction of coiled baskets, and tree resin was applied to waterproof some vessels (Bunnell 1990:89; Clark 1907:71). Clark (1907:69) suggested that decorative patterns woven into baskets were symbolic and followed traditional designs, although some had "so ancient an origin that Indians of the present day do not know what many of them are intended to represent." Some changes in basketry motifs and vessel shape occurred after 1860 in response to production for tourists and collectors (Bates and Lee 1990). Decorative items such as shell beads, glass beads, and feathers were also sometimes used to adorn woven vessels. Yosemite Indian myths suggest that basket-weaving techniques may have been introduced from the south, as one legend of *Tis-sa'-ack* tells of her coming from the "far South" and teaching Yosemite Indian women how to make baskets (Clark 1907:83–85).

Some other vessels for cooking and storage were made of soapstone (steatite), although such vessels were likely much smaller than typical baskets (Barrett and Gifford 1933:211). Stone was also used in the manufacture of knives, arrow points, and other flaked implements. Obsidian served as the primary material in this regard (Barrett and

Gifford 1933:212; see also Bunnell 1990:76). Granite hammerstones and antler tools were used to remove flakes in shaping these stone implements (Bunnell 1990:123). Ground-stone milling tools were made of granite or pumice. Arrow shafts were made from young shoots that were scraped, trimmed, and, if necessary, straightened through heating and bending (Barrett and Gifford 1933:217; Bunnell 1990:122; Clark 1907:74). The latter task was facilitated by use of perforated or grooved stones of steatite or pumice (Barrett and Gifford 1933:213). A stone point was attached to the shaft with sinew, and feathers were used for fletching (Clark 1907:74). Barrett and Gifford (1933:219) suggested that arrows were made by specialists. Cedar was used for locally produced bows (Clark 1907:72), with sinew applied to the back and the bowstring made of sinew or twisted milkweed (*Asclepias* sp.) fiber (Barrett and Gifford 1933:216; Bates 1978). Milkweed cordage also served as tumplines for burden baskets and other tasks. Other items of vegetal materials included soaproot *(Chlorogalum pomeridianum)* brushes, mats, and nets (Barrett and Gifford 1933; Powers 1976:352), and wooden fire drills (Perlot 1985:218). Clothing worn in colder months, armor, and blankets were generally made of buckskin or rabbitskin (Gordon-Cumming 1886:69; Perlot 1985:220; Powers 1976:351), although Barrett and Gifford (1933:211) also reported fur blankets of bear, deer, mountain lion, and coyote, as well as feather blankets. Bunnell (1990: 17, 19, 248) noted that western clothing and woolen blankets were items commonly stolen in raids on trading posts and mining camps (see also Perlot 1985:262), supplementing those produced by Indians. Personal adornment for both men and women included tattoos and the use of feathers for pierced earrings, with females using shells and males using face painting for additional ornamentation (Perlot 1985:80, 235).

As suggested by the diverse array of raw materials used and the ethnohistoric observations of encampment food and equipment, the bounty of local resources was clearly augmented by trade for or direct access to nonlocal materials. Bunnell (1990:76) concluded that obsidian, pumice, and salt were acquired from the eastern side the Sierra Nevada (see also Bunnell 1990:121; Clark 1907:22; Muir 1894; Taylor 1932). Rabbitskin blankets also may have come from this same source, as did brine fly larvae available seasonally at Mono Lake (Bunnell 1990:75; Clark 1907:46; Hutchings 1888:427–428). Marine shell ornaments and glass beads were procured from coastal groups (see Clark 1907:23), and the closest steatite and chert sources lay in the Sierra Nevada foothills to the west as well. Barrett and Gifford (1933:256) suggested that "trade between Miwok and Mono friends was a matter of reciprocal gifts," and people of many different groups came to Yosemite Valley to trade (Barrett and Gifford 1933:129; Clark 1907:51; Steward 1933:257, 325). In return for exotic materials, Yosemite Indians provided various foodstuffs, such as acorns and manzanita berries, as well as baskets and "arrow-wood" (Bunnell 1990:122). Yosemite people may also have served as intermediaries in exchange of items such as shell beads from the Pacific coast to the Great Basin.

WHO WERE THE AWAHNICHI?

Material and documentary records that address the question of Awahnichi ethnicity and culture change consist of local Yosemite Valley data that have been given fuller scope through augmentation with regional archaeological and ethnographic information. Working back and forth between the local and regional allows archaeology and ethnography to be reconciled to a common scale and also tacitly acknowledges that the Awahnichi, like all California native people, did not live in isolation but rather were part of a larger sphere of demographic and economic interaction. Archaeological studies in Yosemite Valley and the greater Yosemite region provide time depth for various broad cultural patterns of which ethnohistoric and ethnographic observations are the latest part. Although the groups present and cultural identity of native people may have changed over the course of millennia, investigations confirm that many of the traits and practices of Yosemite Indians observed and recorded in documents after 1850 had their roots in traditions that date back hundreds or even thousands of years. Particularly important, archaeological evidence reveals that many of the elements of Yosemite Indian life recorded by ethnographers were in place at least as early as A.D. 1350. For example, reliance on acorns; use of bedrock mortars, bow and arrow technology, small obsidian projectile points, steatite vessels and ornaments, and marine shell beads; and logistic organization of settlements are all evident. Although such similarities do not demonstrate cultural continuity with other practices observed after the Gold Rush, all regional archaeologists agree that the Me'-wuk are represented and that they were firmly established in the region by at least this time. Furthermore, ethnohistoric and ethnographic observations of other aspects of material culture, Yosemite Indian mythology, and use of the *-tcī* suffix for the Awahnichi also support affiliation of this group with Miwok speakers.

Given the paucity of archaeological evidence from sites dating to the Protohistoric period (A.D. 1800–1847), however, it is unclear how the picture of Yosemite Indian life after 1850 drawn from ethnohistoric accounts and historical photographs relates to life prior to the introduction of Old World diseases or, even, to just before physical incursion of nonnative people fifty years later. Some of these traits, however, likely predate physical invasion by nonnative people or their diseases. Moreover, although the "ethnographic present" of ethnographers conforms well to the very detailed portrait of native life at the Gold Rush provided by Bunnell and Perlot, reliance on "memory culture" confounds our ability to know which aspects of ethnography relate to life before the "black sickness," after disease-induced depopulation but prior to 1851, after the Gold Rush, or to some combination of all three. Still, ethnographers were able to infer some practices from linguistic evidence rather than informants that appear to be of some antiquity. For example, Gifford (1926b) was explicit in his attribution of village life to contact stress among the Me'-wuk, and comparison of Bunnell (1990) and Perlot (1985) with respect to village life confirms this conclusion. Similarly, Gifford (1926a:141) made specific reference to a time "before the whites" when discussing marriage practices, which places such traits prior to the Gold Rush, at least.

In fact, ethnographic and ethnohistoric observations suggest a series of changes resulting from colonial encounters. Primary among these were the mixture of languages, word borrowing, and further development of dialects; territorial and *nena* realignment; alteration of settlement strategies, including different settlement types and postmarital residence patterns; changes in house construction; escalating intergroup violence; the introduction of domestic animals into the diet; and, perhaps, the need for greater plant management or, at least, shifts in diet resulting from lack of access to traditional gathering places. Ethnographic studies also demonstrate the ongoing process of cultural adaptation and change in traditional activities in the late 1800s and beyond, including the incorporation of new practices in basket production (e.g., Bates and Lee 1990) and the adoption of nonnative material culture such as fishing technology and clothing. Cultural features that may have remained intact during the late 1700s and early 1800s, and probably stayed much the same up until the late 1800s or early 1900s, include patrilineal descent and leadership, the construction of the assembly house and sweathouses, shamanism, marriage practices such as exogamy, membership in moieties, mortuary and mourning practices, use of traditional materials with only minor nonnative additions (i.e., glass beads, woven fabrics), production of traditional implements, and exchange relations. Fortunately, tradition was also preserved in mythology and native oral history. The question is which of these changes, if any, were due to disease-induced depopulation? And, conversely, which traditions were maintained despite the pressures of depopulation? These observations provide a starting point for further archaeological inquiry into the cultural consequences of disease-induced depopulation among the Awahnichi.

CHAPTER 5

Peopling the Past

Brief ethnohistoric references and intriguing dendrochronological observations comprise meager, but important, clues regarding the timing and magnitude of Yosemite Indian depopulation resulting from the introduction of an Old World pathogen. Although they do not provide quantitative information on population size, these data indicate that severe population decline occurred around A.D. 1790 to 1800 and precipitated temporary abandonment of Awahnee. The account of Chief Tenaya suggests population loss from an undetermined fatal disease as well as additional mortality due to intergroup violence generally coincident with the "black sickness" (Bunnell 1990:64–65).[1] When Yosemite Valley was permanently reoccupied a generation later, human population was still small compared to earlier times. Tenaya followed the medicine man's advice to welcome strangers into his band and thereby augmented intrinsic population growth. Yosemite Indians eventually reflected a composite group of people from the western and eastern Sierra Nevada and adjoining areas, who maintained their home far away from European colonists. Initially, these native people reforged the small tribelet settlements like those that had prevailed prior to demographic collapse, but life eventually centered around larger villages. Additional changes to daily life and culture resulted from the later incursion of miners into the goldfields of the Sierra foothills and ultimate occupation of Yosemite Valley by nonnative people as well.

Ethnographic data suggest that the native inhabitants of Awahnee were vulnerable to catastrophic depopulation given their social organization. If cultural traits observed after 1850 existed prior to the influx of nonnative pathogens, small group size and the exogamous moiety system would have made Yosemite Indians particularly susceptible to the amplification of minor demographic perturbations into major problems. In the case of exposure to non-age-specific disease such as smallpox or measles, small population size would have worked against Yosemite Indians by undermining caregiving and potentially reducing group size to such an extent that internal capacity to rebound was impossible. If surrounding populations were affected at the same time, the problem of rebound would have been exacerbated due to the lack of suitable mates outside the moiety or tribelet. Relative geographic separation and sparse population made the penetration of infectious Old World diseases less likely, but interaction that was fostered by exogamy—such as kin-based trade—suggests mechanisms for exposure. On the other hand, once exposed, Yosemite Indian people would have had to cope with the effects of swift-moving diseases in relative isolation. In other instances, exogamy may have been an advantage, such as when catastrophe was limited to just one tribelet or if females within the tribelet were more vulnerable than males. In any event, exogamy created a larger reproductive group that could foster population rebound (see Moore 2001).

Historical demography—the use of quantitative demographic data available in historical narratives or documentary records—has been employed most often to assess the magnitude of colonial-era native population decline (e.g., Cook and Lovell 1991; Dobyns 1983; Ramenofsky 1996; Upham 1992). For example, rough population estimates noted in early expedition chronicles and subsequent enumerations in the journals of explorers or settlers have provided "before" and "after" snapshots of regional population size. As discussed by Henige (1998), however, calculation of population decline based on such methods is highly suspect, since it is often unclear how contemporary observers defined a population geographically, biologically, or culturally, whether observers were referring to the full population or simply a subset such as adult males, and how estimates of "warriors," for example, might relate to the entire population of native men, women, and children. Conversely, censuses and records of births, baptisms, marriages, and deaths maintained by government agents or religious officials provide much more precise accounts. These records also allow for derivation of statistics on population structure (i.e., age, sex), fertility, mortality, nuptiality, and perhaps migration—in other words, the full suite of demographic factors that contribute to changes in population size through time. Thus, detailed consideration of the timing and process of native demographic collapse has been undertaken in some cases (e.g., Walker and Johnson 1992, 2003; Milliken 1995), although such studies are only possible in postcontact institutional settings such as missions where these records were generated.

To assess the magnitude and understand the potential cultural consequences of colonial-era Awahnichi depopulation, it is necessary to develop archaeological data that expands on the initial glimpses of Yosemite Indian demography available through native oral history and ethnohistory. Archaeology provides quantitative information on relative population size and growth rates sufficient to place the event of colonial-era population decline in long-term perspective and to demonstrate how this experience fits within the history of Yosemite Indians. Demographic archaeology presents formidable challenges, however, ranging from definition of a biologically or culturally meaningful population to selection of appropriate proxy measures to determine population size, since individuals themselves cannot be counted. It is difficult enough to take a census in modern urban societies where political or social boundaries are known, residences are fixed, and counts reflect just a single year, so it not surprising that the task of determining population size in past times is even more complicated. And since the methods and assumptions underlying any demographic archaeological study are critical to establishing confidence in subsequent interpretations, it is worth considering these issues in depth prior to presenting the quantitative analysis of Yosemite Indian colonial-era population change derived from archaeological data.

HOW DO WE COUNT PEOPLE?

Demographic archaeology is about counting "things"—proxies or items that have a known mathematical relationship to the number of people that produced or used them. Simply speaking, more things equal more people, and fewer things equal fewer people. Cross-cultural ethnographic and ethnoarchaeological studies establish the validity of specific measures as population proxies and demonstrate how differences in economy, architecture, proxemics, and environment affect each measure.[2] In addition, ethnographic data are sometimes used to convert proxy quantities into estimates of absolute—rather than relative—population size. Demographic archaeology is also about counting a proxy within a specified period of time that is compatible with the scale of analysis. Temporal spans of equal length are necessary for equivalent statistical representation through time, and such periods should be of relatively short duration so that the proxy represents a meaningful population. If the proxy counts span too long a period, fluctuations in population size within the period are masked and demographic traits of one population are blended with those of another. Finally, the proxy measure must be counted within a geographically relevant area that encompasses all or a representative sample of the territory of a breeding population. That is, a biological population must be defined, and this is usually minimally based on continuity in material culture across space and through time. The primary methods used to estimate population size from archaeological data are site frequency, settlement size, habitation area, room counts, artifact frequency, midden volume, site-specific carrying capacity, burial frequency, and regionally aggregated dates.

Demographic archaeology is a minefield of ethnographic data gaps and potential methodological pitfalls—including issues of archaeological site formation and representation, serial use and use-life of elements serving as proxies, and the sufficiency of cross-cultural studies supporting certain proxies. Within this minefield, sampling strategies and assumptions invoked in paleodemographic studies have been the lightening rod for often harsh critiques (e.g., Henige 1998; Petersen 1975). All methods of estimating population from archaeological remains are subject to problems of representation and preservation that can undermine confidence in results. And many proxy measures of population—such as those that depend upon permanent architecture or the presence of cemeteries—are most applicable to sedentary groups, unlike the Indian people of Awahnee. Other methods require good preservation of organic remains, including bone and shell, and these materials are uncommon in archaeological sites in Yosemite Valley. The deterioration of organic remains also undermines use of radiocarbon dating for demographic reconstruction in this area. On the other hand, good temporal control of proxies in the Yosemite region is possible with obsidian hydration dating. And the geographic boundedness of the valley—defined by 600-meter-high cliffs and rugged, inhospitable terrain immediately upriver and downstream—serves as a convenient mechanism with which to define the "population" in this case. Although Yosemite Indian population was not closed in the sense of individual entrance from or exit to surrounding groups, it is assumed here that any such flow related to exogamous marriage and was thus reciprocal and generally equivalent.

Given the various challenges of natural and cultural site-formation processes, spatially and temporally representative sampling, and fine-grained chronological control in demographic archaeology, I based the Yosemite Indian demographic analysis on two proxies so that each could be checked against the other. The first proxy was the frequency of debitage discarded at occupation sites. The second proxy was a modified measure of habitation site frequency that took site size into account. This adjustment to the site-based proxy was necessary, because the size of sites varies greatly within Yosemite Valley. Such variation not only reflects differences in population aggregation and dispersal during different eras but also relates to partially overlapping occupation episodes that indicate periodic reoccupation of several especially desirable locales over centuries or millennia. A population proxy based only on site frequency would ignore the issue of population distribution within the valley, while a proxy based on total site area would not equate with population size due to the problem of sequential reuse of only portions of the entire site area. Furthermore, it was not possible to use an areal proxy based on the size of habitation space for each episode of occupation, since broad horizontal data necessary to define the size of each component were not available for sites in Yosemite Valley. Instead, for sampling purposes, I subdivided the surface area of larger sites into a series of smaller "subsites" and determined the presence or absence of use within these smaller occupation areas through time. That is, the number of subsites occupied during a given period served as a proxy for the size of the population within Yosemite Valley at the time. Regional ethnographic observations—which likely reflect postcontact village life—were insufficient to determine a minimum village size for definition of subsites.[3] Therefore, subsites were defined based on a trimodal pattern of archaeological site area recognized in Yosemite Valley (Hull 2002:206). Using these data, maximum subsite size was established at approximately 9,000 square meters. Sites encompassing a greater area were split into the minimum number of zones of equal size necessary to approximate this target subsite area. This procedure mitigated the effects of population distribution and site reuse that would otherwise confound a site-based approach to demographic reconstruction in this region.

HOW DO PROXIES RELATE TO POPULATION SIZE?

Both the debitage and subsite frequency proxies represent the consumption of a resource by Indian people in a manner that is directly related to population size. In the case of debitage, the resource consumed was abundant, high-quality obsidian that was used to manufacture tools for local domestic tasks. Although access to the obsidian quarries east of the Sierra Nevada was not possible during the winter, there was more than enough material transported into—or scavenged from cultural deposits within—Yosemite Valley throughout the rest of the year to supply annual needs. Subsite frequency, on the other hand, represents the consumption of land for habitation purposes. Within the restricted topographic setting of Yosemite Valley, land—unlike obsidian—was a limited resource for native people.

Such differences between obsidian and land with respect to resource abundance result in distinct mathematical relationships to population size for each proxy (Hull 2002:238ff). In the absence of other factors that would change the relation between the number of people and consumption of a resource as population increased or decreased in this region, I expected per capita consumption of toolstone to remain relatively constant. That is, a linear relationship existed between population size and obsidian debitage frequency, since this resource was abundant ($y = b_0 + b_1*x$; where x is population size, y is debitage frequency, and b_0 and b_1 are constants).[4] Given the limited availability of habitable terrain, however, I expected per capita consumption of land to decrease with increasing population. Up to a certain point, existing villages could continue to expand in size to keep pace with population increase. Or the growing population could split or fission into new habitation sites within Yosemite Valley as resource or social pressures within the parent site became too great. Beyond this point, however, people living within this circumscribed area were unwilling or unable to physically expand or fission. Population either ceased to grow due to positive or preventative checks on mortality and fertility under conditions of resource stress, or people migrated elsewhere if there were not social restrictions on such movement, or the growing population was packed ever more densely within any given site so as to avoid degrading the environment and compromising subsistence resources in the surrounding terrain. Rather than defining a linear relationship, this demographic accommodation to a limited resource defines a nonlinear, power-function ($y = b_0*x^{b_1}$; where y is subsite frequency) or logarithmic ($y = b_0 + b_1*\ln[x]$)

relationship between population size and subsite frequency. In order to use both the debitage and subsite proxies and compare data, these two different mathematical relationships between population and resources had to be anticipated.

The site-based proxy is perhaps the less controversial of the two approaches I employed to examine Yosemite Indian demography, although the nonlinear relationship of site frequency, site area, or habitation area to population size has not been acknowledged in previous applications of site-based proxies in demographic archaeology. In addition, issues of site function, land use, representative sampling, and geomorphological factors had to be addressed to establish the efficacy of this proxy for Yosemite Indians. Regional archaeology and ethnography indicate seasonal shifts in residential location as well as possible changes in settlement strategies through time. Intensive occupation of substantial villages was the norm in midelevation areas such as Yosemite Valley during the Late Prehistoric 1 (1200 B.C.–A.D. 650) and Late Prehistoric 3 (A.D. 1350–1800) periods. Task-specific logistical sites and temporary camps are also expected within such a settlement system (Binford 1980), however, and it was necessary to avoid sampling these sites for the population reconstruction—just as a modern census would not count people at both their home and workplace, or hotel while traveling on business. Fortunately, temporary camps were unnecessary and unlikely within the confines of Yosemite Valley, since all areas were easily accessible from a village. And archaeological data are sufficient to distinguish residential from logistical sites in this area so that task-specific locales could be excluded from sampling. Logistic sites in the Yosemite region include isolated milling features with little or no associated lithic debris, biface caches, and specialized lithic reduction locales—more typical of higher-elevation areas closer to eastern Sierra quarries—that are recognized by extremely dense concentrations of biface thinning debitage of only one obsidian source material (see Hull, Bevill, Spaulding et al. 1995). Settlement during the Late Prehistoric 2 period (A.D. 650–1350) was more ephemeral than the immediately preceding and subsequent periods, and few data are available for settlement strategies during the Early or Middle Prehistoric periods. Unlike the Late Prehistoric 1 and Late Prehistoric 3 periods, use during these other eras appears to represent a residentially mobile settlement pattern in which logistic sites were unnecessary. Thus, all sites in Yosemite Valley dating to these periods likely represent habitation sites. Easy access to all subsistence resources within the confines of Yosemite Valley from a residential locale would have precluded the frequent relocation of such villages—something that might have artificially inflated the number of sites relative to population size in comparison to periods during which a logistical settlement strategy pertained. I assumed that subsite areas represented domestic rather than communal space, since ethnographic data suggest that nondomestic activity areas such as assembly houses were rare and that storage facilities were maintained off-site.

The population proxy based on debitage frequency required even more rigorous consideration of assumptions than the site-based measure, since many factors other than population size could have affected per capita consumption of toolstone and where material was discarded on an annual basis. These parameters include changes in lithic technology such as a shift from core- to flake-based reduction; potential changes in material acquisition, including scavenging; shifts in the types of tools produced; variable artifact use-life; increased production for exchange; and the presence of lithic craft specialists. Archaeological data for habitation sites in Yosemite Valley do not reveal significant diachronic changes in technology related to the nature of the parent material reduced (Nilsson et al. 1999), and dominance of obsidian indicates that issues of variable artifact use-life—often associated with the qualities of various lithic materials—are not relevant. In addition, there are no diachronic shifts in technology in Yosemite Valley that signal production for exchange, the development of lithic craft specialization for nonlocal use, or the adoption of new tool types that required significantly more or less raw material for production. This is not to say that artifact types did not change over the millennia of human use in Yosemite Valley or that the percentage of items ultimately destined for exchange was constant. Rather, these data simply support the assumption that per capita consumption at residential sites to meet local needs or to acquire desired nonlocal items in exchange for lithic artifacts did not vary significantly and unidirectionally through time on a regional level.

It has been argued elsewhere that flakes would be smaller—if not fewer—at sites dating to the Late Prehistoric 2 and Late Prehistoric 3 periods due to the shift from dart to arrow technology (e.g., Jackson and Holson 1984). But there is no quantitative evidence to support such an assertion in Yosemite Valley (Hull, Hale et al. 1998:123; Hull, Bevill, and Kelly 1995:81) or elsewhere in the southern Sierra Nevada (e.g., Skinner 1986:585). Lithic material needs on a per artifact basis may have decreased through time due to this shift in hunting technology and decreasing projectile-point size. But the greater fragility of smaller, thinner points characteristic of arrow use—and the concomitant unsuitability of such small points for subsequent reworking after use damage—may have required consumption of a generally similar amount of lithic material for both arrow and dart points on a per capita basis. And the emphasis on projectile points that underlies the assertion of decreasing consumption of lithic material overlooks the many other formal and expedient tools manufactured and used for domestic tasks. There is no reason to think that production of projectile points dominated the consumption of lithic material to such an extent that changes in hunting technology would dictate overall consumption patterns.

Seasonal site use can also affect the debitage proxy, since some debitage produced on an annual basis was deposited in higher- or lower-elevation zones occupied at different times of the year. The potential for year-round occupation and patterns of seasonal resource availability suggested that residential sites in Yosemite Valley were occupied from the late fall through early spring. Archaeological data indicate that diverse procurement, processing, manufacturing, and food consumption activities were undertaken in these villages (Hull, Bevill, and Kelly 1995; Hull, Hale et al. 1998; Montague 1994, 1996; Mundy and Hull 1988). I assumed that there were no unidirectional shifts through time toward or away from use of Yosemite Valley in the summer by the entire population. Although specific sites or components within sites may have witnessed slightly longer or shorter duration of occupation from year to year relative to any other component, the examination of regionally aggregated—rather than site-specific—data mitigated against temporal bias resulting from varying annual cycles of occupation. Proximity to high-quality lithic sources, apparent lack of specialist production, and the persistence of a hunting and gathering economy for the entire span of traditional native use in Yosemite Valley also suggested that residential sites express lithic resource use within a relatively limited range of lithic consumption.

Finally, differential access to obsidian quarries also did not influence the amount of obsidian exploited by the native people of Yosemite Valley. Geochemical source analyses indicate a regular decrease in source-specific use with distance from the quarry (see Ericson 1981; Hull and Roper 1999), and this pattern is consistent with local exploitation and unrestricted access to material (see Basgall 1989; Bettinger 1982). Given the availability of good-quality lithic materials and cultural factors such as intermarriage that would have favored interaction with neighbors to the east, I concluded that scavenging or reworking of debitage was unlikely on a large scale, although scavenging may have been prompted by minor seasonal or annual shifts in obsidian availability due to snowpack that precluded trans-Sierra travel to quarry areas. The ready access to the quarries is also borne out by the fact that lithic assemblages in Yosemite Valley are nearly 100 percent obsidian. And there is also no evidence for the replacement of obsidian with manufactured glass for tool production by Yosemite Indians during the colonial era, as has been noted at archaeological sites in the Sierra foothills (e.g., Wallace 1970). Regional archaeological data demonstrate that materials were partially shaped at the quarries before introduction to the sites in the western Sierra and, thus, per capita consumption of obsidian in Yosemite Valley for domestic needs did not differ significantly through time. All of these observations supported the efficacy of debitage frequency as a proxy for Yosemite Indian population.

SAMPLING AND CHRONOLOGICAL CONTROL OF PROXY MEASURES OF POPULATION

As this review highlights, the two proxies selected for study of colonial-era Yosemite Indian population decline were built on regional archaeological knowledge developed over several decades. Potential biases have been considered and assumptions have been invoked to enable their accurate use in Yosemite Valley. Diachronic studies of technology, settlement, and exchange were all critical to the identification of factors that might have led to errors in the demographic reconstruction. These data confirmed that such biases either did not pertain in this case or were such that the regional—as opposed to site-specific—demographic study overcame potential problems. Synthetic studies provided the necessary context for assessing site-formation processes and establishing reasonable assumptions. Beyond the identification of appropriate proxies, however, it was also necessary to address issues of sampling and temporal control for the two population measures.

A temporally and geographically representative sample of habitation sites was selected for both the debitage and subsite frequency proxies. Sixty-three cultural deposits likely representing residential sites have been identified through multiple archaeological surveys of Yosemite Valley since 1952 (Hull and Kelly 1995).[5] An additional 35 sites—including isolated stationary milling features, one human burial, and several nonnative sites—lack lithic debitage and were excluded from demographic sampling. The 63 residential deposits encompass 106 subsites that measure approximately 9,000 square meters or less in area. A 15 percent random sample of these subsites (n = 16) was selected for the population study, with this sample fraction based on expected artifact recovery. Debitage samples from each of the 16 subsites were collected from a 1-by-1-meter unit excavated in 10-centimeter arbitrary levels to the base of the cultural deposit.[6] Unit sediments were screened through 3-millimeter mesh to recover artifacts. These units were generally placed in areas of relatively high surface or subsurface artifact density within each subsite, with subsurface information available for some sites as a result of previous augering of deposits (Hull 2002:208). Random sampling of subsites provided the unbiased geographic cross-section of Indian occupation within Yosemite Valley, and the vertical excavation strategy furnished the temporal cross-section of each deposit. Still, extremely early deposits may be underrepresented in the demographic sample, since they may be deeply buried and thus not visible during surface surveys.

The vertical column provided obsidian debitage for dating via obsidian hydration analysis, thereby establishing the chronology of both subsite occupation and debitage production. Consistent with previous regional research results, nonobsidian debitage accounted for less than 1 percent of the total debitage collection from any subsite. A 10 percent sample of the total debitage collection was selected from every 10-centimeter level for 15 of the subsites, and a 5 percent sample was drawn from the remaining subsite due to the unexpectedly dense concentration of lithic debris in this deposit. Only artifacts visually characteristic of Casa Diablo obsidian were selected, since reliable obsidian hydration rate formulas for other obsidian source materials present in Yosemite Valley archaeological sites are not available. Casa Diablo was the most common lithic material used by the Indian people of the valley, however, so there was no difficulty achieving the desired sample size. Geochemical study of a subsample of 100 visually identified items confirmed that at least 95 percent—and perhaps as much as 97 percent—of the sample did indeed derive from this quarry (Hull 2002:218). The full range of technological debitage types and flakes of various sizes were encompassed by the stratified random sampling of Casa Diablo debitage, thereby avoiding any potential temporal biases related to technology.

The debitage selection procedures resulted in a sample of 2,235 specimens for obsidian hydration dating. This dating method is based on the fact that a freshly exposed surface of obsidian absorbs water from the surrounding environment—or hydrates—to create a visually distinct band or rim that increases in thickness through time. Fresh surfaces are created during the production of flaked stone tools, and thus the thickness of the hydration rim indicates the amount of time that has passed since the tool or flake was produced. A small thin section is removed from the edge of an artifact, and the thickness of the hydration rim on each side—that is, on each original artifact surface—is measured in microns. Multiple measurements of the hydration rim are taken along each face to provide a mean hydration measurement for the artifact. If a flake was not scavenged or subject to environmental factors that affected the hydration band, the thickness of the rims on each face are approximately the same. In some cases, however, the thickness of the rims on opposite faces are quite different, and such disparity may reflect specific procurement or manufacturing behaviors such as scavenging. Hydration may be absent from an artifact due to postdepositional processes such as burning, and rims less than 0.7 microns in thickness could not be discerned with the optical equipment employed in this study. In both of these cases, the piece was recorded as having "no visible hydration." The hydration rim can also be difficult to measure if the diffusion front is vague due to burning or weathering. No measurement of the hydration band thickness can be made in these cases.

The rate at which water diffuses into the rock surface varies between obsidians from different quarries, so the geochemical source of the stone must be determined to accurately interpret hydration measurements. The rate of hydration for any given obsidian source material also slows over time, as the diffusion of water into the surface decreases as the thickness of the hydration band increases. Finally, the rate of hydration for any artifact is sensitive to the temperature of the surrounding environment, with the process occurring more swiftly at higher, rather than lower, temperatures.[7] Therefore, I converted the hydration measurements to absolute dates for the population analysis using a nonlinear, temperature-dependent hydration rate formula for Casa Diablo obsidian developed specifically for application to sites in the Yosemite region (Hull 2001b). It has been demonstrated repeatedly that empirically based methods such as this avoid substantial errors and problems common to rates based on laboratory induced hydration (e.g., Hull 2001b; Rogers 2006), and the rate formula used in this study has also been confirmed by ongoing archaeological investigations in

Yosemite Valley. Provenience-specific temperature estimates were based on linear regression equations of surface and subsurface temperature data by depth for various microenvironments and depositional contexts within Yosemite Valley.[8] With temperature estimates so calculated, age estimates were derived in calibrated radiocarbon years before present (i.e., before A.D. 1950). Due to the nonlinear nature of the hydration process and limitations of the optical equipment employed to measure hydration rims, late dates are more precise than early dates. But the large sample of debitage, the protocols for data analysis, and the focus especially on the colonial era reduced the potential interpretative errors resulting from this phenomenon (see Hull 2002).

DEPICTING POPULATION SIZE THROUGH TIME

Diachronic population profiles for each proxy were developed by counting the number of pieces of debitage produced or number of subsites occupied within 50-year increments. Time increments shorter than 50 years are beyond the resolution of the obsidian hydration dating technique, and longer temporal increments result in data reduction that distorts the subsite proxy and is too severe for analysis of colonial-era depopulation (Hull 2002:242). If an item produced two different hydration bands—suggesting the possibility of material reuse—both dates were counted, since I assumed the item was scavenged from the same locale.[9] If one side of the thin section had no visible hydration, I also treated this measurement as if it represented a separate rim. And each piece lacking visible hydration on both faces was also counted. Exceptions to protocols for pieces with no visible hydration were made only if it was evident that hydration on one or both sides was not visible due to problems with thin section preparation or if the absence of hydration was anomalous for the provenience from which it derived. For example, it was assumed that lack of hydration on pieces recovered from deep cultural deposits resulted from damage to the hydrated surface rather than from relatively recent production of the flake.[10] Since pieces with rims less than 0.7 microns (i.e., lacking visible hydration) represent production after A.D. 1850, counts for pieces with no visible hydration that were not excluded for contextual reasons were distributed across the 50-year interval from A.D. 1850 to 1900. The span from A.D. 1900 to 1950 was excluded from such extrapolation, since Indian use of obsidian is not indicated for this era in historical documents and photographs.[11] Although obvious anomalies were omitted based on provenience or evident specimen-preparation problems, it is likely that some of the specimens with no visible hydration do not represent the period from A.D. 1850 to 1900. They simply could not be excluded based on either of these criteria. Thus, the inclusion of pieces with no visible hydration in the proxy counts likely overrepresents actual population during this 50-year period, but to exclude them altogether posed the risk of underrepresenting population at that time.

The protocols for including both primary and secondary rims for pieces with multiple hydration bands, for excluding anomalous pieces with no visible hydration, for omitting specimens with diffuse hydration or other issues that prevented accurate band measurement, and for doubling the 5 percent sample from one subsite to approximate the 10 percent sample collected from other subsites resulted in a total set of 2,978 obsidian hydration dates spanning the last 12,000 years. Dates older than 3550 B.C. were excluded from the population analysis, however, since earlier occupation in Yosemite Valley has yet to be documented with unequivocal archaeological evidence. In addition, the low frequency of dates from such early times suggested that they might represent items scavenged from outside Yosemite Valley or be noise in the data due to postdepositional processes such as burning. Thus, the final sample documenting Yosemite Indian population for the last 5,500 years encompassed 2,931 dates.[12]

The debitage frequency analysis included all obsidian hydration dates in this sample.[13] The site-based proxy simply counted the number of subsites occupied during each 50-year interval, as determined by the presence of one or more pieces of debitage dating to that period. For this proxy, each subsite was treated equally in the analysis, regardless of the amount of debitage related to each episode of use or the actual size of the subsite. For the sixteen subsites examined, area ranged from approximately 530 to 9,000 square meters, with a mean of 7,300 square meters. The large, random sample of dates—unparalleled in most demographic archaeological studies—revealed multiple occupation episodes of variable duration for each subsite.

Finally, for each proxy measure, I smoothed the raw frequency data with a three-point moving average.[14] This procedure reduced the statistical noise in the population profiles, such as that potentially resulting from limitations in hydration measurement procedures and date derivation (see Hull 2002). Thus, the population measure derived for each 50-year increment (see appendix A) represented the mean of the immediately predating, corresponding, and immediately postdating frequency for that time interval. These curves provided relative trends of rate and timing of population growth or decline rather than absolute population numbers (see Ramenofsky 1987). No attempt was made to quantify the number of flakes produced by an individual or individuals and to thereby extrapolate the number of producers represented. Nor was there any attempt to establish the number of people per subsite. Thus, the analysis avoided construction of arguments based on potentially weak cross-cultural generalizations that are significantly influenced by the organization of technology, the lithic material available, resource abundance, and intrasite proxemics. The population profiles are geographically unique signatures of trends that cannot be quantifiably compared to, or contrasted with, any similarly constructed characterizations outside the Yosemite region.

CAUSES OF COVARIATION IN PROXY MEASURES

Although the availability of obsidian and land within Yosemite Valley suggested that both debitage and subsite frequency have a direct mathematical relationship to population, the two measures were assessed against each other to ensure that this assumption was correct. I reasoned that correlation between these two data sets would be evident if these proxy measures were reflecting the same underlying factor—increase or decrease in one proxy would be mirrored by coincident increase or decrease in the other. And given the assumptions underlying the analysis and the sampling strategy employed, the predominant process reflected by such covariation would be population growth and population decline. Since independent data sets were not available for this comparison, the total obsidian hydration sample was divided into two data sets for this evaluation. Thus, each data set encompassed eight subsites selected at random. Since it was anticipated that subsite frequency was related to population size—and therefore to debitage frequency—in a nonlinear fashion, the natural logarithm of both the debitage and subsite frequencies within each 50-year increment over the last 5,500 years were compared in the covariation analysis. High positive correlation of the two proxies (correlation coefficient $r^2 = 0.839$), indicated that these measures tracked each other fairly well, as an increase or decrease in one data set was mirrored in the other.

These results were consistent with the hypothesis that both proxy measures reflected population growth and decline, but I also considered whether these measures were responding to some other potentially linked traits. Were there factors other than change in population size that could account for patterns of coincident increase and decrease in debitage and subsite frequency through time? Changes in subsite frequency might reflect shifts in settlement patterns or duration of occupation, rather than simply changes in population size. And changes in debitage frequency might be related to technological shifts or changes in production for exchange. But should changes in settlement result in changes in lithic technology, or vice versa, to account for the observed covariance?

The simplest explanation for increase and decrease in the number of residential subsites occupied from one time increment to the next—independent of population growth or decline—is a shift in settlement mobility. On an annual round or even somewhat longer basis, more residential subsites are abandoned and new subsites are occupied within a more mobile system if there was no tendency to reoccupy the same area as part of a seasonal round. By this same logic, less mobility results in fewer residential subsites. Population aggregation or dispersal unrelated to mobility changes could also alter subsite frequency. Greater settlement aggregation would result in a decrease in site—and perhaps subsite—frequency within either a more sedentary or a more mobile system. The potential disparity in subsite frequency between the two extremes of residential mobility versus sedentism, and between dispersed versus aggregated population, might be mediated by local pressures of resource depletion (e.g., fuel) or sanitation concerns relative to habitable space or investment in dwellings, storage facilities, stationary milling features, or other nonportable site furniture.

The duration of occupation at any given residential site by Indian people might differ significantly between mobile and sedentary systems, and therefore this factor could affect the amount of debitage deposited at a subsite. But there is no reason to expect correlation between settlement strategy and lithic consumption on a regional scale such as that observed in the two population proxies for Yosemite Valley. In fact, if greater residential mobility is a factor at all in lithic production, it would result in *decreasing* debitage frequency at any given subsite with concomitant *increasing* subsite frequency—exactly the opposite of the high positive covariation observed in Yosemite Valley. Still, it is possible to envision various scenarios such as tool sharing in more sedentary systems or aggregated habitations that could result in coincident decreasing consumption of lithic material and site (if not subsite) frequency. Greater residential mobility might also lead to more frequent access to lithic sources and, therefore, to more wasteful use of obsidian, thereby resulting in coincident increase in both debitage and subsite frequency. In the case of wasteful use, at least, debitage frequency and subsite frequency could covary positively. But it is unlikely that tool sharing or wasteful raw-material use would be significant enough to account for the patterns observed in the Yosemite Valley data or even to overwhelm or distort the impact of frequency changes due to population size. In addition, the potential bias of population aggregation was addressed, in part, by the subsite sampling approach, and topographic circumscription and distance to lithic resources suggest that mobility shifts are probably not a major concern with respect to toolstone consumption in Yosemite Valley.

Changes in production for exchange could have resulted in escalation in debitage production independent of local population size, and the shift from the atlatl and dart to bow and arrow might have decreased debitage frequency. Although it is possible to offer various scenarios that could result in correlation of debitage and subsite frequency based on such lithic consumption changes, such speculation is without foundation in extant archaeological or ethnographic evidence for the Yosemite region. For example, specialist production for exchange might result in correlation of subsite and debitage counts if competition led each specialist to maintain a separate habitation site. Such a strategy seems unlikely, however, given distance to consumers living in the Central Valley and areas even farther west (see Jackson 1974; Jackson and Ericson 1994), and there is no evident advantage or necessity to maintaining separate habitations. Likewise, one might speculate that the shift to the bow and arrow could have reduced the need for communal hunting so that groups tended to splinter into separate habitation sites. In fact, however, it is difficult to imagine how such factors of lithic technology and settlement could be directly—or even fortuitously—linked on a regional scale over thousands of years to account for the observed covariance in subsite and debitage frequency. In light of this assessment, I concluded that the observed highly positive covariation between the debitage and subsite frequency revealed by the independent data sets resulted from shifts in population size rather than from some other factor. But because production of a flake occurred at a moment in time—whereas a subsite was occupied over years, decades, or even centuries—I assumed that debitage frequency was a better indicator of population than subsite frequency (see Hull 2002:247).

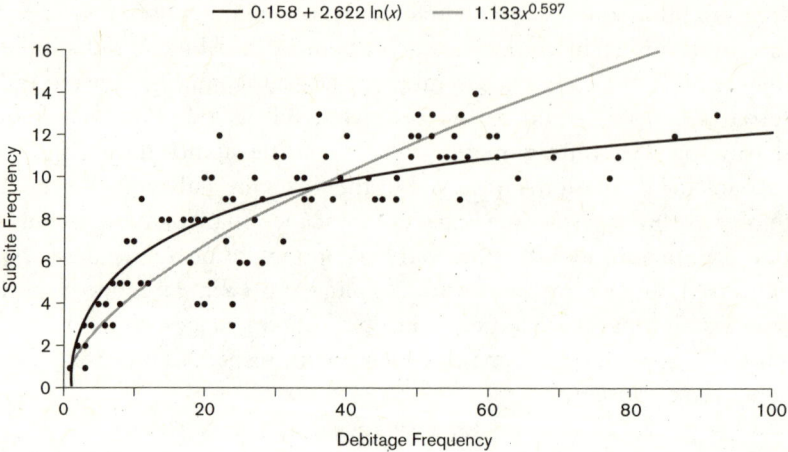

FIGURE 6. Scatterplot and nonlinear regression of debitage and subsite frequency data.

Examination of subsite frequency relative to the debitage frequency for the entire sample of more than 2,900 obsidian hydration dates also clearly revealed the nonlinear relationship between population size and resource consumption that was anticipated for native use of Yosemite Valley (figure 6). The data showed that subsite frequency kept pace with increases in debitage frequency at a decelerating rate. This indicates that people were settled more densely within habitation areas to conserve land as the population grew. Nonlinear regression of the proxies provided two potential mathematical equations to describe this relationship—one a power function and the other logarithmic.[15] Each of these formulas allowed the subsite proxy to be calibrated to the debitage proxy.[16] Smoothed frequencies—incorporating the logarithmic calibration adjustment for the nonlinear nature of the subsite proxy—were considered as a percentage of the maximum population (p_{max}) rather than as raw numbers. Given the logarithmic relationship of subsite frequency to population size, calibrated subsite frequency that exceeded debitage frequency for any given 50-year interval indicated an era of lower than average site-specific population density. Similarly, those temporal intervals with subsite frequency lower than debitage frequency represented episodes of higher than average site-specific population density (see Hull 2005).[17]

The use of p_{max} rather than simple frequency provided a standard currency for discussion of population size and allowed assessment of rates of population growth and decline. Growth rates were derived using an exponential population growth equation drawn from population biology:

$$p_t = p_0 e^{rt}$$

in which p_t is the ending population at time t, p_0 is the starting population at time zero, e is the base of natural logarithms, r is the rate of population growth, and t is the elapsed time in years. For any period of elapsed time (t), r was computed from the known starting and ending population figures. And r was then used to calculate the population doubling time (t_{double}) via the equation

$$t_{\text{double}} = \ln(2)/r$$

This expression—which represents the number of years it takes for a population with a particular growth rate to double in size—serves as a convenient statistic with which to assess the potential perception of population change by individuals in that population.

THE NUMBERS SPEAK

Statistical analysis of the two proxy population measures—and evaluation of these data in light of regional archaeological information and mathematical models of resource consumption—underscore the strength of the methodological approach employed to address the first two key issues of the timing and magnitude of disease-induced depopulation in Yosemite Valley. Estimates of population size, growth rates, fertility, and life expectancy that can be derived via these methods—rather than representing absolute figures—primarily serve as a basis for discussion by placing the colonial-era experience within the context of Yosemite Indian demographic history spanning several millennia. The concept of magnitude, for example, encompasses both the quantitative effect of disease and the qualitative reaction of the participants that was based, in part, on past experience with similar phenomena. Thus, assessing the magnitude of colonial-era depopulation with archaeological data not only requires estimates of the starting population size (as a percentage of $p_{\max}$) and the percentage of population loss due to introduced disease, but also knowledge of whether—and how recently—Yosemite Indians had dealt with other population declines.

The long-term view and focus on the specific demographic history of these people through archaeology differs from most other studies of colonial-era depopulation (cf. Kulisheck 2005). This diachronic perspective permits consideration of past experiences that might have had relevance to decision making during colonial times. Native perception and practices are acknowledged and assessed. Decisions of survivors were not made in a vacuum—rather, they were carried out within a tradition of understanding and within a particular environment of options. What were options in this case? What did past experience suggest was the best course of action? The assumptions, sampling, and testing of archaeological methods that are necessary to frame the discussion within this native perspective can appear overwhelming. But they may seem less daunting if we recognize that historical demographic research and even a modern census requires similar diligence in planning and execution if it is to serve as a useful tool for understanding demographic and social processes.

CHAPTER 6

A Tradition of Survival

Archaeological Evidence for Awahnichi Depopulation

Both idiosyncratic episodes and enduring trends in population growth and decline through time reflect demographic behaviors of birth, death, and migration. These processes result, in turn, from individual decisions based on immediate circumstances and needs, personal life-histories, and collective group experience and memory. Age at marriage, female health and nutrition, birth spacing, contraception, abortion, and cultural norms of family size all affect fertility rates. And interpersonal violence, infanticide, exposure to fatal disease, medical treatment for the sick, and care of the elderly affect mortality. The age and sex of individuals within a population also profoundly affect the expression of such decisions, as well as choices regarding migration. Therefore, as we consider colonial-era demographic change for the Awahnichi and other Native American groups within the three alternate scenarios—early devastating successive pandemics, early isolated exposure to nonnative pathogens with subsequent rebound, or late sustained decline from multiple causes—all of these processes must be kept in mind. Depopulation evident in the archaeological record may have resulted from increased mortality, decreased fertility, emigration of people to another area, or some combination of these factors. Likewise, any apparent maintenance of or rebound in population in the wake of fatal encounters could have been facilitated by decreased mortality, increased fertility, or immigration of individuals into the population from another area. The quantitative picture of Yosemite

Indian demography provided by archaeological data spanning the last 5,500 years demonstrates that colonial-era depopulation was just one of many demographic events related to such personal actions or reactions. And the long-term perspective shows that it was not necessarily the most significant of such events.

COLONIAL-ERA DEPOPULATION: HOW DOES IT FIT INTO YOSEMITE INDIAN HISTORY?

The debitage proxy reveals several relatively brief episodes of minor population decline and subsequent rebound prior to A.D. 1800, with a loss and recovery of 5 to 10 percent of the maximum population (p_{max}) over 100 to 250 years in each event (see figure 7). Such episodes occurred at 3375 B.C., 2225 B.C., 1375 B.C., 1075 B.C., 325 B.C., 25 B.C., and A.D. 325. Although quantitatively small relative to p_{max}, some of these drops—particularly those relatively early in time—represent major proportional losses of at least 25 percent of the population present immediately prior to decline. In addition, at least one sustained population decline without subsequent rebound began around A.D. 500. This decline was one of the most substantial in the history of the people of Awahnee, and it entailed a 35 to 40 percent initial drop in population size before temporary cessation was achieved around A.D. 675. A slightly less substantial decline of approximately 30 percent of p_{max}—or nearly 50 percent of the existing population—followed between A.D. 650 and 1000, after which the population recovered slightly and then continued to decline more slowly until A.D. 1375. Subsequent population increase until A.D. 1600 was followed by decline again around A.D. 1750 to 1800. And it is this final decline—which corresponds to the date of native population loss indicated by ethnohistoric, genealogical, and dendrochronological information—that documents the magnitude of colonial-era population decline.

The population loss at that time—measured from the previous population high at A.D. 1600—was at least 10 percent of p_{max} or about 25 percent of the population present. The decline in the late 1700s was probably even more severe, but the brevity of the experience makes it difficult to capture with archaeological data. Disease-induced mortality, exile, and reoccupation occurred within only 20 years, so the 50-year interval encompasses an average for that span—including the starting population, loss due to introduced disease, and additional decrease due to temporary abandonment—rather than the absolute nadir result-

A Tradition of Survival

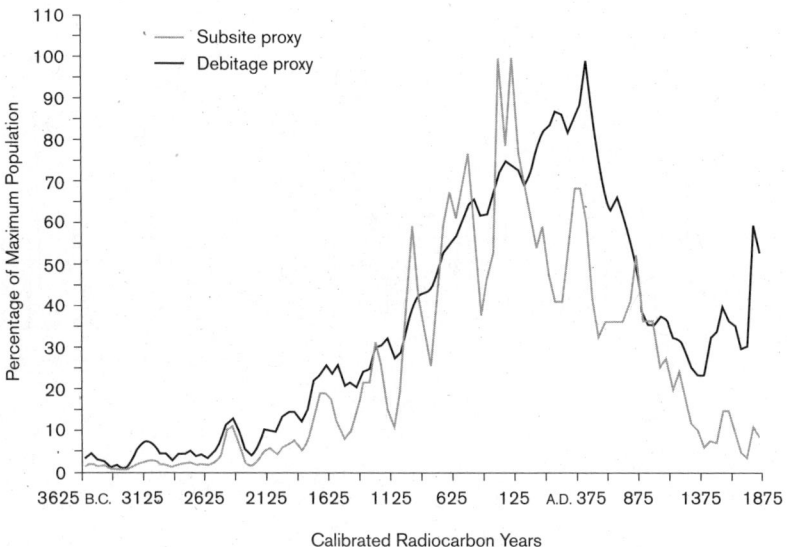

FIGURE 7. Diachronic trends in debitage and calibrated subsite frequency data as a percentage of maximum population.

ing from mortality alone. In addition, three-point averaging coupled with the likely overrepresentation of samples with no visible hydration (placed within the increment from A.D. 1850 to 1900; see chapter 5) tends to dampen the true magnitude of decline and to pull the nadir and post–A.D.1800 population higher than it actually was relative to other periods. In fact, inferring disease-induced mortality greater than 25 percent for Yosemite Indians is not unreasonable, since estimated mortality rates from epidemic smallpox in virgin soil conditions—such as those that prevailed in Yosemite Valley—range from 10 to 100 percent. Mortality estimates for measles and pneumonia in such circumstances range from 10 to 25 percent, which is also consistent with the minimum level of mortality estimated for Yosemite Indians (Bianchine and Russo 1995; Ramenofsky 1987; see also Stearn and Stearn 1945; Thornton et al. 1991).

Sample size for the debitage proxy data prior to 950 B.C. is too small to confidently derive population growth-rate estimates from, but such statistics calculated for the last 2,900 years of Yosemite Indian history are likely more robust. Negative population growth rates for the various episodes of population decline ranged from −0.0002 to −0.0054, or an annual decrease of 0.2 to 5.4 individuals per 1,000 persons in the

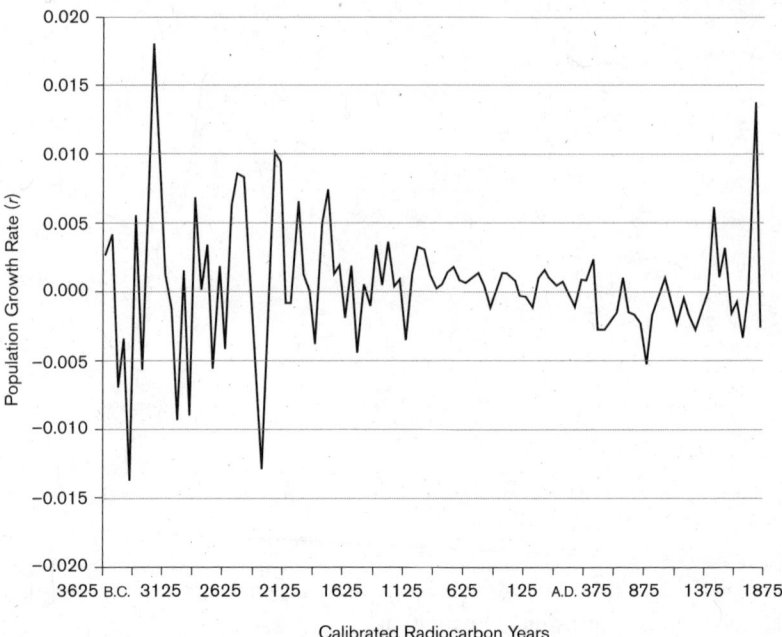

FIGURE 8. Diachronic trends in population growth rates per 50-year increment based on the debitage population proxy.

population (see figure 8). Placed in long-term perspective, the rate of decline due to the introduction of nonnative disease and coeval violence during the colonial era was not especially dramatic relative to earlier periods of population decline. Given the difficulties in establishing the nadir population size, the maximum possible population growth rate for this colonial-era episode was 0.00029 and was likely even lower than this. The growth rate for the preceding 50-year period—likely reflecting some of the colonial-era decline but less affected by possible overrepresentation in later increments by the inclusion of specimens with no visible hydration—was -0.003547. A sharp rebound at the rate of 0.01386 followed colonial-era population decline, and this rate of growth was not matched at any other time in the preceding 4,000 years. Use of no visible hydration data within the A.D. 1850 to 1900 increment may have inflated this postcolonial growth figure somewhat, but such unusually high growth rates are expected in postcatastrophe contexts. For example, cross-cultural studies indicate that increased fertility due to new marriages and younger age at marriage (Livi-Bacci 1997:55)—as well as cessation of lactation amenorrhea associated with prolonged breast-feeding—are common following significant population loss. And mortality is somewhat lower in the aftermath of, and recovery from, disease events because particularly vulnerable individuals have been removed from the population. In fact, such phenomena suggest that the magnitude of postcolonial Yosemite Indian population growth is an even more telling signal of the potential severity of the preceding catastrophe than the quantitative data for the decline itself. Knowledge of the population structure of survivors would be required to determine the specific contribution of short-term Awahnichi fertility and mortality to demographic recovery. On the other hand, the important contribution of immigration cannot be ignored in this case, since ethnohistoric accounts specifically identify such behavior. Furthermore, even if the postdisease population rebound were partially due to immigration, higher rates of intrinsic natural growth are also expected. This is because immigrants tend to be younger, more vigorous, and therefore more fertile than the general population from which they derive (Livi-Bacci 1997:104). Immigrant contribution via fertility would be less significant, however, if immigrants themselves were epidemic survivors of all ages, rather than the self-selecting vital individuals typical of migration in other contexts. If the quantitative data are accurate, this last spurt of growth brought about a doubling of Yosemite Indian population in only 50 years.

Other peaks in population growth rates—revealed by the debitage data spanning the last 2,900 years—occurred on cycles of approximately 300 years (see figure 8). Positive growth rates during these times ranged from 0.001212 between A.D. 1100 and 1050 to 0.00640 at circa A.D. 1475. The latter figure represents a doubling time of approximately 110 years, while the former indicates doubling of the population in approximately 570 years. Both of these events were much less dramatic than colonial-era population rebound, and this cyclical pattern may reflect density-dependent feedback cycles rather than catastrophic events (Hull 2005). Similar to postdisease population recovery during the colonial era, the population increase that began around A.D. 1450 and immediately preceded colonial-era decline also represents a somewhat unusual rate of growth in the scope of Yosemite Indian demographic history. Once again, migration may underlie this pattern, as this particular episode could relate to immigration of the Southern Sierra Me'-wuk into the area. However, the timing is several hundred years later than expected based on linguistic data (Hull 2002).

Comparison of Yosemite Indian archaeological data with ethnographic observations for the Dobe !Kung of southern Africa, the Ache of Paraguay, and the Hadza of eastern Africa indicates that population growth-rate estimates for the distant past—if not the colonial era—in Yosemite Valley are somewhat lower than rates recorded for these three extant hunter-gatherer groups. Overall, Yosemite Indians are most similar to the !Kung, who had a growth rate of 0.00263 at the time demographic data were collected (Howell 1979:215). Based on the debitage proxy, this is a figure approximated by Yosemite native populations multiple times between 1000 B.C. and A.D. 450, as well as around A.D. 1575. The Yosemite proxy data also suggest population growth rates that even exceeded the !Kung figure as recently as A.D. 1575, and postcolonial Yosemite Indian population rebound was at an even greater rate. In fact, the rate of rebound is similar to the growth rates estimated for the Hadza and forest Ache. A growth rate of 0.013 was observed among the Hadza (Blurton Jones et al. 1992:172) and a growth rate of 0.016 was recorded for the Ache (Hill and Hurtado 1996:415). Population growth rates as high as these two ethnographically observed figures, however, were unusual in the demographic history of Yosemite Indians. And such spurts in growth within this native population were not only rare, but relatively short-lived. In addition, two peaks in growth rate in the last 500 years that exceed that recorded for the !Kung were likely due to immigration rather than simply intrinsic growth. Therefore, natural population growth represented at other times was slow indeed.

Even the !Kung rate is at the high end of the general range of population growth revealed by the Yosemite debitage proxy data over the last 2,900 years. But this fact is consistent with Howell's (1979:70) observation that postcolonial decline in mortality among the !Kung accelerated their population growth relative to earlier times. In addition, Howell (1979:215) noted that the growth rate she observed was not representative of the entire history of the !Kung, since fluctuations in populations growth were likely. Rather than concluding that the Yosemite Indian population data are in error or abnormally low for a hunting and gathering population, growth rates for extant hunter-gatherer groups are probably unusually high because of the postcolonial social changes documented by ethnographers (Pennington 2001), the relatively limited span of time over which ethnographic data were collected, and the assumptions and methods invoked by ethnographers to derive demographic estimates in the absence of direct observations. Even differences between the Hadza and !Kung have been the focus

A Tradition of Survival

of much speculation and debate (see Blurton Jones et al. 1992:176ff), with arguments for and against the "representativeness" of either as a hunter-gatherer population.

The subsite proxy expresses somewhat more volatility than the debitage proxy, although most episodes of decline in the former data set are mirrored at less amplitude in the latter (see figure 7). The subsite proxy suggests more radical declines for these periods, with more than 40 percent loss of p_{max} and a negative growth of -0.01017 in one case. In addition, the subsite data indicate sharper increases when growth was evident. Periods of particularly strong growth were revealed from 2500 to 2400 B.C., 1050 to 950 B.C., 250 to 200 B.C., and A.D. 1550 to 1600, with positive growth rates exceeding 0.012 for several 50-year periods. The most substantial, uninterrupted declines in Yosemite Indian population occurred between 950 and 750 B.C., 500 to 350 B.C., 150 B.C. to A.D. 100, and A.D. 350 to 600. Numerous lesser declines and rebounds are also evident in the subsite proxy, particularly when population was apparently at or near maximum. In addition, decline occurred from A.D. 1600 to 1800. This final decline took population down to its lowest level in nearly 4,000 years. If accurately registering colonial-era population decline, the subsite proxy suggests a particularly calamitous event in terms of both the size and rate of population decline. The negative growth rate for the 50-year period ending circa A.D. 1800 was -0.007628, while that of the preceding interval less affected by no visible hydration data extrapolation was -0.015256. Postcolonial population estimates in this case, however, may be underestimated due to the shift to village life and concentration of Yosemite Indian people into just a few locales after A.D. 1850 (Hutchings 1888). That is, site-specific population density was abnormally high at that time relative to earlier periods of Yosemite Indian history, and this would tend to pull down the postcolonial index and result in a higher negative population growth rate. So, while the debitage proxy may overestimate postepidemic population recovery due to the analysis protocols for specimens with no visible hydration, the subsite proxy underestimates postepidemic recovery as a result of cultural factors. Analysis of the subsite proxy using longer time intervals also confirmed that this measure is less secure than the debitage proxy due to such fluctuations in site-specific population density (see Hull 2002).

Many of the periodic declines evident in both the debitage and subsite proxies occurred within the span of 200 years. Given the resolution of the data, this probably indicates single events or similar short-term patterns that would have been perceptible to the Indian people at the time they occurred. In the absence of other contextual data, however, it is difficult to know which declines reflect higher mortality, decreased fertility, increased emigration, or some combination of these factors. Based on the more secure debitage proxy, the colonial-era experience was not as severe in terms of either amplitude or rate of decline as some population decreases that occurred earlier in time. In addition, population fluctuations did not dominate Yosemite Indian demography. Instead, they occurred on the order of every 600 years or more and they overlaid a longer-term trend of increase and decline (Hull 2005). In short-term perspective, significant population fluctuations on the order of 50 to 100 years were not a regular occurrence for the native inhabitants of Yosemite Valley, although sustained population declines were experienced. In fact, when viewed within the perspective of the entire span of Yosemite Indian demography, short-term depopulation during the colonial era came on the heels of partial rebound from a dramatic and sustained decline in population size, which began around A.D. 500 and did not ameliorate until A.D. 1450.

FERTILITY AND MORTALITY: THE COLONIAL-ERA EXPERIENCE IN PERSONAL TERMS

Assessment of fertility and mortality patterns hinted at by the estimated growth rates helps place the Yosemite Indian colonial-era demographic experience in even more personal terms. Mortuary populations are usually necessary to derive fertility or mortality rates from archaeological data. In the absence of such remains, I used general demographic models and compared Yosemite Indians with other preindustrial populations around the world. Population growth rates for a closed population (i.e., no immigration or emigration) reflect the dynamic between fertility and mortality, with growth related to these demographic factors via the following equation:

$$Rl_a = e^{rT}$$

in which R is the number of daughters per woman in the absence of mortality (i.e., the gross reproduction rate [GRR]), l_a is the probability of survival from birth to the average age of childbearing a for females in the population, e is the base of natural logarithms, r is the population growth rate, and T is the average length of a generation (Livi-Bacci 1997:20). Each of these demographic parameters is related, in turn, to other measures of fertility and mortality for a population (Livi-Bacci 1997:20). For example, T generally ranges from 27 to 33 years and is approximated by the average age of childbearing. Similarly, l_a is strongly correlated with e_0, life expectancy at birth, since most girls in a population will live to reproductive age only if e_0 significantly exceeds age at first menarche. Finally, R is related to the total fertility rate (TFR), which is a measure of the total number of births per woman in the absence of mortality. The ratio of TFR to R is 2.06, because female births account for slightly less than half of all births for humans under natural conditions. Since l_a is related to e_0 and R is related to TFR, e_0 and TFR can be used to express r, the population growth rate.

This dynamic between fertility (TFR) and mortality (e_0) for populations with a generational length of 29 years—slightly greater than the 27.4 years observed by Howell (1979:215) for the !Kung—is shown graphically in figure 9.[1] This illustration includes data from various historical preindustrial populations and conjectured prehistoric populations provided by Livi-Bacci (1997:20) as well as information for four extant hunter-gatherer groups—the Ache, Agta, Hadza, and !Kung (see Pennington 2001). Relatively low positive growth rates below 0.01 existed even for agricultural populations of Europe prior to the Industrial Revolution. For these historical agrarian populations, however, growth rates span the entire range from 0.0 and 0.01. These reflect e_0 figures between approximately 22 and 42 years and TFR from slightly more than 4 to just less than 6.5 offspring. Livi-Bacci (1997:20) suggested that "Paleolithic" (i.e., hunter-gatherer) and "Neolithic" (i.e., early agricultural) people had relatively high mortality (e_0 less than 20) that was minimally compensated for by high fertility, although these figures are speculative rather than based on any paleodemographic data. In fact, Howell (1973:261–262, 1976:33) suggested that e_0 of 18 to 20 years is the minimum possible for viable positive population growth in light of normal hunter-gatherer fertility.

Extant hunter-gatherer populations reveal e_0 ranging from 24 to 37 years, and TFR ranging from 4.7 to 8 births (see Pennington 2001). The Ache of Paraguay are very unusual for all of these populations in terms of fertility—whether hunter-gatherers or agriculturalists—although their fertility is comparable to that of the high-mortality Yanamamo of southern Venezuela and northern Brazil (see Neel and Weiss 1975). This cross-cultural analysis suggests that the Ache are probably not a good analog for Yosemite Indians in terms of fertility and mortality (cf. Hill and Hurtado 1996:193, 251). Furthermore, comparison of causes of mortality between the Ache and !Kung suggests that the latter are more likely to succumb to disease, particularly at a young age. The Ache are more prone to violent or accidental death regardless of age (Hill and Hurtado 1996:174). In light of this observation and the closer affinity of Yosemite Indians to the !Kung in terms of growth rates, there was also probably relatively little violent death among Yosemite Indians.

In the absence of quantitative data on TFR and e_0—which are difficult to derive for prehistoric populations even under the best circumstances—it is hard to determine where the Yosemite Indians' colonial-era experience falls within the range of trade-offs of fertility and mortality. The population growth rates throughout Yosemite native history were close to 0.0, however, and define a fairly narrow range around this figure. Population growth rates for Yosemite Indians ranged from -0.003547 to 0.013863 for the last 500 years—that is, an annual loss of roughly 3.5 individuals or annual increase of as many as 14 people per 1,000 individuals in the population. The highest value is in part related, however, to input from immigration rather than just intrinsic growth. Therefore, consideration of such high values within the model of natural growth is inappropriate. In addition, the relatively high growth at circa A.D. 1450 could be due to immigration of Me'-wuk into the southern Sierra Nevada rather than intrinsic growth. Therefore, scope is limited here to the remaining rates in this span (i.e., 0.003382 and lower) and takes into account a likely range of 18 to 30 years for e_0 among hunter-gatherers—that is, between the posited minimum viable e_0 and !Kung life expectancy. Under such circumstances, estimated r figures derived from the debitage proxy suggest a TFR of 4 to 6 offspring for Yosemite Indian women (see figure 9).

A family with 6 offspring was probably the maximum size at the time European disease was introduced. Infant mortality from causes other than the "black sickness"—and the fact that not all couples would have completed their reproductive span—would have resulted in somewhat smaller actual family size when catastrophe struck. There was no way to confirm such fertility figures archaeologically, but ethnohistoric and ethnographic information for Yosemite Indians suggest that this estimate of TFR is not too far afield. For example, Clark (1907:24) noted that Yosemite Indian dwellings housed 6 individuals. Likewise, Chief Tenaya's family encompassed 4 adult children, although this number may represent offspring from more than one wife. In light of likely infant mortality, however, the survival of 4 children to adulthood sug-

A Tradition of Survival

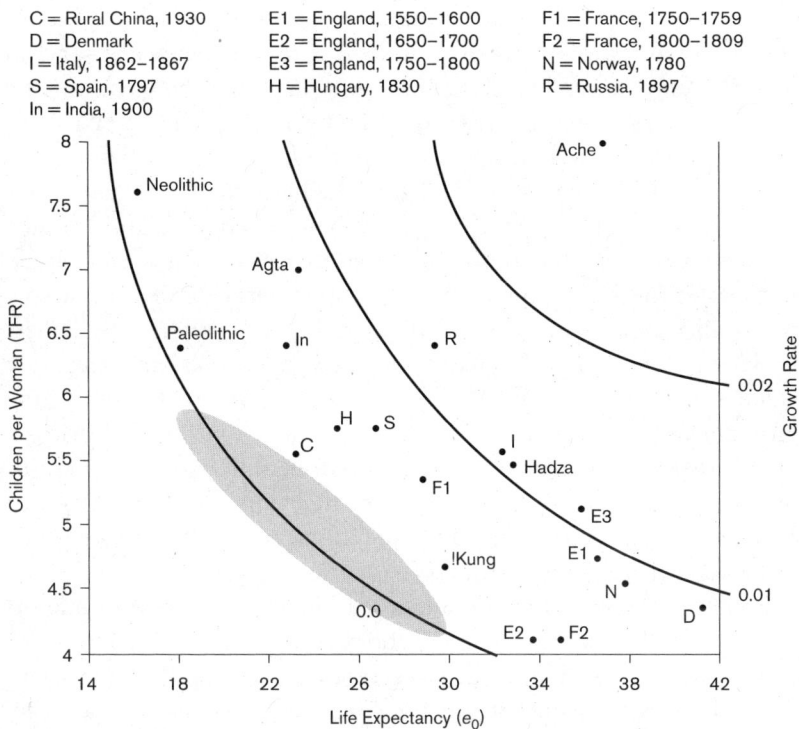

FIGURE 9. Relationship between total fertility rate (TFR) and life expectancy at birth (e_0) in historical and modern nonindustrial populations, including likely range for Yosemite Indians indicated by shaded oval (after Livi-Bacci 1997: figure 1.8b).

gests that TFR was probably greater than 4. Merriam (1899–1902) also noted 4 offspring within the Austin family living at Bull Creek, another unidentified Me'-wuk family at Mariposa, and a third family residing on Chowchilla Creek in 1902. In fact, this was the only family size Merriam specifically recorded—on other occasions he only indicated "several" children present.

Estimates of the probability of female survival to average age of childbearing (1_a) over the last 2,900 years can be derived by applying minimum and maximum intrinsic growth-rate estimates from archaeological data and the range of 4 to 6 offspring to compute R. With an assumed generation length of 29 years, the probability of survival is between 44 to 57 percent when TFR is 4 and only 29 to 38 percent when

TFR is 6.[2] That is, more offspring were necessary to achieve the inferred growth rates for Yosemite Indians if the probability of survival to average age of childbearing was low. Changing the length of the generation to as few as 25 years or as many as 33 years (see Livi-Bacci 1997:20) has relatively little impact on these probability figures, nor does even shorter generational length. The low end of these two probability ranges pertains to the era of disease-induced population decline between A.D. 1750 and 1800 and, given that proxy data probably do not reflect the true magnitude of this short-term decline, these low probability figures (i.e., 29–44 percent) likely represent the highest probability of survival to childbearing age for the cohorts affected by colonial-era disease events. Thus, one can imagine that many young girls did not survive to childbearing age due to introduced disease, while other women may not have survived the full span of their reproductive years. There were at least three other times in the more distant past, however, when similar dire conditions may have prevailed (i.e., A.D. 550, A.D. 925, and A.D. 1325).

So how did colonial-era population decline figure into the trade-off between fertility and mortality? Fatal introduced disease contributed to a significant decline in life expectancy at birth (e_0), but this was a very brief change since it was not followed in the next 50 years by subsequent waves of Old World pathogens. If total fertility rate (TFR) had been essentially constant during earlier periods of Yosemite Indian history, shifts in population growth rates such as those revealed by the debitage proxy were caused by only relatively small fluctuations in e_0. Factors such as proscriptions on age of marriage, season of conception, appropriate behavior following the birth of a child, capacity to provision a family without significant modification to settlement and subsistence regimes, or similar cultural factors—all recorded in regional ethnography—would tend to maintain a constant TFR over the course of Yosemite Indian history. Large changes in e_0—but relative stability in r, such as that prevailing for Yosemite Indians—would only occur if TFR was not culturally constrained. Thus, the dramatic decline in e_0 due to European disease was probably unusual in Yosemite Indian history except in cases of catastrophe. If e_0 dropped below 16 years of age as a result of epidemic disease mortality, capacity to maintain postdisease population size—let alone recover to predisease population size—would have been virtually impossible (see figure 9). Augmentation of the Yosemite Indian population from outside was necessary to maintain a viable population.

TRADITIONS AND DECISIONS: THE DEMOGRAPHIC SIGNIFICANCE OF COLONIAL-ERA POPULATION DECLINE

Computer simulations of growth and decline for small populations further support these conclusions regarding experience and decision making in the context of colonial-era epidemics. And these techniques provide one final means by which to assess the significance of Yosemite Indian colonial-era population decline. Such studies also offer some perspective on the potential influence of exogamy and other marriage rules in this particular demographic situation. These trials rely on either known or postulated schedules of age-specific fertility, mortality, and population age structure, referred to as "lifetables," as well as knowledge or assumptions about marriage rules. For example, simulation programs have been used to study the long-term consequences of age-specific fertility and mortality recorded for extant hunter-gatherers (e.g., Howell 1979). And model lifetables that encompass different theoretical levels of age-specific fertility and mortality thought to approximate past conditions are employed for more general discussions not linked to a specific group.

In archaeological studies, age-specific fertility and mortality figures are sometimes derived from cemetery populations, but this is not an option in Yosemite. In addition, given the evident demographic impact of contact with agricultural or industrial societies on extant hunter-gatherers, census information for postcontact Yosemite Indian families is inappropriate for derivation of age-specific fertility and mortality estimates for a simulation. Rather, the results of previous simulation studies of small populations (based on model lifetables) and estimated population size for Yosemite Indians (derived from archaeological data) provide the means to address potential vulnerability of such a population to extinction in the face of colonial-era epidemic disease. Based on the growth rate from initial occupation around 3550 B.C. to the population zenith at A.D. 600 and an estimated founding population of 25 individuals, p_{max} was approximately 1,000 individuals (Hull 2002: 254). Since the population at A.D. 1800 was about 30 percent of p_{max}, the population numbered approximately 300 people as a result of the immediately preceding population decline. As discussed above, this estimate represents the maximum population size at that time, since the true severity of decline is probably masked by data analysis procedures, by the relatively brief duration of the event, and by the nature of subsequent population recovery.

Morgan (1974) provides a particularly useful simulation analysis of population size over several hundred years for small, closed populations practicing monogamy. This simulation was based on age-specific fertility and mortality rates consistent with a population growth rate of 0.005. Although the archaeological data for Yosemite Indians suggest an even slower rate of population growth—and it is unlikely that this, or any, population remained closed in the long term (Morgan 1974: 37)—this research provides a basis for discussion. Morgan drew on two model lifetables from Coale and Demeny (1966)—one reflecting relatively high fertility and mortality (the "South 1" model) and another reflecting relatively low fertility and mortality ("South 24"). Within the high fertility-and-mortality regime, an initial population of 200 individuals with equal representation of males and females at the beginning of the simulation became extinct within approximately 350 to 450 years. If differential growth rates applied to each sex either through natural or cultural factors, however, extinction occurred even more swiftly, within 300 to 400 years. For the low fertility-and-mortality regime, only one in five trial populations of 200 individuals also eventually became extinct within the time span of the simulation, and this single population required slightly over 900 years to suffer this fate (Morgan 1974: table 1). At the same time, however, even the low fertility-and-mortality regime indicated significant fluctuation in vital rates—such as crude birth and death rates—for short periods of time. Therefore, Morgan (1974:25) noted that the data for this regime

> also suggest that the initial size of the population is of some importance in determining the fate of the population experiencing stochastic variation in vital rates. A smaller population implies a smaller pool of eligible mates for a given individual, especially when criteria for eligibility are not relaxed. Furthermore, that segment of the population (married females of certain ages) which is solely responsible for renewal via the production of births may very likely contain too few or even no members during the early years of a population, especially under a regime of continuing high mortality.

He also observed that such "stochastic variability of the vital rates and numbers of marriages, [affects] . . . the numbers and composition of future cohorts, [and] . . . contributes to amplitude of oscillations in the age classes which results in increased variability of population numbers while the population is small and far from age-structure equilibrium" (Morgan 1974:29). A population of at most 300 Yosemite Indians and growth rates consistent with a midrange fertility-and-mortality regime suggest years to "extinction" in this case somewhere between the high and low estimates of Morgan (1974). Alternately, the low population growth rates in Yosemite Indian populations overall—below Morgan's target of 0.005—suggest that his simulations are somewhat optimistic relative to the Yosemite case. Although population was somewhat on the rebound after A.D. 1450, Yosemite Indian population was not large enough to withstand the impact of significant mortality due to introduced pathogens. Thus, the Awahnichi were particularly vulnerable to demographic collapse, and this may explain why Chief Tenaya's father and the other survivors opted to temporarily leave Yosemite Valley rather than attempt to rebuild a viable group within their traditional territory.

Comparison with computer simulations also confirms that the unusually high mortality that resulted from the influx of nonnative disease severely undermined the viability of the small Indian population remaining in Yosemite Valley after disease-induced decline, regardless of the underlying fertility and mortality regime. In addition, if high mortality persisted—such as might be anticipated in the context of violent interaction with nonnative peoples—rebound would have been all the more difficult. Even minor stochastic variation in vital rates after disease events—which is both expected and magnified in the small populations—would have been potentially calamitous in such circumstances. The previous nadir of population size at A.D. 1450 may have been similarly detrimental in the long term, although it is unclear if a high- or low-mortality regime was in effect at that time. If low mortality prevailed, internal rebound to the subsequent population levels around A.D. 1650 would have been possible. But if a high-mortality regime pertained, augmentation from the outside would have been necessary at that time as well.

These observations can also be contrasted with the simulations of Thornton and colleagues (1991), who specifically addressed the issue of disease-induced population decline due to smallpox in virgin-soil conditions. Age-specific mortality under such conditions is between 20 and 25 percent for people aged 5 to 19, approximately 35 percent for people aged 20 to 29, 40 percent for the very young (< 5 years of age) and those individuals between 30 and 40 years of age, and over 50 percent for individuals older than 40 (Thornton et al. 1991: table 1). Utilizing a starting population of 5,000 individuals and a growth rate of 0.005, Thornton and his colleagues found that population rebound was complete within approximately 70 years following an epidemic, if there were no subsequent epidemics. The significance of large initial population size to survival is clear, however, given the strikingly different outcome of this simulation compared to Morgan's (1974) analysis of a small population with the same growth rate. At lower growth rates, Thornton and colleagues (1991) found that the population recovered only slightly in the 100 years following an epidemic if the population growth rate is zero or not at all if the rate is −0.005. But the population was not in any immediate or even long-term danger, since approximately 3,000 individuals were still present.

This latter population size was derived for all four growth scenarios considered by Thornton and colleagues—encompassing growth rates ranging from −0.005 to 0.01—based on the estimated 40 percent decline from the initial population of 5,000 individuals. This percent decline is somewhat higher than the 25 percent drop evident in the Yosemite Valley debitage proxy data, although the archaeological data may underestimate this proportional loss for reasons previously discussed. In addition, as Thornton and colleagues noted, such mortality figures are dependent upon the initial population age structure. If Yosemite native populations actually did experience somewhat less overall mortality than the 40 percent indicated by Thornton and colleagues, those populations may have had a slightly higher proportion of individuals within those age groups (i.e., 5 to 19 years of age) more prone to survive non-age-specific epidemic disease such as smallpox. Conversely, given Tenaya's account of warfare generally coincident with the "black sickness," increased mortality rates for men—or perhaps all adults—of reproductive age might be anticipated.[3]

Additional simulations that take various marriage restrictions into account (Morgan 1974) also suggest that long-term postdisease Yosemite Indian population viability was unlikely if cultural proscriptions on marriage similar to those recorded ethnographically were in place and adhered to. Morgan considered the effects of incest prohibition, clan exogamy, and remarriage on long-term viability of small populations. Incest was broadly defined to "exclude matings among individuals related within three generations" (Morgan 1974:30), such as first cousins, uncles and nieces, and closer relatives. His focus on clans derived from his work with the Navajo, who maintain four such divisions, but similar consequences likely pertain in the moiety system of the Me'-wuk.

Using a starting population of 200 individuals and assuming a low fertility-and-mortality regime, Morgan (1974) found that groups were almost always destined for extinction within 400 years when exogamy was practiced. In fact, the best expectation under such restrictions was almost no growth over the 600-year simulation period. If exogamy rules were ignored, simulations indicated that the result was almost always long-term positive growth. Morgan (1974: table 3) found growth rates for 10-year periods never exceeded 0.015 when exogamy was maintained, and this observation is commensurate with the maximum rates for Yosemite Indian populations suggested by archaeology. Where exogamy was not maintained, average population growth rates in simulations ranged from 0.004 to 0.034 and were generally greater than 0.02 (Morgan 1974: table 7). The effects of adhering to or ignoring remarriage or incest restrictions were relatively minor compared to the importance of exogamy.

Although it is difficult to apply these simulation results directly to Yosemite Indians, since there are no data regarding marriage rules in the distant past, these data suggest that exogamy may have been an additional factor playing into the decision making of Yosemite Indians in the aftermath of epidemic disease. Because Yosemite Indians were already vulnerable to "extinction" due to small size, stochastic fluctuation, and slow growth, any additional restrictions on mating would have been especially problematic. Earlier in time, any short-term declines may have been offset by the ability to find mates outside the group, effectively making the reproductive population larger. During the colonial era, however, the incursion of nonnative people effectively reduced the reproductive population both physically and culturally through the disruption of traditional cultural systems and social relations. Infiltration of nonnative people also likely affected exogamy practices and thereby made such small populations even more vulnerable by reducing the size of the reproductive group. The decision by the Awahnichi to temporarily relocate to other areas that still had intact populations suggests that maintenance of traditions such as exogamous marriage practices was of primary importance—perhaps even greater than their desire to maintain their residence in Yosemite Valley, although their population may have been too small for recovery even if marriage rules had been relaxed.

SURVIVAL OF THE YOSEMITE INDIANS

The archaeological data confirm colonial-era depopulation around A.D. 1800 and suggest a minimum 25 percent decline in the population at that time. Substantial rebound followed, although this was probably made possible, at least in part, by immigration. Population declines of similar scale and more modest rebounds occurred several times in the more distant past, but in long-term perspective these perturbations were both rare and relatively insignificant. Thus, native people residing in Yosemite Valley when colonial-era disease struck were not preadapted to population decline. They had not experienced other significant short-term fluctuations within their lifetime or even several generations and thus could not draw upon such experience in colonial-era decision making. On the other hand, the Indian people of Awahnee had coped with substantial population loss for many generations in the more distant past, and this history was preserved in native oral tradition rather than personal memory. One story of Tis-sa'-ack notes population decline from starvation, drought, and other natural disasters that likely corresponds to the substantial population loss between A.D. 500 and 1450 (see Hull 2002:305–312). In this sense, colonial-era demographic decision making was part of long tradition of survival that built on the past.

The specific demographic history that led to relatively small population size by A.D. 1600 made the Awahnichi particularly vulnerable to colonial-era demographic catastrophe, whether through introduced disease or some other phenomenon. In earlier centuries, such vulnerability may have been offset by the ability to find mates from outside the group or to augment the group through immigration, effectively making the reproductive population larger. For example, the relatively high growth rate after A.D. 1450 suggests prior augmentation of population from elsewhere. During the colonial era, however, the landscape of native California was changing, and there were not the same opportunities of survival through intermarriage. And later incursion of nonnative people effectively reduced the reproductive options within and between native communities even further.

By A.D. 1800, the Awahnichi population declined to less than 300 people due to the introduction of nonnative disease. Such small population size occurred only one other time after initial colonization of Yosemite Valley by Indian people more the 4,000 years earlier. The small size of the population in the 1700s was due in part to the dramatic and sustained decline in population from A.D. 550 to 1450, from which the Awahnichi had only partially recovered by A.D. 1600. In light of their slow overall population growth, this small initial population size at the time European disease struck made action imperative—they did not constitute a sustainable population in the short term and perhaps even in the long term. Given the disruption of native peoples to the west, ethnohistoric information confirms that the safest remaining option was exercised—many survivors went east for relief from mortality and the chance to rebuild a viable population and community. When the ancestors of the Awahnichi returned to Yosemite Valley a generation later, they drew on the wisdom of their elders and further augmented their population from outside. In the face of this initial colonial assault, the Indian people of Yosemite Valley were making decisions—based on immediate conditions—that provided for their survival and drew on the experience of past generations.

The comparative ethnographic data from other hunter-gatherer groups suggest that the native people of Yosemite Valley experienced very modest growth and decline in the short term throughout their history. In addition, growth-rate estimates over the multimillennial span of human occupation suggest that the colonial era was demographically distinct more for unusual growth than for the decline. This swift rebound after A.D. 1800 was probably due to multiple factors but was likely prompted especially by subsequent immigration of other Indian people into the area, either through their individual presence within the population or their subsequent contribution through reproduction. As Yosemite Indians welcomed others into their community and the additional assaults of colonialism elsewhere in Central California nipped at the heals of these strangers, Yosemite Valley was an attractive destination. This phenomenon of relatively explosive colonial-era population increase prompted by immigration challenges the notion that it was simply depopulation that defined the demographic experience of native people in the wake of disease-induced colonial encounters in North America. Instead, it may have been that subsequent explosive growth due to the reshuffling of the native geography—rather than, or in addition to, population loss—was the important demographic process in this context.

Estimates of female fertility during this time suggest that less than one-third of girls survived to reproductive age and many women of childbearing age perished. Both of these factors severely undermined the demographic recovery of the Awahnichi through intrinsic population growth. And continued low fertility and high infant mortality after the Gold Rush, due to the lack of access to staple food resources and exposure to harsh conditions, are also suggested by ethnohistoric observations. Perlot (1985:224, italics original) noted Scipiano's plea to let the Yosemite Indians gather acorns in the foothill areas around Mariposa

> where *Nang-Oua* (God) calls them, since he plants their food there, for, he [Scipiano] said, the *nang-a* (the man, the Indian) is not a *hin-hin-meti* (bear) of the mountains, he is born in the plains and flats which you now take from him. He has had to take refuge in the mountains, where he never came except during the days of sun (summer) to refresh himself; our women that *Nang-Oua* gave us that we would remain without end (so that our race could perpetuate itself) have more trouble remaking us (giving us children), because they have to give birth in the cold (the snow), and the *piquini* (the child) perishes.[4]

Disregard for marriage traditions such as exogamy might have facilitated demographic recovery of Yosemite Indians without augmentation from outside, although Yosemite Indians' small population size and low growth rate made that difficult even if such proscriptions had been relaxed. Thus, in the immediate wake of epidemic disease, the Awahnichi were faced with difficult decisions between maintaining residence in their homeland or maintaining traditional cultural practices. Although they chose the latter in the short term to facilitate survival, they exercised the former option once their population was sufficient to reestablish residence in Yosemite Valley with the support of immigrants who might not otherwise have been welcomed into the group.

ASSESSING SCENARIOS OF DEPOPULATION

We now return to the three hypotheses of the demographic consequences of colonial-era disease in North America suggested by ethnohistory, archaeology, and computer simulations. The first hypothesis holds that Old World disease preceded direct contact, resultant population declines were severe and sustained, and significant cultural change was inevitable. The second hypothesis also indicates that disease spread prior to face-to-face encounters and brought about severe population decline, but this event was not unique within the history of specific groups and therefore did not necessarily result in significant cultural change. Finally, the third hypothesis suggests that exposure to nonnative disease was not early, and thus cultural change during the colonial era was unrelated to disease-induced depopulation.

The archaeological data presented here demonstrate that the Yosemite Indian experience is consistent with the hypothesis that nonnative disease introduction was both early and significant in terms of the magnitude of population loss. Clearly, depopulation predated direct contact and, in the absence of the immigration, population decline would have been even more catastrophic, if not fatal, to the cultural and biological survival of Yosemite Indians even though the group declined by "only" 25 percent. Thus, the third hypothesis is not substantiated in this case. Rather, the second hypothesis, which suggests early colonial-era catastrophic loss in the long-term context of general population oscillations, is closer to observations. Still, this also is not a completely satisfactory hypothesis, since *frequent* fluctuation in population size did not occur. Instead, small initial population size was the significant factor in determining the cultural response of Yosemite Indians to colonial-era disease and depopulation. A similar demographic crisis of unknown cause had been dealt with as recently as 300 years prior to colonial-era decline, however, and significant depopulation had occurred in the more distant past.[5] Therefore, consistent with the expectations of the second hypothesis, the potential consequences of population decline were likely readily recognized, and cultural alternatives and solutions may have already been in place to remedy the situation. For example, kin relationships may have already existed with surrounding groups. Given these observations, the second hypothesis is also better than the remaining hypothesis, which holds that the scale of colonial-era population loss was unique and would have resulted in severe cultural consequences. Clearly, such population decline was not unique, although colonial-era decline may have been somewhat more swift than that experienced in the more distant past. Cultural consequences may have had as much to do with the rate of decline and rebound as they did with potential preadaptation to decline. Thus, the issue of the potential cultural consequences of colonial-era depopulation among the Yosemite Indians is taken up in the next two chapters.

CHAPTER 7

Daily Practices in a Changing World

Archaeology reveals that Yosemite Indian colonial-era depopulation was substantial but that subsequent rebound was also swift and significant. This demographic recovery was facilitated by a series of decisions and actions that provided for both short-term security and long-term survival. Did these and other choices at that time affect daily practices in the short term or long term? Or did population decline affect culture in ways beyond the control of those who survived? Researchers who favor the catastrophic view of native depopulation in North America argue that significant cultural consequences were the inevitable outcome of such a devastating event and that changes occurred even in the absence of coincident or subsequent direct involvement with colonists (Dobyns 1983:342–343). Given the swift action of infectious fatal disease, they contend that cultural changes would have been rapid and that marked discontinuity should be visible in the archaeological record. Thus, archaeology contributes another thread to the tapestry of Yosemite Indian colonial history—it provides a picture of whether, and how, native culture changed as a result of this colonial assault.

What cultural changes were brought about by this demographic event? And were cultural shifts after depopulation a reaction only to the demographic impact of disease, or were later incursions of nonnative people responsible for some or all of the cultural changes among Yosemite Indians during the early 1800s? In order to formulate an archaeological research strategy sufficient to recognize evidence for disease-induced cultural changes in Yosemite Valley, I first needed to develop expectations for such change. This analysis drew on ethnohistoric information for Yosemite Indians as well as other native people in North America. Yosemite data were most germane, of course, in part because other sources often pertain to stratified societies (e.g., Dobyns 1983). But the cross-cultural synthesis identified an array of factors potentially contributing to change—factors not necessarily evident in Yosemite Indian ethnohistory alone. Archaeological information for the Yosemite region augmented these local ethnohistoric observations and provided additional detail regarding the consequences of colonial encounters in this case.

Other colonial-era native cultural changes recognized in the literature may have resulted from subsequent or coincident subjugation of Indian people by colonial powers or the economic involvement of native people with colonists. Conversely, initial population size, high disease-induced mortality, postdisease conditions of population growth and fertility, and immigration necessary to reestablish a viable population may have influenced the pace and direction of cultural shifts in Yosemite Valley and other regions of North America noted in ethnohistoric accounts in the wake of Old World epidemic disease. For this study, then, processes of direct contact were kept separate from those resulting only from demographic factors of fertility, mortality, and migration related to the assault of nonnative pathogens. Potential cultural consequences of disease-induced depopulation include population aggregation with or without emigration, creolization and ethnogenesis, shifts in external relations and regional interaction, decreasing cultural diversity, and despecialization and simplification of social structure. Some of these shifts resulted from conscious choices made by survivors. Others were simply outcomes that resulted from the skills, knowledge, and proclivities of individuals who survived. Each of these expectations for cultural change—and their potential archaeological manifestations in Yosemite Valley—is reviewed here. In addition, the social and spatial scale at which these processes emerge in systemic and archaeological context is considered, and the specific archaeological methods used to identify them in Yosemite Valley are discussed.

AGGREGATION AND EMIGRATION

One of the most common responses to depopulation identified in ethnohistoric accounts was the aggregation of surviving people within a few existing villages or new settlements (see Dobyns 1983:302, 1991; Smith 1987). For example, this process was observed among the Upper Creeks of the interior Southeast, the Caddoan-speaking peoples of east Texas and Arkansas, and some Iroquoian groups of the Northeast. As a process, aggregation might have been an attempt to maintain an optimal or sufficient population size for the social or political functions of the group. Conversely, simple household survival could have been the critical factor. In the wake of introduced European disease, households may have been unable to provide for surviving members on their own (Laslett 1984), and there was little potential to rebuild households without augmentation of the extant population through aggregation. Such aggregation also could have resulted from the need to maintain a sufficient population size for community-based subsistence strategies—for example, communal game drives or agriculture made possible by the maintenance of collective irrigation systems—or, even, as community defense against native or nonnative aggression. And from a strictly demographic viewpoint, computer simulations suggest that if population size dropped near or below some critical mass due to cultural proscriptions on marriage and the existing demographic regime of fertility and mortality, aggregation was necessary for long-term biological survival of the group. Thus, the size of the surviving population—as well as the previously existing social system and potential motivation to rebuild such a community—dictated whether aggregation was related to cultural concepts of appropriate settlement size and social function (see Dobyns 1983:303; Galloway 1995:131) or instead addressed immediate necessities for access to mates, subsistence provisioning, and biological survival of individuals, households, or groups (see also Perttula 1991:515).

The geography of aggregation was also a choice dictated by social or biological needs. This decision may have favored continued residence within the traditional territory of the group affected or could have entailed emigration to a neighboring area. Dobyns (1983:311; see also Dobyns 1991:550) suggested that marginally productive areas of a group's territory were abandoned in favor of environments more productive for basic subsistence needs. But a host of other factors likely affected such a decision, including previous investment in community infrastructure, proximity to nonnative peoples, social or environmental circumscription, the impact of epidemic disease on neighboring peoples, and external relations with other native groups that affected options for resettlement. And if emigration occurred, displaced survivors might still have maintained ties to their traditional territory and even might have attempted to exert control over or defend that land in absentia (Dobyns 1983:311). Such maintenance of ties to ancestral lands derives from a strong connection to place in preliterate societies, often manifest, for example, in repeated occupation of camps or villages to "presence" the users on the landscape, make evident their connection to particular places, and act as a mechanism of social reproduction (see Ingold 1993; J. Thomas 1993; Tilley 1994).

Even if groups settled elsewhere, aggregation alone might not constitute colonial-era cultural—as opposed to simply geographical—change. Culture may only have altered if existing power relations between previously autonomous groups were renegotiated, if people relocated to a very different environment, or if geographic change within their traditional territory or elsewhere necessitated settlement shifts and reorganization. Such factors would have consequences for authority, the organization of labor, and daily practices. Such cultural changes are separate from those related to amalgamation of communities with very different customs as part of population aggregation, which are considered separately here as creolization. Instead, aggregation is defined as a geographic reorganization of survivors with a shared cultural identity that had potential cultural implications manifest in internal, rather than external, negotiation (cf. Dobyns 1983).

So what are the potential cultural changes and archaeological manifestations of aggregation with or without emigration? Within both scenarios of aggregation—in a new territory or simply within a portion of traditionally occupied lands—population aggregation within one site or area would result in abandonment of other sites. If in situ aggregation occurred, fewer residential sites would be present relative to predisease times, but the same day-to-day activities would be represented at such sites. Still, there might be changes in the size of habitation sites, with size of reconstituted settlements dependent upon prevailing marriage rules, regional or community organization of labor, and other factors. For example, ethnohistoric information for the Pima of Arizona suggests that pre- and postdisease settlement size may have differed (Dobyns 1983:304)—that is, people may not have reestablished settlement conditions exactly like those that prevailed before European disease struck—although simulations suggest that flexibility to downsize settlements might not have existed in the case of small-scale societies such as the tribelets common to much of native California. Aggregation facilitated by emigration, on the other hand, would result in the absence of evidence for permanent or prolonged habitation within a traditional homeland or changing patterns of land use within the ancestral territory in either the short or long term. Changing land-use patterns would result because daily life now centered around residential bases located in a new, distant area. Nonresidential logistic sites or temporary camps might supplant residential bases within the traditional territory, and thus a different array of activities would be evident at pre- and postdepopulation archaeological sites within the homeland. Such shifts in land use would also have consequences for the organization of technology in both the traditional and adopted territory (see Binford 1978, 1979, 1982; R.L. Kelly 1988). For example, bifacial cores suitable for transport over longer distances from villages might have been used instead of less-efficient multidirectional cores.

As in many other areas of North America, Yosemite Indian ethnohistory indicates that aggregation was a key element of postdisease decision making and that emigration was the initial mechanism of aggregation in this case. Chief Tenaya's father and others headed east to Mono Lake, and other Awahnichi likely settled in Sierra areas to the north and south of Yosemite Valley. The tie of the Awahnichi to their traditional places was strong, however, as evidenced by their return to Yosemite Valley after only one generation in exile and Tenaya's observation that a few individuals continued to visit the valley even during this time. Therefore, aggregation in this case represents a short- rather than long-term geographic shift, and control of the land may not have been relinquished easily, even in the short term. The short-term pattern, then, would be either an absence of use or a change in settlement patterns. If ties to Yosemite Valley were maintained from residential bases in the Mono Basin, changes in the frequency or type of nonresidential sites in the valley would have followed depopulation. For example, during exile Indian people might have established nonresidential logistical sites related to hunting or gathering in Yosemite Valley, whereas habitation sites were previously used in this region. Since settlement shifts following depopulation were temporary, however, such movement might not even be visible archaeologically at residential and nonresidential locales in Yosemite Valley. If evident, I anticipated short-term changes in regional settlement with respect to decreased residential presence, followed by the reestablishment of the same or a somewhat altered pattern of settlement upon return.

In the absence of other factors influencing village location, I expected settlement location upon return of Tenaya's band to be reorganized in a shift away from less marginal subsistence or habitation areas to primary focus of settlement in more productive or otherwise desirable locales. Given the tendency for reiterative site use as a method of social reproduction, swift and dramatic population decline due to epidemic disease followed by exile might have resulted in the loss of the collective group memory that maintained these relationships to the land—in spite of possible attempts to maintain ties to Yosemite Valley in some form in the generation following depopulation. Thus, reoccupation by Tenaya's group might have occurred at different sites within the valley than habitation prior to disease contact, although focus on reoccupation of particularly desirable locales might make this less evident. Fewer residential sites were probably reoccupied or created, although this would have depended upon the size of the returning population, as augmented by immigrants from surrounding groups. And such immigration represents a second wave or process of aggregation in this case, which may have had further implications for settlement organization. Regardless of the specific details of settlement use, abandonment, and reuse, the issue of aggregation has to be approached from a regional perspective, focusing on the number, location, size, duration of use, and function (e.g., residential versus nonresidential) of settlements and other sites in pre- and postdisease contexts within Yosemite Valley. Temporal resolution is critical to such an analysis.

CREOLIZATION AND ETHNOGENESIS

Creolization is the blending of cultural traits—including language—of immigrants and their hosts as a result of aggregation of two or more ethnic groups. Ethnogenesis is the formation of a new, shared group identity either to unify the aggregate or to permanently divide factions (Hill 1996), encompassing practices and changes in material culture that may or may not result from creolization. That is, ethnogenesis is a conscious decision not just in practice but also in concept, whereas creolization implies no a priori realignment of group, as opposed to individual, identity. Individuals directed these processes through choice and negotiation, and creolization in particular was probably a common theme in postdisease native contexts due to the prevalence of aggregation as a response to depopulation. Dobyns (1983:306) suggested that such cultural changes occurred for both the hosts and newcomers, as the latter were converted from strangers to kin. For example, creolization likely entailed changes in marriage rules to allow intermarriage and a redefinition or emergence of new social classes or factions during reorganization. But creolization could also encompass an array of daily practices, including dietary preferences, hunting and gathering techniques, and production of manufactured items that in part may have been influenced by the availability of natural resources previously exploited within a traditional territory. Dobyns (1983:311; see also Dobyns 1991:551) described this as "dilution" of existing cultural distinctions brought about by intermarriage of individuals from two cultures, and this process resulted in the emergence of a new, distinct culture rather than the total loss of one culture to the other. Dobyns thus conflated creolization and ethnogenesis, when in fact the latter need not have been an inevitable outcome of the former. Conversely, Dobyns (1991:551) also suggested some lag time in creolization (i.e., ethnogenesis) and the likely persistence of "latent ethnic diversity" for some time in multiethnic communities. And it was this latter tendency, he argued, that resulted in factionalism such as that recognized within some historic Indian groups.

This may be too simplistic a view of creolization and ethnogenesis, since it doesn't take into account the complexity of social negotiation, preexisting relations, the maintenance of cultural identity despite changing practices, and the context in which changes occurred. For example, did creolization occur within households or at a higher level of social organization? And how were negotiations of daily practices affected or dictated by age or gender? Any such processes were clearly dependent upon who was aggregating, environmental conditions and available resources, preexisting cultural relations between the groups, and whether such physical relocation was viewed by the participants as a short- or long-term solution to the demographic crisis. Dobyns (1983) approached colonial-era relocation as if all moves were permanent shifts, but the Yosemite Indian story suggests that emigration and aggregation may have been viewed as a temporary solution to an immediate problem. In the case of small populations vulnerable to amplification of minor demographic perturbations into potential crises, kinship systems with symbols that permitted "differential claims on the resources of others . . . as hedges against extinction" (Hammel and Howell 1987:46) may have been in place. This allowed for group fusion in times of scarcity. If this were the case in Yosemite or other native colonial-era settings, immigrants and hosts may have already shared traits and symbols so that "dilution" might be neither evident nor relevant. Native people recognized affinity but also maintained separate identities. And the very notion of "dilution" distracts from the process of cultural negotiation and formation of new cultures and identities—including the development of entirely new practices—rather than the implicit "watering down" of existing cultures.

In the case of the Awahnichi, settlement was relatively swiftly reestablished within their traditional territory, and distinctive cultural practices and identity may have been maintained during exile in anticipation of return. In such circumstances, there was probably a tendency toward the maintenance of distinct ethnic identities or traditional practices rather than assimilation into or mixing with the culture of the host group, if local conditions of subsistence and settlement allowed. Separate villages or neighborhoods in the host area might even be anticipated. That is, while aggregation on a local level involved consolidating settlements, aggregation on a regional level such as that entailed by emigration might simply have meant relocating but not necessarily inhabiting the same villages as their hosts. The potential for such proclivities toward identity maintenance or lack of creolization is further suggested by archaeological studies of multiethnic communities in colonial contexts, where just such practices have been inferred (e.g., Deagan 1983, 1995; Lightfoot et al. 1998). These studies also suggest that it might be more appropriate to consider the locus of identity at the individual rather than the group level—where creolization is born in the domestic, rather than public, sphere (Lightfoot and Martinez 1995; Lightfoot et al. 1998). Ethnogenesis, on the other hand, is a collective acknowledgment of such aggregate change in the public arena and in interactions beyond the group. Again, an anticipated stay of only one or two generations may have been a significant factor here, as well as the flexibility to enter and exit the host territory at will. The important point is that aggregation and emigration do not a priori equal assimilation, creolization, or ethnogenesis, and evidence for such processes should be sought archaeologically.

In the Yosemite Indian case, I anticipated that potentially distinct traditions of the Awahnichi (Me'-wuk) and Kuzedika (Mono Paiute) converged during the self-imposed exile of the disease-ravaged group to the Mono Basin. It was not clear, however, that blended villages developed in the Mono Basin, as relocation may have simply facilitated access to mates while also providing distance from perceived threats of illness in Yosemite Valley. Such segregation is hinted by the fact that subsequent occupation in Mono Basin by Tenaya's band in 1852 entailed access to particular areas and, perhaps, residential segregation as well (Bunnell 1990:265). It is also significant that although some potential language mixing or borrowing is indicated by the reference to Tenaya's "Paiute jargon" (Bunnell 1990:63), the Miwok language was still sufficiently intact in the Yosemite area to be used by Tenaya when speaking to Maj. James Savage's Indian interpreters and to be later recorded by ethnographers. Bunnell (1990:179) made it clear that Tenaya spoke both Awahnichi and Paiute, reflecting the multiethnic household and community in which he was raised. Therefore, this language retention probably indicates the intention of the Awahnichi descendants to return to Yosemite Valley. Likewise, Tenaya's story suggests that he and his paternal family were still identified as Awahnichi—and others may have been as well—since he was prompted to return by the elderly medicine man.

Due to the practice of exogamy and the need to reestablish a viable population, it was likely that numerous multiethnic households with Awahnichi and Paiute members developed on the eastern side of the Sierra Nevada in the years after introduced disease struck. Many such families and households were probably transplanted to Yosemite Valley upon the return of Tenaya's group. If patrilocality was the rule for both the Mono Paiute and Awahnichi at that time, many surviving Awahnichi women may have remained in the east. And households established in Yosemite Valley upon Tenaya's return may have consisted primarily of Mono Paiute women and Me'-wuk men. Thus, we might anticipate more differences in pre- and postdisease practices of women rather than men in archaeological sites in Yosemite Valley. The relatively high postdisease population growth rate, however, suggests significant immigration that encompassed more than just the households of male Awahnichi descendants from the Mono Basin. And other returning descendants may have spent intervening years with Me'-wuk people to the north or Monache people to south rather than with the Paiute to the east. In addition, it is unclear whether traditions of the Awahnichi, Mono Paiute, and others were sufficiently distinct prior to migration to be readily distinguishable archaeologically in postdisease settings. This is particularly true in light of archaeological evidence for interregional exchange between the Awahnichi and people of the eastern Sierra, San Joaquin Valley, and California coast. Finally, were multiethnic households unique to the postcolonial era? Or, since previous kin ties may have existed as a "hedge against extinction," were such households also present in the past? Archaeological study was necessary to demonstrate if creolization occurred, if individuals maintained their traditional practices and cultural identities, or if new traits were simply introduced within households. Fortunately, the prevalence of multiethnic households identified in colonial-era research elsewhere in North America provided direction for archaeological study of creolization in Yosemite Valley (e.g., Deagan 1983, 1995; Lightfoot et al. 1998). Such studies focus on intrasite use of space and daily practices.

EXTERNAL RELATIONS AND REGIONAL INTERACTION

Shifts in external relations and regional interaction in the wake of colonial-era depopulation may have occurred due to native population movements and presence of nonnative people in close or distant territory. These factors may have permitted access to materials not available in predisease times or may have restricted access to those that were previously available. And changing external relations would be anticipated in a postdisease context because of the need to exploit specialists or use products from elsewhere, since some specialists would no longer be present within the population (see Dobyns 1983:332). Survivors might not be self-sufficient in the short term or even the long run, and exchange with neighbors would be required. Dobyns (1983) suggested this to a certain extent when he discussed decreasing diversity of native artifact forms because of the incorporation of nonnative implements into the economy. His focus on nonnative items, however, distracts from the underlying demographic cause for such change, which pertains even when nonnative goods were unavailable. Rather than attributing such shifts to economic involvement with colonists, acquisition could have been related to strictly demographic factors, since population decline in some areas may have facilitated or prompted population movements that brought new groups into contact or cut off traditional interactions. From this perspective, even colonists can be viewed as new immigrants providing access to different resources for use in traditional cultural practices by surviving native people. In colonial-era research, the focus has generally been on native and nonnative interaction, but by taking a longer-term view and acknowledging that such change likely preceded face-to-face encounters, such expectations apply equally well to native interaction and access to different native goods.

Relations between native groups may also have been marked by decreased competition for natural resources in the aftermath of epidemics, with a concomitant decrease in native warfare (Dobyns 1983:333). This would be especially true if new ties were forged through intermarriage necessary for population survival. Conversely, native population decline was often coincident with nonnative population increase in adjacent areas, and this could have prompted more tension between surviving native groups as they fought over the available land, subsistence resources, or assets used to trade with colonists. The latter instance pertains, for example, to tribes engaged in the deerskin trade in the interior Southeast. Such intergroup tensions were particularly likely in the Yosemite region, where transplanted native people could occupy land beyond the immediate threat of colonists but not beyond the potential ire of resident Indian people who may not have been amenable to the presence of such intruders. And population aggregation and short-term geographic contraction may have temporarily opened up territory for other neighbors that then prompted a response by people who previously controlled such land. For the newcomers, it was a choice of enemies or threats, and by the Gold Rush, nonnative population was growing rapidly, putting ever more pressure on native groups. Overall resource competition, if not population, may have been increasing, and increased conflict was likely between Indians and with colonists. In an area—or during a brief era—still free from the direct or indirect pressure of colonists, however, decreased competition would be expected.

Evidence of postdisease escalation in competition and tension in Yosemite Valley is difficult to develop via archaeology due to the lack of human remains that might provide direct evidence of physical violence. External relations in the form of trade, however, can be assessed, as this issue has been the focus of much archaeological research in the region (see Hull and Moratto 1999). In Yosemite Valley, I anticipated that goods traditionally acquired from the west might be unavailable or that different goods might have been acquired from other groups to the west in the wake of epidemics. This is because demographic shifts and population movements likely pertained to both suppliers—particularly those within the direct influence of the Spanish—and consumers such as the Yosemite Indians. For example, temporary exile from Yosemite Valley may have resulted in the dissolution of some ties to the west that were not easily reestablished after return to the valley, given colonial-era turmoil. Or, westerners may have no longer sought goods that Yosemite people could provide, if they had developed new ties with other groups or found substitute goods through colonial contacts. For example, native people of the San Joaquin Valley may have replaced obsidian tools with those of manufactured glass or metal, whereas marine shell beads may no longer have been available to the native people of the Sierra Nevada. Items traditionally acquired from the eastern Sierra such as obsidian, on the other hand, might not reflect such pre- and postdepopulation distinctions or loss, particularly since ties in this direction were probably strengthened through intermarriage at that time. As these examples illustrate, changing external relations and access to nonlocal materials in the wake of depopulation could reflect either choice or accident, unlike some of the other factors considered.

THE FOUNDER EFFECT IN DECREASING CULTURAL DIVERSITY

Because survivors of infectious disease constituted a smaller population than existed previously, it is likely that these individuals did not retain all of the knowledge or continue all of the practices that the group had prior to this event. This is due to the founder effect, a phenomenon wherein a subset of a population expresses less diversity than the original population from which it derived. In evolutionary biology—the field in which this concept was defined—less genetic and phenotypic diversity results from migration or some other factor that separates some individuals from the parent population. If such separation is maintained for a sufficiently long time, speciation may result (Mayr 1942). When applied to culture, as in the current case, founder effect refers to less cultural diversity within the population subsample (Dunnell 1991:570), and resulting discontinuity between parent and daughter population might lead archaeologists to conclude that a new *culture* emerged. Such decreasing cultural diversity is not the same as Dobyns's (1983:306) concept of decreasing diversity, however, which relates to intermarriage, creolization, and thus, to the reduction of "the number of surviving ethnic groups and . . . [lessening of] an earlier cultural and linguistic diversity." This latter concept applies to intergroup, rather than intragroup, processes and reflects choice rather than accident. Decreasing cultural diversity due to the founder effect is random, although nonnative disease probably disproportionately affected the very old, who likely held special knowledge or skills (Dunnell 1991:571; see also Dobyns 1991:552; Trigger 1966:439–440). Applying the notion of the founder effect to cultural as opposed to genetic content (see Dunnell 1991:571), such a process could result in the absence of some traits or practices exhibited in predisease times. Or the founder effect could manifest practices or skills in different proportions on an intracommunity basis in either the short or long term than might have prevailed in the original population. In the wake of depopulation, there would be less variation in skill levels between individuals and, perhaps, an overall decrease in skills or knowledge held by the group. And decreasing intragroup diversity would likely be more pronounced within complex societies in which some knowledge was held by only a few individuals or by particular groups within the society (Dobyns 1983:332; Dunnell 1991:573). Conversely, if knowledge had been spread early, often, and equally among the members of a group—as in the case of gender roles in hunter-gatherer bands (Dunnell 1991:573)—we might not expect the founder effect to be as significant in postdisease cultural change. In fact, it might even be that such a strategy of knowledge sharing existed as part of preadaptation to small population size and the biological vulnerability deriving therefrom.

Founder effects with respect to material culture may have been short-lived, as new experts emerged through necessity or individual commitment to the development and acquisition of skills that could no longer be depended upon from other individuals. On the other hand, negative consequences with respect to esoteric knowledge may have been permanent, since such knowledge was held by a few and not openly discussed or publicly demonstrated. For example, certain ceremonies may have simply ceased, since there were no survivors with knowledge necessary for their perpetuation. Or objects may have been imbued with different meanings in pre- and postdisease cultural contexts, since traditional understanding was prone to loss through the founder effect. And even if particular artifact types continued to be used or manufactured, they may have been used in different ways than in the past. Due to systemic discontinuity (see Dunnell 1991:571), archaeological assessment of colonial-era culture change in Yosemite Valley and elsewhere must address such underlying practices and understandings (see Schiffer 1976). To do so requires a contextual approach rather than simple material or morphological analysis (see Hodder 1991; Lightfoot et al. 1998). For example, were objects made and used in the same social spaces that they were prior to the impact of depopulation?

Decreasing cultural diversity as a random process would have resulted in both short- and long-term changes in Yosemite Indian culture. In the short term, I anticipated changes in material culture due to the loss of highly skilled individuals. This change would have been short-lived, as such skill could be reestablished after sufficient time and investment in these arts. Long-term changes in practices would be evidenced by either the loss of traits or changes in meaning indicated by the context of artifact use. Archaeological assessment of decreasing diversity among Yosemite Indians is confounded somewhat by the potential addition of practices through intermarriage of Awahnichi with neighboring people. That is, some traits may have been "lost" while others of similar function were "gained," particularly those related to practices critical to individual survival or maintenance of the community. Pre- and postdepopulation comparisons were important to recognizing the source of such changes, and temporal control was critical, as only short-term change was likely for some aspects of decreasing intragroup diversity.

DESPECIALIZATION AND SIMPLIFICATION OF SOCIAL STRUCTURE

Whereas decreasing intragroup diversity represents a stochastic process brought on by small group size, despecialization represents the termination of a practice or role due to lack of demand for the products or the processes it entails. Despecialization was a choice of people rather than an accident of history. Some researchers have focused on despecialization as manifest in the replacement of traditional objects with those of nonnative manufacture (Dobyns 1983:331). Access to new—presumably more desirable—goods would have decreased demand for the production of items for which such nonnative substitutes could be found. For example, if shell or stone beads were replaced by glass beads, artisans responsible for production of traditional beads would no longer be required. Broader implications with respect to despecialization, however, are not necessarily restricted to interaction with colonists. Such a process is also expected as population size declines and simplified social structure results. Goods related to certain roles or practices would no longer be required, and "decreasing demand and opportunity for social and economic specialization [may have made] . . . survivors necessarily jacks of more and masters of fewer trades than their forebears" (Dobyns 1991:552). Support for full-time and, perhaps, even part-time specialists would fade, particularly within a hierarchical system in which the individuals or classes of people requiring these locally produced goods would themselves no longer be supported.

In fact, despecialization has generally been conceived as particularly relevant to hierarchical societies that supported craft specialists. Thus, this concept is somewhat more difficult to apply to the Yosemite Indian case than either creolization or decreasing diversity from the founder effect, because there is no evidence of such a structure for the Awahnichi. As defined here, despecialization does not entail an outright loss of a skill within the community (i.e., related to decreasing diversity) but rather a lack of demand for that skill in the short or long term. So, even without a hierarchical organization, part-time specialists might not have been in demand. A more generalized toolkit was expected in postdepopulation archaeological contexts in Yosemite Valley, either because survivors were "jacks of all trades" or because fewer types of objects were manufactured even for personal use and specialized tools were not required for this smaller array of personal goods. Despecialization might also be evident in an overall decrease in technological skill in manufacturing, with individuals performing tasks at which they were not especially proficient. Thus, despecialization is evident in artifact and assemblage diversity as well as in technological practices and skills in manufacture and use.

Simplification of social structure in the aftermath of depopulation was also a process of social supply and demand. Dobyns (1983:328) concluded that such simplification was likely because "interaction between a hundred people is inevitably far simpler than interaction between a thousand or ten thousand inhabitants of a single human settlement." For example, deurbanization might be one form of simplification, although time lags in change might be apparent "due to inertia and human conservatism" (Dobyns 1991:550). A corollary of such simplification is that access to and control of labor for corporate projects, such as construction of irrigation systems or ceremonial structures, might no longer exist. This suggested that simplification was potentially visible archaeologically on an intersite basis, particularly in the investment of corporate structures and facilities. Therefore, simplification might not apply to the Yosemite Valley case, since the Awahnichi had a relatively simple social structure lacking such major corporate investments prior to depopulation. It was anticipated, however, that due to likely tribelet organization any such changes would relate more to regional rather than local or site-specific phenomena.

CONSEQUENCES FOR INDIVIDUALS, HOUSEHOLDS, AND GROUPS

This review reveals that some cultural changes expected in the wake of depopulation—such as emigration, creolization, ethnogenesis, and despecialization—relate to decisions of the survivors in the face of changing circumstances. These changes involve perception, needs, and actions.

Still, although conscious decision making is recognized in many cases, it was often a far cry from choice as we generally conceive of it—options may have been severely limited by basic needs for survival in swiftly changing conditions. For example, emigration was a decision but may have been the only viable option. Other changes, such as decreasing diversity, are simply stochastic processes that may not have been recognized by Indian people at the time and thus may not have been subject to response. Nevertheless, they affected culture in the wake of fatal disease. Postdepopulation cultural shifts also varied with respect to their locus of change—whether impact was manifest at the individual, household, or group level. Aggregation and external relations were regional phenomenon, simplification of social structure was a local process, and despecialization and creolization probably were especially germane to households and individuals. Thus, colonial-era culture change represents a complex—and group-specific—process of action and accident on multiple levels, and many of these same processes may have also occurred in precolonial native contexts in the wake of local catastrophe.

Fortunately, many of the expectations of culture change in the aftermath of colonial-era population decline have potential material consequences that can be sought archaeologically on an intrasite, site-specific, local, or regional scale. For example, aggregation is manifest in regional settlement patterns and site constituents, external relations are evident in regional patterns of exchange, and creolization is indicated in the organization of household labor and mundane practices of daily life. Issues of temporal resolution are problematic, however, given the swift and potentially short duration of some changes. In addition, study of colonial-era culture change that resulted from depopulation rather than direct encounters presents a challenge to conventional archaeological approaches to culture contact and colonialism. Such changes unfolded in a context where nonnative goods were unavailable, and therefore the materiality of experience was retained in traditional objects rather than nonnative goods. Thus, such study must look beyond macroscale economic models and the incorporation of nonnative objects. Culture change must be assessed in actions—that is, in the practices that define culture by engaged and thoughtful people—within a particular historical setting. Yosemite Indians were aware of the significance of depopulation to their community and the implications of this event for short-term, if not long-term, survival. They made decisions with these issues in mind. And the importance of agency and decision making by native people to colonial-era culture change underscores the significance of individuals and household activities in understanding this process. This perspective contrasts with focus only on the societal level, as was common to acculturation approaches that dominated studies into the 1980s and still often overshadows more recent culture-contact research.[1] Individuals, not cultures, interact and have goals or agendas in such contexts (Schortman and Urban 1998:108).

Thus, from cross-cultural analysis of ethnohistory and archaeology, two scales of archaeological analysis emerged from the expectations of postdepopulation culture change for native people of Awahnee: (1) intrasite analysis to assess identity and practices on an individual and household basis; and (2) intersite analysis to explore aggregation, settlement patterns, social structure, and external relations at the group level. The most profound changes that represent conscious choice rather than accident relate to the articulation of different cultural traditions. Multiethnic households, with potentially fluid membership but a common residence, negotiated roles in cooperative tasks and shared goals. These households developed through intermarriage following short- or long-term population aggregation. Such aggregation brought together individuals who "enact[ed] and construct[ed] their underlying organizational principles, worldviews, and social identities in the ordering of daily life" (Lightfoot et al. 1998:199). In essence, these daily practices are "surface phenomena" of traditions with "deep, meaningful referents" (see Shennan 1993:58), of which individuals enacting such traditions may not even be aware (Bourdieu 1977). People with different cultural traditions and attributions of meaning to daily practice organize their social environment and conduct themselves in potentially distinct ways. They embody the structure of long-term tradition in everyday actions. Short-term idiosyncratic or superficial change in actions or organization may occur in the context of depopulation—with or without intercultural articulation—but the potential enduring deep structural changes especially relevant to anthropological analysis must be demonstrated in the long term rather than assumed from archaeological data manifesting such practices. Therefore, daily practices and routines after disease-induced depopulation that were evident in the archaeological record had to be contrasted with predisease situations and long-term trends that both revealed and defined the structure of Awahnichi culture prior to depopulation.[2]

Defining culture as practice—rather than as only a material or adaptive phenomenon (see Trigger 1989)—highlights the reiterative (i.e., reproductive) and spatial component of everyday existence, as people organized domestic, recreational, and ceremonial activities within their households and communities. And the "little routines" of daily life in such contexts accumulate material evidence particularly suited to archaeological study, since these mundane acts account for the bulk of the objects, features, and debris produced and deposited. Thus, it was important and informative for the archaeological study of Yosemite Indians to consider the spatial organization indicated by the construction, maintenance, and abandonment of public structures, dwellings, extramural space, and trash deposits. In pre- and postdepopulation settings, the spatial arrangement and relationship of implements or debris, for example, can indicate changes in the organization of domestic labor and the decisions made by people. Such choices were based on their cultural traditions and perceptions within a social environment potentially substantially altered by depopulation.

Archaeological analysis of cultural practice within native households in Yosemite Valley was undertaken through block excavations sufficient to reveal spatial patterning and depositional events, especially those of household units. Such exposures allowed comparison of the context of artifacts, ecofacts, and features; their spatial relationships to each other; and their relationship to the built environment.[3] Three-dimensional recording of cultural objects and features also contributed to this contextual approach, although previous site disturbance, sandy sediments, and the rodent activity common to Yosemite Valley undermined horizontal and vertical integrity somewhat. Still, general isopleth plots depicting the spatial density of items based on excavation unit recovery were used to augment three-dimensional data and to define activity areas that were then compared on a constituent and more detailed spatial basis. The organizational principles of households and communities in pre- and postdepopulation times that were revealed through such analysis addressed the construction and maintenance of age, gender, faction, class, and other social relationships within and between individuals and households that may have undergone change in the wake of depopulation. Such shifts may be manifest particularly in creolization, despecialization, or simplification, although the latter is perhaps most relevant to a larger scale of analysis than the individual and household.

One of the primary emphases of households is cooperation in the procurement, processing, cooking, and consumption of food. Thus, archaeological focus on food-preparation areas greatly contributes to reconstructing social relations within the household (Netting et al. 1984: xxii; Hendon 1996:48). Although subsistence choices are ultimately dictated by available resources, preference in resource selection or relative incorporation of specific foods into the diet is based on a variety of cultural factors—such as notions of appropriate foods, processing technology, and communal versus individual hunting strategies. In addition, different means of processing and consumption can pertain to the same foodstuffs within different cultural traditions. Therefore, subsistence patterns manifest through comparison of floral, faunal, and artifact assemblages derived from dwelling units may reflect shifts in cultural traditions of household members or household size and organization due to depopulation.

Analysis of faunal samples provided the bulk of the direct subsistence information for Yosemite Indians, although these data were augmented by analysis of limited macrofloral samples. Both of these data sets provided qualitative and quantitative data on species and elements exploited, while the faunal assemblage also documented cultural modification (e.g., butchering, fractures, burning) that signal cultural preference in processing and consumption at the household level. In addition, given the promise of crossover immuno-electrophoresis (CIEP) in previous Yosemite subsistence studies (Hull, Roper et al. 1999), this technique was also applied to examination of subsistence. An extract (antigen) of protein residues present on an artifact is tested against antibodies of known faunal or floral species. If the unknown antigen reacts with a known species antiserum, then protein residues of that species were retained on the artifact.[4] Such residues may indicate faunal or floral resources processed with each implement or could reflect organic materials used to haft the tool to a handle or shaft.

Households also share in other domestic activities such as construction of shelter, manufacture of vessels, and tool production. Material culture and the built environment of households reveal the wealth or status of their members in addition to cultural affiliation. Individuals undertook these tasks and so it is important to consider technology and identity expressed through the manufacture and use of material objects. As noted by Sinclair (2000:196), "technology is not simply a body of explicitly formulated and objectively described knowledge. It is a suite of technical gestures and knowledge that is learned and expressed by individuals in the course of social practices. Technology is one of the social processes by which individuals negotiate and define their identities, in terms of gender, age, belief, class, and so on." Raw materials, manufacturing implements and techniques, and tool use form a "constellation of knowledge" for individuals (Sinclair 2000). In light of such perspectives, intra- and intersite comparison of material culture of Yosemite Indians was explored through technological and functional analysis of flaked stone tools and debitage. For this study, a focus on lithic items was necessary, since objects of organic materials are not well preserved in most Yosemite Valley deposits. With respect to flaked stone technology, the strategy employed recognized various stages in the manufacturing process in both the tool and debitage assemblages as well as particular manufacturing features (e.g., notching, bipolar breakage).[5] Such distinctions addressed technical decisions, sequencing, and desired outcomes.[6] In addition, morphological and metric traits addressed tool function and use-life that relate to activities undertaken, material acquisition, and other factors. These technological data for tools were augmented by CIEP results, which contributed to defining function for intra- and intersite comparisons.

Spatial, technological, and other specialized analyses of ecofacts and artifacts recovered through broad horizontal excavations at pre- and post-depopulation deposits provided for exploration of household activities, intrasite spatial patterns, daily practices, artifact context, and individual identity. These analyses addressed culture change at the microscale. The qualitative and quantitative spatial array of artifacts and ecofacts contributed to recognizing activities represented, to defining single- or multitask activity areas, and to inferring the possible skill, gender, or age of individuals represented. Such conclusions were facilitated through reference to regional archaeological data spanning centuries or millennia, native oral tradition, and general ethnographic and ethnoarchaeological information (e.g., Binford 1980; R. L. Kelly 1995). Based on expectations for population-related culture change, it was anticipated that several issues and questions could be addressed in this way. For example, were shifts in the organization of space, subsistence practices, and material culture indicated? How might such changes relate to the intermarriage with people living east of the Sierra in the face of population loss? Are there differences in tasks associated with women rather than men, which might be related to intermarriage and postmarriage residence patterns? Was greater craft specialization and skill indicated by the presence of more specialized tools types (e.g., drills) in predisease settings? Did a shift away from such specialization reflect a change in social organization or traditional knowledge? And finally, were multitask activity areas or tools more common in postdisease settings?

Given these expectations, in the case of the Awahnichi it was desirable to have a predisease and postdepopulation perspective not only for Yosemite Valley but also for the Mono Basin. This work required a view of both the Mono Paiute and Me'-wuk peoples for comparison and discussion of native culture change in Yosemite Valley in the wake of depopulation. Data from Yosemite Valley were developed expressly for this study, although data on earlier centuries and millennia prior to the introduction of European disease were also available from previous regional research (see Hull and Moratto 1999). Some existing colonial-era data for the Mono Basin were available from Arkush (1995), although his research was conducted utilizing a theoretical perspective incompatible with the current research. Therefore, little spatial data was available for assessment of the systemic context of items recovered from the deposits he studied. In addition, his temporal placement of "precontact," "protohistoric," and "postcontact" sites was based to a certain extent on the incorporation and representation of nonnative artifacts and is therefore tautological when applied to the issue of culture change.

Recognition of the potential changes in settlement and external relationships due to depopulation required a different scale of analysis than that relevant to individuals and households. This larger scale of interaction pertains to the relationship between households that comprise a village or group as well as to relations of Yosemite Indians with groups in surrounding areas. Therefore, although not relevant to as many of the expectations of postdepopulation culture change as microscale action based on identity and household activities, such issues were significant to culture change. And these factors were addressed at a regional level with different types of archaeological data. Given expectations for postdisease cultural change, most important in this regard were settlement data, including number, size, location, and function of sites. These traits address population aggregation and potential shifts in village size as well as possible settlement strategies adopted to access Yosemite Valley from a distant residential base. Likewise, obsidian hydration information and analyses of artifact assemblages contributed to assessment of changing settlement patterns within Yosemite Valley. These temporal data were also used to explore reiterative use of sites that may indicate attachment to place and identity maintenance at the group level. Conversely, disjuncture in settlement reuse could indicate discontinuity in such traditions.

Similarly, Yosemite Valley residents participated in long-distance exchange as both producers and consumers. Demographic changes both within Yosemite Valley and in surrounding areas may have altered such interaction. Access to nonlocal resources was assessed through diachronic comparisons of raw-material types, artifact morphology, and technological traits that indicate the form in which items were acquired. At a regional scale, settlement data also addressed these issues, including aspects of settlement mobility and territorial circumscription. Fortunately, regional interaction has been the subject of significant previous research in the Yosemite area. Random samples of debitage for X-ray fluorescence analysis were selected from pre- and postdepopulation contexts to assess potential shifts in external contacts through trade. Artifact assemblages also included shell and stone beads likely acquired from the west.

Even at this broader analytical scale, it was essential to establish temporal control and to assess the representative nature of spatial data. At a minimum, pre- and postdepopulation deposits had to be discernable and separable either stratigraphically or on the basis of obsidian hydration data. The regional perspective, however, provided more flexibility with data from the more distant past, as only broad trends were sought. Conversely, the spatial aspect was somewhat more problematic, as existing data do not represent a random sample of sites and the complex use-histories of village locales indicated by obsidian hydration dating suggested that substantial sampling might be required to clearly delimit site size, for example, in pre- and postdepopulation times.

ANTICIPATING SCALES OF YOSEMITE INDIAN CULTURE CHANGE

Given Tenaya's account of the Awahnichi response to the "black sickness," Yosemite Indian postdisease culture change was probably dominated by the consequences of short-term relocation and intermarriage with people to the east. The loss of traditional knowledge due to the vulnerability of a small population is also germane, although to a lesser extent. This would also be more difficult to gauge with archaeological data. Likewise, the potential loss of external connections with neighboring groups to the west is relevant, as such groups endured their own demographic and cultural changes that affected surrounding people (see Phillips 1993). At the intrasite level, archaeological data address daily practices reflecting the "little routines" embedded in the "deep structure" of culture, with individuals making decisions in light of short-term circumstances and long-range plans. Potential changes include organization of domestic labor, craft specialization, changes in traditional craft skill after the loss of specialized knowledge, shifts in family or household size, and intermarriage with people of other cultural traditions. Significantly, just such changes have been observed by ethnographers in basketry traditions of the Yosemite Indians at a later date (see Bates and Lee 1990). At the intersite level, we might expect changes in settlement patterns, external relations, and exchange.

Archaeological fieldwork for this study entailed shallow but broad excavations at one predepopulation site (Hol'-low) and one postdepopulation site (He-le'-jah). Although assessment of the type and quantity of nonnative goods formed an element of the analysis—particularly with respect to external relations—the focus was on identifying activities and context of use in pre- and postdepopulation contexts within Yosemite Valley. Context of use was facilitated through in situ mapping of artifacts and more general isopleth maps based on excavation unit recovery. This process permitted analysis of artifacts and ecofacts in both density and kind. Were the same activities undertaken in pre- and postdepopulation settings? What did spatial and assemblage data indicate with respect to the organization of activities, household dynamics, and domestic life? Did use of nonnative items by Yosemite Indians simply reflect the incorporation of raw materials available within a shifting economic sphere, or fundamental changes in economic activity and social organization? Although only two sites within Yosemite Valley contributed to the detailed picture of immediate pre- and postdepopulation life, the interpretive value of these data was enhanced by the fact that these observations were embedded within a larger study of regional context.

In keeping with the perspective of culture as practice, an appraisal of colonial-era culture change at the level of the individual or household was juxtaposed with patterns at a larger scale and in a broader temporal framework. This was crucial for understanding the significance of population change to cultural change, recognizing which options may have been available, and identifying what changes were actively instituted. Three broad types of culture change were anticipated at the microscale in the wake of depopulation: (1) creolization or development of multiethnic households through intermarriage with neighboring peoples; (2) decreasing diversity in practices or skill due to random loss resulting from decreasing population size; and (3) despecialization deriving from the lack of demand for skills related to practices no longer supported after severe population loss. Creolization, in particular, was expected to be visible archaeologically in the routines of daily life and the organization of space within households at He-le'-jah and other sites occupied during the 1800s, as people with different cultural traditions came together. Decreasing diversity, on the other hand, is a stochastic process reflecting accident rather than choice and would be potentially evident in comparison of tool manufacture and use in pre- and post-depopulation contexts. Finally, despecialization was anticipated to be manifest in individual skill and the range of objects produced. The areas excavated within both Hol'-low and He-le'-jah represented domestic activity areas, and hearths identified at each provided spatial focus for assessing household practices. Comparison at the general level of the village considered the activities represented and how different tasks were accomplished. Assessment of the organization of activities within the household involved examining the site-specific hearth contexts and use of space around these features. Finally, focus on specific traits of individual implements and tool assemblages addressed creolization, despecialization, and decreasing diversity.

With microscale individual and household practices established, analysis then shifted to the local and regional level. Several potential consequences of catastrophic depopulation in the colonial era—or the even-more-distant past—played out and were best addressed at the regional rather than site-specific or intrasite scale. In the Yosemite case, the aggregation and emigration of people in the wake of depopulation was expected to be manifest in regional settlement patterns. Shifts in external relations and regional interaction were also anticipated, evident in the incorporation of exotic materials or the production of items for exchange identified through intersite comparison. Finally, simplification of social structure might have occurred, although simplification is less germane to the native people of Yosemite Valley than in some other areas of North America. Such change would be evident in settlement patterns, including investment in communal facilities such as assembly houses at one or more villages. These and the other potential shifts at the regional scale were assessed, in part, with extant archaeological data for the Yosemite area augmented by the results of excavations at Hol'-low and He-le'-jah.

For the macroscale analysis, external relations were considered first, with particular focus on acquisition of obsidian and nonnative goods. This was followed by assessment of potential changes in settlement, especially site location, reiterative village use, and construction of intrasite features. These broad issues could not be addressed as comprehensively as I had hoped, as it was often necessary to rely on existing archaeological information that lacked good temporal control. In addition, such data do not represent a random sample suited to statistically defensible conclusions. Data from the excavations at Hol'-low and He-le'-jah contributed somewhat, however, particularly with respect to regional interaction. In addition, information from these sites permitted reference to microscale observations that addressed macroscale patterns. For example, these additional data provided a picture of the form in which materials were acquired and the context of use in the colonial era. This latter element was critical, since it was not just the presence of such items that was important but also how items acquired from elsewhere were integrated into daily practice.

The analytical dialectic between pre- and postdepopulation materials and periods fostered by an approach utilizing archaeological data, ethnohistoric accounts, ethnographic observations, and native oral traditions provided for a better understanding of both the recent and distant past. And the fifty-year lag time between the introduction of virulent disease and the invasion of the Sierra Nevada foothills by miners allowed the consequences of these two assaults of colonialism to be examined separately in Yosemite Valley. This study was complicated, however, by the fact that this colonial-era demographic event was very brief and subject to rapid population recovery. The same swift change and recovery might also pertain to the cultural effects of depopulation, making population decline nearly invisible in the archaeological record. Both short- and long-term cultural consequences of disease-induced demographic change had to be considered and demonstrated in the Yosemite Indian case.

CHAPTER 8

Hol'-low and He-le'-jah

Cultural Continuity and Change

In the early 1600s, the Awahnichi were living in a world of relative plenty and calm, having maintained their community from one generation to the next through a precipitous decline in population during the previous millennium. They lived in about twenty camps and villages in Yosemite Valley, one of which was Hol'-low (cave).[1] This village was situated near the eastern end of the valley on an open, sunny slope dotted with oak trees and conifers. The nearby creek was shaded by stands of pine and cedar that lined the sandy banks. A large rockshelter decorated with red paintings—from which the village took its name—was present at the edge of an extensive jumble of the huge boulders that had fallen from the cliffs above no more than fifty years before. A few additional boulders, deeply embedded in the surrounding sediments through centuries of deposition, studded the gentle slope below. Here, multiple families lived at least part of each year, occupying a few houses scattered across the flat. Women pounded acorns into flour in the mortars present on two of the larger rocks within the village. At mealtime, food was prepared and consumed in baskets and steatite bowls around household hearths. Robes and baskets, bows and arrows, flaked stone tools, and other implements were manufactured around the hearths and in the open space between the houses. Abundant obsidian and a few chert flakes and tools lost or discarded throughout the flat bear witness to this handiwork. The obsidian may have been acquired through trade with neighbors or procured directly by the Awahnichi through trips to the eastern side of the Sierra in the summer months. The stone and shell beads adorning the baskets and apparel stored in the houses were acquired from trading partners to the west.

By 1800, the world of the Awahnichi was a different place. The descendants of the survivors from the 1600s had faced their own demographic crisis within just one generation—devastating disease transmitted from distant European colonists. As in the past, survivors had made decisions in the wake of population decline that would shape their destiny as individuals and a group in both the short and long term. Survival initially required rebuilding their community through intermarriage with people in the Mono Basin and elsewhere. Although the Awahnichi had interacted with—and perhaps even intermarried among—neighboring people before, interaction now was probably more extensive and profound than at any other time in the recent past. Emigration and intermarriage brought the disparate languages and cultures of the men and women of the western and eastern Sierra together in nearly every household. After more than fifteen years of self-imposed exile elsewhere, reoccupation of Yosemite Valley in the 1800s was tentative at first. By circa 1820, for example, the village of He-le'-jah (mountain lion) was one of perhaps only six camps occupied by the returning Indian people.[2] Located in the central portion of Yosemite Valley, this village was tucked between steep cliffs to the north and the slow waters of the meandering river to the south. A rockshelter that could have provided sanctuary for one family or several adults was present at He-le'-jah, situated on the slope at the lower margin of an oak- and conifer-studded boulder field. It was less than half the size of that at Hol'-low, but it served as shelter for the Indian people living here during the late winter and perhaps at other times of the year. A hearth was situated near the front of the rockshelter to protect the fire from the elements but to keep smoke from filling the small space of the refuge, the ceiling of which was so low that an adult could not stand upright. People worked at tasks out of the elements or in the shade of the shelter during the day and by firelight at night, making arrow points, weaving baskets, and preparing food with handstones and other utensils. Farther back in the shelter, food and gear were stored, and the people made their beds while the fire kept the nighttime chill at bay. And like their ancestors at Hol'-low, these people pounded acorns in one of the dozen mortars present on two boulders in the nearby flat, manufactured stone tools, and traded for shell beads and obsidian.

Thus, in many ways, daily life at He-le'-jah was similar to the routines of more than two hundred years earlier at Hol'-low. But there were subtle signs of change in this hinterland of colonial California that presaged the greater shifts that would come after the influx of miners into the Sierra foothills. For instance, there were changes in the items acquired, produced, and consumed by Indian people and in the typical practices of everyday life and shared residence in a diverse community. Archaeological exploration of postdisease, colonial-era culture change began around one hearth in each of these villages, examining the "little routines" of daily practice that defined the collective identity, life, and world of native people. The scope then expanded beyond the village to study the settlement strategies within Yosemite Valley and native interaction with close and distant neighbors both before and after disease-induced depopulation. The hearth at Hol'-low was located on a bench created by a large boulder on which women pounded acorns. Archaeological excavation here encompassed a 16-square-meter area in two intersecting trenches and a block excavation around the hearth. The hearth at He-le'-jah was within the rockshelter and was exposed by excavation of a 9-square-meter trench that bisected the shelter from front to back. An adjacent 0.375-square-meter area exposed a storage feature nearby. Because each hearth was a center of household activity, archaeological data from these villages provide a glimpse of the daily life of individuals and households that were separated by only about two hundred years in time but by very different circumstances.

DAILY LIFE WITHIN THE VILLAGE

Due to the differences in preservation of organic remains between the open deposit at Hol'-low and the rockshelter at He-le'-jah, comparison of domestic activities at these two villages focused on stone tools and debitage. The flaked stone tool assemblages at both sites were dominated by edge-modified flakes (EMFs) used for a variety of cutting and scraping tasks (see table 2). Most of these implements were not intentionally shaped, but rather their edges were simply altered by use. Arrow points and bifaces—which included finished tools as well as roughouts in various stages of manufacture—were somewhat less common. Finally, drills and gravers accounted for the remainder of the flaked stone tools used, although both types were rare. The frequency of these various objects indicated that expedient flake tools were used and discarded most often. In contrast, relatively few specialized implements were produced and used—especially those tools such as drills, which were not subject to frequent damage due to use. Still, the debitage

TABLE 2.
Frequency of Flaked Stone Tool Types
at Hol'-low and He-le'-jah

Object	Hol'-low	He-le'-jah
Bifaces		
Type 2 (early percussion)	1 (0.5%)	1 (0.6%)
Type 3 (late percussion)	3 (1.6%)	3 (1.9%)
Type 4 (pressure)	16 (8.3%)	13 (8.4%)
Type 5 (pressure, flake blank)	8 (4.2%)	22 (14.2%)
Indeterminate	2 (1.0%)	
Drills	3 (1.6%)	2 (1.3%)
Edge-modified flakes		
Abraded edges	114 (59.4%)	66 (42.6%)
Intentionally retouched edges	18 (9.4%)	8 (5.2%)
Abrasion and retouch on edges	11 (5.7%)	14 (9.0%)
Gravers	1 (0.5%)	
Projectile points	15 (7.8%)	26 (16.8%)
Total	192	155

assemblages indicated that production of bifacial tools was the focus of most manufacturing activity (see table 3), with the flaking debris often scavenged for use as expedient tools. That is, flakes were probably not made expressly for use as such tools, but were simply useful byproducts of biface and projectile-point manufacture. Both percussion reduction and final pressure thinning and shaping of bifaces were carried out. In addition, cores were sometimes reduced. Fist-sized granite hammerstones found at both sites were used for flaked stone tool production.

Thus, the lithic assemblages and other village features—such as the presence of mortars—indicated that manufacturing and processing activities were conducted at these sites. These observations were consistent with domestic use in residential settings. In addition, since the same types of tools were used and were present in roughly equivalent proportions at each village, the types of activities carried out at these locales were probably very similar as well. There was little difference between domestic activities undertaken at villages prior to and following colonial-era depopulation. This conclusion was further supported by more detailed data for particular artifact types within these broad flaked stone tool classes. For example, biface types indicative of various stages in the tool production process were present in similar proportions

TABLE 3.
Proportional Representation of Debitage by Technological Type
and Reduction Stage at Hol'-low and He-le'-jah

	Hol'-low				He-le'-jah			
Technology/Reduction Stage	Obsidian	Chert	Basalt	Quartz	Obsidian	Chert	Basalt	Quartz
Early core percussion	1 (0.0%)		6 (12.2%)		2 (0.1%)	2 (5.3%)		
Late core percussion	30 (0.6%)		5 (10.2%)		20 (1.3%)			
Indeterminate core percussion	12 (0.2%)		4 (8.2%)	5 (26.3%)	7 (0.5%)	1 (2.6%)		
Early blade percussion	3 (0.0%)				4 (0.3%)			
Late blade percussion	6 (0.1%)				5 (0.3%)			
Early biface percussion	338 (6.9%)	1 (1.4%)	1 (2.0%)	2 (10.5%)	186 (12.1%)	5 (13.2%)		
Late biface percussion	414 (8.4%)	3 (4.3%)	4 (8.2%)		219 (14.3%)	2 (5.3%)		
Indeterminate biface percussion	827 (16.9%)	1 (1.4%)	8 (16.3%)		210 (13.7%)	2 (5.3%)		1 (15.5%)
Late uniface percussion					5 (0.3%)			
Early biface pressure	1625 (33.1%)	27 (38.6%)			509 (33.2%)	12 (31.6%)		
Late biface pressure	663 (13.5%)	24 (34.3%)			75 (4.9%)	8 (21.1%)		
Indeterminate pressure	34 (0.7%)	1 (1.4%)			5 (0.3%)	1 (2.6%)		
Indeterminate percussion	425 (8.7%)	8 (11.4%)	20 (40.8%)	11 (57.9%)	170 (11.1%)	4 (10.5%)	4 (100%)	6 (75.0%)
Bipolar	2 (0.0%)		1 (2.0%)		22 (1.4%)			
Undetermined	527 (10.7%)	5 (7.1%)		1 (5.3%)	94 (6.2%)	1 (2.6%)		1 (12.5%)
Total	4907	70	49	19	1533	38	4	8

(see table 2). Pressure-flaked bifaces that reflected the final stages of tool manufacture were most common, and this was consistent with the prevalence of biface pressure flakes in the debitage assemblages. The relative representation of pressure-flaked bifaces made on flake blanks (Type 5 bifaces) constituted the only major difference between the villages for this particular class of tools. More of these specimens were present at He-le'-jah than at Hol'-low. Rather than representing a distinction in tool function and site activities, this likely indicated less complete pressure reduction of the bifaces at He-le'-jah, with the relict flake scar of the parent piece still visible. In contrast, more complete pressure thinning resulted in pressure-flaked bifaces (Type 4) common at Hol'-low. Many of the pressure-flaked bifaces at these two sites appear to be projectile points broken during manufacture.

The only distinction in activities carried out by the occupants of these two villages was indicated by use-wear on edge-modified flakes, and this was a subtle difference. Some of these tools had edge rounding that reflected the processing of soft materials. Others exhibited step flaking along the working edge, since they were used on hard materials. A few tools had both stepping and rounding (see table 4). Tools with step flaking, rounding, or both were much more common at Hol'-low than at He-le'-jah, and those with rounded working edges were especially prevalent at the older village. In contrast, the tools at He-le'-jah rarely exhibited use-wear. Thus, use of edge-modified flakes sufficient to create such wear was more common at Hol'-low. Since both types of wear occurred in nearly equal proportions at this site, both hard and soft materials were commonly worked by the villagers. And edge-modified flakes with only abrasion or intentional retouch—but not both—were also more prevalent at Hol'-low (see table 2). Thus, all of these observations suggested that any given tool was primarily used for just one task rather than a variety of tasks at Hol'-low, and that these tools were used more exhaustively than at He-le'-jah. Coupled with the presence of finely shaped drills and a graver, the use-wear on (see table 4) and modification of (see table 2) the edge-modified flakes at the older village suggested that people undertook more diverse and intensive processing activities here. The tool assemblage from He-le'-jah also included bone tools such as awl tips and a spatulate utensil, however, and this hinted at more diverse activities at this later site than indicated by flaked stone tools alone.

The paucity of well-worn edge-modified flakes used for specific processing tasks at He-le'-jah (see table 4) could relate to decreasing diversity

TABLE 4.
Frequency of Use-wear on Edge-modified Flake (EMF)
Tools at Hol'-low and He-le'-jah

Use-wear	Hol'-low	He-le'-jah
Rounding	30 (21.0%)	2 (2.3%)
Stepping	31 (21.7%)	9 (10.2%)
Rounding and stepping	7 (4.9%)	3 (3.4%)
None	75 (52.4%)	74 (84.1%)
Total	143	88

in material culture or despecialization. In the latter case, such a pattern might indicate that the items produced with such tools were no longer required for either local use or exchange. Or, if due to decreasing diversity, artisans responsible for using edge-modified flakes may not have survived to pass on their knowledge of products or production methods to the succeeding generation. Conversely, the introduction of different processing techniques through intermarriage could also account for such a shift in tool representation, with implements other than stone tools used for these tasks. It was difficult to attribute such distinctions in edge-modified flake traits to a specific cause, since similar data on use-wear from previous studies in Yosemite and surrounding regions were lacking. In fact, the low frequency of edge-modified flakes with clear use-wear at He-le'-jah could have been due to factors unrelated to the range of activities undertaken. For example, people may have had access to at least some metal tools by the time the village was occupied, and this could have resulted in less reliance on expedient flake tools for processing tasks. Or access to textiles may have reduced the need to process skins, and this might account for the presence of very few edge-modified flakes with rounding. If either of these hypotheses is correct, fewer edge-modified flakes would exhibit wear indicative of prolonged tool use, and this class would be less prevalent in the assemblage as a whole. In contrast, native access to nonnative weaponry was probably limited, and therefore the greater representation of projectile points and pressure-flaked bifaces at He-le'-jah than Hol'-low may reflect the continued need to manufacture and use these traditional tools for defense and the procurement of game. So, although distinctions in the flaked stone tool assemblages between these two sites might reflect some shift in practices related to creolization or despecialization, the evidence could instead reflect access to nonnative materials such as metal and textiles. Therefore, shifts could be due to external relations rather than population-related phenomenon specific to Yosemite Valley. Such differences could also be related to the duration of habitation or the importance of tasks given the season of occupation or gender of occupants.

Artifacts other than flaked stone tools also indicated potential creolization or changes in daily practices. For example, the use of milling slicks in addition to mortars could be a late phenomenon related to the blending of different vegetal food-processing technologies through intermarriage (cf. Haney 1992). This was suggested, in part, by the prevalence of such features in Yosemite Valley and areas to the north inhabited by the descendants of the Awahnichi (see Hull, Roper et al. 1999). Such features were rare or absent to the south of Yosemite Valley. Since Mono Paiute people of the eastern Sierra never abandoned the use of handstones and millingstones in favor of mortar technology for processing seeds (e.g., Arkush 1995), Awahnichi intermarriage with Mono Paiute people could have resulted in the continued reliance on milling rather than pounding technology in the multiethnic households of Yosemite Indians. The presence of suitable bedrock outcrops for milling slicks, however, may have obviated the use of portable millingstones typical on the eastern side of the Sierra (cf. Haney 1992). The potential for greater change in female rather than male practices after disease-induced depopulation in Yosemite Valley—due to intermarriage of Awahnichi men and Mono Paiute women and patrilocality—could be indicated by this pattern and, perhaps, by the differences in edge-modified flake use-wear. Due to the difficulty of dating stationary milling features, this possibility could not be explored in detail. But a cursory review of regional archaeological site information indicated that milling slicks were present at a number of sites in Yosemite Valley, including Hol'-low (Hull and Kelly 1995). In fact, nearly 54 percent of such features occurred at archaeological sites linked to ethnographic villages (see Hull and Kelly 1995), and an additional 18 percent were located at a village site occupied after 1930 (Hull and Kelly 1995:50). These observations suggested predominant use of milling slicks in colonial and postcolonial contexts, likely as a result of demographic changes. Several small boulder features with single milling slicks also occurred within rockshelters, and such shelters were commonly used as dwellings during the colonial era (see "Regional Settlement" below).

The use of pumice handstones by Yosemite Indians may also have been a colonial-era or postcolonial practice related to milling rather than pounding of vegetal foods in multiethnic households. Pumice abraders were found in deposits postdating A.D. 1100 in the Mono Basin (Arkush 1995), and a pumice handstone was recovered from the northern area of the village of Soo-sem'-moo-lah in the central portion of Yosemite Valley (Hull and Kelly 1995:32).[3] Although this site was probably not occupied when the Mariposa Battalion arrived, it was the location of the Indian village throughout much of the subsequent three decades and may also have been occupied earlier. The only other pumice milling implement recovered in the Yosemite region was geochemically identified as deriving from Mono Craters (Mundy 1992:87). As this geologic source only formed six hundred years ago, this tool was also relatively recent. These observations suggested that pumice milling tools may have been introduced into Yosemite Indian households through intermarriage with women of the eastern Sierra.

In contrast, certain implements that might be expected in the case of intermarriage with Mono Paiute people in the wake of disease were notably absent from these two villages and other sites in Yosemite Valley. No native brownware ceramics were used by the occupants of either site, despite the fact that such vessels were used at the same time and somewhat earlier by Paiute people living on the east side of the Sierra Nevada (Weaver 1986). Arkush (1995) observed brownware sherds in protohistoric and Late Archaic contexts in the Mono Basin (i.e., circa A.D. 500–1800). These ceramic vessels were manufactured farther south in the Owens Valley (e.g., Eerkens et al. 1999), however, and were not as common in areas to the north (Weaver 1986). Ceramic vessels never enjoyed acceptance in the Yosemite area, as only one ceramic sherd has ever been found in this region (Fitzwater 1962:246). Since brownware vessels were not an item of local manufacture within the Mono Basin, it may not be surprising that intermarriage of Awahnichi and Mono Paiute failed to introduce these objects into Yosemite Valley.

Finally, although issues of preservation undermined comparison of game procurement practices, processing, and consumption by the occupants of these two villages, some general observations were possible. The combination of faunal remains and organic residue results from Hol'-low indicated exploitation of deer, rabbit, canid (i.e., dog or coyote), porcupine, and bear by the residents. Only two of these species—porcupine and rabbit—were clearly indicated by faunal remains (see table 5), and the absence of organic residues on projectile points failed to link any

TABLE 5.
Types of Faunal Remains Recovered at Hol'-low and He-le'-jah

Common Name or Description	Identification	Hol'-low	He-le'-jah
Horse	*Equus* sp.		1 (0.1%)
Black-tailed deer	*Odocoileus hemionus*		2 (0.2%)
Unknown deer	*Odocoileus* sp.		1 (0.1%)
Deer size	Order Artiodactyla (family indeterminate)	1 (0.6%)	2 (0.2%)
Deer/pronghorn size	Medium artiodactyl		7 (0.8%)
Coyote, dog, wolf	Family *Canidae* (genus indeterminate)		13 (1.5%)
Coyote, dog, wolf size	*Canis* sp.		3 (0.3%)
Porcupine	*Erethizon dorsatum*	11 (7.0%)	
Raccoon size	Order Carnivora (family indeterminate)		2 (0.2%)
California or black-tailed jackrabbit	*Lepus californicus*		1 (0.1%)
Jackrabbit/hare	*Lepus* sp.	1 (0.6%)	2 (0.2%)
Douglas squirrel	*Tamiascurius douglasii*		2 (0.2%)
California ground squirrel	*Spermophilus beecheyi*		11 (1.2%)
Western gray squirrel	*Sciurus griseus*		5 (0.6%)
Unknown squirrel	*Sciurus* sp.		1 (0.1%)
Deer mouse	*Peromyscus maniculatus*		1 (0.1%)
Elk, horse size	Very large mammal		1 (0.1%)
Deer size	Large mammal	6 (3.8%)	97 (10.9%)

Deer to dog size	Medium-large mammal	6 (3.8%)	215 (24.2%)
Canid size	Medium mammal	8 (5.1%)	156 (17.5%)
Rabbit size	Small-medium mammal	3 (1.9%)	41 (4.6%)
Small rabbit/rat size	Small mammal	10 (6.3%)	111 (12.5%)
Pocket mouse size	Micro mammal	10 (6.3%)	
	Indeterminate mammal		40 (4.5%)
	Medium-large bird		2 (0.2%)
Large perching birds	Medium bird		5 (0.6%)
Perching birds	Small-medium bird		5 (0.6%)
Small perching bird	Small bird	2 (1.3%)	34 (3.8%)
Rat/gopher size	Medium rodent	1 (0.6%)	8 (0.9%)
Mouse size	Small rodent		13 (1.5%)
Rats, mice, gophers	Rodent (family indeterminate)		4 (0.5%)
Lizards, snakes	Order Squamata (suborder indeterminate)		1 (0.1%)
Suckers, minnows	Order Cypriniformes (family indeterminate)		1 (0.1%)
	Medium fish		14 (1.6%)
	Small fish		1 (0.1%)
	Fish (order indeterminate)		3 (0.3%)
	Indeterminate vertebrate	99 (62.7%)	84 (9.4%)
Total		158	890

of the other species directly to procurement. Rather, the residue results associated many of these animals with processing tools rather than with implements used for procurement or consumption. For example, deer and rabbit residue were identified on drills, suggesting modification of skins for clothing or other use rather than simply butchery of the animal. The same functional associations may have pertained to the numerous edge-modified flakes with positive residue results. Therefore, the introduction of organic residue data was not directly equivalent to inferences based on faunal assemblages, although use of such animals for subsistence was likely. The faunal assemblage from He-le'-jah indicated that diverse mammal species were consumed, including deer, canid, rabbit, horse, and squirrel (see table 5). Birds and fish were also eaten. Numerous fragmentary faunal remains—too incomplete for identification to family, genus, or species—also underscored the importance of mammals of various sizes in the diet of residents of both Hol'-low and He-le'-jah. Small-to-medium sized mammals were most evident in the sample from the older site, and use of large mammals appeared more common at He-le'-jah. Perhaps the availability of large mammals increased after human decimation from disease, or perhaps smaller human populations allowed for narrower diet breadth and focus on more efficient hunting of large mammals.

Consumption of horse and squirrel by the residents of He-le'-jah was distinct, but exploitation of horse was clearly related to availability rather than cultural shifts deriving from depopulation. The presence of squirrel at He-le'-jah and absence of such remains from Hol'-low, on the other hand, could simply be due to differential preservation of these small bones in the two deposits. Finally, the absence of evidence for bear at He-le'-jah—which was indicated by residue results from Hol'-low—could be due to season of occupation. Dental increment analysis of a deer tooth from He-le'-jah indicated that the rockshelter was probably occupied, at least in part, during the late winter, since that animal was killed sometime between February and April. Bears would be in hibernation at this time. All of these observations suggested that differences between the faunal assemblages at the two villages could be due to preservation of faunal bone and other noncultural factors, rather than relating to differences in the diet of Indian people in pre- and postdepopulation times. Unfortunately, the poor quality of faunal remains at Hol'-low precluded consideration of potential differences in processing or consumption of game that could reflect subsistence preferences of people with different cultural traditions.

DOMESTIC ACTIVITY AROUND THE HEARTH

The hearths at Hol'-low and He-le'-jah were well-defined concentrations of ash, charcoal, and discolored soil. At Hol'-low, this feature consisted of charcoal, very dark grayish brown soil mottled with gray ash, some scattered fire-affected granite cobbles and decomposing granite sand that derived from additional fire-affected rock, and an underlying compact, baked sediment. Located between 7 to 17 centimeters in depth within the deposit, this hearth measured approximately 100 by 60 centimeters and was completely exposed through excavation. Radiocarbon assays of two charcoal samples collected from this feature—coupled with dendrochronological dating of the trees in the rockfall on this site—established the age of circa A.D. 1600 to 1620 for this hearth. A large portion of the hearth at He-le'-jah was exposed by the excavation trench. This feature consisted of a concentration of light gray ash and charcoal that was situated between 11 and 20 centimeters in depth. It measured an estimated 90 centimeters in diameter, including the unexcavated portion that extended about 15 centimeters west of the trench. Radiocarbon analysis of a charcoal sample and associated temporally diagnostic artifacts indicated that this hearth dated to circa A.D. 1820.

Comparison of the flaked stone tools recovered in the hearth areas at these two villages reinforced the distinctions evident in the complete site assemblages (see figure 10). That is, there was slightly greater emphasis on processing activities around the hearth at Hol'-low, in contrast to somewhat more focus on manufacturing and procurement tasks in the hearth area at He-le'-jah. But the same range of activities was undertaken around the hearths at both sites. There was also not much distinction between the flaked stone tool assemblages in the hearth and nonhearth areas within these villages. Only a slight contrast between these zones was noted at He-le'-jah, where debitage was much more dense in the hearth area than in the nonhearth area (Hull 2002:495). Debitage density was slightly greater in the hearth area than the nonhearth zone at Hol'-low as well, but this pattern was not as dramatic as that observed at He-le'-jah. The greater focus of manufacturing activity in the hearth area at the younger site might be due to the greater organization of space or need for light within the confines of the rockshelter as opposed to the open deposit at Hol'-low.

Isopleth maps (maps 5 and 6) based on excavation-unit artifact frequency also indicated the importance of hearths in defining the use

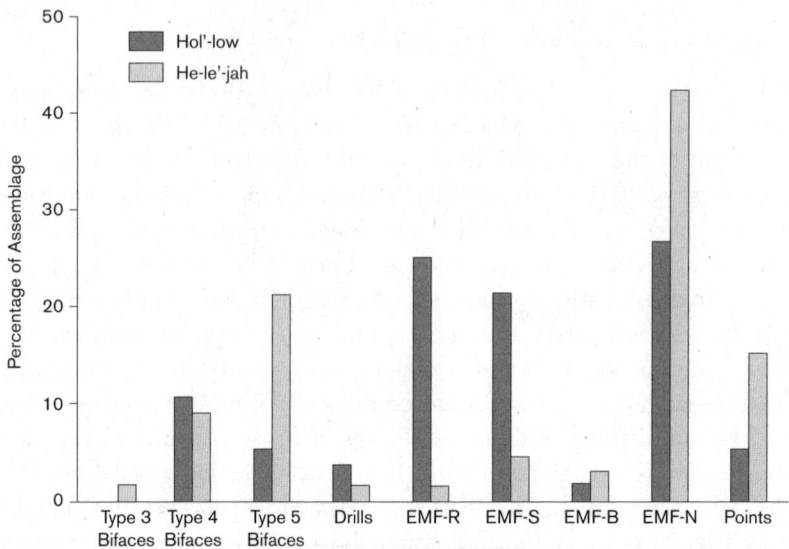

FIGURE 10. Comparison of flaked stone tool assemblages from the hearth areas at Hol'-low and He-le'-jah. EMF = edge-modified flake; EMF-R = rounding; EMF-S = stepping; EMF-B = both rounding and stepping; EMF-N = no use-wear.

of space at these two sites. At both Hol'-low and He-le'-jah, faunal remains, ornaments, and edge-modified flakes, in particular, clustered in these areas. Steatite beads, the only ornaments recovered at Hol'-low, were especially common directly south of the hearth at this site. Two lesser clusters of beads occurred 2 to 4 meters to the north. In contrast, the hearth area at He-le'-jah did not demonstrate an unusual propensity for ornamental objects, although there was a clear concentration of shell beads and ornaments and, to a lesser extent, bone beads in this area. Glass beads clustered here but also occurred in the rear of the rockshelter away from the hearth (see map 6). Steatite beads were found from the central portion of the rockshelter to the apron. Faunal remains clearly clustered in the hearth area at Hol'-low, and such debris was prevalent around the hearth and on the apron in front of the rockshelter at He-le'-jah. Bone awl tips were also common on the apron at the younger site. These patterns could relate to spatial separation between processing and consumption areas at He-le'-jah or, alternately, to the cleaning of the hearth area to remove excess debris within the confines of the rockshelter. Regardless of cause, similar patterns of multiple faunal concentrations were not evident at Hol'-low.

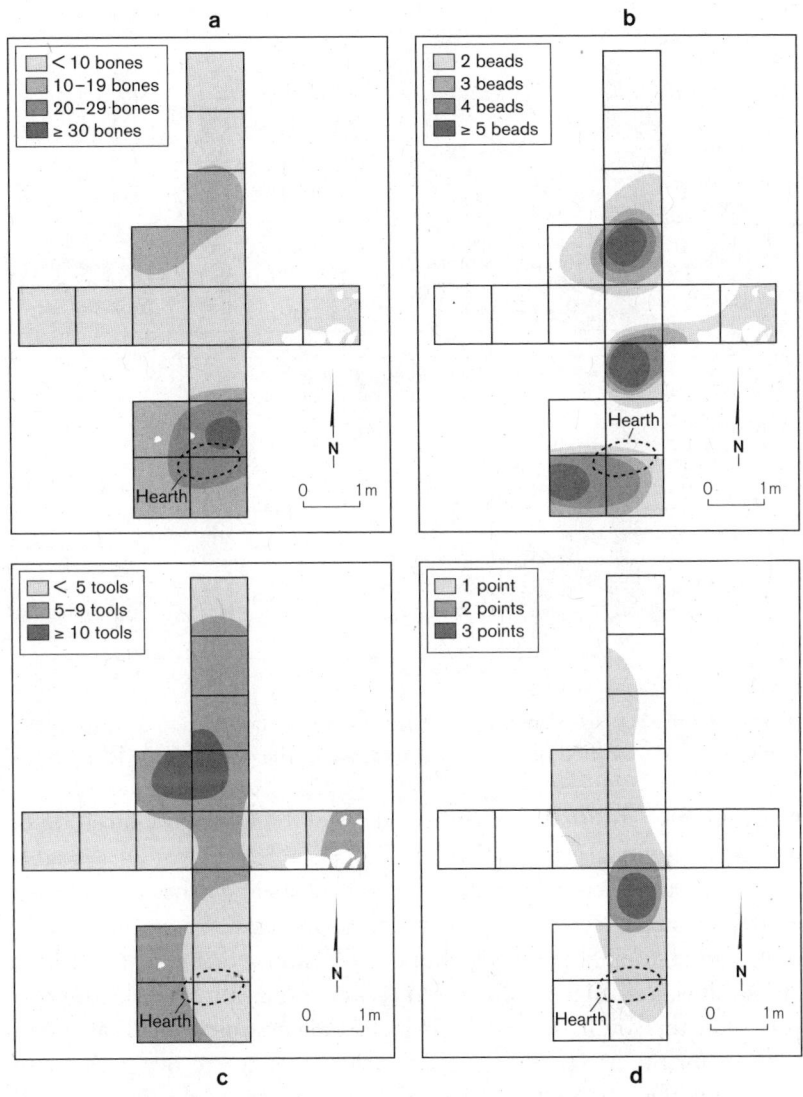

MAP 5. Isopleth maps depicting the density of: (a) faunal remains; (b) steatite beads; (c) edge-modified flake tools; and (d) projectile points at Hol'-low.

Therefore, different practices might be indicated. The apparent absence of disposal areas at Hol'-low, however, could also be due to the limited extent of excavation at this site and more expansive use of space in this open context.

Many tools within the hearth area at Hol'-low were recovered in

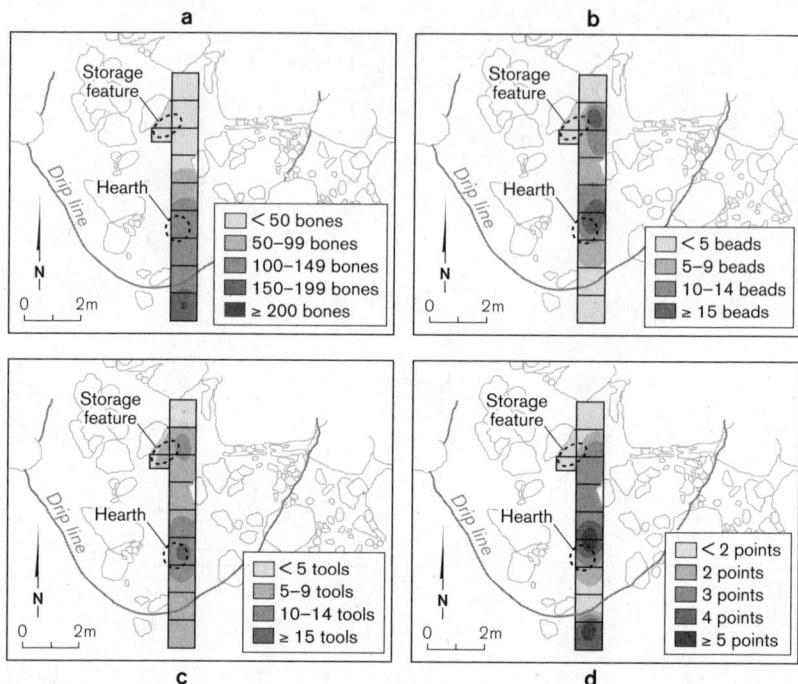

MAP 6. Isopleth maps depicting the density of: (a) faunal remains; (b) glass beads; (c) edge-modified flake tools; and (d) projectile points at He-le'-jah.

situ, and this permitted even finer analysis of the spatial organization of domestic activity around the hearth. Comparable data were unavailable for He-le'-jah, since the less compact sediments and other factors such as artifact size affected recovery of objects in place. A concentration of flaked stone tools was noted around the eastern portion of the hearth at Hol'-low, and edge-modified flakes were especially prevalent in this zone. On the south side of the hearth, flaked stone tools that tested positive for the presence of organic residues tended to occur closer to the feature than did tools that lacked such evidence of use. On the north side of the hearth, the reverse trend was observed. Rabbit residue was particularly well represented in this latter area, whereas edge-modified flakes with evidence of deer residue tended to occur south of the hearth. The two stone drills were located to the northwest of this feature, and I concluded that this might indicate the spatial segregation of the tasks undertaken with these tools. The presence of implements with residues from plants also suggested additional processing activities around the hearth at Hol'-low, if not elsewhere within the village. These results were less secure than those for faunal species, however, since two of the three species identified are not native to the region.

In light of these observations, hearths were clearly the centers of activity in both villages. Multiple tasks were performed either simultaneously or at different times around the hearth at Hol'-low, with diverse manufacturing, processing, and consumption tasks carried out. There was also some spatial segregation of different tasks. Despite the apparent level of activity, the space was not cleaned to remove faunal remains or other debris, although poor preservation of dietary bone and the limited excavation area may have undermined my ability to recognize such practices. That is, disposal areas at some distance from the hearth may have been used. In contrast, activities around the hearth at He-le'-jah were less diverse, and people focused especially on manufacturing flaked stone tools and consumption of game. Of course, possible cleaning within the rockshelter and dumping of debris on the apron may have distorted this view somewhat. Abundant faunal remains and debitage were present on the apron, however, and occurred in quantity comparable to that observed within proximity to the hearth.

These data indicated greater diversity in household practices in predepopulation times and therefore possible shifts in, or loss of, some activities through accident or choice after the colonial assault of disease. The small sample size and lack of comparative information for surrounding site areas, however, made such conclusions tenuous. This was particularly true since these villages might have been used in different seasons, as this would affect the type and scope of activities conducted, regardless of the era of occupation. Although dental increment analysis indicated occupation of He-le'-jah in the late winter or early spring, at least, the season of occupation for Hol'-low was unknown.

INDIVIDUAL SKILL IN FLAKED STONE TOOL PRODUCTION

Colonial-era native depopulation could have resulted in collective loss of knowledge or skill either due to choice or accident. Regardless of the specific processes involved, such shifts would be apparent in changing tool manufacture and use, and evidence for special products, skills, and particular proficiency might be absent in postdisease times. Such consequences are less germane to the day-to-day tasks evident at Hol'-low and He-le'-jah, since such routine skills were probably shared by multiple individuals within a household or group. In addition, any loss of skill in the long term seems unlikely, since many if not most Yosemite people emigrated to the eastern side of the Sierra where similar daily practices were unaffected by depopulation. Thus, practitioners would have been available to share technical knowledge with immigrants, as necessary. Still, practices may have differed somewhat from similar Awahnichi traditional ways. And despite the potential to reacquire knowledge and the apparent utilitarian nature of the tools involved, it could be that some objects—for example, projectile points—also had significance within other realms, such as the establishment and maintenance of cultural identity (see Shackley 2000 and references therein). In this case, greater investment in manufacturing of such items may have existed in predisease, or even postdisease, settings. Therefore, potential distinctions in apparent investment and skill were assessed even for tools related to mundane tasks.

Specialized implements used to manufacture more exclusive products that were most likely affected by depopulation—since knowledge of their manufacture may have been invested in only a few individuals—were absent from these sites. And it was necessary to limit analysis for those tools that were present to only locally produced items or the tools used to produce them. It was relatively easy to exclude some items—such as steatite beads—that almost certainly were manufactured elsewhere, given the lack of evidence for local production and the exotic raw material. The locus of production for other tools, such as projectile points, was more difficult to discern. Therefore, the focus was on evidence for differential skill and particular practices manifest in debitage and tool fragments that were clearly related to on-site manufacture. Other finished tools that might or might not have been produced at Hol'-low and He-le'-jah were considered secondarily.

Three specific technological traits of flaked stone tool manufacture were used as clues to the skill of the flintknappers and their investment in flaked stone tool production. I focused on the production of formed tools rather than expedient implements due to the relatively great representation of bifacial technology in the debitage samples from both sites. The first trait was the presence of transverse parallel pressure flakes. These are thin, parallel-sided, comma-shaped flakes that result from the production of fine, ribbon-flaked bifaces that require adept technical skill and knowledge to produce. The second characteristic I considered was the regularity of flake scar patterning on tools—the more regular the flake scars, the more time invested and skill involved in tool production. Nonpatterned flaking results from expedient and opportunistic reduction to derive the desired tool form. Collateral flake scars represent regular flake removals perpendicular to the long axis of the tool. Greatest investment and planning in tool production is indicated by oblique flake scars that extend across the face of a tool at a consistent, acute angle to the long axis, or by chevron flake scars that are oblique removals that meet at a right angle at the longitudinal axis of the biface. Finally, I examined tools and debitage for evidence of manufacturing errors. In this case, the presence of nonstrategic overshot flakes was used as one indicator of such mistakes. Overshot damage results when a biface thinning flake travels too far across the piece and removes a portion of the opposite edge. Sometimes, overshots are intentional, as they can be used to remove irregular masses or stepped areas on the biface surface. For the most part, however, these flakes indicate an error that may or may not have been overcome as production of the tool progressed. In some instances, the damaged area can be further worked to remove the overshot flaw, but in other cases, the tool is irreparably damaged and must be discarded. Perverse breaks also indicate a manufacturing error. This directional fracture from the tool edge generally indicates inappropriate force during pressure flaking or tool notching. Such damage is almost always fatal to use of the tool for its originally intended purpose and is especially common in pressure flaking and notching of projectile points. Thus, this trait served as another indicator of manufacturing skill.

Numerous small transverse parallel pressure flakes of obsidian were produced by the residents of Hol'-low. This type accounted for nearly 4 percent of the total obsidian debitage sample and 8 percent of the obsidian pressure flake collection. A few notching flakes were also observed and, together with the small size of the transverse parallel pressure flakes, these data indicated that the finely flaked small projectile points were probably produced. The flaking pattern on projectile points from this village confirmed this conclusion, as most of these tools exhibited both collateral and oblique flaking rather than unpatterned flaking or only collateral flaking. The oblique flaking likely resulted in the production of the transverse parallel pressure debitage. At least one Desert Side-Notched projectile point found at Hol'-low was an exceptionally well-made tool that exhibited fine flaking and remarkable symmetry in both plan view and profile. The abundance of transverse parallel pressure flakes relative to finished tools, however, indicated that many of the bifacial items produced were probably removed from the site. Pressure-flaked bifaces from Hol'-low exhibited much less precision and investment in manufacture than projectile points—perhaps because they were broken before production was finished. Pressure-flaked bifaces made on flake blanks had unpatterned flaking or simple edge modification, while the other pressure-flaked bifaces primarily exhibited collateral flaking. Two of these latter bifaces, however, had both oblique and collateral flaking, and two others exhibited ribbon flaking consistent with fine manufacturing techniques.

In contrast, the obsidian debitage assemblage from He-le'-jah contained only six transverse parallel pressure flakes. These flakes accounted for less than 1 percent of the obsidian debitage sample and only 1 percent of the obsidian pressure flake collection. Only half of these were small flakes indicative of final tool production, and this suggested relatively little investment in fine tool manufacture. This conclusion was further supported by the fact that most of the projectile points exhibited collateral rather than oblique flaking. Still, two of the projectile points exhibited chevron flaking—a trait indicative of exceptionally careful work and a feature not observed at Hol'-low. In addition, overshot damage on one of these tools clearly indicated manufacture or reworking on-site rather than importation of this finely worked piece from elsewhere. Therefore, there was more disparity in the investment in biface manufacture by the residents of the He-le'-jah, with either relatively rough or particularly fine flaking evident on individual tools. Similar to Hol'-low, most of the pressure-flaked bifaces were collaterally flaked, and only four of these tools exhibited oblique flaking.

Evidence for likely manufacturing errors at Hol'-low was limited to just three overshot flakes—one of which removed a point tang—and one perverse fracture on a pressure-flaked biface. Overshot flakes comprised less than 1 percent of the total obsidian debitage from this site, and the single biface accounted for only about 3 percent of the total biface collection. Although only six overshot flakes were observed at He-le'-jah, one Cottonwood Triangular projectile point exhibited overshot damage, two Desert Side-Notched points had perverse fractures, and six pressure-flaked bifaces had similar breaks, including four tools manufactured on flake blanks. Thus, more than 10 percent of the projectile points and more than 15 percent of the bifaces at He-le'-jah exhibited manufacturing errors. This suggested substantial production failures related to the knapping skill of the people living at this village. Thus, depopulation appears to have had a negative effect on flaked stone tool manufacturing skill. This may have been due to a decision to invest less time in tool production and the maintenance of skill, or it could have resulted from a stochastic loss of technical knowledge necessary for particularly successful manufacturing.

Other reasons unrelated to depopulation could also account for some of these observations. Transverse parallel pressure flaking, regular flake scar patterning, and manufacturing errors—as well as traits such as more extensive working of a tool indicated by invasive flaking and the absence of relict scars—are not due only to manufacturing skill. These practices can also be affected by the availability of raw material. Small parent pieces likely available in times of material shortage, for example, would have precluded more thorough working and fine ribbon flaking. Although the influence of this factor was not assessed quantitatively, evidence for bipolar reduction indicative of potential material shortages was recognized at He-le'-jah in particular. A bipolar break was observed on a biface fragment, two bifaces were manufactured on bipolar flakes, and one bipolar core and several bipolar flakes were present. Thus, material shortage likely contributed to some of the technological observations at He-le'-jah, especially manufacturing errors and flake scar patterning on bifaces. Manufacturing errors revealed by debitage were relatively rare at both sites, however, and this attested to the overall skill of the flintknappers. In light of such skill, lack of investment in fine tool finishing by the residents at He-le'-jah was either a conscious choice based on perceived needs or resulted from limitations imposed by the smaller size of the parent material available. On the other hand, differences between these two sites in the relative occurrence of manufacturing errors on tools were more pronounced. Therefore, shifts in degree of skill or technical knowledge are likely responsible. Unfortunately, lack of comparable studies for other, well-dated sites in Yosemite Valley—particularly single-component assemblages—made it impossible to determine whether differences were simply idiosyncratic and individual or if they were a depopulation-related phenomenon.

As noted above, technological analysis of finished tools with an eye to the potential loss of skill through choice or accident was more problematic, since such items may not have been locally produced. Still, the projectile points used by the site occupants revealed an interesting pattern. Nearly 15 percent of the Desert Side-Notched projectile points from He-le'-jah exhibited serrate edges (figure 11), but no such projectile points were found at Hol'-low. This observation prompted a review of regional archaeological literature, which demonstrated that serration of such points was a colonial-era phenomenon (Hull 2004). Serrate Desert series points have been found throughout the Yosemite

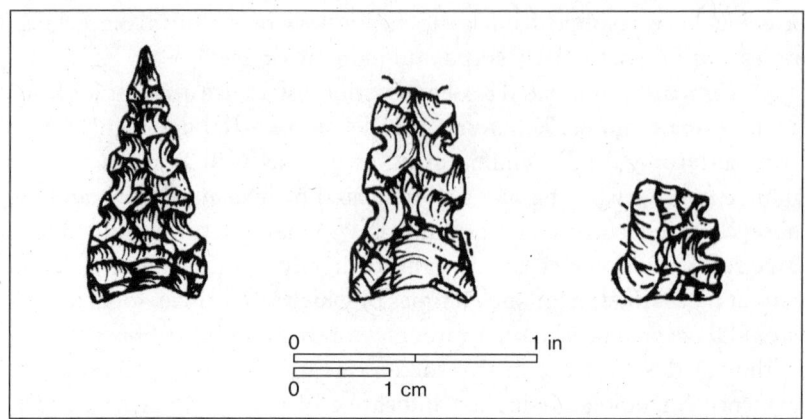

FIGURE 11. Serrate Desert Side-Notched projectile points from He-le'-jah.

region, often in association with glass beads or other artifacts indicating very late use. Serrate Desert Side-Notched points have also been found in late contexts near Mariposa and at Buchanan and Hidden reservoirs in the southern Sierra foothills. To the north, serrate Desert Side-Notched points have been recovered from villages on the lower Stanislaus River and include some made of bottle glass (Van Bueren 1983:106). Serration of Desert Side-Notched points was relatively rare east of the Sierra Nevada, and these points were notably absent from the colonial-era deposits in Mono Basin examined by Arkush (1995).

In light of these data, serration of Desert Side-Notched points was a colonial-era practice related to factors deriving from the west rather than east of Yosemite Valley. The geographic distribution—which extended from at least the lower Cosumnes River watershed on the north to the Fresno River on the south—was generally coincident with Central and Southern Me'-wuk traditional territory, although the northernmost zone was within Plains Miwok territory (Hull 2004; see map 3). This latter zone was also the area to which Indians in the missions of the San Francisco Bay area likely fled, however, and archaeological data from the San Joaquin delta indicate an earlier tradition of projectile-point serration just to the west (e.g., Heizer 1941; Moratto 1984). Leaf-shaped, stemmed, and corner-notched varieties of Stockton Serrate projectile points were the primary forms produced by people of the San Joaquin delta from at least A.D. 700 to 1690. In contrast, from circa A.D. 1350 until the historical period, unserrated Desert Side-Notched and Cottonwood Triangular points were used by people of the central and southern Sierra as well as by Indians of the Great Basin. Serrate Desert Side-Notched points limited to colonial-era contexts in the central Sierra Nevada reflect a blending of projectile-point traditions of delta people with those of the mountains—that is, serration traditionally used with Stockton Serrate points was transferred onto Desert Side-Notched points. Given likely population displacements and demographic responses to colonialism, this practice may have resulted from Awahnichi intermarriage with or exposure to individuals fleeing from Spanish domination. The fact that chevron flaking was also observed only on points from He-le'-jah may indicate that this manufacturing feature was an additional tendency in tool production of westerners at that time. Data examined were insufficient to determine whether serration of Desert series points slightly predated, or was coincident with, colonial-era population movements in the Central Valley. If the latter case, then the cultural identity of the residents of He-le'-jah is somewhat uncertain. And this has potential implications for assessing the degree of—and causes for—change in pre- and postdepopulation technical knowledge and skill observed within Yosemite Valley. In addition, colonial-era influence or immigration from the west could have a bearing on the presence of a breccia mortar and nonnative goods at He-le'-jah (see "Regional Interaction and External Relations" below).

REGIONAL INTERACTION AND EXTERNAL RELATIONS

Geochemical study of obsidian tools and debris has been used for more than twenty-five years to address regional interaction and external relations in the Yosemite area, particularly with respect to interaction with people of the eastern side of the Sierra where this material originated (Hull and Roper 1999). However, random sampling of debitage for geochemical analysis—the practice most useful to such studies—has only been incorporated into research designs relatively recently in Yosemite. And site- rather than component-specific sampling has been the norm, even when random sampling has been undertaken, because mixing of deposits is common. Such practices in prior work hampered a diachronic view of obsidian use in the current study, but geochemical analysis of a random sample of debitage from Hol'-low and He-le'-jah provided baseline data for the most recent past. In fact, these samples encompassed all of the debitage of sufficient size for X-ray fluorescence analysis from the hearth areas. These geochemical data were augmented by visual characterization of the entire obsidian debitage and tool assemblage based on translucency. This technique has been used with success in previous studies in Yosemite Valley, although such methods describe general tendencies rather than rigidly bounded types (see Hull and Roper 1999:303). In general, opaque material tends to derive from the Casa Diablo quarries, which encompass the Lookout Mountain, Sawmill Ridge, and Prospect Ridge subsources (see map 4). Semitranslucent obsidian is common to the Bodie Hills source, and material from Queen (Truman Meadows) and Mount Hicks are usually translucent. Some Bodie Hills glass can be opaque or translucent, however, and some obsidian from Queen and Mount Hicks can be semitranslucent. In addition, Mono Craters and Mono Glass Mountain material may be opaque or semitranslucent (Hull and Roper 1999:303). And visual ascription of any source becomes more problematic as debitage size decreases, since even opaque obsidian flakes may be thin enough to pass light.

Geochemical analysis revealed that flintknappers working around the hearth at Hol'-low were primarily using Mono Craters obsidian, although material from Casa Diablo (Lookout Mountain), Bodie Hills, and Queen were also reduced (see table 6). The dominance of opaque material most typical of the Casa Diablo source in the total obsidian debitage sample, however, suggested that Mono Craters obsidian may have been somewhat better represented in the geochemical sample than in the site assemblage as a whole. Such representation could result if Mono Craters obsidian was more prevalent in the larger size classes suitable for X-ray fluorescence analysis or if it was more common around the hearth than across the entire site. At He-le'-jah, on the other hand, obsidian geochemistry revealed that Casa Diablo (Lookout Mountain) glass dominated the debitage sample from the hearth area, although Mono Craters obsidian was also prevalent. The remainder of the sample included material from Bodie Hills, Queen, and Mount Hicks. Again, possible discrepancy between the visual and geochemical results due to lithic tool-production technology or intrasite distribution was indicated, since semitranslucent obsidian accounted for the bulk of the debitage from He-le'-jah.

Although the differential representation of Casa Diablo and Mono Craters obsidian was the most obvious contrast between these two villages, these data were most striking in the distinction of both sites from many previous assemblages studied. Geochemical data for other sites in Yosemite Valley indicated that Casa Diablo rather than Mono Craters obsidian was the primary material used by the people living in this area

TABLE 6.
Proportional Representation of Obsidian
Source Materials in Debitage Samples
from Hol'-low and He-le'-jah (%)

Obsidian Source	Hol'-low	He-le'-jah
Casa Diablo	20.0	47.6
Bodie Hills	13.3	14.3
Queen (Truman Meadows)	6.7	4.8
Mono Craters	53.3	28.5
Mount Hicks		4.8
Unknown	6.7	

(Hull and Roper 1999: figure 9.5). The unusually high proportion of Mono Craters obsidian at both Hol'-low and He-le'-jah, then, suggested a temporal trend not previously identified in the region. And a similar pattern was indicated by Arkush's (1995) research at sites in the Mono Basin that postdated A.D. 1100. In fact, closer inspection of other existing geochemical data from Yosemite Valley and elsewhere within the region—including information for temporally diagnostic artifacts such as projectile points and flakes dated by obsidian hydration analysis—also supported relatively intensive exploitation of this source late in time (Hull 2002; Hull and Roper 1999; see also Brady 2006). In one sense, these results were not surprising, since high-quality Mono Craters obsidian was only available after formation of Panum Dome circa A.D. 1395. The significance of abundant Mono Craters glass at both Hol'-low and He-le'-jah is that this volcanic activity in the Mono Basin prompted a major realignment in the geography of obsidian procurement within approximately two hundred years, presumably because material was equal in quality to that of Casa Diablo, the next closest source. The slightly closer proximity of Mono Craters to Yosemite Valley prompted people to shift their obsidian procurement to that quarry.

Regular exploitation of this source both pre- and postdated the introduction of disease into Yosemite Valley and depopulation, so the shift to Mono Craters glass could not be linked to this demographic event and potential changing external relationships deriving therefrom. On the contrary, the significant feature here was the general consistency between Hol'-low and He-le'-jah in this regard as well as in the representation of lesser source materials. This suggested that access to these eastern Sierra obsidian sources or acquisition of finished tools from people controlling these sources was not affected by depopulation. Rather, the prevalence of Mono Craters obsidian relative to Casa Diablo was related to the availability of higher-quality glass from this closer quarry in the relatively recent past (see Hughes 1989:4). Both Yosemite and Mono Basin data suggested particular use in the last five hundred years. The use of pumice handstones—probably made from material from this source area—may also be related to the availability of this stone after the most recent eruption of Mono Craters, or this could be due to the introduction of new milling technology due to intermarriage (see "Daily Life within the Village" above).

Still, there were some differences in obsidian acquisition between the pre- and postdepopulation occupations that manifested themselves in the debitage technological data. In particular, bipolar reduction constituted a rare, but potentially significant, practice at He-le'-jah and was evident in both tools and debitage. This technique reflected exhaustive use likely related to material shortage and scavenging of available tools and debitage for production of new implements. The use of bipolar reduction by the residents of He-le'-jah indicated that access to exotic materials, including obsidian, was limited. Although this may have been caused by depopulation and realignment of external relations, it was difficult to imagine this as a factor affecting acquisition of materials from the east. Mono Craters is located only 60 kilometers east of Yosemite Valley and was readily accessible via Mono Pass (see map 4). In fact, given such proximity, procurement may have been direct rather than through exchange. If exchange was required, however, material shortages after depopulation could have resulted if Yosemite residents were unable to provide suitable items in exchange. Such inability might have resulted from a reorganization or loss of domestic labor. Alternatively, it could be that residents of He-le'-jah maintained stronger ties to the west rather than the east, as suggested by the presence of serrate Desert Side-Notched points. In this case, ability to acquire goods from the east such as obsidian could have been undermined. This seemed unlikely, however, given native oral tradition on intermarriage with people in Mono Basin. Instead, the simplest explanation for material shortage evident at He-le'-jah was environmental rather than cultural. That is, material shortage was simply due to occupation during the late winter. In this circumstance, trans-Sierra travel to access obsidian sources in the Mono Basin or Long Valley would have been difficult and necessitated scavenging for artifact production.

This could account for the slightly greater prevalence of Casa Diablo obsidian, which would have been readily available for scavenging from numerous sites within Yosemite Valley.

With respect to external relationships to the west, the presence of nonnative implements was a good indicator of the existence of such ties. Access to these items by Yosemite Indians prior to 1830 was only possible through native interaction rather than nonnative contacts or "acculturation." Small blanket and clothing fragments were found at He-le'-jah, as were a ceramic pipe bowl fragment, a hook garment closure, a needle, five cut nails, and iron fragments.[4] In addition, axe-cut cedar bark used for a storage feature and other cut wood noted in previous work at the site clearly indicated access to metal tools by the residents. By far the most common and least equivocal indicators of continuing contacts and interaction with people to the west were glass beads. More than seventy of these beads were recovered at He-le'-jah, and similar specimens have been found at other sites in Yosemite Valley and the greater Yosemite area (see Gassaway 2005; Hull 2000). Glass beads may have been acquired individually, as lots, or attached to objects such as baskets, skirts, hairnets, or flicker-feather headbands. Most of the glass beads were nontubular monochrome drawn beads (Class II) of various colors, although nontubular polychrome drawn beads (Class IV), tubular monochrome drawn beads (Class I), and plain monochrome mold-pressed beads (Class MPI and MPII) of various colors were also present.[5]

Arkush (1993) argued that glass beads were likely acquired by native people of the western and eastern Sierra through exchange with Yokuts traders from the Central Valley. Although difficult to establish archaeologically, this conclusion seems reasonable given the distance of Sierra people from Spanish colonial outposts and the low potential to interact with nonnative peoples penetrating the interior due to the sporadic and often hostile nature of such incursions. Travel to the coast to acquire such items directly was also unlikely, given the threat of the missions and the involvement of interior Indians in horse theft in the Central Valley. The recovery of a horse tooth—and, perhaps, horse bones in the form of remains identified only as "very large mammal"—indicated that livestock was brought into Yosemite Valley "on the hoof" in the 1820s, perhaps via trading partners to the west. The presence of shell beads and ornaments also revealed the maintenance of traditional trading relationships to the west, although such items at He-le'-jah might represent heirlooms. These ornaments included eight *Olivella* beads of types H1a, H1a or J, H1b or H2, G1, and K1, as well a small clamshell disk bead and *Haliotis* ornament fragments.[6]

If the nonnative objects were indeed acquired from native traders, the residents of He-le'-jah maintained relatively robust external contacts with the people to the west, despite new challenges faced by the occupants of the Central Valley, including their own demographic crises. Clearly, new items were added to the inventory—if glass beads were not attached to the primary objects of exchange—and trade in other items such as shell beads may have declined. Exchange endured, and the residents of Yosemite Valley were evidently capable of providing suitable items in return when necessary. Such continuity suggested that the temporary exodus to the eastern side of the Sierra was not sufficiently disruptive or enduring to dissolve relations with people to the west or to prevent reestablishment of such ties after return to the west side of the mountains. The immediate predepopulation context of exchange with the west could not be adequately assessed with data from Hol'-low because the perishable shell beads that were likely important items of trade were absent. But this aspect of regional interaction apparently continued much as it had prior to Awahnichi demographic collapse despite the turmoil of the late 1700s and early 1800s. It was unclear, however, whether the same was true later in time when people in the Central Valley evidently sustained their own particularly calamitous population collapse in the early 1830s (Cook 1955).

Continuity in external relations with people to the west, however, may be somewhat less secure than it might appear. The presence of serrate Desert Side-Notched points at He-le'-jah could indicate that residents were, in fact, westerners themselves. It may be that both beads and horses were acquired directly in the Central Valley and brought along during retreat into the Sierra by such westerners escaping colonial aggression. And the breccia mortar recovered from He-le'-jah in the 1950s (see Hull 2002:440) is also unusual for the Yosemite area and may indicate introduction of this tool from the west through population movements. Use of portable mortars was a practice common to people of the Central Valley but was not necessary in the Sierra Nevada where bedrock outcrops suitable for mortars were abundant. The influx of immigrants from the west after the Awahnichi returned to Yosemite Valley may have facilitated ongoing exchange with native people of the Central Valley. In this case, the potential influence of the temporary exodus of the Awahnichi to the east and elsewhere might not have been significant to postdepopulation relations. It was not possible to determine if archaeological observations reflected the presence of westerners or if they pertained to the reestablishment of old exchange patterns. The spatial organization of activities in both pre- and postdepopulation sites, however, indicated that the context of use for beads and beaded objects did not change. At both Hol'-low and He-le'-jah, such items were frequently, but not exclusively, used adjacent to hearths that served as the center of domestic activity. The distribution of shell beads, in particular, indicated a hearth emphasis at He-le'-jah, but the absence of such items at Hol'-low—likely due to poor preservation in the open deposit—precluded assessment of any shifts in meaning ascribed to such objects acquired through trade or the practices associated with them.

REGIONAL SETTLEMENT

Analysis of disease-induced settlement shifts that reflected emigration, aggregation, or potential loss of connection to place required data on the number, location, size, and function of sites that dated to both pre- and postdepopulation times. Obsidian hydration information and temporally diagnostic artifacts specific to the colonial era permitted this examination. With these temporal data, it was possible to explore changes in the duration of occupation at particular villages, reiterative site use, and the geography of pre- and postdepopulation settlement. In-depth analysis of site function was not undertaken, since a substantial regional diachronic database and detailed component-specific functional interpretations were unavailable. Still, general observations with respect to potential settlement function and changes in village life in the wake of disease were possible.

Obsidian hydration data not only confirmed Chief Tenaya's account of emigration and subsequent return to Yosemite Valley but also provided evidence of settlement aggregation in the recent past. The Awahnichi temporarily abandoned habitation in Yosemite Valley around A.D. 1790, moving to the eastern side of the Sierra and perhaps elsewhere. Relatively few, if any, sites were occupied in Yosemite Valley for about twenty years thereafter. Settlement aggregation upon return was indicated by the juxtaposition of the debitage and subsite population proxy measures. This analysis suggested that site-specific population density following depopulation was greater than that common throughout much of Yosemite native history and, to a lesser extent, even immediately prior to depopulation. This trend toward greater population density within villages was initiated at least 350 years prior to colonial-era depopulation. Therefore, this practice could have related to arrival of the Me'-wuk in the central Sierra Nevada or to some other phenomenon rather than being just a postdepopulation practice.

Settlement location and reiterative use were addressed with the random sample of subsites used in the demographic study. In this case, it was necessary to identify particular components at each site to assess reoccupation or establishment of new sites. Issues of obsidian hydration sampling, instrument measurement error, and variation of hydration band thickness around the mean due to increasing date error with age complicated this analysis. Following Hull, Hale, and colleagues (1998:107), I assumed "individual episodes of use would define a normal curve varying around the mean . . . [and] such mean peaks would emerge from . . . smoothed [data] . . . , which was essentially defined by partially overlapping normal curves of various components present." Still, occupational episodes represented by high frequencies of debitage could "swamp" components that preceded or followed them if these other episodes of use were relatively ephemeral—that is, some components might be overlooked. Maximum frequency "peaks" evident in site-specific hydration data were identified as components, with intervening "valleys" assumed to represent statistical noise or the absence of occupation. Each component peak was plotted as a "pulse" of site use, although individual occupations so represented likely varied in actual duration within the 50-year increment in which they fell. This analysis provided for assessment of potential shifts in the locus of use within Yosemite Valley through time.

Indian people engaged in episodic reuse of all of the sampled habitation sites within Yosemite Valley (figure 12). But no village sustained use for more than approximately 150 years at a time, and most were occupied for 50 years or less during any given episode. The minimum number of occupational episodes at any village was three, at Haw-kaw-koo'-e-tah (CA-MRP-79), but most sites witnessed at least six periods of habitation during the past 5,500 years. Several villages were occupied at any given time, and there were no geographic trends in preference for eastern, central, or western zones through time. Indian people occupied several villages between A.D. 1600 and 1750, immediately prior to colonial-era depopulation. These villages included use of the eastern portion of We'-sum-meh' (CA-MRP-70), the northern area of Kom'-pom-pa'-sah (CA-MRP-67), the western portion of Ah-wah'-ne (CA-MRP-196 EU14), the northeastern zone of Ah-wah'-ne (CA-MRP-56 EU8), and the

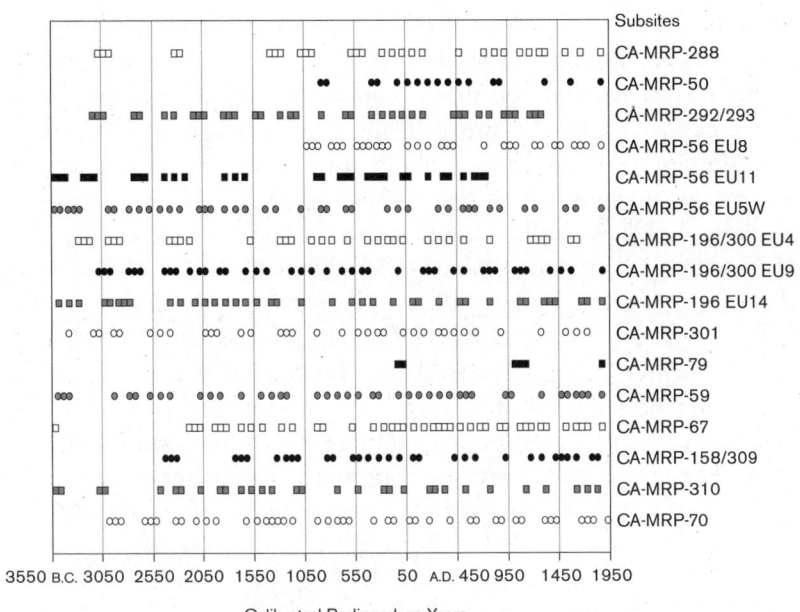

FIGURE 12. Subsite temporal components based on obsidian hydration dates.

southern portion of Koom-i-ne (CA-MRP-59).[7] Site CA-MRP-310 (no ethnographic name) also witnessed use at about this same time. In contrast, only one or two locales in the random sample, including the rockshelter at Aw'-o-koi-e (CA-MRP-158/309) and perhaps CA-MRP-310, revealed occupation between A.D. 1750 and 1800 in the immediate wake of depopulation. Colonial-era use of Aw'-o-koi-e also did not reflect reoccupation of a site occupied immediately prior to depopulation. The last prior use of this area dated between A.D. 1600 and 1650 or slightly earlier. As many as nine locales in the random sample—including Kom'-pom-pa'-sah (CA-MRP-67), the western and northeastern portions of Ah-wah'-ne (CA-MRP-196 EU14 and CA-MRP-56 EU8), and the southern portion of Koom-i-ne (CA-MRP-59)—were occupied at various times after A.D. 1850.

These data suggested that villages other than those occupied by Indian people at the time disease struck may have been inhabited upon initial reoccupation of Yosemite Valley. Still, such habitation occurred in areas that had been used at other times in the more distant past, so any postdepopulation trends might simply be idiosyncratic rather than intentional or due to a loss of connection to place. Extrapolation of these data for the entire valley suggested that at least six—and perhaps as many as twelve—villages were occupied upon initial permanent reoccupation of the valley.[8] It was difficult to assess site data with respect to expectations of aggregation in—or, in this case, reoccupation of—less marginal environments (see Dobyns 1983:311), since all sites witnessed complex use-histories. And such expectations were less germane to Yosemite Valley than to some other areas of North America, since the territory involved was small and all areas could be accessed easily within a two-hour walk of any village. Still, final population aggregation after A.D. 1850 tended to occur on sites that had witnessed the most sustained pulses of occupation in the more distant past. These may have been especially desirable locales, and thus Yosemite Indians may have preferred to inhabit these areas—if not immediately after reoccupation, then somewhat later. For example, the reiterative use of the western portion of Ah-wah'-ne (CA-MRP-196 EU14) over the last 5,500 years—an area that was also reoccupied in the early 1800s—suggested that it was a relatively desirable locale.

The obsidian hydration data for the random sample of subsites provided for extrapolation and inferences of number, location, and use-histories of villages for the entire valley. These data also contributed to assessment of postdepopulation settlement patterns in an even more concrete way when coupled with the distribution of glass beads. These observations filled out the picture of postdepopulation settlement and were also augmented by dendrochronological data on fire-scar frequency indicative of native burning and land use during this period. Milling slicks were considered as another potential indicator of postdepopulation occupation, but the use of these features may have persisted well past the time of nonnative incursion into the valley (see "Daily Life within the Village" above). Thus, use of slicks might track somewhat later settlement patterns as well. Since milling slicks—unlike certain types of glass beads—could not be confidently linked only to the colonial era, they were not incorporated into the settlement assessment. In contrast, glass beads of the types considered in this study were primarily used in California between A.D. 1770 and 1834. The frequency of beads in each deposit in Yosemite Valley was not relevant, as some sites were represented only by surface collection while others were subject to more extensive controlled excavation. Rather, the importance was with respect to site location and the types of features occurring at these sites. Glass beads have been found at nine sites in Yosemite

Valley, including Ah-wah'-ne, He-le'-jah, Ho-low (CA-MRP-82), Loi-ah (CA-MRP-92/H), the westernmost portion of Koom-i-ne (CA-MRP-163), CA-MRP-190/191 (no ethnographic name), Sap-pah'-sam-mah (CA-MRP-71), CA-MRP-55/H (no ethnographic name), and CA-MRP-902/H (no ethnographic name) (Gassaway 2005; Hull 2000; Elena Nilsson, personal communication 2006). The four glass beads from Ah-wah'-ne, however, represent two disparate subsite zones within the village area, both of which happened to be included in the hydration sampling undertaken for the demographic reconstruction.

Most of the sites with glass beads were located in the central to eastern portion of Yosemite Valley, where most of the archaeological sites identified as residential locales are situated. Only two sites with glass beads, Sap-pah'-sam-mah (CA-MRP-71) and CA-MRP-55/H, were located near the western end of the valley. Obsidian hydration data available for all of the locales except Loi-ah (CA-MRP-92/H), Sap-pah'-sam-mah (CA-MRP-71), and CA-MRP-55/H suggested that each had been subject to occupation at various times in the past.[9] In fact, the striking pattern that emerged from these data was not geographic tendencies within Yosemite Valley but rather that rockshelters were associated with many of these sites. Rockshelters were used at four of these villages[10]—He-le'-jah, Ho-low (CA-MRP-82), the westernmost portion of Koom-i-ne (CA-MRP-163), and CA-MRP-55/H—and the Mariposa Battalion found the old Indian woman still living in the rockshelter at Hol'-low. These locales account for approximately 17 percent of all such sites identified in Yosemite Valley, most of which have not been subject to archaeological study to determine their age. In addition, obsidian hydration data for Aw'-o-koi-e (CA-MRP-158/309) indicated that this village may have been used during the colonial era as well. In contrast, the remaining sites with glass beads lacked rockshelters and accounted for only 5 percent of open deposit sites in the valley. Coupled with the observation of basketry fragments at and apparent late use of the rockshelter at Hol'-low, these data suggested that there was a particular preference for the use of rockshelters in the wake of depopulation. This pattern might reflect a decision to minimize investment in architecture and construction, perhaps due to other demands on short labor. Or such a trend might indicate shorter duration of occupation, perhaps even representing sporadic use from afar between A.D. 1800 and 1820. Another alternative was that rockshelters were occupied by westerners seeking refuge in Yosemite Valley. Finally, if the data from He-le'-jah are representative, such use might reflect winter occupation. All of these scenarios were speculative, however, and could not be assessed with the available settlement data.

The final line of evidence bearing on settlement changes in the wake of depopulation comes from dendrochronology of fire scars on old- and intermediate-growth timber located in the western portion of Yosemite Valley (Gassaway 2005). Such blackened areas typically occur near the base of a tree if it has been exposed to flames insufficient to actually kill it. Therefore, the frequency of scars on a tree indicates the number of fires to which it has been exposed, including fires of both natural (e.g., lightening strikes) and cultural (e.g., Indian burning) origin. Counting the number of tree rings and location of scars within the sequence of rings establishes when each fire occurred. Study of nearly sixty trees revealed that fires were common in Yosemite Valley, but topography and fire history suggested that most if not all of these conflagrations were due to cultural rather natural causes such as lightening strikes. The valley is too deep for lightening strikes to routinely reach the valley floor, and no lightening-ignited fire has been recorded there since the 1930s; thus, Gassaway (2005) concluded that most of the scars resulted from fires intentionally set by native people. Given sampling methods and the likely loss of older trees to decay, this cultural activity was especially apparent after A.D. 1765 but was probably common in the more distant past as well (Anderson and Carpenter 1991). By the late 1800s, however, traditional Indian burning was terminated and fire suppression was instigated by the National Park Service.[11] In fact, the data suggested that fires may have been set nearly every year after A.D. 1800, and thus Gassaway (2005:112) concluded that Indians never ceased to inhabit the valley.[12] Since this conclusion is at odds with Reynolds's (1959) earlier dendrochronological work in Yosemite Valley as well as with the demographic reconstruction based on archaeology, another interpretation of the data may be more persuasive.

Many of the scar events that dated between A.D. 1798 and 1819 were marked by just one tree, rather than multiple trees, within the sampling units. And many of these single scars correspond to dendrochronological dates for initiation of the intermediate-age conifer stand identified by Reynolds (1959: table 12). Where multiple scars for any given date within this span were found, however, there were rarely corresponding intermediate-age growth starts (figure 13). Thus, these "spikes" of scar dates may represent the fires set by native people during this period, while the single dates may reflect isolated lightening strikes, insults other than fire, or noise in the data due to different methods used by

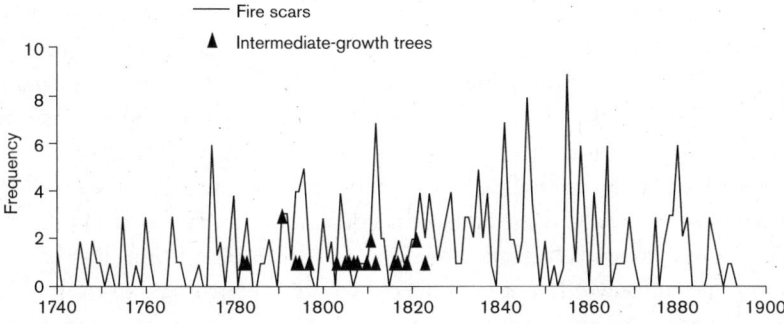

FIGURE 13. Comparison of fire-scar frequency and intermediate-age conifer-stand start dates.

the two analysts in Gassaway's (2005) study, the diverse conifer species sampled, or complacent microenvironments. And each "spike" within the entire period from A.D. 1765 to 1880 reflects a consistent season of ignition, underscoring their identity as events. These fires were set approximately every four to six years between A.D. 1820 and 1847. This same fire interval is evident from A.D. 1795 to 1804. In contrast, no major fires occurred between A.D. 1781 and 1794, and only one major fire was ignited between A.D. 1805 and 1820. This latter conflagration was a very localized fire started sometime during the fall or winter of A.D. 1812. About half of the preceding and subsequent fires represented by the date spikes were also set during these seasons, and the other major fires were ignited in the late summer.

In fact, only three fires clearly occurred between A.D. 1798 and 1819, when the Awahnichi were likely still occupying the Mono Basin. These fires occurred at A.D. 1800, 1804, and 1812, respectively. Thus, rather than reflecting sustained occupation, the "filtered" dendrochronological data indicate that Indian people visited Yosemite Valley at least three times during exile and continued to manage the vegetation either for their ongoing subsistence needs or in anticipation of permanent return. Such infrequent visitation is consistent with Tenaya's statement to that effect (Bunnell 1990:65). At other times during this period, fires were rare or absent. The only other period after A.D. 1798 that witnessed similar depressed fire activity was between A.D. 1851 to 1854. This was the time when Yosemite Indians were forced to contend with the Mariposa Battalion—including finding temporary asylum in Mono Basin—and suffered decimation at the hands of the Mono Paiute. Thus, this is a good analog for the events—also revealed in the filtered fire-scar data—that took place nearly fifty years earlier. In addition to being less frequent—approximately seven years passed between the fires set from A.D. 1804 to 1820—burning may also have been more localized.

If vegetation-management practices were pursued in the absence of sustained habitation, the use of rockshelters rather than construction of dwellings may have facilitated this activity. Fires were often set in the late fall or winter, and the late-winter occupation of He-le'-jah is generally consistent with the fire-scar data on season of ignition despite the fact that winter would not have been the optimal burning season. It may be that other logistic sites were used in Yosemite Valley in conjunction with burning, but since random sampling for the demographic study did not consider nonresidential deposits, it was not possible to explore such land-use practices in the wake of depopulation. At a minimum, these results suggest that the Awahnichi maintained their connection to Yosemite Valley while in exile, presumably in anticipation of their permanent return. That being the case, they may also have maintained their culture and identity while living elsewhere, and creolization may be less evident as a result. Such attachment to place was specifically discussed by Bunnell (1990:197), who noted that the "colony originally established by Ten-ie-ya . . . [was] attached to this valley as a home. The instinctive attraction that an Indian has for his place of nativity is incomprehensible; it is more than a religious sentiment; it is a passion."

A SENSE OF PLACE AND PURPOSE

This assessment of the cultural consequences of colonial-era depopulation at both the micro- and macroscale provided an intriguing picture of daily life both within households and communities in the centuries surrounding the colonial encounter. Distinctions between life prior to and in the wake of disease were subtle, and numerous factors other than depopulation could have contributed to such differences. These include site seasonality, preservation of organic remains, and simply idiosyncratic differences due to the limited sample for these two periods and even the more distant past. Archaeological data are unable to address some elements of potential colonial-era change suggested by ethnographic and ethnohistoric observations, such as those related to language, territoriality, or intergroup violence. Conversely, the data do provide insights on other practices that were expected loci of either change or stability. For example, the appearance of milling slicks argues for a pattern of patrilocal postmarital residence predating the Gold Rush, at least, if these features are related to Mono Paiute wives. And despite the absence of house features, changes in dwellings are indicated by the sudden use of rockshelters for habitation. Expected changes are also evident in the incorporation of domestic animals in the diet and the adoption of nonnative material culture, while anticipated continuity is demonstrated in the production and use of traditional implements and regional exchange.

Data at the microscale, encompassing household practices, hearth-centered activity, and individual skill, indicated minor differences between people occupying Hol'-low and He-le'-jah. At the household level, there were differences in the emphasis on and conduct of processing activities, with such practices more diverse and intensive in predepopulation times. In this case, the availability of metal tools and other nonnative objects such as textiles might have contributed to diachronic trends. Focus on activities centered on hearths indicated much the same pattern evident at the larger spatial scale, although flaked stone and, especially, faunal remains may have been removed from the hearth area at He-le'-jah. The data pertaining to individuals rather than households or entire communities were the most intriguing, as they suggested some deliberate or accidental loss of flaked stone manufacturing skill after depopulation. This was indicated by reduced investment in fine tool production and more manufacturing errors. Interpretations in this arena were complicated by the possibility that residents at He-le'-jah were immigrants or marriage partners from the west. Certainly, some blending of cultural traditions of people of the Sierra Nevada and the San Joaquin delta were indicated. Although ethnohistoric accounts indicate that Tenaya welcomed outsiders into his band, the extent of such influence was not anticipated, and regional context for colonial-era changes in the Central Valley are necessary to better interpret these observations. In addition, the manufacturing activities may have been affected by the seasonal availability of obsidian. The season of occupation and potential functional differences pertaining thereto could not be assessed.

At the microscale, then, some distinctions in flaked stone tool and faunal assemblages were suggested, but attributing these differences specifically to depopulation was difficult. In fact, such trends could be due to season of occupation, access to nonnative tools and materials, interaction with native people from the west, and numerous other factors. In addition, any distinctions in artifact assemblages that were apparent might not have been significant to daily practice. More important were possible distinctions in skill or investment in tool manufacture that were not so easily dismissed by other potential causes. In this case, however, material shortage potentially resulting from seasonal restriction from obsidian sources on the east side of the Sierra was also a factor. Even if all differences are attributed to depopulation, such shifts appear relatively minor in the full scope of daily life and may only represent short-term changes that could have been or were subsequently reversed.

At the regional scale, there were no major shifts in external relations, access to exotic materials, or settlement patterns upon reoccupation as a consequence of depopulation. In fact, in this regard life went on much as it had before disease struck. Continuity in exchange with people to both the east and west was revealed, although access to nonnative materials also occurred after depopulation. Such items were probably obtained via traditional native traders, and there was no evidence to suggest that the incorporation of such items significantly altered daily life of the Yosemite Indians. In fact, spatial data for ornaments at Hol'-low and He-le'-jah suggested no difference in the likely context of use despite the shift from steatite to glass beads. In the short term, Awahnichi descendants apparently maintained ties to Yosemite Valley and continued vegetation-management practices from a distance, even though they did not permanently reoccupy the valley until about A.D. 1820. Perhaps the most substantial evidence for settlement change during this time was the reliance on rockshelters. This may have been related to a need or desire to minimize investment in architecture. Other factors such as site seasonality also may have contributed to this pattern. Permanent resettlement was established in areas that had witnessed occupation on numerous occasions in the more distant past. There was no particular tie to specific locales occupied just prior to depopulation, perhaps due either to deliberate avoidance of such sites or to no remaining attachment to place in the collective group memory. As noted above, however, there are many potential explanations for such a change that may or may not have a direct relationship to depopulation.

The story of the Awahnichi, then, is one of cultural persistence—with only the subtlest of changes in daily life—despite significant population decline. Short-term decisions to relocate and intermarry with people of other groups, made necessary by the dire biological circumstances, entailed no profound changes in daily life and may not have had consequences for other aspects of culture. This conclusion runs counter to many characterizations of colonial-era native cultural change by archaeologists, anthropologists, and historians, which are largely based on cases in which the consequences of introduced disease have not or cannot be disentangled from impacts due to other factors such as economic, religious, or social interaction with colonialists or neighboring native groups enmeshed in such relationships. Once again, the data are consistent with the hypothesis that disease-induced depopulation occurred prior to face-to-face encounters with colonists but that histories of survival and endurance provided for cultural continuity even in the face of short-term changes and demographic catastrophe. Determining if this was unique to Yosemite Indians requires more careful evaluation of other cases of possible colonial-era population collapse—a task taken up in the next chapter.

CHAPTER 9

The Colonial Experience

*Epidemic Disease and Cultural Outcomes
Elsewhere in North America*

Decisions made by the Awahnichi and other North American Indians in the aftermath of colonial-era disease were based on experience. For some, cultural mechanisms for survival in the face of demographic perturbations were already in place. They had endured similar circumstances in the past that facilitated their grasp of the problem and their response. For others, this event was anomalous and, therefore, may have been especially difficult to negotiate. Thus, to understand the short- and long-term demographic and cultural consequences of this particular facet of colonialism, we cannot detach Indian groups from their unique history. Any cross-cultural comparisons that seek to understand the cultural outcomes of colonial-era native demographic change in North America are only possible if each group is considered within its specific context. Both the common and the unique cultural and historical threads of disparate cases must be identified. Such assessment—drawing on archaeology and native oral tradition—must take into account the particular colonial aggressor (people, purpose, or pathogen), the sequence and timing of nonnative disease and physical incursion by colonists, traditional knowledge of similar demographic circumstances, evidence for native cultural flexibility, and the likely options for biological and cultural survival at the time disease struck. Context serves to identify the factors that produced similar or different outcomes in various cases and, in so doing, fosters anthropological understanding of European colonialism as a process in North American Indian cultural history.

The magnitude of mortality from introduced disease within Indian communities and its effects on culture were mediated by numerous situational factors, including extant population density, settlement patterns, geographic isolation, environmental productivity, subsistence strategies, preexisting disease load, regional interaction, and political organization, to name just a few (Stannard 1991:523; see also Ramenofsky 1987, 1990, 1991). These interpretive considerations are in addition to group history and the knowledge preserved in native oral tradition and called upon by charismatic leaders, which figured into the response to such a crisis. The contention that significant culture change was inevitable ignores diversity of both situation and experience and harkens back to acculturation research of the 1930s in which change was deemed both inevitable and unidirectional (see Cusick 1998a, 1998b; Dunnell 1991:573). Such a predetermined view discounts the temporary nature of cultural adjustments given the inherent flexibility of groups with a history of demographic challenges or cultural dynamism. In fact, the critical element in the case of colonial-era depopulation was likely that insufficient time elapsed to reverse consequent, otherwise short-term, cultural adjustments prior to physical impingement by Europeans. Archaeological methods inhibit the recognition of these shifts for what they actually were—part of dynamic rather than static native histories. There was potential to reverse short-term trends initiated by native decision making in the immediate wake of disease, particularly given sufficient time before direct interaction with colonists to negotiate such accommodations free from the additional pressures of colonial occupation.

The significance of Old World disease to anthropological understanding of colonial-era culture change and the process of colonialism, then, is not limited to whether the earliest European presence immediately led to down-the-line spread of disease into the interior of the continent. Focus on this issue is critical primarily to estimation of precontact native population size, which is central to the contact-era population debate. Clearly for the Awahnichi, immediate disease exposure was not the case, since many of the Spanish missions had been established in California at least twenty years before the "black sickness." Rather, the issue of relevance is whether Old World disease preceded direct contact sufficiently (e.g., by more than one generation) so that the effects, if any, were both realized and accommodated through various cultural means. In addition, we must determine if these responses represent deep structural changes or simply surficial adjustments in the short term. The Yosemite Indian case suggests the latter, but to fill out the diverse picture of North American Indian disease-induced depopulation and culture change at a distance from colonists, we must consider native oral history and archaeological evidence of other cases of disease infiltration prior to face-to-face encounters or sustained nonnative occupation within a region. Yosemite Indians were different from many other native groups that have been subject to ethnohistoric and archaeological assessment of colonial-era depopulation. The Awahnichi were foragers rather than farmers, and thus their story provides an important contribution to anthropological understanding of colonialism. How representative is their experience in the panoply of native colonial experiences in North America?

Few cases of European disease preceding face-to-face encounters or sustained interaction between Indians and colonists have been documented archaeologically, either because evidence has not been sought or because temporal information has been insufficient to the task. For example, chronologies often rely on the proportionate incorporation of nonnative items into daily life, but this is ultimately tautological when materialist approaches to culture change—encompassing European goods—are then invoked. And even in cases where disease-induced depopulation has been examined, the use of extant archaeological data rather than the development of statistically defensible demographic sampling undermines confidence in conclusions. This practice has resulted in often harsh critiques (e.g., Henige 1998). Much of the literature on colonial-era native depopulation instead derives from ethnohistory or is more broadly speculative based on epidemiological possibility rather than specific material evidence. Such study is further complicated by the fact that "first contacts" or potential avenues for the spread of nonnative disease in North America were often in coastal areas and along major inland waterways such as the St. Lawrence, Mississippi, and Missouri rivers. Thus, the sequence of disease introductions represents a perplexing history within North America. Disease in some areas—for example, the interior Southeast—may have been introduced from more than one direction. Likewise, the "interior" of one era or generation—for example, the middle Mississippi River valley—was the landfall of the next wave of colonialism. There is no single "ground zero" in either time or space after the Columbian landfall from which to consider and track the spread, demographic impact, and cultural consequences of introduced diseases.

Here, I consider ten case studies from seven interior regions of

The Colonial Experience

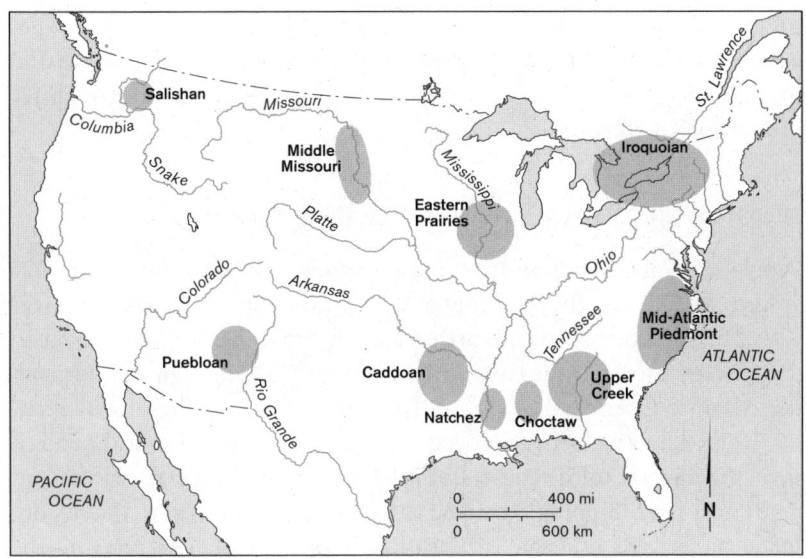

MAP 7. Ten case-study areas of interior native peoples with possible precontact infiltration of Old World fatal disease.

North America that either might, or have been claimed to, document infiltration of precontact disease: the interior Northeast, mid-Atlantic Piedmont, interior Southeast, Eastern Prairies of the upper Midwest, middle Missouri River, Columbia Plateau, and Southwest (see map 7). For each of these cases, I summarize archaeological and historical evidence for the continuity or change within these societies in the centuries leading up to potential encounters with nonnative disease, assess similar evidence of disease transmission in each case, and explore the short- and long-term cultural consequences of fatal disease in the absence of physical incursion or a sustained, local colonial presence. Thus, this analysis considers the key issues of the timing, magnitude, and cultural consequences of disease-induced depopulation that collectively establish which of the three scenarios of colonial-era demographic decline pertains—early demographic and cultural collapse, early exposure with population rebound and cultural persistence, or late demographic and cultural decline from multiple causes. For each case, the colonial encounter is placed within the context of Indian demographic and cultural developments leading up to that time and is discussed with an appreciation for regional native and nonnative interactions that contributed to the cultural outcomes. This assessment of multiple cases provides for comparison with the Yosemite Indian experience and, in turn, the Awahnichi story can be used to understand and disentangle the dual forces of colonialism for these and other native groups in North America.

IROQUOIAN TRIBES OF THE INTERIOR NORTHEAST

People speaking northern Iroquoian languages lived in the major river valleys and along the lakeshores of the middle St. Lawrence River watershed of northeastern North America, from the Richelieu River to the eastern shores of Lake Huron (see map 8). Although inland from the Atlantic Ocean, this region of temperate mixed forest is bisected by the St. Lawrence River, which is a rich fishery and natural conduit from the interior to the coast. Both the abundant natural resources and ready access to shipping attracted early European interest in the region. Jacques Cartier's multiple explorations along the St. Lawrence in the mid-1530s and early 1540s were the first European forays into the area. These endeavors brought him into contact with northern Iroquoian people and may have introduced fatal disease among some native people on the lower St. Lawrence,[1] although no archaeological data have been developed to document such outbreaks. Substantial influence of Europeans within native communities in this interior region only came after the founding of French settlements along the St. Lawrence began in 1608. The French came to exploit fisheries and furs, and their efforts included establishing trade with, and initiating Jesuit missionary activities among, the Iroquoian-speaking Wendat (Huron) and Algonquian-speaking groups who lived north of the St. Lawrence River in what is today southern Québec and Ontario. The French also aligned militarily with their new native trading partners in enduring possibly centuries-old conflicts with traditional Iroquoian enemies to the south of Lake Ontario. And they established several forts and missions in the region over the next century to help maintain their economic hold on the region against competing European colonial interests.

The Dutch established Fort Nassau on the Hudson River directly east of the northern Iroquoians in 1614,[2] in an effort to support initial trade with the Algonquian-speaking people of the region. By the 1620s, this colonial presence had attracted participation by native people to the west, including exchange with the Iroquoian people of upstate New York. The Dutch maintained their economic activities in the Hudson River region until they lost control of their colonial holdings in North

The Colonial Experience

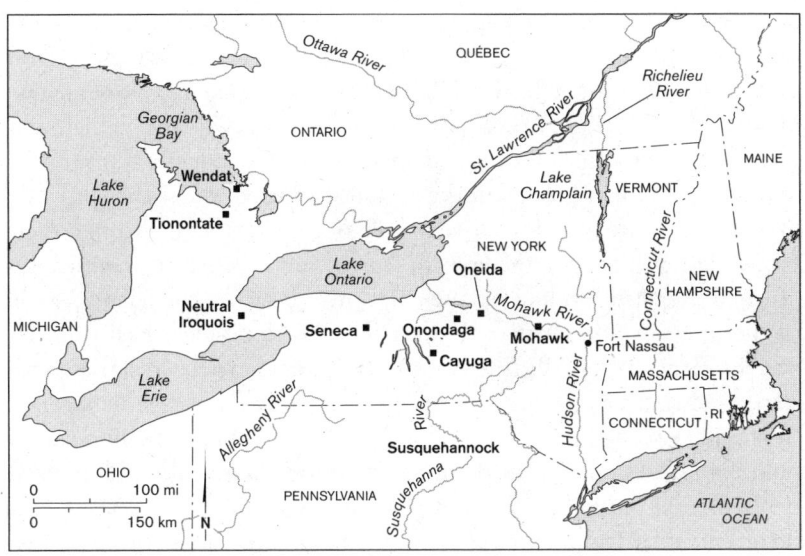

MAP 8. Iroquoian case-study area.

America to the British in the 1660s. The British, in turn, initiated trade with Algonquians of the Chesapeake region south of the northern Iroquoians after the founding of Jamestown in 1607, but their reach only extended north into Iroquoian country after the establishment of trading posts farther inland beginning in the 1630s (W.C. Johnson 2001:79). Even the early British colonial presence influenced existing interior native trade relations between the Algonquians and the Iroquoians as far away as upstate New York, however, with archaeological evidence indicating a prolonged episode of decline in the marine shell trade via the Iroquoian-speaking Susquehannock of the upper Potomac and Susquehanna drainages to the Seneca south of Lake Ontario during the early to mid-1600s. Access to marine shell by the Seneca thereafter may have only been secured through aggression against Monongahela middlemen (W.C. Johnson 2001:80), although the timing of renewed access to shell from the Chesapeake region coincides with historically documented disease among interior tribes of the Northeast. Thus significant, if temporary, changes in long-standing economic relations occurred even prior to a British colonial presence within Iroquoian territories (W.C. Johnson 2001:80).

As native populations shifted within the region during the mid-1600s, groups such as the Mohawk sought to expand their territory to the north and west, acquiring land sufficient to support their members (Starna and Brandao 2004). This aggression led to escalating cycles of violent, armed conflict between the northern Iroquoian people of upstate New York and neighboring native groups allied with the French and ultimately led to the substantial displacement or conquest of Iroquoian and non-Iroquoian groups in the region. Participation in the fur trade and access to firearms by native people of the Northeast through their trade relationships with the French, Dutch, and British also significantly affected the need for, and balance of, power between the native people of the interior Northeast on both a short- or long-term basis (Starna and Brandao 2004). By the 1700s, Iroquoian groups residing both north and south of the St. Lawrence River found themselves embroiled in wars between the British and French. Such dynamic economic and political factors make it difficult to disentangle native disease-induced depopulation in this region from physical incursion of colonists, direct involvement of Iroquoian people in colonial enterprises, or centuries-old native conflict further facilitated by access to firearms.

There was a dynamic history of native occupation in this region in the millennium leading up to European colonization, including population movements, consolidation of tribes, and formation of powerful intertribal political alliances. These trends unfolded on a backdrop of continuity in daily life and social organization; thus, there is a history of both native cultural stability and change. Archaeological evidence indicates that Iroquoian-speaking people were relatively recent arrivals to the interior Northeast, with data suggesting their immigration into the area from the south around A.D. 900. They brought with them a horticultural tradition based on maize and production of ceramics as well as village life and longhouse architecture indicative of the matrilineal social organization observed later by European traders and missionaries. Settlement centered on village clusters, with abandonment of specific settlements after a few decades of use. Such abandonment was prompted by declining agricultural productivity of immediately adjacent fields or depletion of other local resources such as fuelwood. There are also some evident changes in settlement location through time, however, apparently reflecting efforts to balance access to prime agricultural soils with the need for defense against aggression of neighboring tribes. Specifically, for a time, settlements shifted away from valley bottoms to more defensible locales on adjoining bluffs or hills at some distance from the floodplains.

Some of these changes may have been due, in part, to the onset of the

Little Ice Age circa A.D. 1450, which shortened the growing season and decreased crop yields in this more marginal area for maize agriculture. In fact, many of these cultural changes were part of a broad pattern of geographical contraction observed throughout the interior Northeast at that time. Native people either left areas altogether or consolidated settlements in place to facilitate continued reliance on agriculture. In areas such as southern Ontario, deteriorating agricultural conditions precipitated a return to hunting and gathering and a reliance on large game rather than small game among some groups. This subsistence shift also necessitated changes in settlement location, in particular, and a decrease in house size is also evident (Fitzgerald 2001). Climate change with the onset of the Little Ice Age may account for increasing tension and conflicts between native peoples in the region, and such stress may in turn have contributed to political confederation of the Mohawk, Oneida, Onondaga, Cayuga, and Seneca within the League of the Iroquois (also called the Five Nations) as a deterrent to intertribal violence.[3] Iroquoian confederacies also formed to the east, with four tribes coming together as the Wendat (Huron), two tribes constituting the Tionontate (Petun), and a third confederacy later known by the French as the Nation du Neutre (Neutral Iroquois; see Warrick 2003:260; Fitzgerald 2001:37–38). The relative peace that prevailed within confederacies thereafter facilitated the move from defensive hilltop locales back down to valley agricultural land, although conflicts may still have occurred between confederacies. By the time of Columbus's landfall, numerous northern Iroquoian tribes with distinct identities were present, with each formed through the merging of smaller local groups within discrete regions surrounded by generous buffer zones used for hunting. In addition, the confederacy of the Five Nations was already beginning to coalesce or had already been established, representing a larger scale of sociopolitical integration within the region (see Bradley 2001:30, citing Tuck 1971; see also Snow 1996).

The most detailed studies of northern Iroquoian colonial-era demography focus on two groups: (1) the Mohawk, who lived along a 75-kilometer-long stretch of the Mohawk River near the town of Amsterdam in what is now east-central New York State (Snow 1995, 1996, 2001); and (2) the Wendat-Tionontate (Huron-Petun), who lived on the southeastern shores of Lake Huron in southern Ontario near present-day Midland (Warrick 2003) (see map 8). Although some of the details of migration and disease for the Mohawk provided by Snow (1995, 1996) are specific to this group, they may serve as a model for other Five

Nations peoples, at least until the mid-1600s. Jordan (2006) cautioned, however, that the Mohawk colonial experience should not be generalized for all Iroquoian groups, since their geographic situation was unique, and thus their experience with European colonialism was different than that of Iroquoian peoples to the west. Similarly, Warrick's (2003) analysis of the Wendat-Tionontate provides a picture for the northernmost Iroquoian groups or other native people allied with the French, while also allowing comparison with colonial-era demography of the Five Nations. In both studies, demographic inferences based on archaeology were complemented by historical records, which provided detail on migrations also evident in material culture. Snow (1995, 1996) argued that thorough demographic reconstruction was possible in the Mohawk region because all Mohawk villages have been identified in the archaeological record[4] and fine-scale chronology has been established through a combination of radiocarbon dates and diagnostic items of European manufacture.[5] Although Warrick (2003:265) could only claim that more than 60 percent of all Wendat-Tionontate villages were represented in his study, he relied on village area, longhouse hearth density, burial, and documentary data on family size to establish population trends through time. Similar to Snow's work, chronology for this reconstruction was based on radiocarbon dates, ceramic seriation, and glass beads.

Snow's (1995, 1996) reconstruction indicated that during the fifteenth and early sixteenth century, several villages were dispersed throughout the length of Mohawk territory. Subsequent nucleation to just two villages occurred between A.D. 1525 and 1560, perhaps as a result of changes within matrilineages that facilitated population aggregation and management of larger social groups (Snow 1996:170). But overall population size remained relatively constant until circa A.D. 1580, when the population grew nearly 25 percent. Given such swift increase, local Mohawk population was evidently augmented by incorporation of people from elsewhere rather than just intrinsic growth. Snow (1996:169) concluded that the newcomers may have been St. Lawrence Iroquoians, who were displaced by Mohawk aggression aimed at providing them access to trade with the French along St. Lawrence River. Interestingly, these refugees or captives seem to have been incorporated into just one—rather than both—of the Mohawk villages that existed at that time.[6] This may suggest maintenance of a distinct subcommunity in the short term.

The Mohawk population continued to grow from approximately 2,000 to more than 7,500 people over the next fifty years, again largely due to immigration in response to French attacks on neighboring people, Iroquoian aggression against other groups, or a desire for greater involvement by the Mohawk in colonial trade (Snow 1996:172). This movement included settlement of Oneida people within Mohawk territory, establishing their own village at least until A.D. 1635 (Snow 1996: table 1). Given the significant contribution of immigration, it is impossible to determine if any population decline due to decreasing fertility or increasing mortality occurred simultaneously for the resident Mohawk people prior to A.D. 1634. In fact, Snow (1996) concluded that the only evidence for increased mortality reflects the historically documented smallpox epidemic of A.D. 1634—that is, epidemic disease did not infiltrate the Mohawk region prior to direct and sustained encounters with nonnative people through trade. At this time, archaeological evidence indicated a substantial decline on the order of 60 to 75 percent of the population, presumed to be wholly attributable to mortality rather than also entailing emigration. Thereafter, the population continued to decline, although at a less alarming rate. Once again, however, augmentation from outside continued, including incorporation of some Wendat around A.D. 1655, partially at the urging of the Jesuit missionaries (Snow 1996:175–176). As before, the many refugees may have maintained separate communities within Mohawk territory, at least in the short term, as indicated by distinctive Wendat material culture at one site. There is also evidence, however, of likely incorporation of outsiders into existing Mohawk villages (Snow 1996:176). Despite the continuing influx of refugees, wars, disease, and colonial settlement took their toll on the Mohawk, and population continued to gradually decline thereafter.

Subsistence practices for tribes of the League of the Iroquois remained constant throughout the colonial era, but material culture began to change beginning in the late sixteenth century due to incorporation of people from the north and south (Bradley 2001:31). Settlement also changed, particularly in response to the political situation of the region, including access to nonnative traders, hostility or alliance with native neighbors, and village sizes necessitating more frequent moves since swidden agriculture depleted proximate fields. Significantly, however, both Snow and Bradley did not recognize change in internal sociopolitical organization until after sustained involvement with colonists. This change is apparent in the decline of matrilineal descent and authority—indicated in part by changes in architecture—which was probably attributable to factors other than disease-induced demographic change. In particular, male-dominated colonial society was unwilling to acknowledge or unable to recognize female authority, and this undermined the dominance of women leaders through individual native male access to goods and power via trade. There were also changes in ritual practices due to the incorporation of other native peoples into Mohawk and other Iroquoian groups. Bradley (2001) noted stability in location and thus identity for the Onondaga, however, even as ethnicity was shifting with the incorporation of captives and refugees from surrounding groups. He observed that "one was considered Onondaga if one lived with, and was accepted by, the people of the great hill [from which they took their name and identity], regardless of one's origins" (Bradley 2001:30). This same observation may well apply to other native groups within this and other regions.

Population estimates for the Wendat-Tionontate derived from archaeological data reveal a demographic history similar to that of the Mohawk. Uninterrupted and relatively steady population growth is documented beginning around A.D. 1100 and continuing until A.D. 1500, with small, statistically insignificant fluctuations in the subsequent 130 years. Population peaked at more than 33,000 individuals. Catastrophic depopulation is evident after A.D. 1633, when the population declined by more than 60 percent. Juvenile mortality rose significantly around A.D. 1636 (Warrick 2003). This population decline led to settlement aggregation, and bioarchaeological data indicate a possible concomitant decline in household size by approximately 40 percent (Warrick 2003:267). These observations suggest that the Wendat-Tionontate were unsuccessful in their attempts, if any, to rebound from this demographic catastrophe, perhaps because they had maintained a relatively stable population with low to no growth in the 150 years leading up to this event. Consistent with the archaeological findings, historical records document that a series of fatal diseases spread through Wendat-Tionontate communities between A.D. 1634 and 1640. Moreover, descriptions suggest that each episode represented a different malady and, thus, each inflicted maximum devastation due to the lack of even recently established immunity (Warrick 2003:265). Some diseases were clearly introduced via native intermediaries from French, Dutch, and British sources, since permanent colonial settlement of the region not occur until the late seventeenth century. Depopulation among the Wendat-Tionontate continued in the decade between initial disease-induced depopulation and colonial settlement due in large part to aggression from the south by the Five Nations.

In summary, archaeological evidence for both the Mohawk and Wendat-Tionontate reveals significant depopulation beginning with fatal epidemics in A.D. 1634 rather than any earlier decline due to introduced pathogens.[7] Multiple diseases were introduced in a series of waves within less than a decade, with relatively short intervals between each episode. Combined with the relatively low intrinsic population growth rates that likely prevailed prior to disease, these repeated assaults made internal population rebound unlikely without relocation, amalgamation, or augmentation of population through forced or consensual immigration of neighboring peoples. The Mohawk were successful for a time through their often aggressive pursuit of new community members, and the Onondaga followed a similar tack. The Wendat-Tionontate, on the other hand, relocated either with other Iroquoian groups such as the Mohawk or struck out on their own to areas to the west. In the latter case, Branstner (1992) argued that the Tionontate did not significantly alter their practices of settlement, subsistence, technology, and perhaps even ideology as a result of disease-induced depopulation, coincident Iroquoian aggression, and subsequent interaction with French missionaries, despite their substantial displacement to the west. In contrast, Bradley (2001:31) observed significant shifts within Onondaga culture—including changes in settlement, mortuary practices, and material culture—in the decades following incorporation of outsiders and concluded that "the social implications of these changes must have been staggering." Thus, the different decisions made by various northern Iroquoian groups in the face of depopulation had very different outcomes with respect to identity and culture in both the short and long term.

SIOUAN PEOPLES OF THE MID-ATLANTIC PIEDMONT

The Piedmont of Maryland, Virginia, and North Carolina is a land of rolling hills between the low coastal plain to the east and the Appalachian belt of ridges and valleys to the west. Numerous rivers—from the Susquehanna River in the north to the upper tributaries of the Cape Fear River in the south—flow east to the Atlantic Ocean (see map 9). A rich mixed-hardwood forest dominated by oak, hickory, and pine once blanketed the terrain. Colonial activity of the British and, to a lesser extent, the Spanish had a profound, if not immediate, effect on the Indian people who lived along the majors rivers and smaller tributaries of the Piedmont. Historical accounts from as early as the late 1500s

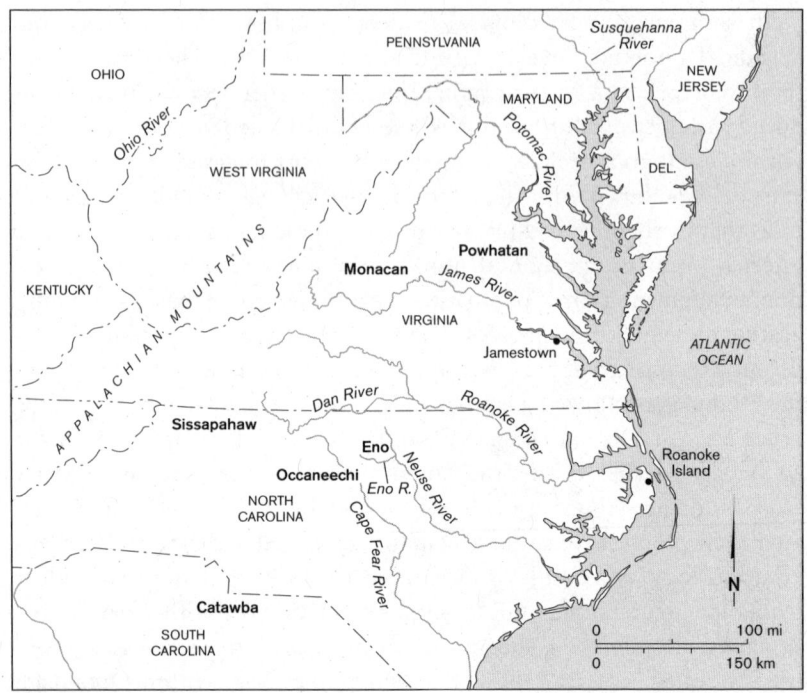

MAP 9. Mid-Atlantic Piedmont case-study area.

often refer to these native groups, although much remains uncertain about their sociopolitical organization and even their linguistic affiliation. Scholars generally believe that these people were Siouan speakers, whose culture developed in situ during the preceding Woodland period (ca. 1000 B.C.–A.D. 1600).[8] Groups include the Monacan, Occaneechi, Eno, Sissapahaw, and Catawba as well as several others known to later British explorers and traders.

The archaeological record for Siouan groups of the Piedmont documents a varied diet of both wild and domestic plants as well as use of terrestrial game and aquatic resources such as freshwater shellfish and fish. Agriculture based on maize, beans, squash, and sunflower was in place by at least A.D. 1000, although the importance of these domesticates increased through time. In addition, the smaller, dispersed homestead clusters typical of life before circa A.D. 1400 gave way to more nucleated settlements of circular houses within palisades thereafter. Mortuary customs prior to colonial incursion varied somewhat through time, reflecting more or less investment in the excavation of pits or chambers for the dead. By A.D. 1600, burial practices generally entailed interment within deep chambers that were placed within and around domestic structures inside the village palisade. These communities were not part of complex chiefdoms like many peoples of the interior Southeast and Mississippi River valley. Rather, many groups were likely tribes or, as Hantman (2001) has argued for the Monacan of the middle James River area, simple chiefdoms.

Early incursion by explorers into the interior Southeast as well as somewhat later European settlement on the mid-Atlantic coast—including the establishment of the short-lived Spanish mission of Ajacan on the lower James River in A.D. 1570 and the equally transitory English colony at Roanoke Island established in A.D. 1585—evidently had little or no effect on native people of the mid-Atlantic Piedmont (Hantman 2001; Ward and Davis 2001). Subsistence, settlement, burial practices, and exchange persisted much as they had prior to these initial tentative probes of the region by outsiders. And equally important, there is no archaeological evidence for depopulation at this early time, such as might be expected from down-the-line transmission of fatal diseases from coastal peoples along traditional trade routes. Ward and Davis (2001:125) suggested that such early disease spread might have been inhibited, in part, by the relatively small size of village populations and the fact that the territory did not open up to sustained interaction with Europeans until the mid-1600s.

British traders began to push into the Piedmont after securing a treaty with the Powhatan of coastal Virginia in A.D. 1646. This led to the establishment of several forts and trading posts on the eastern margin of the Virginia Piedmont (Hantman 2001:115). Archaeological evidence for introduction of fatal diseases only appears in the southern mid-Atlantic Piedmont sometime between circa A.D. 1670 and 1700. And this is substantiated by the written accounts of traders, who noted substantial population decline in the decades between their visits to individual villages. Thus, disease after A.D. 1670 could have resulted from either direct contact with traders or through down-the-line transmission between native people after the British were well established on the coast. In the Piedmont region, such devastation is evident in the archaeological record in substantial cemeteries—often placed outside the village palisade—and sometimes relatively little investment in mortuary ritual. This latter conclusion is indicated by shallower graves and the common restriction of grave goods to few individuals. Thus, death was not so swift or disease so demoralizing to the survivors as to preclude proper treatment of the dead, but shifts in mortuary behavior are indicated.

Despite significant loss of life after A.D. 1670, the archaeological record of the southern mid-Atlantic Piedmont also reveals continuity in daily practices, including settlement, subsistence, architecture, storage, and technology. On the other hand, community cohesion may have suffered, since the frequency of roasting pits that are thought to relate to communal feasting activities decrease (Ward and Davis 2001:132). Communities were likely struggling to cope with depopulation, and population movements are indicated in both the distribution of ceramic types and historical accounts. For example, the Occaneechi moved into the Eno River region from the Roanoke River area to the northeast after A.D. 1676 (Ward and Davis 2001:132; see map 9). Such migration and aggregation of people of different cultural traditions may account for two separate cemeteries at one village on the Eno River dating to this time, or such segregation may have resulted from two separate epidemics during the course of occupation there (Ward and Davis 2001:132). Second waves of disease are also suggested by age-specific mortality patterns for the individuals buried at a site on the upper Dan River. The relatively high percentage of subadults suggested that adults withstood the pathogen due to prior immunity, while the younger generations lacked such protection (Ward and Davis 2001:137). By the early eighteenth century, most survivors of various Siouan tribes of the southern mid-Atlantic Piedmont had migrated south to be incorporated within other groups, or they had been removed to other areas under colonial protection (Ward and Davis 2001:141).

To the north, settlement of Jamestown on the James River in A.D. 1607 initiated colonial-era culture change in the adjacent Virginia Piedmont somewhat earlier than in North Carolina. Unfortunately, the archaeological record of this region is very sparse and does not lend itself to the detailed study of demographic and cultural change that is possible to the south. This is due, in part, to active geomorphology and the long history of agricultural development in the major river valleys that has obscured or destroyed archaeological sites located in these primary occupation zones. As in the southern mid-Atlantic Piedmont, however, the archaeological record for the Late Woodland period (ca. A.D. 900–1600) documents cultivation of maize, beans, squash, and sunflower, and agricultural produce was augmented by hunting and use of wild plants in the diet. Likewise, Indians lived in small village clusters or homesteads that lined the rivers, with circular to oval post dwellings. Increasing diversity in architecture, ceramics, and other aspects of material culture suggests that these societies were also developing more social inequality within groups (Gallivan 2004). Burial practices were somewhat more diverse than in the southern Piedmont and included simple pit burials within and adjacent to villages, rock-cairn burials, and burial mounds. The latter often served as the resting place for hundreds or even thousands of individuals. The largest of these mounds were created after A.D. 1400, whereas smaller mounds were located to the west in the ridge and valley area prior to this time. It is perhaps significant that burial practices at these mounds shifted from individual primary interment to mass secondary interments through time, although there was a return to individual interment "in the historic era" (Hantman 2001:121). Mass secondary interments might signal high mortality events such as those expected with introduced disease; alternately, such practices may indicate less ready access to burial mounds by Indian people after migration or displacement in the face of colonial encroachment. In the latter case, the remains of individuals may have had to be moved to the mounds after initial interment elsewhere.

Such archaeological observations have not prompted regional specialists to conclude that fatal nonnative disease is, in fact, represented in the northern Piedmont. Still, settlement patterns indicate that the Monacans abandoned the Virginia Piedmont by A.D. 1650. Most, if not all, Monacans relocated to the south and west along trade routes in the Roanoke and Shenandoah river valleys to facilitate participation in the growing deerskin trade. These people had previously acted as suppliers or middlemen in the copper trade with Powhatans of the coastal plain, but their position was undermined by access to European copper after the establishment of Jamestown.

In summary, the archaeology of the southern mid-Atlantic Piedmont—coupled with ethnohistoric records—provides irrefutable evidence for the infiltration of nonnative disease into interior areas. Unlike the interior Southeast, there is unequivocal bioarchaeological evidence for such events in the Eno and Dan river areas, at least. But the exact timing of epidemics remains unclear, and they may have occurred at a time when the influence of Europeans was increasing—in this case, trading and the acceleration of the deerskin and pelt trade as well as escalation in slave raiding. Thus, it is difficult to determine if the cultural effects were due to disease-induced depopulation or were related instead to direct interaction with British traders or changing intertribal relations due to nonnative economic incentives. The timing and impact of disease to the north is even less certain. Shifts in population to south and west such as that undertaken by the Occaneechi is also seen in southward movement of the Monacans. The potential contribution of introduced disease in the latter case has not been demonstrated and, in fact, is more commonly attributed to native power relations and jockeying of individuals and groups for choice positions in colonial trade. In addition, these patterns may be part of a broader trend of regional abandonment witnessed as early as the 1500s in Maryland and evident by A.D. 1630 in the upper Potomac River country (Wall 2004:96). There, such regional relocation may be related to Iroquoian aggression from the north.

COMPLEX SOCIETIES OF THE INTERIOR SOUTHEAST

No other region of North America has witnessed as much determined interest and research on disease-induced native population decline and resultant cultural change as the interior Southeast. Inland from the gulf coastal plain, this region stretches from the headwaters the Savannah River in South Carolina on the east to the tributaries of the Mississippi River in east Texas and western Arkansas on the west. In between lie the bluffs and basins of the eastern side of the Mississippi River, the upland prairies of northern Mississippi, the Piedmont of northern Alabama and Georgia, and the ridge and valley system of eastern Tennessee. Here, archaeological evidence dating to around A.D. 1400 has revealed a series of complex (including paramount) and simple chiefdoms,[9] in which people lived in multiple satellite villages and farmsteads organized around civic-ceremonial centers with platform mounds. Native people practiced maize agriculture and produced a variety of locally distinctive ceramics identified by differences in temper and decoration. These settlements and civic centers were clustered on fertile floodplains within the major river valleys, whereas much of the surrounding terrain was devoid of human occupation. Instead, these intervening zones were used for hunting and also acted as buffer areas between chiefdoms. Long-distance trade networks with chiefdoms situated in the Mississippi River drainage as far north as the Ohio River served to distribute exotic materials such as marine shell and copper used by elite individuals, with some raw materials conveyed via these networks originating from areas as far away as the Great Lakes.

All of the chiefdoms of the interior Southeast emerged around A.D. 800 to 900 from local Late Woodland groups (Galloway 1995:49). But each had a unique history of development, the details of which are more or less understood based on the extent of archaeological research in each area. Some chiefdoms show cycling, as the primary civic-ceremonial center of one polity gave way to another and thus became subordinate to the new center. In other regions, evidence indicates that some chiefdoms had devolved back into tribal societies by A.D. 1500, as construction and use of the public architecture indicative of central political control of labor ceased and people aggregated into large villages in upland areas. Some of this cycling or change may have been due to the fact that interior chiefdoms were part of the larger network of elite Mississippian communities. Change elsewhere within this web caused perturbations in southeastern polities as internal and external power relations altered. This was particularly true with respect to changing access to exotic goods, which functioned as items of prestige and authority for the chiefs. It has also been suggested that chiefdoms—not just in the Southeast but as a sociopolitical form in general—were intrinsically unstable societies (see Blitz 1999; Galloway 1995:67ff; Scarry 1996). Developing from tribal societies, chiefdoms may fail to make the further transition to a state-level society because of limited local biotic potential. Some chiefdoms in the Southeast evidently returned to tribal organization after their large populations depleted the local environment through overproduction of maize and degradation of the floodplains. The resulting loss of productive capacity undermined their ability to support the complex sociopolitical system that was in place. The shift from chiefdoms to tribal societies in some areas of the Southeast also may have been due to deteriorating climatic conditions, including the onset of the Little Ice Age around A.D. 1450.

This ebb and flow of some chiefdoms—between simple and complex organization—or the outright collapse of sociopolitical structure of others is evident in the archaeological record of the Southeast prior to even the earliest possible incursion of European disease or people into the area. This fluidity complicates interpretations regarding the infiltration or impact of nonnative disease prior to face-to-face colonial encounters in this region, especially since little direct archaeological evidence exists for population decline due to fatal decease resulting from either initial contacts with explorers or down-the-line transmission from the Spanish missions of the coastal or peninsular zone of La Florida. It is often unclear if the cultural changes that occurred during the late sixteenth and early seventeenth centuries were simply due to regional patterns of chiefdom cycling or collapse, or if they reflect the impact of introduced disease through inadvertent transmission. There were also large-scale population movements within and into the region over significant distances in the seventeenth century, and this has made tracking the specific colonial-era cultural developments of the Caddoan-speaking, Muskogean-speaking, and other native peoples who inhabited the area by the early 1800s particularly challenging for regional archaeologists. On the other hand, initial contact of early Spanish explorers with numerous chiefly societies in the interior Southeast was followed by nearly one hundred years of physical isolation of Indians from colonial peoples after Juan Pardo's expeditions of A.D. 1565 to 1568. This allows for a unique "before and after" snapshot of native cultures potentially affected by disease based on historical records rather than just archaeology.

Galloway (1995:131) suggested that even the initial, brief encounters with European explorers—and the knowledge of Spanish colonists to the south and east—"preconditioned" the Indian people of the interior Southeast to colonialism and set this process in motion in the absence of sustained physical interaction. She also concluded that Indian anticipation and adjustment to this new colonial reality on the distant landscape made native people better able to cope with disease-induced population loss when it did eventually arrive. If her hypothesis is correct, even depopulation may not have been a cause of culture change. This is an interesting thesis, although severe population decline may not have been anticipated as an inevitable outcome of impending colonial encounters—despite potential knowledge of the ravages of disease elsewhere. And if it was deemed inevitable by native people, such knowledge may have prompted flight rather than cultural accommodation.

The discussion here focuses on four of the more thoroughly studied cases of native colonial experience in the interior Southeast that may have been significantly influenced by the early introduction of fatal Old World diseases. These chiefdoms or their immediate precolonial descendants were antecedents of the Upper Creek, Choctaw, Natchez, and Caddoan peoples. The conclusion that all of these groups were chiefdoms at the time of contact with the earliest explorers is somewhat problematic, as the Spanish were inclined to interpret or expect political organization consistent with the city-state polities of the Iberian Peninsula that prevailed at that time (Galloway 1995:110). That is, the designation of *chief* may have been a misnomer, perhaps attributing more authority to community leaders than they actually commanded. As evidence, Galloway (1995:111) argued that the very persistence of the Hernando de Soto corps in their four-year journey across the Southeast

The Colonial Experience

likely resulted, in part, from their failure to find paramount—rather than simple—chiefdoms capable of supplying significant labor necessary for exploitation in the *encomienda* system previously instituted by the Spanish in Mesoamerica and South America.[10] And the absence of paramount chiefdoms may also be indicated by chronicled settlement patterns in certain regions at that time.[11] This historical conundrum of native sociopolitical organization at contact is also compounded by the focus of much archaeological study on civic-ceremonial mound sites and cemeteries, to the detriment of research on habitation sites. Significantly less is known about potentially simpler societies or the daily life of chiefly subjects, whereas much more has been inferred about complex groups and their ceremonial centers.

Upper Creeks

The Upper Creeks were a confederation of Eastern Muskogean-speaking peoples who inhabited what is now east-central Alabama in the area of the Coosa, Tallapoosa, and Alabama rivers by the late 1600s (see map 10). The "Creek" designation was a late appellation used by British settlers of South Carolina, and this term also encompassed the Lower Creeks of central and western Georgia. The Indian people themselves self-identified by their *talwa* (town group) or larger regional affiliation such as Abihka, Alabama, Okfuskee, and Tallapoosa (Waselkov and Smith 2000:242). Archaeological and ethnohistoric data demonstrate, however, that even these tribal groups were relatively new manifestations or recombinations of descendants of various chiefdoms such as Coosa, which had existed as recently as the time of Soto's *entrada* through the region in A.D. 1540. Although the Soto chroniclers may not always have been correct in identifying true chiefdoms, the "province" of the Coosa traversed during the journey was sufficiently politically organized to warrant recognition as such.[12] The Coosa chief controlled mound and village centers over a considerable area (Hudson, Smith et al. 1985) and was able to provide both porters and supplies for the subsequent leg of Soto's journey west. This was in contrast to some other leaders of the interior Southeast, who could not muster such control of labor and therefore likely oversaw only simple chiefdoms or tribal societies at that time.

Archaeological evidence for the decline of the Coosa chiefdom in the face of colonial pressures—including possible exposure to fatal disease as a result of relatively brief encounters with Spanish explor-

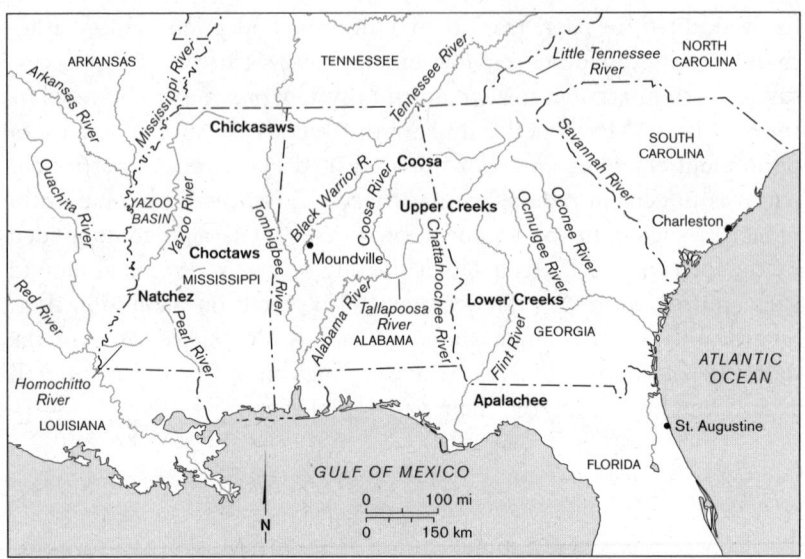

MAP 10. Upper Creek, Choctaw, and Natchez case-study areas.

ers—and the reemergence of these people as one of the Upper Creek tribes has been developed by Smith (1987, 2001, 2002; Waselkov and Smith 2000). Focusing on settlement hierarchy and distribution, burial customs, and migration as indicators of disease-induced depopulation, he observed decreasing site size and number, the termination of mound construction and cessation in use of civic-ceremonial mound sites, and the interment of more than one individual in a grave, presumably due to high mortality events. All mound construction ceased by A.D. 1630, and the construction of new mounds—as opposed to simply adding to existing mounds—stopped at least thirty years earlier (Smith 1987:92). At the same time, human population concentrated in smaller zones within such civic-ceremonial centers, although similar demographic shifts also occurred between A.D. 1350 and 1500, prior to any possible European influence (Smith 1987:71). Fewer—but not smaller—habitation sites also appeared around A.D. 1630, suggesting population aggregation, particularly in the western portion of what had been the Coosa province at its apogee (Smith 2001). Mass or dual burials were somewhat more common between A.D. 1525 and 1565, and from A.D. 1600 and 1630, coincident with these other signs of chiefdom collapse.

Smith (1987:75) concluded that abandonment of areas was the surest sign of disease-induced depopulation following the establishment of La Florida, since such population movement was not readily recognizable in the more distant past.[13] For example, he concluded that the establishment and abandonment of the King site, a large, palisaded settlement on what is now the northern Alabama-Georgia line coincided with pandemics of A.D. 1539 and 1564 posited by Dobyns on the basis of regional historical accounts (Smith 1987:79). And Smith suggested similar coincidental patterns of relocation and subsequent abandonment at other sites despite the fact that such correlations necessitate greater chronological accuracy than is available from archaeology and assume that correlation was cause. Likewise, as he acknowledged, archaeological evidence for early disease-induced depopulation among the Coosa is equivocal at best. For example, the lower proportion of young children and adolescents in the burial population at the King site relative to precontact populations is directly counter to expectations for non-age-specific disease, such as a "virgin-soil" epidemic, despite the fact that mass or multiple burials are present.

The apparent cultural decline prior to direct, sustained European contact that Smith attributed to introduced disease is also suggested by historical, rather than simply archaeological, data. The account of the expedition of Tristán de Luna from A.D. 1559 to 1561 noted fallow fields, smaller populations, and less chiefly authority among the Coosa than had been demonstrated just twenty years earlier during the Soto *entrada* (Smith 2001:130). Unfortunately, we have no comparative data for the more distant past to know if defiance by commoners such as that observed by Luna was unusual. And by A.D. 1568, the Juan Pardo expedition witnessed fully functional chiefdoms in the Coosa area (Smith 1987:87; cf. Galloway 1995:160). This observation suggests a potential reversal of fortune for the Coosa chiefs if there was indeed a lapse in power less than a decade earlier. The wider distribution of European trade goods beyond elite control evident in the archaeological record by A.D. 1600 is a stronger indicator of increasing sociopolitical change than the documentary record, as is the decline in production and exchange of native exotic goods by the late 1600s (Smith 1987:144). Both of these observations, as well as cessation of mound construction, serve as compelling evidence for degradation of the native sociopolitical systems of the interior Southeast beginning in the late sixteenth or early seventeenth century, rather than coincident with earlier European exploration (see Smith 1987:27, 103). In fact, greater access to highly valued trade goods may explain the collapse of chiefly authority (e.g.,

Wesson 2001)—that is, disease-induced depopulation need not have been the underlying cause.

Despite potential power shifts and turmoil during the sixteenth century, the Indian population remained substantial and the Coosa maintained their residence in the same general area into the early 1600s. That is, cultural change during the early to mid-1500s could have been due to chiefdom cycling rather than disease-induced decline. But even Galloway (1995:5) conceded that the "Mississippian Decline"—which spread from the major center of Cahokia near present-day St. Louis beginning in A.D. 1200 to Moundville in northwestern Alabama by A.D. 1500—cannot completely account for the subsequent depopulation evident in chiefdoms of this portion of the interior Southeast during the colonial era. She concluded that the Soto expedition was likely not the vector of disease in the Coosa area, since the Spaniards had been on their journey for more than a year by the time they reached this region and any contagion among the party had probably run its course (Galloway 1995:107–108). Still, disease transmittal via swine that accompanied the corps cannot be discounted (see Ramenofsky and Galloway 1997). In addition, Galloway (1995:159) did not see historical evidence to support significant depopulation prior to A.D. 1560. Instead, archaeological evidence supports major cultural changes in the mid- to late sixteenth and early seventeenth centuries, including aggregation of local and immigrant people in the Coosa River valley. These immigrants moved south into the region from the Little Tennessee River as a result of hostile Cherokee invaders. The Cherokee, in turn, were responding to trading opportunities with the British, who were by then settled on the mid-Atlantic coast and adjacent interior from Virginia to South Carolina. And by the mid-1600s, the Upper Creeks (i.e., Alabamas) themselves were thoroughly engaged in trade with Spanish missions to the south via Apalachee middlemen (Smith 1987:106; Waselkov and Smith 2000:248). In subsequent decades of the seventeenth and eighteenth centuries, archaeological traces of the ancestral Upper Creeks document their continued migration farther south along the Coosa River, down into the Alabama River drainage, and east up the Tallapoosa River (Smith 2001, 2002; see map 10). Historical sources also confirm substantial population movements during the latter half of the seventeenth century, with migrations primarily in response to physical threats and slaving raids of armed allies of the British. The Creek Confederacy accrued through alliances over time and was largely in place by the 1680s (Smith 1987:139). This is revealed archaeologically by more standardized ceramics (Smith 1987:141), perhaps developing due to greater communication facilitated by the confederacy or the Creeks' desire to establish their identity as a people.

The consolidation and movement of the Upper Creeks during the late sixteenth and early seventeenth century, then, was part of a broader regional pattern of southward movement among all Creeks either in response to aggression from the north, opportunities created in the south by the decimation of other tribes by disease, or both (Smith 2002). For example, historical documentation of town names—which people maintained as they moved—indicate that some Lower Creeks probably had their origins in Talisi (Worth 2000:272), a center located on the middle Coosa River in Soto's day. That is, these people moved southeast to the Chattahoochee River area (see map 10), just as Upper Creek ancestors were also moving south from even farther north. On the Chattahoochee River, resident Hitchiti speakers also moved south during late 1500s, as indicated by both archaeological evidence and native oral tradition (Worth 2000:273). There was substantial reduction in population—perhaps due to nonnative disease—in the Lower Creek region of the lower Chattahoochee River along the Alabama-Georgia border sometime between A.D. 1550 and 1650 (Worth 2000:269), and this is documented by a dramatic decline in number of habitation sites and a concomitant collapse of chiefdoms indicated by cessation of mound construction. By A.D. 1692, the lower Chattahoochee River was largely abandoned, as Lower Creek people had moved east to the Ocmulgee and Oconee river region of central Georgia to participate in trade with the British (Smith 2002; Worth 2000:279).

Clearly, migration and aggregation were not unusual processes among the Creeks by the late 1600s, and aggregation at least was a practice evident elsewhere in the Southeast in the centuries before European exploration. Sociopolitical organization had also undergone profound change, although again, such change was not unprecedented in the dynamic cycles of the Coosa and other Southeast chiefdoms. On a more intimate scale, archaeological evidence indicates some changes in domestic architecture by A.D. 1700, but other household practices such as pottery production reflect remarkable continuity in the face of other changes (Waselkov and Smith 2000:257). Thus, cultural stability was maintained in everyday life by Creek women through their domestic activities such as agriculture and ceramic production despite the changes affecting sociopolitical organization and settlement (Worth 2000:284; see also King 2006; Wesson 2001, 2002). Conversely, men became entangled in the colonial deerskin trade, and their roles within both the household and society were changing. So, both cultural change and continuity are evident among the Upper Creeks.

Significant depopulation from introduced disease as well as later violence likely contributed to collapse of ancestral Upper Creek chiefdoms initially identified by the Soto chroniclers, but when did European disease actually strike? The Tascaloosa polity encountered by Soto near the headwaters of the Alabama River immediately after his venture with the Coosa may have "disappeared" after Soto and before Luna (Galloway 1995:159). The cause of this change is unknown, however, and may reside in the eastward emigration of individuals of Talisi and other villages who later emerged as Lower Creeks. Based on native resistance encountered by the Pardo expedition of A.D. 1567–1568 as they traveled west into present-day Georgia, Galloway (1995:162) suggested that "perhaps they were crossing a sort of 'disease front' [and] peoples [such as the Coosa] on the other [western] side of the front may already have begun to defend themselves against encroachments of refugees" destined for the Creek Confederacy whose groups had already succumbed to disease-induced depopulation. That is, significant epidemics had not yet occurred among ancestral Upper Creeks in the 1560s. Conversely, Smith (1987) argued for a somewhat earlier spread of disease all the way to the Coosa River region. Certainly, available archaeological and historical data suggest earlier decline of the Creeks than the more westerly Chickasaws and Choctaws, who experienced documented decline beginning in the late 1600s, well after their full involvement with the colonial processes of slaving and the deerskin trade. The archaeological evidence for the Coosa, however, could be taken to support demographic collapse as late as A.D. 1630. To the south, the Lower Creek area may indicate early influence of introduced disease from Spanish missions—perhaps from the Apalachee missions built in the 1600s or even from the Atlantic coast mission settlements of La Florida such as St. Augustine, which date back to the 1560s. Galloway (1995:167) noted increased trade resulting from the Spanish mission presence, and escalating interaction between ancestral Lower Creeks and the Spanish settlers may have led to the early spread of nonnative disease there, if not farther north.

Lag time, if any, between the introduction of fatal disease and physical incursion by native (if not nonnative) aggressors into the Upper Creek region of the interior Southeast was probably short—on the order of decades rather than centuries. Such colonial-fueled aggression makes

The Colonial Experience 245

any assessment of change attributable to introduced disease and consequent depopulation difficult, if not impossible, with currently available data. Likewise, the paucity of archaeological and ethnohistoric data for the region north of the Coosa in Tennessee, Kentucky, and West Virginia also hampers our understanding of broader regional dynamics at that time. At the very least, Galloway (1995:200) concluded that once southeastern chiefdoms collapsed in the face of disease or other causes during the colonial era, their reconstitution as chiefly polities from the resulting tribes was unlikely. This was not due to depopulation per se but rather from their growing participation in trade with European colonists and the ready access to trade goods by most, if not all, members of these native societies. Such access effectively undermined the acquisition and control of prestige items by leaders—preventing their ascendancy as chiefs—and served to perpetuate the Indian role as suppliers of raw materials to Europeans (see also Galloway 1995:350; Wesson 2001).

Choctaws

Farther west, the ancestors of the Choctaws were also unlikely to have suffered the fate of early fatal disease due to the Soto *entrada*, as Soto did not reach the Choctaw homeland until the winter of A.D. 1541, more than one year into his trek.[14] And other expeditions such as that of Luna from A.D. 1559 to 1561 did not journey so far west (Galloway 1995: figure 4.1). West of the Mississippi River, ships and crew captained by Alonso Álvarez de Pineda explored the gulf coast of what is now Texas in A.D. 1519, and survivors of the ill-fated gulf expedition of Pánfilo de Narváez briefly settled on the Texas coast near present-day Galveston between A.D. 1528 and 1532.[15] There is no indication from archaeology or native oral tradition, however, that fatal disease passed east from this quarter into the Choctaw area, either through direct contact with colonists or down-the-line transmission via native trade from Mesoamerica (see Galloway 1995:136). Finally, the Spanish missions that probably served to introduce disease into Lower Creek area in the late sixteenth or early seventeenth century were less of a factor for Choctaw demographic history given their distance and the focus of Choctaw colonial interaction with the French rather than Spanish. For the Choctaws, depopulation due to colonial encroachment probably did not occur until the late 1600s and was likely due to multiple causes associated with colonialism, although there had been a history of demographic change in the region even prior to Columbus's landfall.

Galloway's (1995) study of the origins of the Choctaws through archaeology, historical records, and native oral tradition reveals a potent confederation that aligned with the French and subsequently garnered the attention of other colonial powers. Ultimately, however, they fell victim to rapacity of U.S. expansion and forced relocation in the early 1800s. Archaeological evidence indicates that the Choctaw homeland of the upper Pearl River of east-central Mississippi (see map 10) was largely devoid of human use during the Mississippian period, since it lacked broad alluvial valleys necessary to support the agricultural productivity required of Mississippian chiefdoms (Galloway 1995:124). Instead, several chiefdoms existed to the east and west prior to A.D. 1500, including groups in the Yazoo Basin of northwestern Mississippi and the Moundville culture of the Black Warrior River in northwestern Alabama. It was in the latter area that the Choctaws had their roots.

Moundville flourished from A.D. 800 to 1500 (Galloway 1995:31), but with the collapse of this chiefdom many of the people moved downriver into the middle Tombigbee and lower Alabama river areas of western Alabama (see map 10). Settlement hierarchy disappeared at that time, mound construction and craft specialization ceased, and burials no longer encompassed the variety of mortuary practices indicative of status differentiation that prevailed up until that time (Galloway 1995:71). All of these changes suggest significant political shifts and simplification of social structure prior to any possible European influence in the region. Despite changes in settlement and sociopolitical organization, however, subsistence remained much the same, including continued reliance on maize agriculture (Galloway 1995:64). Thus, many other facets of daily life also likely remained relatively unchanged. Conversely, the new practice of urn burial of infants and disarticulated adults emerged, and Galloway (1995:139) suggested that this relatively expedient mortuary practice may have been in response to epidemic disease.

Sometime in the late 1600s—perhaps in response to disease threats from La Florida that were already devastating gulf coastal tribes—additional migration occurred as the people of the middle Tombigbee and lower Alabama rivers pushed northwest into the upper Pearl River region (Galloway 1995:203). They joined others who were already settled in the northwestern Choctaw prairie homeland, although sociopolitical organization, settlement, and subsistence practices of the residents and newcomers were similar. In this new territory, as many as fifty autonomous tribes maintained large villages and emerged in historical documents of the late seventeenth century as the "Choctaw." The first use of this term to denote the people of this region was in A.D. 1686, in the annals of the expedition of Marcos Delgado from the Apalachee mission in northern Florida (Galloway 1995:20), and this collective self-identity seems to have formed sometime between the late 1500s and mid-1600s (Galloway 1995:170). The French established "first contact" with the Choctaws in A.D. 1699 and alliance by A.D. 1702 (Galloway 1995:183). The British, on the other hand, established a trading post among the neighboring Chickasaws by A.D. 1700.

Some Choctaw ancestors may have been part of the "Pafalaya" simple chiefdom or tribal group noted in the Soto chronicles, which Galloway (1995:124) placed in the middle Tombigbee Valley area. Any contact they had with Soto was relatively brief, however, and they had no interaction with subsequent Spanish explorations. In fact, the Choctaws themselves were not pulled directly into the colonial intrigue of the interior Southeast until forced to contend with British-inspired slave raids of their Chickasaw neighbors to the north in the late seventeenth century. After the establishment of Charles Town (i.e., Charleston) on the South Carolina coast in A.D. 1673, the Chickasaws were recruited by the British to provide Indian slaves for transport to the Caribbean. To facilitate this trade, the British provided firearms to the Chickasaws and their other Indian allies, setting off a chain reaction of violence, resistance, and displacement that forever changed the face of native occupation in the interior Southeast. The Choctaws fell victim to this aggression, but unlike many of the other native groups that suffered the trauma of the slave trade, the Choctaws remained in their territory and the population was augmented by refugees from surrounding areas. Thus, the Choctaws represent the coming together of numerous Western Muskogean-speaking groups, as indicated by an oral tradition that records both their presence in place and immigration into the region.

The timing of catastrophic introduced disease among the Choctaws, if any, remains unknown. It was likely coincident or nearly coeval with the infiltration of Europeans into the region in the late 1600s, however, although Galloway (1995:140) speculated that earlier southward movement from the Tombigbee River into the coastal plain with the collapse of Moundville may have been due to depopulation and the capacity of the coastal plan, a more agriculturally marginal area, to support smaller populations. Thus, population declines, or at least significant demographic shifts, were not uncommon in this area even prior to colonial activities. Unequivocal evidence for catastrophic mortality—dozens of decomposing bodies of individuals struck down by disease—was observed south of the Choctaw region by Pierre Le Moyne d'Iberville at Mobile Bay in A.D. 1699 (Galloway 1995:184), but it is unknown if such disease spread inland via native intermediaries. And Galloway (1995:174) suggested that Choctaw people of the Pearl River may have actually severed connections—dating back to their participation in the Mississippian interaction sphere—with the Natchez people to the west when they were threatened with disease from that quarter around A.D. 1680. In fact, "aggressive boundary maintenance" (Galloway 1995:181) seems to have prevailed for the Choctaws in the 1680s, this time in reference to their interaction with people to the east. New communal mortuary practices evident in the archaeological record and the adoption of a uniform dialect facilitating interaction between Choctaw groups as well as with outsiders (Galloway 1995:346) may have been other mechanisms that supported the formation of Choctaw identity in resistance to native and colonial aggressors. Importantly, the development of such practices was a Choctaw decision to establish their identity as a people distinct from the disparate groups from which they derived, and may also have included shifting material symbols of previous cultural difference to instead denote lineage or moiety affiliation (Galloway 1995:265).

Colonial depopulation likely furthered the loss of sociopolitical complexity that began with the precolonial collapse of the chiefdom that was the Choctaw heritage. Conversely, the daily practices of domestic life, such as subsistence tasks and the production of tools and household goods, were maintained (Galloway 1995:141). And even much of the evident cultural change was not the result of introduced disease—rather, declining population was related to a host of factors, including slave raids and later involvement in the deerskin trade. Economic involvement of the Choctaws and their neighbors with the British and French had demographic consequences and, too, provided for the manipulation of Indian people by colonists and vice versa for political, economic, and social ends. Since there had been fluctuation in population and migration even during the Mississippian period (Galloway 1995:60), the Choctaws were heirs to a tradition of demographic change and accommodation in the not-so-distant past. Galloway (1995:346) posited an explicit recognition of this history by Choctaw people in coping with colonial change when she concluded that marriage of Choctaw women to men of groups to the east may have been seen as "reestablishing older lineage links severed by migration" after A.D. 1500. Still, Galloway (1995:163) concluded that there may have been some cognitive shift among the Choctaws that accompanied demographic change and colonial expansion. She suggested that experience with Soto and likely knowledge of continuing presence of Spaniards to the southeast in La Florida may have led to cultural change such as the "modification of the very concept of novelty into [the elders'] teaching about human conduct in the world" (Galloway 1995:163). She suggested this specifically in reference to diplomatic or intergroup relations, as manifest in dealings with colonists and perhaps even other native groups. Physical displacement of Choctaw ancestors and their ultimate coalescence within their historically known territory, including their eventual use of territory extending west to the Yazoo delta, "made a dramatic difference in how Indian groups viewed themselves and each other [and thus] it also affected how they would deal with permanent European settlers" (Galloway 1995:6).

Similar to the Upper Creeks, then, there is no compelling archaeological or historical evidence for depopulation due to introduced disease among the Choctaws until they—and their neighbors—had established economic and diplomatic relations with European colonists around A.D. 1700. Although permanent nonnative settlement was not yet present at that time, there was regular exchange and other interaction with the French, and a British trading post was present among the Chickasaws to the north. And when depopulation did occur, it was likely due to multiple factors, not the least of which was slave raids. This was offset somewhat, however, by continued immigration into the region by displaced people of the west and east during the eighteenth century. In addition, archaeological data and native oral tradition reveal a history of demographic upheaval and adjustment among the Choctaws and their ancestors, dating back at least to the collapse of the Moundville chiefdom around A.D. 1500.

The Natchez and Their Yazoo Basin Neighbors

The Yazoo Basin and Natchez Bluffs are two distinct physiographic areas on the eastern side of the Mississippi River between the confluence with the Arkansas River on the north and the mouth of the Homochitto River on the south (see map 10). The Yazoo region is characterized by alluvial, swampy bottomland and natural levees with mixed deciduous forest, while the loess uplands of the Natchez Bluffs encompass mixed hardwood forests and pine woodlands bisected by tributaries of the Mississippi River (Brain 1978). Archaeological, ethnohistoric, and ethnographic data reveal a complex mosaic of native cultures within the region, predating French explorer René-Robert Cavelier, Sieur de La Salle's first entry into the area in A.D. 1673. These sources also indicate significant movement of groups within the area before and during the colonial era, but scholars agree that when first encountered by the French the Natchez Indians occupied mound centers located near the present-day city that bears their name. Native oral tradition reinforces Natchez connections to the region prior to European encounters (Jeter 2002:211), and new studies suggest that these people were linguistically distinct from their neighbors, many of whom were later immigrants into the area (Jeter 2002:195). For example, Tunican speakers were relatively recent arrivals into the Yazoo Basin and, eventually, the Natchez Bluffs.

Various reconstructions of the route of Soto have been proposed, but recent work by Hudson and his colleagues (Hudson, DePratter et al. 1989; Hudson, Smith, and DePratter 1990) suggests that the Soto *entrada* passed through the Yazoo Basin. In fact, their six-week encampment in the spring of A.D. 1541 within the province of Quizquiz may have been in this area or somewhat farther north. Brain (1978) links Quizquiz to the Tunica, whereas Jeter (2002:205–206) provides several alternate interpretations based on ethnohistoric data, including possible Natchez affiliation of these people. Similarly, historical reconstructions place the more southerly Quigualtam province of the Soto chronicles either within the Yazoo Basin or in the Natchez Bluffs region. Most scholars agree that Quigualtam was Natchez (Jeter 2002:211). Although Soto never visited the latter chiefdom, both Quizquiz and Quigualtam were still clearly potent and vital polities at the time of Soto's expedition, unlike some other chiefdoms of the interior Southeast that had already vanished or were in decline. The Quigualtam ruler was especially defiant of the Spanish interlopers, sufficiently so to lead the Soto *entrada* to avoid direct interaction. And when French missionaries and traders first arrived in the lower Mississippi Valley in A.D. 1673, the "Natchez" they identified were still inhabiting mound centers and functioning under the strong central authority of chiefly "Suns." This was in contrast to many other groups the French had encountered farther north along the Mississippi, including in the Yazoo Basin. Still, the Natchez may have already incorporated people from disparate groups into their communities by this time (Galloway

1995:174). Within only a few decades, however, the Indian population of the Natchez area had also been decimated, and conflicts with the French had led to the collapse of the Natchez chiefdom and dispersal of the survivors. For example, some Natchez refugees—recognized by their ceramics—settled among the Chickasaws near present-day Tupelo, Mississippi, although even in this circumstance they choose to gather in just one, rather than both, of the Chickasaw village clusters in this area (J. K. Johnson 2000:104).

Historical records suggest that earlier population decline may have occurred prior to French colonial enterprises in the region, if nonnative disease spread out of the Southwest (Dobyns 1983). For example, members of the A.D. 1519 expedition of Pineda along the Texas coast suffered from various maladies that might have been transmitted north via native intermediaries. If any population decline occurred among the Natchez between the expeditions of Soto and La Salle, however, historical records suggest that it was insufficient to significantly undermine the sociopolitical structure of the polity. Population also could have rebounded had there been a significant disease event, given the large initial population size and unlikely secondary waves of disease during this time of little interaction between Indians and colonists here or in immediately adjoining areas (see Thornton et al. 1991). When disease struck in the 1700s, on the other hand, historical accounts indicate that it was swift, persistent, and devastating. Several Natchez chiefs were struck down in quick succession, and native oral tradition notes that the perpetual flame maintained within the temple was finally extinguished (Lorenz 2000:148).

Just as the Natchez were the likely descendants of Quigualtam, so Quigualtam was heir to one of the paramount chiefdoms of the Yazoo Basin or Natchez Bluffs area, archaeologically identified as the Plaquemine culture. Although related to the Mississippian tradition of the interior Southeast and middle Mississippi River drainage, the Plaquemine culture had deeper roots in the region and, in some areas, maintained existing traditions rather than adopting some Mississippian traits. Earliest Mississippian influence appeared in the northern Yazoo Basin around A.D. 1200, with subsequent spread southward. This Mississippian influence in the north is recognized archaeologically by the introduction of characteristic shell-tempered ceramics, reliance on maize agriculture, the emergence of a hierarchical settlement system including ceremonial mound centers, and long-distance exchange of exotic materials among elites. The Plaquemine culture, which persisted in the Natchez Bluffs area into the 1500s, also participated in exchange and shared subsistence and settlement characteristics of the Mississippian tradition, but these people utilized ceramics that were unique to this area.

Regional archaeological research has provided a detailed picture of the rise of Mississippian and Plaquemine cultures in the lower Mississippi Valley as well as long-term patterns of regional settlement that accompanied these cultural changes. Brain (1978) synthesized these latter data, which indicate construction of several mound centers on tributaries close to Mississippi River by A.D. 1300 and substantial populations in both the Yazoo Basin and Natchez Bluffs. During the subsequent century, additional mound centers were built and flourished, apparently in response to the increasing influence of Mississippian culture. After circa A.D. 1400, however, people relocated to newly constructed mound centers situated farther upstream. Still, the regional population remained large. Over time, the number of mound sites declined, centers became more dispersed, and by A.D. 1500 new mound construction was sharply curtailed. This shift coincided with similar decline in Mississippian cultures elsewhere in the Southeast. By the late 1600s, only two major mound centers were still in use.

Brain concluded that ancestral Natchez people occupied the bluffs region throughout this sequence, while the archaeological record of the Yazoo Basin reflected Tunican antecedents. Jeter (2002) built on this earlier work to discuss even broader-scale regional population movements from western Arkansas to the Natchez Bluffs. He offered various scenarios of cultural affiliation and population movements into and within the region, each of which has implications for understanding demography during the colonial era. Of primary import here is his suggestion that "Northern Natchezan" people occupied the trans-Missippian region from the Arkansas River south to the Yazoo River mouth. That is, both the Natchez Bluffs and the Yazoo Basin were occupied by Natchezan peoples, with the northerners displaced by native immigrants into the Yazoo area or simply consolidating in the Natchez Bluffs after circa A.D. 1500.

Ramenofsky (1987) undertook archaeological study of contact-era native depopulation in the lower Mississippi Valley, including the Natchez region, Yazoo Basin, and adjacent areas to the west and north along the Mississippi River. Chronological control for the population reconstruction relied on radiocarbon dates, pottery seriation, and the presence of certain nonnative goods. Ceramics and radiocarbon dates formed the basis for defining the prehistoric Mississippian component dating from ca. A.D. 1200 to 1541, although these two dating methods proved somewhat less useful for establishing two later periods of interest. Instead, the protohistoric period, spanning the approximately 130 years between initial Spanish and French incursions, was defined primarily by presence of ornamental metal bells and glass beads of European manufacture. Similarly, early historical native occupation after the French colonial presence was identified by more diverse European goods serving a wide range of utilitarian tasks. Based on site counts, which were the only data available to serve as a population proxy, Ramenofsky observed significant decline after A.D. 1541 and modest population rebound after A.D. 1700. These data suggested catastrophic depopulation through exposure to disease vectors in the Soto expedition, through subsequent down-the-line disease transmission from other areas in the absence of face-to-face encounters with Europeans, or both.

Although Ramenofsky concluded that population rebound after A.D. 1700 probably reflected sampling problems rather than true patterns, she was satisfied that the significant decline during the protohistoric period reflected depopulation due to introduced disease. Further, she noted that such a conclusion was especially likely given the focus of much regional archaeology on ethnohistoric sites. That is, despite the fact that such sites were probably overrepresented in her sample, population decline was not only evident, but dramatic. While this interpretation ignores extended use of some sites—and therefore the presence of prehistoric components at some of these same "protohistoric" sites—there is another chronological issue that suggests that the data may not be as robust as Ramenofsky suggests. Specifically, the reliance on nonnative goods to distinguish prehistoric from protohistoric components assumes there was uniform access to and spread of such items throughout the area. In fact, such goods were probably extremely rare, at least during the early protohistoric period, as Spanish and French goods were only available via distant overland contacts with the missions of La Florida or transmission along the Mississippi River from the north. If such goods were not readily available to most, if not all, of the native population of the lower Mississippi Valley at that time, then many protohistoric components would be incorrectly identified as prehistoric. This effectively inflates prehistoric site counts, while at the same time undercounting protohistoric components. If such temporal problems contributed to the pattern of dramatic decline during the protohistoric period, then we can conclude that population decline was probably much less dramatic or, even, that such decline did not occur until much later. Furthermore, if this is the case, then "rebound" during the historic period disappears and instead simply reflects the end of a regional trend in demographic decline.

The broad geographic scope of Ramenofsky's study—from Memphis, Tennessee, to northern Louisiana—also lumps multiple distinct histories of peoples and polities within the mosaic of colonial-era disease, including possible southern Natchez persistence as groups farther north dealt with an influx of native people from areas perhaps as far away as the Ohio River valley (Jeter 2002:215–216). Since Ramenofsky's pioneering study, work by Jeter (2002) and others has suggested a much more complex pattern of regional population disruption, movement, and reorganization spanning decades and centuries both before and after the Soto *entrada*. In fact, Galloway (1995:139) contended that diachronic demographic trends during the protohistoric period may be related to the long-term trend in population decline beginning centuries earlier (see Brain 1978; Mainfort 2001), and that any decline in population size among the Natchez following Soto and prior to French colonization was "serious" but not "catastrophic" (Galloway 2002:237; see also Brain 1978:358). For example, continuity in burial practices "may point toward lesser disease impact" between initial Spanish and French exploration (Galloway 2002:240). In fact, Galloway (2002:241) concluded that the Natchez maintained continuity in both their internal and external relations even after the substantial disease-induced depopulation of the early 1700s. She observed that "the strength of historical developments and cultural patterns, combined with the relatively steady state of the underlying subsistence base, seems to have kept individual groups on the same paths they had already defined for themselves" (Galloway 2002:241). The role of Natchez women and kinship relations probably played an important role in maintaining such continuity (Galloway 2002:247), while the maintenance of strong ties to their ancestral territory—dating back at least to the Plaquemine culture—may also have contributed to Natchez persistence following the devastation of disease (Galloway 2002:246). In this respect, the Natchez truly did stand out from their newcomer, native neighbors.

Caddo

Archaeological evidence and ethnohistoric accounts of the Spanish and French—dating from as early as the Soto *entrada,* which was under the command of Luis de Moscoso after the death of Soto a few months

The Colonial Experience

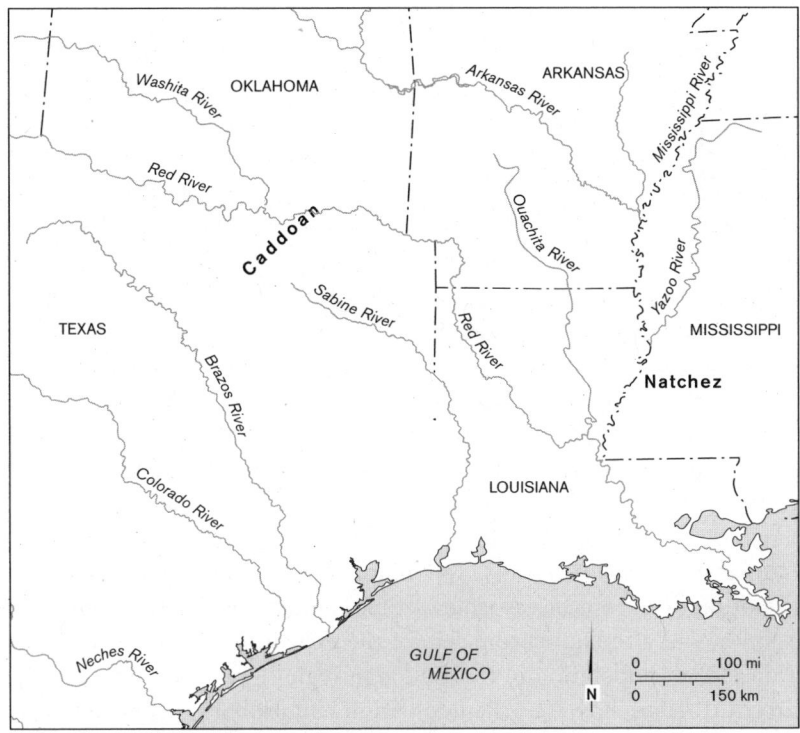

MAP 11. Caddoan case-study area.

earlier—provide a picture of the complex societies of Caddoan-speaking peoples inhabiting the forested uplands of what is now east Texas, southeast Oklahoma, western Arkansas, and northeast Louisiana. *Caddo* was a term coined by the French from a local native language and encompassed numerous polities that self-identified by an array of local names, several of which were recorded by the Soto chroniclers. These people lived in dispersed rural villages and farmsteads that were associated with large, uninhabited civic-ceremonial centers that were, in turn, located in the major river valleys from the Neches River in the south to the Arkansas River to the north (see map 11). Archaeological investigations have documented the development of these societies beginning around A.D. 800. Cultural characteristics included the construction of substructural platform and burial mounds at ceremonial sites, the interment of high-status males and associated retainers or family members in shaft burials in the mounds, residence in small household compounds in outlying settlements, burial of lesser adults in farmstead compounds or rural community cemeteries, and the production of utilitarian and fine ceramics that serve to identify locally distinct traditions likely representing ethnic groups within the larger Caddoan area. Differences in material culture and, to a lesser extent, architecture and inferred sociopolitical organization or status differentiation are evident, but all Caddoan societies were governed by theocratic chiefs who controlled economic, political, and religious life (Perttula 1992).

Caddoan culture was supported by the cultivation of maize and other introduced New World cultigens, while salt production also grew in importance after A.D. 1400. Local products were augmented by exotic raw materials and goods made of marine shell, copper, turquoise, and cotton that were acquired through long-distance exchange. Such trade was particularly robust before A.D. 1400, reinforcing interconnections between Caddoan-speaking groups as well as ties of Caddoan elites to similarly positioned people of other cultural traditions in the Southeast, Southwest, Plains, and middle Mississippi River. Population size of many groups at the time of first contact with the Soto *entrada* is unknown, although chroniclers of the expedition noted substantial, if dispersed, population in the Caddoan region (Perttula 1992:19). By circa A.D. 1690, however, the population had probably dropped to less than ten thousand individuals, most of whom had settled in major river valleys.[16] Historically, ethnographers recognized approximately twenty-five Caddoan-speaking groups in the region, including three "confederacies" that represented aggregations of previously distinct Caddoan peoples who had allied to take advantage of the burgeoning fur trade with the French after A.D. 1685. Mobility facilitating such aggregation was due, in part, to the earlier introduction of the horse from the Southwest, which also contributed to the rise of bison hunting within the northern Caddoan-speaking groups during the colonial era.

Much of the archaeological research on cultural change among Caddoan peoples during the colonial era has been developed by Perttula (1992; see also Perttula 1991, 1993, 2002a, 2002b), who paid particular attention to the potential for change brought about by disease-induced depopulation. Chronology of the colonial era—or as Perttula termed it for this region, the Protohistoric period (A.D. 1500–1683)—was based on calibrated radiocarbon, thermoluminescence, and archaeomagnetic dating; ceramic seriation; and temporally diagnostic projectile points. Ceramics, in particular, were used to define often quite brief periods on the order of a few decades. Still, the exact

The Colonial Experience   257

timing of some cultural shifts and population decline during this era remains uncertain. European goods were not important in Caddoan life until after permanent European occupation in the area and, thus, are not useful for chronology of the early colonial era. Lack of random sampling for regional settlement studies precluded quantitative assessment of population size with archaeological data prior to, during, or after the colonial era, and this was recognized by Perttula as a significant problem with the database. In addition, the bias of many studies toward ceremonial mounds and cemeteries undermined both demographic studies and fuller consideration of the daily practices of Caddoan people. Much research has focused instead on social stratification and sociopolitical organization represented by civic-ceremonial centers. Similar to Smith's (1987) study of the Coosa, Perttula inferred that disease-induced depopulation had occurred early in the colonial era, since significant changes in sociopolitical organization and mortuary practices were evident prior to sustained occupation in the region by the Spanish and French beginning in the early 1700s.

Direct archaeological evidence for introduced disease or population decline is available from only one subarea, the Ouachita River valley in southwest Arkansas (see map 11). Here, mean age at death for the population declined—indicating a greater proportion of deaths among the young—and periosteal lesions on human skeletal remains have been taken as evidence for the occurrence of smallpox within the population sometime between A.D. 1500 and 1650 (Perttula 1992: 132). Significantly, however, archaeological data do not indicate any cultural changes resulting from posited depopulation. Rather, Perttula (1992:227) concluded that "in general the Caddoan populations of the region had adapted well [after the smallpox epidemic] and experienced no diminishment in adaptive efficiency during the Protohistoric period." This included the continued construction and use of burial mounds as well as evident social stratification. That is, supracommunity sociopolitical integration was maintained, and ultimate abandonment of the Ouachita River valley by Caddoan people didn't occur until late 1600s (Perttula 1992:133). And even elsewhere in the Caddoan world there was relatively little or gradual cultural change at that time. For example, Perttula (1992:228) noted evidence in the western Caddoan area of east Texas of "community reintegration . . . , [which] may mean that cultural disruptions and depopulation were not as severe initially among these rural [upriver] Caddoan communities as it [sic] was for some of the Caddoan populations in the major river valleys."

Instead, the major locus of colonial-era sociopolitical change was on the Red River in the central Caddoan area (see map 11). Here, mound construction and use ceased, and shaft burials were either placed in nonmound areas or gave way to community cemeteries with little distinction in individual status evident in grave goods. The shift to a more egalitarian society may have occurred as early as A.D. 1500 in middle Red River area (Perttula 1992:132–133) but perhaps as late as A.D. 1650 downstream in the lower Red River valley (Perttula 1992:121–122). And in the latter area, both apogee and decline occurred during a 150-year span within the Protohistoric period. There were also significant regional settlement shifts due to the abandonment of some areas and population aggregation at a few widely dispersed locales. But local population densities still did not match that achieved earlier in time. It is important to note, however, that archaeological evidence from the Caddoan area reveals that markers of sociopolitical complexity, such as the practice of mound shaft interments, began to decline in some areas as early as A.D. 1300 (Perttula 2002a:54), while in others this practice persisted until the mid-1600s (Perttula 1992:146).

Although such temporal disjunction in initiation of sociopolitical change within Caddoan polities prior to any possible European influence makes attribution of cause for colonial-era sociopolitical change problematic, Perttula (1992) concluded that significant shifts in culture between A.D. 1500 and 1600—such as the abandonment of mound shaft burials and settlement aggregation in some areas—were the result of disease-induced depopulation. This, despite the lack of direct or proxy quantitative assessment of population size. He reasoned that these changes followed the introduction of disease from one or more of the Spanish expeditions between A.D. 1519 and 1683. In addition to Pineda's exploration of the Texas gulf coast south of the Caddoan region (A.D. 1519) and the brief occupation of the same area by survivors of the Narváez expedition (A.D. 1528–1534), documented Spanish colonial ventures included the Soto traverse through Caddoan territory (A.D. 1542) and brief contact with the westernmost Caddoan peoples by the expeditions of Hernando Martín and Diego del Castillo (A.D. 1650) and the expedition of Juan Domínguez de Mendoza and Fray Nicolás López (A.D. 1683) (Perttula 1992:19ff). Alternately, depopulation may have been related to the early spread of Old World disease via native intermediaries from the Southwest after the establishment of Santa Fe by the Spanish in A.D. 1600, as nonnative goods were circulating among Caddoan peoples by the 1680s (Perttula 1992:70).

Regardless of cause of colonial-era native culture change in the Caddoan region, the process was complex and the decisions made were not unique to this period. Settlement aggregation and dispersal were also common later in time, as people adjusted to take advantage of trading opportunities with the French and Spanish. And the same may have applied prior to Columbus's landfall, particularly with the decline of interregional native exchange networks to the east and initiation of salt production around A.D. 1400 or, somewhat later, with the influences of non-Caddoan native people to the southwest who were engaged with Spanish traders by the mid-1500s. In addition, some regional changes clearly predate direct colonial interaction. In the northern Caddoan area, for example, it has been suggested that local droughts between A.D. 1549 and 1577 may be to blame for sociopolitical decline (Perttula 1992:141). Here, there was a shift to more a mobile lifestyle, an increase in hunting, and less reliance on maize agriculture, perhaps due to influence of or threats from people of the prairies to the west. Abandonment of this northern region by Caddoan people began around A.D. 1520 and was complete within one hundred years, with subsequent settlement by non-Caddoan peoples. Could environmental factors have also contributed to or caused the social changes that Perttula (1992) attributed solely to introduced disease and depopulation? Was Caddoan culture change during the colonial era due to deteriorating environmental conditions, catastrophic disease-induced depopulation, the changing economic landscape that emerged with colonial traders, or a combination of these factors? If sociopolitical change cannot be directly attributed to disease because change was underway even prior to Columbus's landfall and regional droughts were influencing actions at an early time in the northern Caddoan area, then how confident can we be that the archaeological evidence from the colonial era relates only to catastrophic disease-induced depopulation?

Minimally, the Caddoan data suggest uneven exposure to introduced diseases and a mosaic response to resulting depopulation. Some groups may have responded with social and settlement changes that suggest a move to less complex, more egalitarian, organization. Elsewhere, no change occurred, even though disease clearly infiltrated these populations. The latter is particularly telling and suggests that local factors such as leadership or isolation from second waves of disease had a significant influence on the direction and pace of population-induced change. If colonial-era Caddoan populations were as large as Perttula would have us believe, then decline in population size was significant.

On the other hand, demographic simulations suggest that such a large population would have rebounded relatively quickly in the absence of subsequent pathogenic assaults (see Thornton et al. 1991). Therefore, the fact that Caddoan populations continued to decline precipitously after A.D. 1685 was probably due to repeated epidemics—which Perttula noted occurred at least once a generation—rather than to the fact that disease was present. Prior to A.D. 1685, on the other hand, disease introduction was evidently rare and unlikely unless transmitted via native intermediaries from the Southwest. And the fact that cultural change was not that significant in many areas during the early colonial era supports that notion that multiple epidemic shocks were unlikely at that time.

The lack of fine chronological detail for prehistory—comparable to that applied to the colonial period—also undermines understanding of how flexible these social systems may have been either in the more distant past or during the colonial era based on past experience. It is also important to consider the timing of cultural change within the context of subsequent settlement in the area by the French and Spanish via missions, presidios, and trading posts. Time lag, if any, between the initial disease assault and any local consequences resulting therefrom—mediated by the actions of leaders, group history and memory, or other factors—may have dictated how well Caddoan peoples responded to epidemics. For example, if fatal disease struck closer to A.D. 1685 than in the 1500s, Caddoan people may not have been able to make sufficient cultural adjustments and demographic recovery prior to European occupation. And even Caddoan cultural change after sustained European contact has been explained by some researchers as entirely consistent with Caddoan dynamics and intergroup interaction extending into the distant past. That is, cultural accommodations are reminiscent of the history of adjustments to trade relationships, shifting power relations, and other processes evident in the archaeological record during the height of Caddoan sociopolitical integration. The argument that depopulation caused significant cultural change is not supported by extant data, which shows evident cultural stasis or rebound in the one case with direct evidence for disease (in the Ouachita River valley). This observation undermines any attribution of cause for irreversible change in later circumstances, with explanations for colonial-era cultural change other than disease-induced depopulation ranging from economic involvement with European colonists to the specific context of leadership to the collapse of interregional networks that reinforced traditional sociopolitical authority.

MULTIETHNIC DYNAMICS ON THE EASTERN PRAIRIES

The demographic history of the native people who lived on the prairies situated west and south of Lake Michigan is a complicated and still poorly understood sequence of population aggregation, dispersal, decline, and migration. This process began in the 1400s due to factors unrelated to European colonialism and simply continued for different, or related, reasons after physical infiltration of French traders and missionaries into the region in the mid-1600s (Brown and Sasso 2001; Emerson and Brown 1992). Earliest European contact in this area occurred with the landing of Jean Nicolet de Belleborne on the western shore of Lake Michigan in A.D. 1634, but the biological or cultural impact of this event, if any, remains to be demonstrated. Rather, the establishment of French missions and trading posts on Lake Superior and Lake Michigan in 1660s initiated sustained interaction between native people and European colonists within the region. Likewise, the A.D. 1673 expedition of missionary Jacques Marquette and trader Louis Jolliet from the western shore of Lake Michigan through present-day Wisconsin and down the Mississippi River to the confluence with the Arkansas River, and their return through present-day Illinois, led to the expansion of French colonial activities in the prairies and areas to the south. Thus, historical data suggest that the late 1600s probably mark the period when colonial-era disease-induced native population decline began in the prairies, just as this period witnessed substantial declines in native population farther south along the Mississippi River after French infiltration (see "The Natchez and Their Yazoo Basin Neighbors" above). The question, however, is whether archaeological evidence tells a different tale of earlier demographic decline.

Archaeological evidence suggests a deep history of occupation within the region by Siouan-speaking peoples, some of whom may have subsequently moved west onto the Plains either prior to or during the colonial era (Brown and Sasso 2001:213). In fact, many of the native people encountered by French missionaries and traders in the Eastern Prairies in the seventeenth century were relatively new arrivals to the area, either representing Algonquian-speaking groups who had migrated west from the central Ohio Valley or Iroquoian-speaking peoples who had entered from present-day southern Ontario. Much, if not all, of the westward migration of Algonquians into this region preceded the Columbian landfall, but the influx of Iroquoian and other native people from the east also continued after European incursions into the Northeast. This colonial-era movement was spurred, in part, by the aggression of the League of the Iroquois following the devastation of disease within those populations in the 1630s (see "Iroquoian Tribes of the Interior Northeast" above). Such demographic dynamism not only makes it difficult to identify in situ colonial-era depopulation due to introduced disease in the upper Midwest, it also hampers attempts to understand subsequent cultural change. Any given village may have witnessed occupation by multiple groups with different cultural traditions either in sequence or simultaneously (Brown and Sasso 2001).

This prairie region encompasses tall-grass uplands, oak savanna, and prairie-woodland mosaic along the streams. This zone stretches from the headwaters of the Illinois and Wabash rivers south of Lake Michigan to the northeast along the upper reaches of the Mississippi River watershed in southern Wisconsin, southeast Minnesota, and northern Iowa (see map 12). Hardwood forests abut the prairies to the north, and to the south, fertile valley floodplains of the Mississippi River and its major tributaries dominated the cultural landscape of this region prior to European colonization. Along these major river drainages of the southern zone, archaeological evidence has documented the rise of Mississippian cultures around A.D. 800, setting in motion the subsequent participation within this tradition of resident groups as far away as the interior Southeast. As noted above, Mississippian traits included the construction of large civic-ceremonial centers in the major river valleys; a hierarchical settlement structure including lesser towns, villages, and farmsteads; dependence on maize, bean, and squash agriculture on the floodplains; and the production of fine ceramic vessels and effigies. These cultural features indicate complex chiefdoms in which long-distance exchange of exotic goods between elites reinforced sociopolitical power and authority.

On the prairies proper, only relatively few, relatively small civic-ceremonial centers appear after A.D. 1000 with the emergence of what is known as the Oneota culture (Brown and Sasso 2001). This represents a fusion of sorts of existing prairie traits and Mississippian influence, although many of the characteristic Mississippian features such as trade of exotic materials and production of fine ceramics are

The Colonial Experience

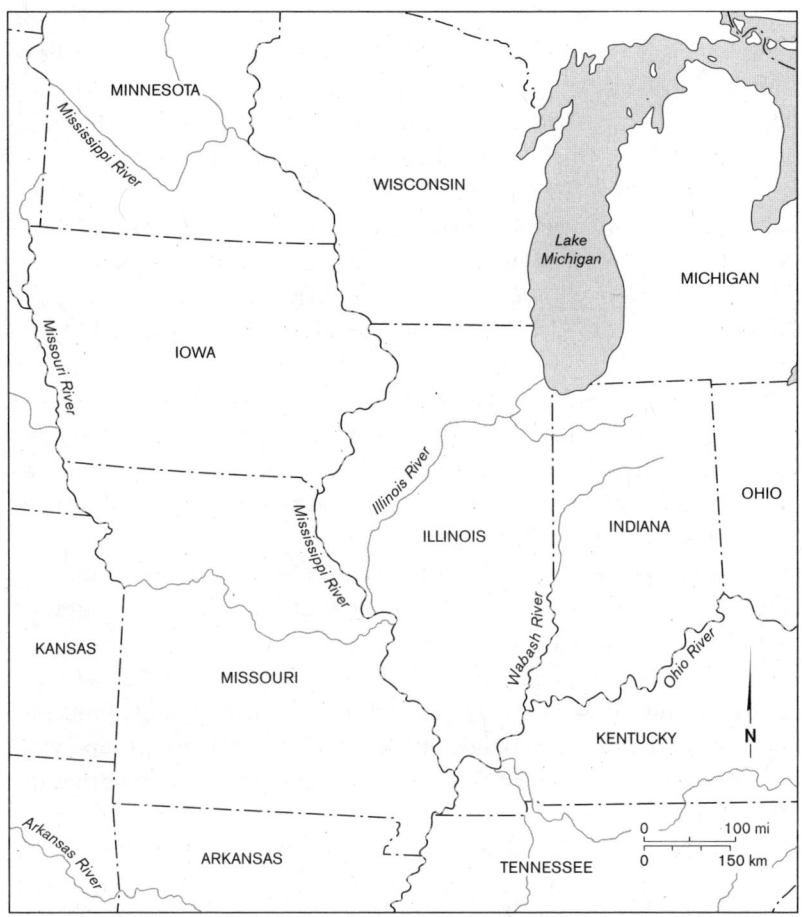

MAP 12. Eastern Prairies case-study area.

less developed in this region. In addition, even after the rise of the more complex sociopolitical structure represented by civic-ceremonial mound sites, there was generally less reliance on maize agriculture by people of the Oneota tradition and greater incorporation of wetland plant resources into the diet. Native people of the prairies also hunted bison after the circa A.D. 1450 onset of the Little Ice Age brought about climatic conditions conducive to bison habitation in the region (Brown and Sasso 2001:224). Oneota culture persisted as tribes rather than chiefdoms into the colonial era and thus is thought to represent the historical development of resident Siouan peoples in the region. Later

Algonquian and Iroquoian immigrants used similar subsistence practices, but their presence is recognized by distinctive ceramics and differences in domestic architecture. Ethnohistoric observations suggest that Indian occupation was concentrated in valley farming communities for a portion of the year, with a shift to dispersed or communal upland hunting for the remainder of the year. Archaeological evidence indicates that settlement architecture was variable in the centuries leading up to European incursion—ranging from small earthlodges to large arbor longhouses—although such shifts likely reflect different populations and migration rather than endogenous change (Brown and Sasso 2001:215).

Regional archaeologists have made repeated attempts to connect pre-Columbian cultural assemblages of this area—distinguished primarily on the basis of ceramics—with specific native groups identified in the region by the French in the seventeenth century. As discussed by Emerson and Brown (1992; see also Brown and Sasso 2001), such research has proven extremely difficult for a host of reasons, not least because of evident discontinuities in material culture due to migration and the replacement of native ceramics with nonnative goods. Thus, determining colonial-era disease-induced depopulation and consequent cultural change is equally complicated by such demographic processes and potential cultural amalgamation, as many of these groups were neither stable nor closed populations and multiethnic communities did form (Brown and Sasso 2001:213). Still, a demographic study of the colonial era was developed for the Eastern Prairie zone by Green (1993), who used calibrated radiocarbon dates and a few thermoluminescence dates to posit a hiatus in occupation between circa A.D. 1550 to 1650, with apparent population rebound thereafter (Green 1993:296). Green was careful to acknowledge, however, that the frequency of radiocarbon dates through time was unreliable for demonstrating diachronic increases and decreases in population. This was because individual sites or components were often represented by multiple dates, thus inflating the dates for that period. Therefore, Green chose to focus on gaps that he determined would represent true instances of depopulation. Furthermore, he attributed the gap in dates to population decline due to introduced diseases prior to face-to-face encounters with Europeans rather than some other cause.

Despite Green's cautions, his study has been criticized on both methodological and interpretative grounds. Critics have pointed to the relatively small sample size—just 39 dates from twenty-four archaeological sites in Wisconsin, 32 dates from Iowa, and 11 dates from Minnesota—as well as the fact that calibration of radiocarbon dates within the period of interest results in broad error ranges that undermine concise chronology (Brown and Sasso 2001:226; Henige 1998:161–162). Interpretive critiques of this demographic reconstruction, on the other hand, have focused especially on the fact that native demographic changes were well underway in this region prior to Columbus's landfall. For example, Brown and Sasso (2001:226) note significant consolidation in regional population during the 1500s, with growth in one area evidently facilitated by movement from, or abandonment of, another area. Such movements undermine assessment of regional demography unless a geographically broad but statistically robust sampling strategy is employed for demographic reconstructions. Such observations suggest that one or more endogenous factors precipitated demographic change in the region and that early colonial-era decline was, in fact, part of this long-term process of population decline rather than reflecting down-the-line disease transmission via native trading partners from the Southeast or Plains. The onset of the Little Ice Age has received the most attention as a causal factor and, certainly, this is reasonable given coeval subsistence shifts with the decrease in temperature and growing season. Green (1993) considered climate change as a factor, but largely dismissed this as a cause in favor of disease (cf. Emerson and Brown 1992:103). His argument was based primarily on the fact that agricultural productivity persisted in several areas despite changing climatic conditions, and he also argued on more general grounds that the effects of slight decreases in seasonal temperatures on maize agriculture remain to be demonstrated rather than asserted.

Still, given these observations regarding long-term history, demographic sampling, and environmental change on the Eastern Prairies, it is difficult to conclude that the available evidence reflects proof of disease-induced depopulation in the sixteenth or early seventeenth century. Likewise, as noted above, population movements into and within the region undermine tracing consequent culture change within any given group that might relate only to population decline. In general, there do not appear to have been any substantial changes in subsistence, settlement, and technology that cannot be explained, at least in part, by the influx of native immigrants from the east during this same period. Subsequent access to, and intertribal competition for, colonial trade brought about somewhat more substantial changes, although cultural continuity is still evident. For example, palisaded villages and episodic population aggregation are evident after the establishment of French outposts in the region, but nonnative materials were often used in traditional ways (Branstner 1992; Brown and Sasso 2001:216; Birk and Johnson 1992:233). Since the Eastern Prairies were an interior area prior to A.D. 1630, any disease introduction at that time would have been through long-distance, down-the-line interaction of native people. After A.D. 1670, however, direct interaction occurred between native people and the French, and so it is more likely that disease-induced depopulation occurred after sustained French presence in the region. Therefore, any consequent cultural changes were likely related to the involvement of native people in the region with colonial economic activities.

HIDATSA, MANDAN, AND ARIKARA OF THE MIDDLE MISSOURI RIVER

The middle Missouri region is a riverine corridor bisecting the northern Plains in present-day North and South Dakota. This stretch extends from the confluence with the Knife River on the north to the White River on the south, and several additional major tributaries draining the Missouri Plateau enter the Missouri River from the west in the intervening zone (see map 13). This region is characterized by grasslands, rolling hills, and sometimes dramatic bluffs overlooking the lower terraces, riparian forests, and floodplains along the river, which eventually flows into the Mississippi River near St. Louis. This territory was inhabited historically by the Hidatsa, Mandan, and Arikara—sedentary horticulturalists and bison hunters who lived in semisubterranean earthlodges within large, palisaded villages situated on the high river terraces.

These people are perhaps best known to contemporary audiences because of their encounters with Meriwether Lewis and William Clark in 1804 as well as depictions of village life in the paintings and sketches of George Catlin dating to the 1830s. European influence on groups of the middle Missouri, however, dates back to the early 1700s, if not before. French trappers working in the lower Missouri region as early as A.D. 1714 were told of Arikara villages upriver but did not venture there themselves. Still, it was clear that the native people of the middle Missouri were already engaged in the fur trade by this time (Parks 2001:366), and the horse had probably been fully integrated into life on the northern Plains via introduction from native people to the south by the late 1600s (Swagerty 2001:260). Earliest direct con-

The Colonial Experience

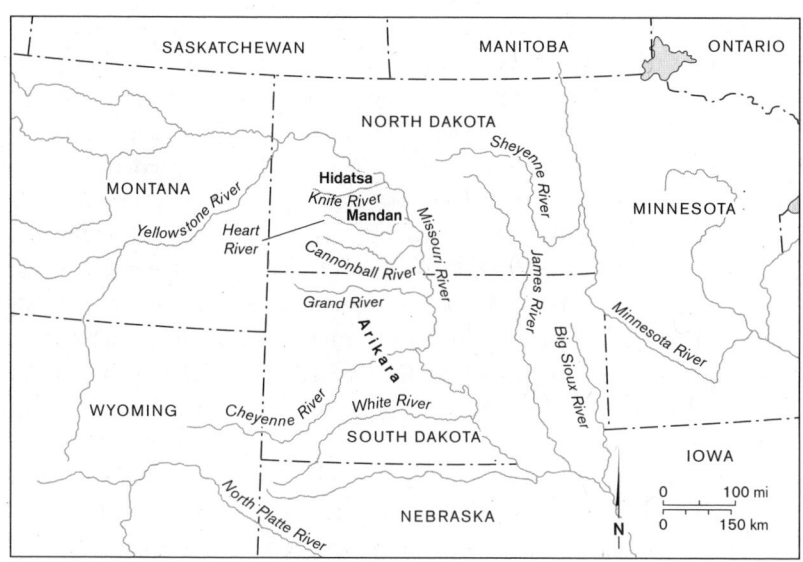

MAP 13. Middle Missouri case-study area.

tact with Europeans came to the Arikara in A.D. 1734 in the person of a French trapper named Bienville (Parks 2001:366). Contact with the Mandan followed in A.D. 1738, with the visit of French fur trader Pierre Gaultier de Varennes, Sieur de La Verendrye. La Verendrye's visit to the Mandan, and those of his sons to Arikara villages downriver during the subsequent decade, escalated participation of middle Missouri tribes in trade with the French along the Assiniboine River to the east. By A.D. 1776, French traders were living within Mandan and Hidatsa villages (Wood and Irwin 2001:349). Nonnative presence in the region was essentially continuous thereafter and likely contributed to well-documented disease introductions, including the catastrophic smallpox epidemic of A.D. 1781. Aggregation and alliance occurred between the Mandan and Hidatsa in the wake of this epidemic; further depredations from introduced disease, and ongoing aggression from mounted hunter-gatherer peoples to the east (Stewart 2001:329). Still, each group maintained separate residences and neighborhoods within the single joint village that ultimately became their home (Stewart 2001:331). In some cases, survivors also attempted to augment declining populations through capture of neighboring women and children (Stewart 2001:331).

Despite the seeming stability of the traditional sedentary horticultural life of the Hidatsa, Mandan, and Arikara, regional archaeology and ethnohistory document a dynamic picture of cultural development and native population movements—if not demographic decline—within the region even prior to nonnative intrusion. The antecedents of the Siouan-speaking Mandan and Hidatsa emerged on the middle Missouri south of the Cannonball River around A.D. 1200, approximately two hundred years after similar villages were first settled farther south in the White River area by unrelated Plains horticulturalists (Wood 2001). All of these people produced pottery; cultivated maize, beans, squash, and sunflowers; hunted bison; and inhabited earthlodge villages sometimes protected by surrounding ditches or post palisades. This way of life had its roots in the Woodland tradition of the plains-prairie interface to the east, and movement of horticultural people into the middle Missouri region was probably facilitated by a shift to a warm, moist climate suitable for agriculture after A.D. 900 (Wood 2001:190). Hidatsa oral tradition and archaeology reveal that multiple migrations contributed to the population over a few centuries.

A return to cooler, dryer conditions after A.D. 1250 initiated a series of even more far-reaching cultural changes in the region. Villagers of the White River faded from history with no clear descendants, while antecedents of Caddoan-speaking Arikara pushed north into the same area from the central Plains. This immigration forced ancestral Mandan and Hidatsa who had expanded as far south as the White River to consolidate their population within fewer, larger settlements in the Heart River area. And it was only after a return to somewhat more favorable climatic conditions after A.D. 1400 that they attempted, unsuccessfully, to reclaim some of the territory lost to the ancestral Arikara in the previous century. Although practicing horticulture, the southern people had a more flexible settlement system that allowed alternate aggregation and dispersal of population as prevailing environmental or social conditions dictated. Krause (2001:205–206) suggested that the occupation of smaller villages over a wider area and more frequent relocation provided one mechanism by which they were able to outcompete their Siouan village predecessors as local food and timber resources declined. In contrast, their northern neighbors opted for wholesale abandonment of areas rather than reorganization (Krause 2001:205). The southern intrusion was clearly an unwelcome encroachment, as violence accompanied this expansion and fortification of northern villages became commonplace. The subsequent introduction of the horse to the northern Plains brought even more conflict, although this time via raids on villages by mounted hunters of the east.

Archaeological assessment of colonial-era demography in the middle Missouri was undertaken initially by Ramenofsky (1987), who relied on population proxies derived from regionally aggregated data on settlement counts, settlement size, and roofed area. Similar to other colonial-era demographic analyses, chronology for the span from circa A.D. 1000 to 1885 encompassed by the study was established using radiocarbon dates, ceramic seriation, seriation of nonnative metal objects, and representation of nonnative goods (Ramenofsky 1987:110). Five periods—ranging from approximately forty to three hundred years in duration—were used to track population size, with minimum, mean, and maximum temporal estimates for each period used for analysis. Since this pioneering work, additional bioarchaeological and ethnohistoric evidence has been brought to bear on this topic, providing much-needed clarity to the general trends first outlined by Ramenofsky. The contribution of alternate data sources was especially important, as much of the archaeological data was equivocal and, in some cases, failed to accurately represent well-documented historical disease-induced population decline. As discussed by Ramenofsky, such errors resulted from problems of temporal representation and sampling as well as possible changes in residential mobility, intrasite proxemics, and domestic space needs through time. Still, regional population trends were developed from quantitative estimates acknowledged as "inadequate," "biased," or "unreliable" (Ramenofsky 1987:116), undermining confidence in patterns inferred for the colonial era.

Ramenofsky (1987:123) concluded that initial disease-induced depopulation occurred perhaps as early as A.D. 1612 to 1680, although temporal estimates for this period allow for initial decline as much as fifty to one hundred years later. Still, even estimates of disease exposure beginning in the 1730s or later suggest potential introduction of fatal disease well in advance of physical incursion of nonnative people into the region. Thus, the data argue for the initial transmittal of disease via native intermediaries, probably as a result of involvement in the fur trade. Significantly, recent ethnohistoric work by Sundstrom (1997), largely drawn from sources of more residentially mobile hunter-gatherer groups of the northern Plains, also demonstrated that significant episodes of disease likely occurred within the region in the early 1700s, if not before. This study relied on "winter counts," pictographic chronologies used by tribes in the area to record and recall historical events. These records revealed a pattern of initial rare and limited outbreaks circa A.D. 1724, perhaps followed by relatively infrequent disease introductions over the next forty years. Repeated catastrophic disease exposures began in A.D. 1780, however, and these multiple episodes prohibited groups from ever managing demographic recovery. The key to permanent and sustained depopulation was frequent introduction and reintroduction of diseases, perhaps as often as every five years (Sundstrom 1997:324). Still, Sundstrom's study also documented the mosaic nature of disease introductions rather than widespread and uniform pantribal disease exposure and death.

Owsley's (1992) bioarchaeological study also seemed to support initially limited, rather than sustained, catastrophic depopulation due to disease exposure, perhaps as early as A.D. 1600 to 1650. In this case, patterns of subadult and adult mortality were consistent with disease introduction, although the lack of similar bioarchaeological data on mortality for precolonial horticultural populations made unequivocal attribution to nonnative disease impossible. It is known, for example, that the shift to village life on the northern Plains several centuries earlier resulted in negative health consequences for many individuals. In addition, as Owsley noted, environmental change, intertribal violence, and even effects on fertility (especially after A.D. 1800) have not been adequately assessed as contributors to colonial-era demographic patterns revealed through bioarchaeology. Populations were apparently on the rebound during the late 1600s, suggesting that disease introduction or reintroduction was not commonplace. Instead, sustained population decline and increased risk of mortality for all age groups is revealed in bioarchaeological data after A.D. 1700 and, especially, after A.D. 1750, including many deaths from trauma rather than disease.

Given the interpretations made possible by use of multiple, diverse data sources, then, there is no evidence for infiltration of continent-wide pandemic disease into the middle Missouri in the 1500s. Disease-induced depopulation during the 1600s, if it occurred at all, was not sustained. Rather, the data indicate prolonged and repeated disease exposure after the establishment of regular trade with Europeans in adjoining regions of the prairies and plains in the 1700s, with irreversible demographic consequences by the late 1700s. The merging of settlement-based population proxies from archaeological data, osteological data, and ethnohistory provides a compelling picture of disease introduction through down-the-line transmission within and between native people prior to either direct interaction with nonnative people

The Colonial Experience

and, especially, prior to sustained European presence in region. In this respect, the experience of native people of the middle Missouri was similar to that of the Yosemite Indians, although on the northern Plains there was more time lag (perhaps one hundred years) between initial exposure (from which they rebounded) and sustained contact. Such early, indirect exposure may be due in part to the presence of horses, the mobility engendered by the use of horses, or intertribal warfare spreading disease more rapidly and distantly on the Plains.

SALISHAN-SPEAKERS OF THE COLUMBIA PLATEAU

On the Columbia Plateau, archaeological study of depopulation due to down-the-line disease transmission has been considered with data from the Chief Joseph Reservoir on the middle Columbia River in north-central Washington (Campbell 1990). This region of lowland shrub steppe is a large basin between the Rocky Mountains and Cascade Range. Major river systems originating in the mountains to the east bisect the area, and these valleys are surrounded by proximate upland grasslands and more distant forests in the mountain ranges. By A.D. 1400, the middle Columbia was inhabited by Salishan speakers, including the Wenatchee, Chelan, and Sinkayuse (Miller 1998:253), all of whom maintained cultural traditions that had deep roots in the region. As early as 3000 B.C., many of the cultural characteristics typical of the people encountered by Lewis and Clark—the first nonnative people to enter the area in A.D. 1805—had already begun to coalesce (Ames et al. 1998). These practices included construction of circular pithouses and a logistical settlement and subsistence strategy focused on relatively fixed, small village locales. By 1900 B.C., these traits had grown even more central to domestic life, and daily practices of these nonagricultural groups also now included dietary reliance on salmon fishing and bulb processing as well as storage of foodstuffs (Chatters 1995). If the ethnographically recorded pattern holds for the more distant past, sociopolitical control was maintained by council at the multifamily village level rather than residing in a hierarchical structure (Walker 1998:5).

Study of demography, climate, and culture on the Columbia Plateau between ca. 4000 and 1 B.C. indicates that these developments were probably a response to changes in the seasonal availability of terrestrial and aquatic resources (Chatters 1995). The native people generally lived in winter villages along the major rivers, whereas summers were spent in upland camps with access to a various plants or game. In the middle Columbia, the use of longhouses also developed around A.D. 1, suggesting multifamily residential units and possible changes in social organization at that time. By A.D. 1400, material culture included small triangular arrow points, exotic goods acquired through long-distance trade, and perishable items such as cordage, mats, baskets, and fishing equipment.

Archaeological evidence for the late prehistoric period (A.D. 1200–1700) developed by Campbell (1990) suggested to her that disease-induced depopulation occurred in the region around A.D. 1525, if not slightly earlier. Specifically, she examined five different proxy measures of population size so that multiple indicators could be compared to establish confidence in population trends through time. These proxies were component frequency, total site area, and accumulation rates for shell, animal bone, and features other than dwellings. Chronology for the A.D. 900 to 1900 span of her study relied primarily on calibrated radiocarbon dates. Statistical error inherent in radiocarbon dating required that each population proxy be calculated for the minimum, mean, and maximum time spans potentially encompassed by each occupational component. Patterns of demographic change were examined using each of these three time scales to establish that increase or decrease in a measure through time was not biased by which chronological method was used. In this, Campbell was satisfied that consistent trends were revealed by most of the proxies. Still, the reliance on fewer than one hundred radiocarbon dates meant that the temporal resolution of results was poor. In fact, greater accuracy and precision in chronology would be required to determine whether or not the depopulation could be attributed to introduced disease or if it was, in fact, initiated prior to any possible incursion of nonnative pathogens (see Campbell 1990:186).

The uneven distribution of features and animal bone among the sampled components undermined their use as indicators of population change. Instead, component frequency, total site area, and shell accumulation served as more robust data sets, with all but the latter demonstrating an apparent decrease in population between A.D. 1425 and 1525, as well as a decline around A.D. 1775 that is consistent with a smallpox epidemic inferred from regional ethnohistoric accounts (see Campbell 1990:22). The shell data suggested that the fifteenth-century decline may have started somewhat earlier, although a population nadir in the early 1500s was apparent in this proxy as well. The component frequency and site area proxies also indicated earlier population oscillations and another substantial decline at circa A.D. 1000, but Campbell (1990:169) chose not to consider the potential cause or significance of this previous decline. And despite the fact that the data suggested that the population nadir in the early 1500s was possibly initiated prior to any possible infiltration of nonnative disease, Campbell (1990:186–187) expressed no doubts that introduced disease was, in fact, responsible for this decline. Likewise, given the general timing, she concluded that this was due to the continental spread of smallpox via the Plains in the early 1520s posited by Dobyns (1983). Significantly, all three of the proxies Campbell ultimately focused on indicated substantial population rebound after colonial-era decline until at least A.D. 1775, suggesting population resilience or augmentation through migration. Campbell was careful to note the coarseness of her chronology, although at least one critic (Henige 1998) ignored this caution.[17]

Campbell's conclusion that the data reflect disease-induced depopulation in the early 1500s is tenuous, given the coarse chronological techniques employed and the history of population fluctuations in the region demonstrated both by her data and that of other regional researchers (see later this section). Still, it is of note that there was a generally coincident shift in settlement initiated between A.D. 1350 and 1450, which is indicated by a dramatic decrease in field camps and corresponding increase in special-purpose sites (Campbell 1990:181). This shift could have been in response to greater resource abundance at particular fishing locales with decreasing regional population (Campbell 1990:188), although Campbell's data also suggest relatively rapid population rebound either through population aggregation or intrinsic growth that might have mitigated any short-term resource gains. Campbell (1990:189) saw this settlement change as a shift to a forager strategy, although the increase in special-purpose sites at the expense of field camps is more consistent with decreasing residential mobility indicative of a collector strategy (Binford 1980). And in any case, Campbell's data argue that this change was set in motion even before any possible infiltration of nonnative disease. Therefore, one can argue that this shift represents cause rather than consequence of later demographic change.

Any analysis of colonial-era culture change on the Columbia Plateau must acknowledge the significant influence of the horse, which sets this region apart from many of the other cases we have already considered. Horses spread north from the Southwest following reintroduction into North America by the Spanish in the early 1500s (Shimkin 1986), and horses were present on the Columbia Plateau by circa A.D. 1730 (Boyd 1998:472; Campbell 1990:19). Native use of horses for transport facilitated swifter travel over longer distances, allowing Salishan people to potentially come into contact with infected individuals who might otherwise have been beyond their interaction sphere. The horse also led to significant cultural changes, including shifts in subsistence, settlement, exchange, warfare, and social organization, including the formation of confederacies (Miller 1998:253; Walker 1998:3). Thus, archaeological assessment of any cultural change prompted by disease-induced depopulation is difficult to detach from coincident changes brought about by the adoption of the horse.

If Campbell is incorrect in her assertion that nonnative disease infiltrated the Columbia Plateau in the early 1500s, her archaeological study and ethnohistoric data still support the spread of nonnative disease via native people prior to physical incursion by colonists (see also Boyd 1998). That is, the A.D. 1775 smallpox epidemic is significant to the colonial experience of Salishan-speaking people in part because it preceded Lewis and Clark by at least thirty years. The issue is did initial colonial-era depopulation destabilize the population and traditional culture of the Salishan people of the Columbia Plateau, or had both rebounded from this initial colonial assault by the time of nonnative infiltration? Furthermore, to what extent did any long-term history of demographic change and accommodation preserved in native oral history, memory, and practices allow native people to deal with the challenges of colonial-era depopulation, whenever it did occur? The long-term view of demography for the Indian people of the Columbia Plateau developed by Chatters (1995) suggests that native people of the plateau had a dynamic demographic history and that factors other than disease could have affected population size at various times, even during the colonial era. A population proxy used in his study based on the frequency of regionally aggregated radiocarbon dates—adjusted based on assumptions about the loss of carbon from archaeological sites and features due to degradation over time—indicated that the initial adoption of cultural practices like those recorded ethnographically in the region likely prompted multiple episodes of population growth. On the other hand, substantial fluctuations in population size occurred between 4000 and 1 B.C., and declines at circa 2000 B.C. and 250 B.C. resulted in temporary or even permanent shifts in subsistence and settlement practices as people coped with imbalances between subsistence resources and population. Thus, this long-term view of regional demography suggests that population fluctuations recognized in the early 1500s—although developed at a much finer temporal scale—may reflect factors other than depopulation due to introduced nonnative disease. In addition, cultural practices may have been in place to deal with the challenges of depopulation, since Campbell (1990) recognized previous declines as recently as circa A.D. 1300.

PUEBLOAN PEOPLES OF THE SOUTHWEST

At the time of Columbus's landfall, both mobile hunter-gatherers and sedentary agriculturalists inhabited the American Southwest. Both had also lived in the region for centuries, if not millennia, and two distinct agricultural traditions were in place—the Hohokam of the Sonoran Desert and the ancestral Puebloan groups to the north and east of the Hohokam. The focus here is on groups of the Puebloan tradition, as these people have been the subject of most prior regional demographic studies. In fact, archaeological investigations have documented a dynamic settlement and demographic history for these people, who did—and still do—occupy portions of the Colorado Plateau, Mogollon highlands, and upper Rio Grande watershed in present-day Arizona and New Mexico (see map 14). This is an arid to semiarid region characterized by pinyon-juniper uplands and deeply incised bedrock canyons. It is dissected by several rivers including the Colorado, Rio Grande, San Juan, Salt, and Gila (see map 14). For agricultural peoples living in the Southwest, these challenging conditions required finding a balance between access to reliable water—more readily available in higher-elevation zones—and temperate microclimates suitable for maize agriculture—more typical of lower-elevation areas.

In this region, Puebloan communities emerged as such around A.D. 750 from the previous Basketmaker tradition, which was characterized by the use of pithouse dwellings and subsistence that encompassed both maize horticulture and use of wild resources (Cordell 1997). The subsequent cultural shift to typical Puebloan life was marked by dietary reliance on maize agriculture as well as the development of substantial above-ground masonry architecture, trade of exotic goods through regional and extraregional exchange, and the introduction of new ceramic wares to augment those already in use. At the peak of their demographic and settlement expanse throughout much of present-day northern Arizona and western New Mexico, multiple "settlement clus-

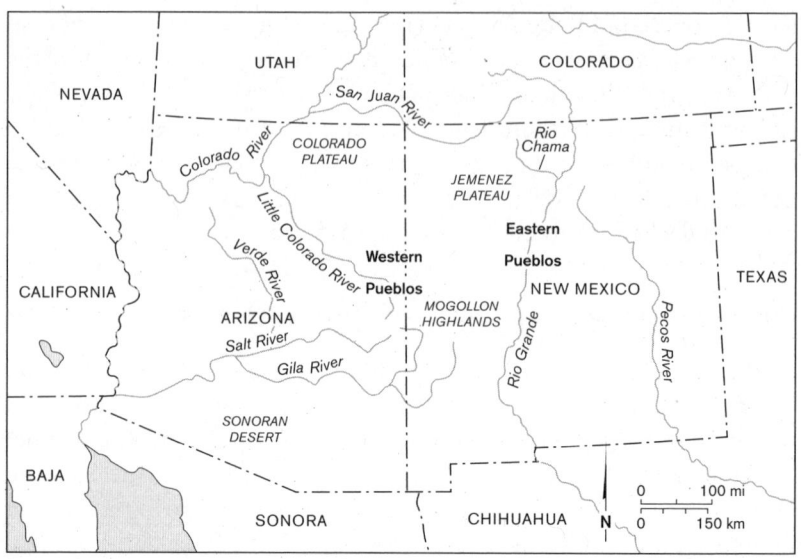

MAP 14. Southwest case-study area.

ters" of Puebloan peoples were linked together by networks of economic and social exchange, similar to the polities of the interior Southeast. In this case, such sociopolitical entities were smaller and less complex, with economic, religious, and social ties rather than political alliances reinforced by extralocal networks. By the late 1400s, approximately twenty Puebloan settlement clusters existed in northern Arizona and New Mexico (Upham and Reed 1989), although this number may have been even greater in the past, prior to population aggregation and reorganization after A.D. 1300. By A.D. 1500, additional significant regional population aggregation had occurred, reducing the number of settlement clusters still further. Concomitant simplification of social networks is also evident, in marked contrast to Puebloan society just three hundred years earlier. Historically, the groups of the Rio Grande drainage, including the Rio Chama and Jemenez Plateau, are collectively referred to as the Eastern Pueblos, whereas the Western Pueblos include Hopi, Zuni, Acoma, and Laguna of east-central Arizona and the adjacent New Mexico border region.

Dating of archaeological sites—and establishing a diachronic picture of the population history of the region—has primarily relied on radiocarbon dating, dendrochronology, and ceramic seriation, although thermoluminescence dating has also recently been incorporated into chronology building in the region. Precolonial population estimates have been based on multifamily pueblo room counts and presumed occupancy rates for such rooms. In contrast, colonial-era population estimates have generally relied on historical documents rather than archaeological data, although specific census data are rarely available from such sources. Earliest encounters of the Spanish with Puebloan peoples occurred between A.D. 1539 and 1542, with a brief but violent encounter with the Zuni by members of the expedition of Fray Marcos de Niza in A.D. 1539 and more sustained interaction with the substantial expedition of Francisco Vásquez de Coronado into western New Mexico between A.D. 1540 and 1542 (Cordell 1989:25). Subsequent, more modest *entradas* in the 1500s included the expedition of Augustín Rodriquez and Francisco Sanchez Chumascado in A.D. 1581, the venture of Antonio de Espejo in A.D. 1582, and the expedition of Gaspar Castaño de Sosa from A.D. 1590 to 1591 (Kulisheck 2005: table 2.2; Ramenofsky 1996:172; Upham 1992:223). Despite these repeated explorations in the region, the first permanent Spanish settlement did not develop until Juan de Oñate established a colony on the lower Rio Chama of northwest New Mexico in A.D. 1598. Prior to this date, population estimates from explorers' chronicles variously relied on approximations of the number of warriors, all pueblo occupants, or residents of particular pueblos, depending on which areas were actually visited and the proclivities of the particular recorder. With permanent Spanish settlement, records improved, including census data recorded by missionaries. Earliest historical estimates of Puebloan population during the late 1500s suggest as many as 117,300 individuals (Upham 1992: table 1), with evident precipitous native population decline following colonization until the Pueblo Revolt of A.D. 1680. This event also led to abandonment of the region by the Spanish for the next twelve years.

Archaeological data indicate that precolonial population of Puebloan peoples was relatively large despite the arid conditions. There were clear fluctuations in population size and the geographic distribution of people through time, however, reflecting responses to long-term changes in local and regional climatic conditions (Dean et al. 1994). Populations were generally on the rise throughout the Colorado Plateau, Mogollon highlands, and Rio Grande area between A.D. 1100 and 1300. Shortly thereafter population began to decline, and settlement aggregation and consolidation occurred in response to adverse climate conditions.

Tracking subsequent colonial-era population trends is confounded by the dynamic demographic history in the seven centuries leading up to initial nonnative exploration (Palkovich 1996:186). In addition, only one archaeological study (Kulisheck 2005) has specifically collected data for, or focused on, the colonial era, and regional archaeologists have yet to develop a chronology that is sufficient to recognize the exact timing of potential catastrophic disease-induced depopulation, as opposed to more gradual population decline (Palkovich 1996:181). Rather, most archaeologists who have contributed to the study of colonial-era depopulation in this region have variously relied on some combination of archaeological, osteological, historical documentary, and epidemiological information.

For example, Upham (1992:229, 230) used room counts from Eastern and Western Pueblo areas, presumed occupancy rates, and some assumptions about depopulation from disease in virgin-soil conditions to infer a population of nearly 200,000 individuals in A.D. 1500. With this archaeological estimate as a baseline, he then contrasted this figure with population estimate of approximately 117,000 Puebloans provided in Spanish documents of the 1500s and concluded that significant depopulation occurred sometime between A.D. 1520 and 1590. Palkovich (1996) chose a more conservative approach to all data sources and was unable to conclude such early population decline. Focusing on the Eastern Pueblos, she suggested that historical records in fact revealed population stability at least through A.D. 1664 (Palkovich 1996:188). She also noted that the long-term pattern of precolonial demographic change precluded attributing colonial-era depopulation wholly, or even partly, to introduced disease (Palkovich 1996:186). Reff's (1992) study of historical epidemics in the Greater Southwest—including northern Mexico—revealed that it was unlikely that fatal Old World disease penetrated the Puebloan area prior to A.D. 1593. Although this could simply be a reflection of the lack of Spanish recorders "beyond the border" of colonized territory, European disease did not seem to spread thoroughly even within the known realm. Finally, Ramenofsky (1996; see also Upham 1986) focused on the epidemiology of the potentially fatal pathogens most likely to have been introduced and considered these data in light of regional archaeological data. Despite prevailing conditions that would have been conducive to the spread of pathogens given native trade and proximity to Spanish routes of travel, Ramenofsky puzzled over the lack of archaeological evidence for severe disease-induced depopulation prior to A.D. 1680. Still, her findings are consistent with those of both

Reff and Palkovich, casting doubt on the accuracy of Upham's (1992) conclusions.

No one disputes that Puebloan peoples suffered significant population decline as a result of European colonization of the Southwest, including substantial depopulation due to the introduction of Old World pathogens. What remains debated, however, is when substantial and sustained disease-induced decline was initiated. In the absence of comparable archaeological data from pre- and postcolonial settings prior to Kulisheck's (2005) recent study, recourse has been to use historical documents. As noted by Palkovich (1996:189), however, population estimates derived from historical records are "inconsistent," and "the true rate of demographic decrease [following Spanish incursions] is masked by census difficulties, social disruptions, indigenous warfare, and other factors" (Palkovich 1996:186). Even Upham (1992:233), who relied exclusively on such documentary sources for his analysis of colonial-era demographic decline, noted that the Spaniards "often underestimated total populations because of their methods of estimation [and] this fact, along with enumeration inconsistencies, obfuscates any attempt to use the data from the narratives in an uncritical manner." In fact, the data marshaled by such studies are only sufficient to indicate substantial disease-induced population loss after permanent Spanish presence in the region circa A.D. 1598. While earlier disease exposures are both possible (Ramenofsky 1996) and even known from A.D. 1638 to 1641 and at A.D. 1670 (Ramenofsky 1996:163), such episodes were not sufficient to lead to permanent catastrophic decline at such an early date (Palkovich 1996:191). This conclusion is further supported by Kulisheck's (2005) study of field houses on the Jemenez Plateau. The multiple indices of economic intensification that Kulisheck used as demographic proxies suggest regional population stability until the late 1600s, with demographic decline only coming after the Pueblo Revolt of A.D. 1680 (Kulisheck 2005:414).

Puebloan peoples were also apparently well positioned to withstand the cultural threats that often accompanied severe depopulation. Palkovich (1996:186) attributed such cultural resilience and continuity to the relatively challenging environmental conditions of the region, which lead to "cultural flexibility." In this sense, although Puebloan peoples were agriculturalists, they may have been similar to equally flexible hunting and gathering peoples who also developed social mechanisms to accommodate local environmental or cultural challenges in precolonial times. Palkovich (1996:191) concluded that "it is reasonable to hypothesize at this point that the long-established pattern of settlement shifts and demographic response to the vagaries of the environment may have served to maintain Pueblo demographic viability in the face of new biological and social disruptions." This could certainly explain why no archaeological evidence has yet been presented to support significant disease-induced depopulation prior to the seventeenth century.

DIFFERENT PEOPLE, DIFFERENT HISTORIES

The ten diverse case studies discussed in this chapter provide intriguing observations about the timing, magnitude, and cultural impact of introduced Old World diseases during the colonial era. Some suggest similarities to the Yosemite Indian case in that disease preceded face-to-face contact, but each is also clearly unique. This overview of archaeological data, native oral tradition, and historical records argues against continent-wide pandemics and instead indicates a complicated mosaic of disease-induced depopulation and cultural responses. The data reveal that lag time, if any, between disease introduction and physical incursion was generally short, except in the case of groups living in the middle Missouri region, the Columbia Plateau, and perhaps in the Caddoan area (although the lag time is shorter than has been previously suggested in some archaeological studies). In these areas as well as others, the presence of the horse evidently facilitated the spread of disease farther in advance of face-to-face encounters. In all cases, however, lag time between disease-induced depopulation and a permanent colonial presence in the region was on the order of decades rather than centuries, just as in the Yosemite situation. Still, since European disease preceded direct contact by more than one generation, the cultural consequences of fatal epidemics were both recognized and accommodated by native people. Many decided to relocate but not necessarily to amalgamate, suggesting that relocation was viewed as a temporary solution.

Although physical presence of nonnative people was not yet established when introduced disease initially struck, native groups affected by epidemics were often already directly or indirectly involved in processes set in motion by colonial presence in adjoining regions, or by European interaction with neighboring tribes through the deerskin trade, fur trade, slaving, or other enterprises. That is, in many areas it is difficult to separate colonial-era disease-induced depopulation from population decline due to other causes. It is also difficult to attribute concomitant cultural change exclusively to epidemic disease, given such cross-entanglement and short lag times between the assault of fatal disease and European incursion. In this sense, the Yosemite case is distinct, since such cultural entanglement was not a factor. Interestingly, where archaeological evidence for depopulation prior to direct encounters is strongest, such as in the southern portion of the mid-Atlantic Piedmont, the record also demonstrates cultural continuity—especially within the domestic sphere—both in the short term and after European encroachment. This same pattern is evident for Yosemite Indians. And in cases such as that of the Caddo and groups of the middle Missouri, there is even evidence for population rebound prior to direct encounters with European people.

This analysis—and the complex picture of native colonial experiences that emerges from it—has been enhanced by placing regional colonial-era events and processes within each group's longer-term history through both archaeology and native oral history. In addition, study of disparate groups with divergent cultural traditions, different long-term histories, and distinct colonial encounters underscores the difficulty in generalizing about the colonial experiences of native people in North America and the process of colonialism itself from an anthropological perspective. These cases range from agriculturalists to hunter-gatherer-fishers and from paramount chiefdoms to band-level societies. Likewise, some were fully sedentary groups, while others were seasonally transhumant. Some had been in place for centuries, while others were more recent arrivals to an area at the time fatal disease struck. Few, however, had experienced long-term population stability, and native people in many regions witnessed significant population movements prior to the Columbian landfall. It is interesting that significant differences in response to the devastation of introduced diseases and consequent depopulation are evident even within proximate groups such as the Wendat-Tionontate and Onondaga, although different colonial allegiances and long histories of enmity between native groups in the region certainly contributed to the group-specific outcomes in this area.

One recurring theme in these ten cases as well as in that of the Yosemite Indians is the ability of people to adapt to changing circumstances—or, more correctly, the ability of the native people to make decisions, chart their own course, and persist in the midst of colonial upheaval, often drawing on a dynamic long-term history and inherent cultural flexibility in order to do so. When data are examined critically from this perspective, population collapse from Old World disease does not take center stage as the inevitable harbinger or catalyst of profound cultural change. Rather, native people were simply "getting on," drawing on their own histories and experiences to do so. And to frame colonial-era experiences of native people as "colonialism" denies dynamic histories and similar experiences and threatens to cast perseverance as resistance to an "other" that, from a native perspective, was not necessarily that different from previous challenges to their survival. It was the forces of colonialism other than initial disease exposure that appear to have ultimately undermined traditional lifeways. Although there are not sufficient historical records or native oral histories to address the specific role of charismatic leaders in the cultural outcomes in many of these cases, the diversity of responses suggests that such figures likely played a role. Thus, this analysis argues for a historical anthropological study of colonialism in North America, including contextualizing the colonial experience of individual groups via the long-term lens of archaeology. These observations, conclusions, and implications are considered in more detail in the next chapter. As the Yosemite Indian case once again takes center stage, we will consider the structural significance of disease-induced colonial-era native culture change and thereby assess the general process and concept of colonialism in North America.

CHAPTER 10

Culture, History, and Colonialism

As we seek to understand cause and effect in the course of humanity, it becomes clear that the processes and events that comprise human experience are embedded within one other, intimately linked, and in many instances perhaps inseparable. When disentangling these elements extends to the unwritten past of indigenous experience in colonial encounters, and the focus is on the dynamics of culture rather than a simple sequence of events, the challenge becomes greater still. Fortunately, archaeological data, native oral tradition, ethnohistoric accounts, and ethnographic observations can all be drawn upon to both tease apart and reveal the circumstances, timing, magnitude, and outcomes of colonial-era native depopulation in North America as both a historical event and an anthropological process. In the case of the Yosemite Indians, this research has encompassed both a long-term context necessary to understand the phenomenon and consequences of colonial-era depopulation, as well as a short-term view of native responses to Old World biological agents instituted at the individual and community level. This approach creates a fuller picture in this particular case, and also provides a richer, more nuanced understanding of native and nonnative interaction in North America in the 350 years following Columbus's landfall.

The introduction of deadly diseases was largely an unintentional consequence of European colonization. And yet, it has been argued that catastrophic depopulation brought about by disease facilitated the expansion and enabled the success of colonists across the continent. Without this advance assault, the relatively small number of European adventurers would have been unable to contend with the thousands of native people encountered locally or the millions of indigenous people across North America. This surely was the case, but to extend this line of reasoning to conclude inevitable and profound native culture change simply as a result of depopulation is taking this argument too far. For example, Galloway (1995:25) concluded that "demographic collapse . . . marked the triumph of European microbes over thousands of years of tradition" (cf. Galloway 2002). The cases considered herein suggest otherwise, as the "small traditions" of everyday life persisted and self-determined identities and demographic responses were negotiated in changing circumstances much as they had been in the distant past. And it was not demography alone that led to the alteration of "big traditions" such as sociopolitical structure and, ultimately, many other aspects of traditional life. Rather, irreversible culture change resulted from being caught up in colonial economic enterprises that often arrived in tandem with, or within a few decades of, disease. Had there been just a single wave of fatal disease, then many native people likely would have recovered long-term cultural stability and most if not all predisease practices if they had been free to do so beyond the many other influences and pressures brought with European colonization. Second waves of disease and exploitation of native resources or labor were the most destructive forces to Indian peoples, leading to prolonged biological and cultural instability and ensuring their inability to withstand in the wake of colonization.

POPULATION DECLINE AND CULTURE CHANGE

This book has explored three different scenarios characterizing the processes of colonial-era population decline and consequent culture change for the Awahnichi of Yosemite Valley, and these scenarios are equally relevant to other indigenous peoples of Americas who encountered European colonists. The first view posits that disease-induced population decline occurred early, prior to face-to-face interaction with nonnative people, and that this demographic event was both unique in the history of the native groups and devastating. Therefore, consequent culture change was inevitable, significant, and irreversible. The second view acknowledges that colonial-era depopulation predated direct encounters with nonnative people and expects that such disease took a heavy toll on human life, but suggests that such an event was not unique. Rather, population fluctuations—and perhaps even severe declines—had occurred in the past. Therefore, cultural consequences were not inevitable and any such shifts identified archaeologically might simply represent short-term or surficial, rather than enduring or deep structural, change. The third view holds that not only was colonial-era depopulation a relatively late phenomenon related especially to direct encounters, but that any disease-induced decline was neither unique nor devastating. Instead, significant population loss occurred as a result of other causes such as deliberate genocide. In addition, any coincident culture change was largely due to factors other than the introduction of nonnative disease and the potential demographic consequences deriving therefrom.

In the case of the Awahnichi, ethnohistoric data and dendrochronological evidence for temporary exile of native people from Yosemite Valley reveal that the introduction of nonnative disease preceded direct interaction with nonnative people in this region. The long-term demographic data developed from archaeological investigations confirm the timing of this event between circa A.D. 1790 to 1800. While the population decline revealed by two separate proxy measures of population size was substantial—representing at least a 25 percent decline in population size—these data also indicate that this was not a unique event. Rather, significant and sustained population decline also occurred after A.D. 500 and continued until at least A.D. 1375, with the population size at the latter time likely as small as that resulting from colonial-era disease approximately four hundred years later. The Awahnichi had only begun to recover from this earlier decline when the colonists' "black sickness" brought further death.

Per archaeological evidence, a particularly important factor in the Yosemite Indian colonial-era demographic experience was that the initial population size was relatively small at the time disease struck. In addition, the population was subject to very slow growth prior to this colonial-era demographic event. Although the specific practices contributing to the low growth rate are not accessible through available archaeological information, this tendency was probably due to cultural practices such as later age at marriage or prolonged breast-feeding, both of which tend to reduce the number of children conceived. Together, the relatively small population size and slow growth rate made the Awahnichi particularly vulnerable to extermination in the face of life-threatening events such as the non-age-specific diseases introduced during the colonial era. Given ethnohistoric and ethnographic evidence for the practice of exogamy, which further narrows the range of mates with whom to rebuild households and domestic life in the wake of depopulation, emigration and augmentation of the population from outside were inevitable choices.

Despite this demographic upheaval, the comparison of daily practices, organization of domestic activities, and external relations in pre- and postdepopulation villages do not suggest any significant cultural shifts in the aftermath of disease. In fact, contrary to expectations for radical cultural changes due to depopulation (e.g., Dobyns 1983; Dunnell 1991), archaeological results reveal that many of the practices evident before population collapse continued to be carried out in the same contexts in the aftermath of population decline, emigration, and subsequent reoccupation of Yosemite Valley. For example, the array of stone tools employed was similar, as were the technologies used to produce these tools. It is also likely that the spatial focus of domestic activity within households was unchanged, although there may have been minor differences in the organization of space. At a larger scale, there is no evidence for dissolution of or changes in external relations, although some people not traditionally occupying Yosemite Valley prior to demographic collapse may have used the area on occasion after this event. Access to exotic goods either through direct procurement or exchange continued much as it had prior to depopulation. Furthermore, while there was access to some new materials such as metal tools and glass beads through trade, the selective incorporation of these items did not represent a fundamental change in the organization of household activities. There is no indication, for example, that such items were used in ways inconsistent with the stone tools and native ornaments they superseded or for tasks not performed in earlier times. Together, these observations suggest that although short-term changes on the scale of one to two generations may have occurred, daily life continued much as it had prior to population collapse. Continuity may also be indicated in settlement organization, descent, and marriage practices, although such conclusions are based on archaeological and ethnohistoric observations as well as ethnographic identification of practices predating the Gold Rush.

Differences that may or may not reflect changes due to depopulation are fairly subtle. These include reduced investment in the manufacture of fine bifacial tools such as projectile points and, perhaps, some loss of knowledge contributing to success in flaked stone tool production through either choice or accident. On a somewhat larger scale, there may have been less investment in architecture or changes in settlement location and seasonal use within Yosemite Valley in the few decades following population decline. Such changes were relatively minor, however, in contrast to the dire predictions of Dobyns (1983; see also Dunnell 1991). In fact, such shifts may simply be idiosyncratic or individual and were in any case likely surficial.

There is circumstantial evidence that even practices potentially detrimental to long-term survival, such as exogamy, were adhered to in the face of great challenges to traditional life in the immediate aftermath of disease. These practices were deeply embedded within Awahnichi culture, perhaps to such an extent that options for change were not even apparent. If such options were contemplated in a decision about whether to discontinue traditional marriage practices or temporarily give up residence within traditional territory, however, it was the latter option that was exercised. The fact that the Awahnichi were able to relocate to the eastern side of the Sierra Nevada even suggests that relationships with these neighbors were in place as a "hedge against extinction" (Hammel and Howell 1987), which made this decision somewhat easier. That is, given the long history of population instability and a memory of difficult times preserved in native oral tradition, existing practices of identity or affinity may have been a conscious decision in light of the vulnerability of such a small group to further demographic catastrophe.

It was only later, when Yosemite Indians engaged in prolonged and often violent interaction with miners and others during the Gold Rush era, that life began to change radically. This is revealed especially poignantly in the memoirs of Jean-Nicolas Perlot (1985), as native people struggled to survive when denied access to traditional hunting and gathering territories. Ethnographers also identified changes in settlement patterns after the Gold Rush based on linguistic evidence (Gifford 1926b). Further gradual changes in daily life occurred as Indian people took advantage of opportunities in the local tourist economy (e.g., Bates and Lee 1990). Such observations are consistent with what Alexander (1998:485) refers to as "cultural entanglement," in which "interaction within an expanding territorial state gradually results in change of indigenous patterns of production, exchange, and social relations." While such change may ultimately manifest significant differences in political and economic power between the parties to the colonial encounter, asymmetry is not characteristic of the original context of contact. In the Yosemite Indian case, the nonnative advantage may only have been possible because of previous decimation due to disease. The processes of change in such interaction can unfold over centuries, while "cultural and ethnic differences are often not marked, and . . . are amenable to mediation through traders and culture brokers in either society" (Alexander 1998:485). Importantly, distance from the colonizing force plays a role in defining whether a relationship is one of cultural entanglement or the oppression and coercion of what Alexander terms "colonization" (see also Rice 1998). Thus, the relative isolation of Yosemite Indians was important to their experience and to the slower tempo of change.

All of these observations indicate that Awahnichi depopulation and cultural change in the colonial era is most consistent with the second hypothesis regarding the process of colonialism. Significant population decline occurred early, prior to direct contact with nonnative people, although the proportional loss may have been somewhat less than that posited elsewhere in North America based on ethnohistoric information. Consistent with the second scenario, population declines occurred in the more distant past, although frequent, substantial fluctuations in population size were uncommon. Consequent short-term cultural adjustments made in the immediate wake of colonial-era disease contact do not appear to have been significant in the long term. In addition, short-term shifts such as emigration did not interfere with or alter daily practices, which continued much as they had in the past. It may be that such endurance reflects a "preadaptation" of the Awahnichi to demographic change, with the tendency for flexibility and resilience rooted in the distant past.

Ethnohistoric information for the Yosemite Indians also highlights the importance of charismatic native leaders and local circumstance in colonial interactions and outcomes. In the case of the Awahnichi, an aged medicine man both prompted and supported the decision of Chief Tenaya and other descendants to return to Yosemite Valley. Kroeber (1921:63) noted that Tenaya "was not only a brave warrior but an unusual personality, who maintained his authority over his people by his native influence and by the respect which he commanded rather than by any legal position." And Kuykendall (1921:13) cited a letter written by Captain Boling in which he noted that the Yosemite Indians' "determined obstinacy is entirely attributable to the influence of their chief." The denigration and loss of their leader during the tumultuous years following their encounter with the Mariposa Battalion was likely

Culture, History, and Colonialism 289

a significant blow to the community. Still, the Awahnichi story demonstrates the potential for strong leadership to enable swift recovery from the destabilizing effects of catastrophic mortality within the span of one to two generations. Therefore, even when significant depopulation occurred, native groups could have substantially rebounded both demographically and culturally prior to face-to-face encounters with colonists. The speed with which this could have been accomplished—in part dependent upon immigration—suggests that such processes would be nearly invisible in the archaeological record unless specifically sought at a fine temporal scale with appropriate methods and sampling. Thus, it is possible that fatal disease infiltrated other areas of interior North America well in advance of direct interaction with colonists, but as yet, such events are undetected archaeologically either because populations substantially recovered or population decline did not result in significant culture change.

CROSS-CULTURAL PERSPECTIVES

These findings, in turn, prompt additional questions with respect to the general colonial experience of native people and the process of colonialism in North America. Is the Awahnichi case somehow unique in the timing, magnitude, and response to colonial-era disease-induced depopulation? What similar decisions or different outcomes should we expect for other groups with significantly different cultural traditions who resided in other areas of North America? For example, are such observations only germane to foragers as opposed to farmers? Certainly, some significant factors, including previous population decline and small group size, do not pertain to all groups. Likewise, there is no ethnohistoric or archaeological evidence to suggest successive waves of disease in the Yosemite region, despite the fact that such processes are hypothesized or documented elsewhere and were probably especially debilitating. But some characteristics of the Awahnichi experience may be more universal, including lag time between the introduction of disease and physical incursion of nonnative people, or the augmentation of population through immigration and intermarriage with people of other groups. Although often relying on much less robust archaeological evidence and lacking ethnohistoric accounts and native oral tradition comparable to that available for the Yosemite, the other ten case studies reviewed in this book suggest that each native group was dealing with the processes of disease-induced depopulation in the specific context of past history, cultural perception, external relations, territorial circumscription, and other factors that affected decision making in each circumstance. Still, some common threads are evident.

Data from areas including the Northeast, Southeast (e.g., Choctaws, Caddo), upper Midwest, Southwest, and perhaps the mid-Atlantic Piedmont indicate population movements and sociopolitical change preceding any possible infiltration of European disease or other influence. That is, native groups had a long tradition of demographic dynamism. In some areas, patterns of demographic and cultural change leading up to the colonial period were initiated in the 1400s or earlier. For the Awahnichi, their immediate demographic history resulted in small population size that made them particularly vulnerable as a viable population when faced with additional loss of life. It is unclear to what extent the preceding demographic events and processes in other regions of North America either destabilized or strengthened native groups prior to their encounters with Old World disease. For example, Iroquoian peoples had a long history of violence and confederation, and some of these actions had either positive or negative consequences to the various parties in terms of the size or distribution of population. Similarly, demographic restructuring of the Choctaw ancestors after the demise of the Moundville chiefdom may have made them more capable of dealing with colonial-era depopulation, since the hierarchical sociopolitical structure characteristic of their Mississippian forebears had already disappeared, and new settlement and subsistence strategies had been organized. On the other hand, population stability apparently pertained to the Coosa chiefdom, but major sociopolitical reorganization initiated earlier within the larger Mississippian arena could have made the Coosa more vulnerable to disease-induced catastrophe at the time disease struck. And all these examples contrast yet again with the Natchez, who maintained the social complexity and robust population of their Plaquemine ancestors well into the colonial era, perhaps because they were not as invested in the Mississippian realm.

Regardless of a group's initial population size, the cases reveal that emigration or aggregation was a common first response in nearly all instances of disease-induced depopulation. This response may reflect something other than a simple biological imperative, since even groups that enjoyed large predisease populations, and so would have been buffered from any imminent extinction in the wake of disease, exercised this option. Still, the Awahnichi example highlights that a critical reason for emigration and aggregation was a low population growth rate, which was typical of this and other North American native cultures. A history of population decline in the past also probably factored into such decisions in many cases. The ethnohistoric and archaeological information for the Awahnichi, Iroquoian groups, Mandan, Hidatsa, and perhaps people of other regions reveal that aggregation was usually viewed as a temporary solution, since immigrants often maintained their own communities and identities side-by-side with their hosts. That is, population movements did not a priori lead to amalgamation, creolization, or ethnogenesis in the short term. In the Awahnichi case, Mono Paiute people provided the refugees with separate land to exploit, just as separate villages were created in Mohawk and Onondaga territory, and Upper Creek ancestors maintained village names even when they relocated. It was only as the further pressures of colonialism came to dominate a region that some of these temporary arrangements became permanent and the social barriers between groups were relaxed or abolished. For example, the "Yosemite" eventually emerged as an identity when demographic shifts—this time as hosts rather than visitors—were made permanent. Similarly, long-term biological, if not cultural, viability of the Choctaws, Onondaga, and Mohawk was made possible by permanently incorporating neighbors and perhaps even strangers or traditional enemies within their groups. Coosa movement, on the other hand, was not a temporary solution—or at least it was not reversed—perhaps because the Coosa did not aggregate with another group or have a similar history of population movement, accommodation, and renegotiation of identity until their ultimate emergence as part of the Creek Confederacy.

Time and again, archaeological information on subsistence and technology (and sometimes architecture, if not settlement patterns and locations) shows continuity from pre- to postdisease times. Thus, it may be that continuity also pertained to other aspects of culture, such as social relations and worldview embodied in such activities. Continuity is revealed by faunal, floral, and flaked stone assemblages from colonial-era villages in Yosemite Valley, and continuity in technology and subsistence from pre-Columbian times through the early colonial period is indicated in the southern mid-Atlantic Piedmont (Ward and Davis 2001), throughout the Southeast (e.g., Perttula 1992; Waselkov and Smith 2000), and in the Northeast (Snow 1996), where ceramic traditions in particular remained sufficiently intact to trace migrations. In other instances, it may be more difficult to recognize continuity when groups relocated to distant areas (e.g., but see Branstner

1992) or where groups moved into or within regions that witnessed a long history of population movements and dynamism (e.g., the upper Midwest). Despite continuity in many practices, there is also evidence for change in internal social relations following—if not yet directly attributable to—depopulation in some regions. For example, indicators of community cohesion decreased, including the number of communal feasting features in the Carolina Piedmont and Iroquoian longhouse size. External relations also changed in many areas as power dynamics within and between groups shifted due to access to nonnative goods, but such changes were not necessarily a population-related phenomenon. Where European influence was absent or not immediately significant in the wake of disease, external relations remained stable, with nonnative goods simply added to the array of already available materials. Clearly, lag time between disease and economic involvement with colonists was brief or nonexistent for much of the interior Southeast, Northeast, and other areas. And in some cases (e.g., among Iroquoian groups), economic interactions actually preceded catastrophic disease. Therefore, it is difficult, if not impossible, to argue that cultural changes were due to mortality alone, and the Awahnichi case suggests that disease would have had no such lasting cultural consequences. And like the Awahnichi, it may not have simply been the magnitude of population decline that mattered to decision making and outcomes in the aftermath of disease but also *who* within the group was struck down. The death of important social, political, or religious leaders would have been especially significant to societies during a time of crisis.

Several characteristics emerge from the Awahnichi case and cross-cultural comparisons as important factors that contributed to the cultural persistence of native groups in the immediate aftermath of disease-induced depopulation. The first factor was attachment to the land and success in maintaining such connections, perhaps due to the influence of charismatic leaders. For example, this appears important to the persistence of the Onondaga (Bradley 2001) and the Natchez (Galloway 2002), who drew on traditions of connection to place through name or practice. Galloway (2002:246) summarized this for the Natchez by noting that, concerning colonial-era resilience of the Natchez relative to more recent immigrants into the lower Mississippi Valley, "one simple difference . . . is obvious: the Natchez still occupied their virtually immemorial homeland, drawing strength from the evidence of their long residence written in the mounds and cleared lands that the French found so attractive." The same may have pertained to the Awahnichi descendants, who maintained ties to Yosemite Valley during their exile and returned to it only a generation later. This attachment to homeland and the strength drawn from connections to the land, however, was always weighed against the threat to security by remaining in place. The physical threat from the League of the Iroquois in the Northeast and vulnerability of people to slave raiding in the Southeast prompted other groups such as the Wendat-Tionontate to relocate rather than maintain ties to traditional homelands. These decisions contributed to their perseverance in the wake of disease.

A second important factor was cultural flexibility while maintaining important practices and traditions that defined communities. Often such flexibility had deep roots in the past, although more recent adaptation to the colonial milieu was possible (see Galloway 1995). Preexisting relations with neighboring groups facilitated survival in turbulent times, but deeply held beliefs and practices were maintained even when a native group resided in proximity to others. The latter situation may have been fostered by the maintenance of separate villages observed archaeologically in some many cases.

The third factor, consisting of subsistence practices, is related to such cultural flexibility. Foraging rather than farming may have allowed for more ease in short-term cultural accommodation, since it facilitated residential mobility. This is evident, for example, in the Eno River region of the Carolina Piedmont, where people were able to relocate and sustain much like the Awahnichi did on the western side of the continent. Similarly, the decreasing reliance on maize and increased use of upland zones by the Choctaws, dating back to the demise of Moundville, may have worked in their favor in the wake of depopulation. But even horticultural societies such as the Iroquoian groups, the Mandan, and the Hidatsa managed in the wake of depopulation, although they may have been drawn into colonial enterprises much sooner—and therefore experienced more rapid and profound change—than did foragers as a result of their settlement and subsistence strategy. Restricted access to land undermined the subsistence base and was a key element in Yosemite Indian cultural transformation, as it was elsewhere. Such limitations necessitated the incorporation of new foods and the initiation of trade or wage labor to acquire substitute foodstuffs, and increased interaction with merchants and others necessitated new forms of dress, among other consequences. The Yosemite Indians experienced all of this change while still encountering resistance or dealing with violence in continued conflicts over land.

A fourth factor was the maintenance or overt renegotiation of identity in changing times. For example, the Choctaws and Creeks actively negotiated new identities with which to move forward as a cohesive whole, creating new confederacies or ethnic groups in response to the incorporation of near or distant neighbors within communities. In other cases, such as the Onondaga, newcomers were subsumed within existing identities of their hosts rather than forging a new collective identity for diverse groups. Still, the sense of belonging and purpose may have been satisfied by either strategy.

The fifth and final factor that contributed to cultural persistence in the wake of disease was the tempo of interaction—cultural entanglement versus colonization in Alexander's (1998) terminology—and the ability of native people to maintain their economic independence and physical distance from colonizers. The participation of other native groups in activities such as slave raiding, however, created additional challenges, since such activities magnified the local effect of colonists disproportionate to their actual numbers. That is, the enlistment of native people in colonial enterprises often brought those effects to the hinterlands in advance of nonnative presence and ultimately made those enterprises successful. Gradual rather than abrupt progression of European influence allowed autonomous adjustments, since "as long as such groups were in a position to manage regional intelligence . . . for their own benefit. . . . 'subaltern' groups have managed to preserve their identities and resist cultural absorption" (Galloway 2002:247). In the long term, however, the various elements that contributed to cultural stability in the wake of depopulation were threatened or destroyed by other aspects of colonialism, including control of native labor or wider access to trade goods, which undermined chiefly authority. Significantly, the labor of Yosemite Indians was never directly controlled or coerced by others, although such participation was often necessitated by circumstance. This contributed to their autonomy, including the maintenance of village life well into the 1900s. Where labor was controlled or even voluntarily redirected toward capitalist enterprises that diverted effort away from traditional practices, erosion of social and gender roles resulted (e.g., Frink 2007; Kardulias 1990; Nassaney 2004).

Previous anthropological and historical study of the cultural consequences of colonial-era native depopulation has suffered from the inability to disentangle depopulation due to introduced disease from the physical incursion of nonnative people. This has resulted in the assumption that the former established irreversible colonial cultural transformations. What the Yosemite Indian data show, however, is that disease on its own was not the "knock-out punch" to the traditional life and culture of many people. Rather, groups weathered this substantial challenge much as they had past assaults, with flexibility and agency, albeit with often severely limited options. Continuity is demonstrated especially in the domestic sphere, and this is critical since the family served as an important locus of identity and a visible measure of continuity and tradition. Changes in daily life and even social structure came only after economic entanglement in nonnative commerce or disenfranchisement as these economic interests were developed or asserted. The importance of colonial-era demographic collapse to Indian people of North America lies not in the magnitude of the collapse—as some determinant of inevitable cultural change and destruction—but in the decisions made in the wake of such depopulation and the efforts of people to reestablish or construct their identities and communities after demographic calamity. Such decisions were affected by the broader regional natural and cultural context as well as by a people's unique history, including their previous experience with depopulation, the character of the group and their leaders, and their ability to make these choices free from the threat of additional attacks either at the hands of colonists or their native allies. These were not static societies, for abrupt and gradual change occurred over the preceding decades, centuries, or millennia. Memory of such dynamism and past challenges was preserved in native oral history, and such memory played a role in the persistence of native culture and identity, just as it does today.

These observations do not diminish the magnitude or trauma of native depopulation. Significant devastation clearly occurred and in many cases was set in motion prior to direct contact. The long-term cultural outcome, however, seems to be due to either further waves of introduced disease that kept many native populations off balance or to the physical incursion by nonnative people and the economic involvement of native people with colonial interlopers. The dual assaults of biological and cultural invasion occurred in relatively quick succession in many places. Where longer lag time is evident, such as in the Caddoan case of mosaic spread of pathogens, there was often some population rebound following disease, cultural accommodation for societies small and large, and no clear irreversible cultural change. This suggests that had there been longer lag time between disease and encounters across the continent—as would have prevailed in the continental pandemic scenario (Dobyns 1983) in the absence of subsequent waves of different diseases—then native groups would have endured relatively intact unless already inherently unstable due to processes in place prior to the Columbian landfall. And importantly, any coincident culture change may not be distinguishable from dynamics set off by incursion of Indian people into a new region in precolonial times, regardless of these people's intent with respect to the resident population.

Since colonial-era demographic collapse and displacement have analogs in the distant past, then perhaps "colonialism" is not a proper representation of these processes, despite being initiated—sometimes at significant distance—by a European presence. But the native colonial experience did begin with this event, even if depopulation began prior to face-to-face encounters and did not entail an intentional act. It is important to appreciate this point, because these initial "encounters" provide necessary context for understanding later engagements between colonists and native people in more traditional colonial settings such as missions, ranchos, and trading posts. That is, we cannot fully understand the relationships of power and resistance in, or even simply "living through," colonialism as we often conceive of it (see Silliman 2005:66) without first appreciating these early demographic seeds of the colonial process. Although some scholars limit the definition of colonialism to settings of power differentials and argue that precontact, disease-induced demographic decline is not part of colonialism (e.g., Silliman 2005:59), to do so ignores the issue of how such imbalances came about in a land where indigenous people greatly outnumbered colonists in all initial encounters and even some enduring relationships such as missions. To disregard the full history of native people, by decontextualizing such "encounters" and ignoring the unique history of each group accessible via archaeology, privileges the intruders rather than native people. Indigenous people of North America had no fundamental experience with "colonists" or "colonialism" and reacted no differently than they would have to any other challenge or catastrophe. The process of colonialism had no meaning within these native societies and thus had to be envisioned, defined, and dealt with as had events of disease or catastrophe in the more distant past. Alexander's (1998) definition of "cultural entanglement" seems a more encompassing view of the colonial process, especially from the perspective of native people. When actually confronted with interlopers rather than simply their biological advance men, the encounter was one of perceived equality—or, more correctly, as one of *greater* indigenous rights—rather than one of imbalance or domination, even in the wake of disease.

If we acknowledge that cultural dynamism is the norm within native forager and farmer communities, we can move away from the fallacy of stability that attributes anthropological significance to events detached from experience rather than to the specific circumstances in which those events occurred. The way in which anthropologists generalize about culture change depends upon which factors (events or circumstances) are given the most weight. Insisting that processes can only be understood in specific context certainly makes such generalization a much more difficult task. Still, to attempt to develop generalizations about both the process and the outcome of colonialism without an appreciation for such context and history would likely prove meaningless to most anthropologists. This echoes Hodder's (2000:31–32) conclusion that archaeologists must move away from exclusive focus on the "grand synthesis of the long term" to also incorporate the "small narratives of lived moments." The Yosemite Indian experience indicates that it is the *convergence* of circumstances that was significant to decision making and culture changes that were ultimately manifest in the archaeological record of the colonial era and, presumably, in the more distant past. The Yosemite Indian case represents the intersection of previous population decline, existing relationships, and charismatic leadership. Archaeologists must acknowledge that such change plays out at a finer temporal scale than is generally sought in archaeological endeavors (that is, within one or two generations) and, hence, may be dependent upon and influenced by specific individuals.

PESTILENCE AND PERSISTENCE

Determining cause and effect is a tricky business even in the recent past, let alone in antiquity. The "historicizing" of anthropology, including detailed consideration of context and circumstance in the lives of individuals, however, allows for critical assessment of the contingent nature of colonial encounters. Such interactions entailed—and distilled within a relatively brief span—processes that occurred in precolonial contexts or over longer periods of time. Because depopulation may have occurred substantially before direct interaction with nonnative peoples, and because deep structural culture change was not a consequence of population collapse, time is a fundamental element to investigation of the colonial experience (see also Ramenofsky 1991:439). Rather than considering time only in "history" as opposed to "prehistory," the importance of time transcends the limits of the contact "moment" to encompass the context, onset, duration, rate, and magnitude of population and culture change evident in multiple data sets and at different temporal scales. Thus, a suitable theoretical approach to colonialism must conceptualize the processes of nonnative interaction and consequent culture change the same as earlier intergroup contacts or cultural transformation (see Alexander 1998), including the recognition of culture change in both the short- term and the long- term (see Lightfoot 1995). It must seek such change in daily practices rather than simply the incorporation of nonnative material objects.

The results of this study confirm that this approach has been successful, particularly with respect to the reconstruction of long-term demographic patterns. Both native oral tradition and additional archaeological data lend support to the trends observed. And the natural features of Yosemite Valley and the abundance of ethnohistoric information, archaeological sites, ethnographic data, and various native oral accounts made the story of the Awahnichi especially well suited to the long-term historical anthropological approach employed in this study. Long-term demographic reconstruction has also highlighted the importance of explicit and well-grounded assumptions about formation of the archaeological record and of making such assumptions clear. Employing an empirical method, the validity of these assumptions could be tested, and this provided great confidence in the interpretations. Significantly, these results confirm that a quantitative approach is compatible with an appreciation for, and incorporation of, both history and agency in explanation.

Assessing colonialism in the fullest sense from "contact" onward[1] is only possible when archaeological data are incorporated into study and when the colonial era is placed in longer-term history. But can such methods can be successfully applied elsewhere? Certainly, developing a substantial sample of calendric dates representing a culturally meaningful and statistically defensible sample was critical to this research. However, such archaeological data are either not available in all areas, or gathering such data is prohibitively expensive given the types of chronological methods that are available. This may prevent completion of similar detailed studies in other cases. Many archaeological approaches to colonial-era demographic and cultural change are hampered by the temporal measuring devices employed. The reliance on phases or potentially nonrepresentative samples of radiocarbon dates undermines the capacity to both develop dynamic pictures of such change and to have confidence that the patterns so revealed provide an accurate picture. In light of such difficulties, the current research was explicitly constructed as a demographic study and employed a chronological tool that provided calendric dates amenable to manipulation at various temporal scales. Colonial-era trends were placed in longer-term perspective. Therefore, the onset, rate, duration, and magnitude of both demographic and culture change could be assessed and, equally important, the data were analyzed at scales commensurate with the lived experience of people. Finally, consequent culture change was examined at the individual as well as the group level to address the diverse spatial scales within which processes of change likely occurred.

A long-term perspective is uncommon to historical anthropological research on colonialism in ethnographic or archaeological analyses. Within this approach, the colonial encounter is best viewed as simply one historical event among many that proximally or ultimately affected the cultural trajectory of both the native and nonnative peoples who were parties to such interaction. Such a perspective counteracts a Eurocentric preoccupation with the impact of Western people, culture, and the "World System" on non-Western peoples of the "periphery" in culture-contact research (Lightfoot and Martinez 1995; Ohnuki-Tierney 1990). And it allows us to move away from a reliance on the problematic "memory culture" of early ethnography, which is detached from specific time and place. If we acknowledge native people as individuals with history, then as Rubertone (2000:435) notes, "rather than insisting that many Native American groups of the postcontact period are historically emergent phenomena whose cultural authenticity is questionable and whose local circumstances are the consequence of European contact and colonialism instead of deep historical roots, they might be more accurately described as people with remarkably complex histories of survival and enduring attachment to community and place."

Certainly, the ethnohistoric account of the Awahnichi indicates just such attachment to place, as the descendants permanently returned to their traditional territory when they were able to do so and have maintained a strong connection to this day. Likewise, the Yosemite Valley archaeological data attest not only to survival of people but also to endurance of culture. Although Awahnichi colonial-era population decline is of anthropological interest and poses interesting challenges to archaeology, it is ultimately a personal story of circumstance, adjustment, and survival. Yosemite Indian cultural history and, in fact, all history is made up of stories that can often only be assessed via archaeology. The challenge is to develop suitable methods and to invoke appropriate perspectives that allow us to tell such stories in a way that reflects their cultural significance to those involved and their descendants in both the short and long term. In the case of the Yosemite Indians, it was the ability to put this demographic event into context—through a long-term view of population size developed through archaeology—that has permitted a fuller understanding of the processes of cultural negotiation and accommodation in changing circumstances.

APPENDIX

Population Proxy Data

TABLE A-1.
Proxy Population Data

Date Interval	Debitage Proxy			Subsite Proxy				
	Frequency	3-pt Average of Frequency	3-pt Average as Percentage of Maximum Population	Frequency	3-pt Average of Frequency	3-pt Average as Percentage of Maximum Population	3-pt Average of Frequency, Calibrated to Debitage Scale	3-pt Average as Percentage of Maximum Population, Calibrated to Debitage Scale
A.D. 1950–1900	3			2				
A.D. 1900–1850	92	39.67	52.89	13	6.33	50.00	10.54	8.93
A.D. 1850–1800	24	45.33	60.44	4	7.00	55.26	13.59	11.52
A.D. 1800–1750	20	22.67	30.22	4	3.67	28.95	3.81	3.23
A.D. 1750–1700	24	22.33	29.78	3	4.67	36.84	5.58	4.73
A.D. 1700–1650	23	26.67	35.56	7	6.67	52.63	11.97	10.14
A.D. 1650–1600	33	27.33	36.44	10	7.67	60.53	17.53	14.85
A.D. 1600–1550	26	30.00	40.00	6	7.67	60.53	17.53	14.85
A.D. 1550–1500	31	25.33	33.78	7	5.67	44.74	8.17	6.93
A.D. 1500–1450	19	24.33	32.44	4	6.00	47.37	9.28	7.87
A.D. 1450–1400	23	17.67	23.56	7	5.33	42.11	7.20	6.10
A.D. 1400–1350	11	17.67	23.56	5	6.67	52.63	11.97	10.14
A.D. 1350–1300	19	19.00	25.33	8	7.00	55.26	13.59	11.52
A.D. 1300–1250	27	22.00	29.33	8	8.00	63.16	19.90	16.87
A.D. 1250–1200	20	24.00	32.00	8	9.00	71.05	29.14	24.70
A.D. 1200–1150	25	24.33	32.44	11	8.33	65.79	22.60	19.15

Period							
A.D. 1150–1100	28	27.67	36.89	6	9.33	73.68	33.09	28.05
A.D. 1100–1050	30	28.33	37.78	11	9.00	71.05	29.14	24.70
A.D. 1050–1000	27	26.67	35.56	10	10.00	78.95	42.68	36.17
A.D. 1000–950	23	26.67	35.56	9	10.00	78.95	42.68	36.17
A.D. 950–900	30	29.00	38.67	11	10.00	78.95	42.68	36.17
A.D. 900–850	34	38.00	50.67	10	11.00	86.84	62.49	52.96
A.D. 850–800	50	42.67	56.89	12	10.33	81.58	48.46	41.07
A.D. 800–750	44	46.33	61.78	9	10.00	78.95	42.68	36.17
A.D. 750–700	45	50.00	66.67	9	10.00	78.95	42.68	36.17
A.D. 700–650	61	47.00	62.67	12	10.00	78.95	42.68	36.17
A.D. 650–600	35	50.67	67.56	9	10.00	78.95	42.68	36.17
A.D. 600–550	56	56.33	75.11	9	9.67	76.32	37.58	31.85
A.D. 550–500	78	65.00	86.67	11	10.33	81.58	48.46	41.07
A.D. 500–450	61	75.00	100.00	11	11.33	89.47	70.96	60.14
A.D. 450–400	86	66.33	88.44	12	11.67	92.11	80.58	68.29
A.D. 400–350	52	63.67	84.89	12	11.67	92.11	80.58	68.29
A.D. 350–300	53	60.67	80.89	11	11.00	86.84	62.49	52.96
A.D. 300–250	77	64.67	86.22	10	10.33	81.58	48.46	41.07
A.D. 250–200	64	65.33	87.11	10	10.33	81.58	48.46	41.07
A.D. 200–150	55	62.67	83.56	11	10.67	84.21	55.03	46.64
A.D. 150–100	69	61.33	81.78	11	11.33	89.47	70.96	60.14
A.D. 100–50	60	58.67	78.22	12	11.00	86.84	62.49	52.96
A.D. 50–0	47	54.00	72.00	10	11.33	89.47	70.96	60.14
0–50 B.C.	55	51.33	68.44	12	11.67	92.11	80.58	68.29
50–100 B.C.	52	54.67	72.89	13	12.00	94.74	91.51	77.55

(continued)

TABLE A-1. (CONTINUED)

	Debitage Proxy			Subsite Proxy			
Date Interval	Frequency	3-pt Average of Frequency	3-pt Average as Percentage of Maximum Population	Frequency	3-pt Average of Frequency	3-pt Average as Percentage of Maximum Population	3-pt Average of Frequency, Calibrated to Debitage Scale	3-pt Average as Percentage of Maximum Population, Calibrated to Debitage Scale
100–150 B.C.	57	55.67	74.22	11	12.67	100.00	118.00	100.00
150–200 B.C.	58	56.33	75.11	14	12.00	94.74	91.51	77.55
200–250 B.C.	54	54.00	72.00	11	12.67	100.00	118.00	100.00
250–300 B.C.	50	50.33	67.11	13	11.00	86.84	62.49	52.96
300–350 B.C.	47	46.67	62.22	9	10.67	84.21	55.03	46.64
350–400 B.C.	43	46.33	61.78	10	10.00	78.95	42.68	36.17
400–450 B.C.	49	49.33	65.78	11	11.33	89.47	70.96	60.14
450–500 B.C.	56	48.33	64.44	13	12.00	94.74	91.51	77.55
500–550 B.C.	40	45.00	60.00	12	11.67	92.11	80.58	68.29
550–600 B.C.	39	42.67	56.89	10	11.33	89.47	70.96	60.14
600–650 B.C.	49	41.33	55.11	12	11.67	92.11	80.58	68.29
650–700 B.C.	36	39.67	52.89	13	11.33	89.47	70.96	60.14
700–750 B.C.	34	36.00	48.00	9	10.33	81.58	48.46	41.07
750–800 B.C.	38	33.33	44.44	9	9.00	71.05	29.14	24.70
800–850 B.C.	28	32.33	43.11	9	9.67	76.32	37.58	31.85
850–900 B.C.	31	32.00	42.67	11	10.33	81.58	48.46	41.07
900–950 B.C.	37	30.00	40.00	11	11.33	89.47	70.96	60.14

950–1000 B.C.	22	25.67	34.22	12	10.33	81.58	48.46	41.07
1000–1050 B.C.	18	21.67	28.89	8	8.67	68.42	25.66	21.75
1050–1100 B.C.	25	20.33	27.11	6	6.67	52.63	11.97	10.14
1100–1150 B.C.	18	24.33	32.44	6	7.67	60.53	17.53	14.85
1150–1200 B.C.	30	23.00	30.67	11	9.00	71.05	29.14	24.70
1200–1250 B.C.	21	22.67	30.22	10	9.67	76.32	37.58	31.85
1250–1300 B.C.	17	18.67	24.89	8	8.67	68.42	25.66	21.75
1300–1350 B.C.	18	18.33	24.44	8	8.67	68.42	25.66	21.75
1350–1400 B.C.	20	15.33	20.44	10	7.67	60.53	17.53	14.85
1400–1450 B.C.	8	16.33	21.78	5	6.67	52.63	11.97	10.14
1450–1500 B.C.	21	15.67	20.89	5	6.00	47.37	9.28	7.87
1500–1550 B.C.	18	19.67	26.22	8	7.00	55.26	13.59	11.52
1550–1600 B.C.	20	17.67	23.56	8	8.00	63.16	19.90	16.87
1600–1650 B.C.	15	19.67	26.22	8	8.33	65.79	22.60	19.15
1650–1700 B.C.	24	17.67	23.56	9	8.33	65.79	22.60	19.15
1700–1750 B.C.	14	16.67	22.22	8	7.33	57.89	15.43	13.08
1750–1800 B.C.	12	11.33	15.11	5	6.00	47.37	9.28	7.87
1800–1850 B.C.	8	9.00	12.00	5	5.00	39.47	6.34	5.37
1850–1900 B.C.	7	11.00	14.67	5	6.00	47.37	9.28	7.87
1900–1950 B.C.	18	11.00	14.67	8	5.67	44.74	8.17	6.93
1950–2000 B.C.	8	10.33	13.78	4	5.33	42.11	7.20	6.10
2000–2050 B.C.	5	7.33	9.78	4	4.33	34.21	4.92	4.17
2050–2100 B.C.	9	7.67	10.22	5	5.33	42.11	7.20	6.10
2100–2150 B.C.	9	8.00	10.67	7	5.00	39.47	6.34	5.37
2150–2200 B.C.	6	5.00	6.67	3	3.33	26.32	3.36	2.84

(continued)

TABLE A-1. (CONTINUED)

Date Interval	Debitage Proxy			Subsite Proxy			
	Frequency	3-pt Average of Frequency	3-pt Average as Percentage of Maximum Population	Frequency	3-pt Average of Frequency	3-pt Average as Percentage of Maximum Population	3-pt Average of Frequency, Calibrated to Debitage Scale	3-pt Average as Percentage of Maximum Population, Calibrated to Debitage Scale
2200–2250 B.C.	0	3.00	4.00	0	2.00	15.79	2.02	1.71
2250–2300 B.C.	3	4.00	5.33	3	2.67	21.05	2.60	2.21
2300–2350 B.C.	9	7.67	10.22	5	5.67	44.74	8.17	6.93
2350–2400 B.C.	11	10.00	13.33	9	7.00	55.26	13.59	11.52
2400–2450 B.C.	10	8.67	11.56	7	6.67	52.63	11.97	10.14
2450–2500 B.C.	5	5.67	7.56	4	4.33	34.21	4.92	4.17
2500–2550 B.C.	2	3.67	4.89	2	3.00	23.68	2.96	2.51
2550–2600 B.C.	4	2.67	3.56	3	2.33	18.42	2.29	1.94
2600–2650 B.C.	2	3.33	4.44	2	2.67	21.05	2.60	2.21
2650–2700 B.C.	4	3.00	4.00	3	2.33	18.42	2.29	1.94

2700–2750 B.C.	3	4.00	5.33	2	3.00	23.68	2.96	2.51
2750–2800 B.C.	5	3.33	4.44	4	2.67	21.05	2.60	2.21
2800–2850 B.C.	2	3.33	4.44	2	2.33	18.42	2.29	1.94
2850–2900 B.C.	3	2.33	3.11	1	1.67	13.16	1.78	1.51
2900–2950 B.C.	2	3.67	4.89	2	2.33	18.42	2.29	1.94
2950–3000 B.C.	6	3.33	4.44	4	2.67	21.05	2.60	2.21
3000–3050 B.C.	2	5.33	7.11	2	3.67	28.95	3.81	3.23
3050–3100 B.C.	8	5.67	7.56	5	3.33	26.32	3.36	2.84
3100–3150 B.C.	7	5.33	7.11	3	3.00	23.68	2.96	2.51
3150–3200 B.C.	1	3.33	4.44	1	2.00	15.79	2.02	1.71
3200–3250 B.C.	2	1.33	1.78	2	1.33	10.53	1.57	1.33
3250–3300 B.C.	1	1.00	1.33	1	1.00	7.89	1.38	1.17
3300–3350 B.C.	0	1.33	1.78	0	1.33	10.53	1.57	1.33
3350–3400 B.C.	3	1.00	1.33	3	1.00	7.89	1.38	1.17
3400–3450 B.C.	0	2.00	2.67	0	2.00	15.79	2.02	1.71
3450–3500 B.C.	3	2.33	3.11	3	2.00	15.79	2.02	1.71
3500–3550 B.C.	4	3.33	4.44	3	2.67	21.05	2.60	2.21
3550–3600 B.C.	3	2.67	3.56	2	2.00	15.79	2.02	1.71

Notes

1. DISENTANGLING COLONIAL ENCOUNTERS

1. Various terms can, and have been, used to refer to the span of time encompassing the period after Columbus's landfall but prior to direct contact between colonists and native people, the establishment of permanent colonial outposts in a particular region, or "the production of detailed historical documents" for a given geographic area (Wesson and Rees 2002:1). *Contact* can be ill-defined or subject to debate, however, if the timing of nonnative disease infiltration is unknown or if it is not deemed to constitute contact. Since this span of time varies greatly within the Americas due in part to which terminal "event" is used to define the era, it is impossible to define a single "period" for the purposes of discussion on a continental or hemispheric basis. In addition, using A.D. 1492 as a starting point is equally fraught with problems, since the effects of the European presence in the Americas on native people were often not initiated until centuries later. That is, the Columbian landfall had no immediate significance to the history of many native groups. Some archaeologists use the term *protohistoric* when referring to the period "between contacts and colonies" (Wesson and Rees 2002:1), but some Indian people find this term offensive since it implies a lack of history prior to the arrival of Europeans in the Americas. Therefore, *protohistoric* is avoided in favor of *colonial era* and *contact era*, which are used more or less interchangeably in the current text. Both of these terms are meant to encompass the period that began with the earliest effects of the European presence on native people within a specific geographic region, whether that influence came at a distance or through direct interaction and whether it ended with the establishment of permanent nonnative domestic communities in native territories and successful or unsuccessful attempts to confine local Indian people to reservations. Since the timing of such initial effects is one of the central questions explored in this book, we

shall see how "contact" is a date subject to revision. Historical background for the various case studies presented provides detail on the span of time roughly encompassed by the colonial era in different regions. Although *colonial era* may appear to privilege Europeans in the encounter similar to *protohistoric,* use of former term is deemed appropriate since it is the process of colonialism that is under scrutiny.

2. Statistics on mortality for introduced diseases most prevalent during this period include 10 to 25 percent expected mortality for measles, 10 to 40 percent mortality for epidemic typhus, 20 to 25 percent mortality for both pneumonia and plague, and anywhere from 10 to 100 percent expected mortality for smallpox (Ramenofsky 1987: tables 46, 49, and 51).

3. Genetic research is also making significance contributions to our understanding the post-Columbian spread of infectious diseases among Native American populations as well as related potential morbidity and mortality. In this case, genetic variability of the pathogens themselves has led the conclusion that the particular subspecies or strain of a pathogen could have been important in determining the extent of Native American mortality in any given epidemic (Ramenofsky et al. 2003).

4. Examples of archaeological studies of New World population decline that consider the interactions of environment, host, and parasite that are emphasized by epidemiologists include Newson (1993) and Ramenofsky (1990, 1996).

5. Alchon (2003) provides a succinct and useful summary of this debate and various population estimates in the appendix of her book.

6. Although Ramenofsky and colleagues (2003) make the intriguing observation that spread of some infectious Old World diseases such as influenza might be facilitated by migratory waterfowl or some domesticated animals (see also Ramenofsky and Galloway 1997).

7. Ramenofsky (1987; see also Ramenofsky 1996) provides a useful summary of the communicability of certain pathogens. Smallpox is most apt to be communicable long after initial appearance within a population, as this disease can survive in a dried state without a host for up to two years. She notes that smallpox in other than the dried state is communicable for 9 to 14 days (3 to 7 days for other forms), whooping cough is communicable for 4 weeks, and measles is communicable for 7 to 14 days, similar to scarlet fever. Influenza has a somewhat shorter period of communicability of only 1 to 3 days.

8. Studies of the potential spread of Old World diseases in advance of face-to-face contact between native and nonnative people draw especially on pathogenic and ethnohistoric data, although Ramenofsky's (1987) study is primarily archaeological. Dobyns (1966, 1983) estimated that the pre-Columbian population in the Americas was more than 90 million people (18 million in North America) and that introduced diseases reduced this number by as much as 97 percent. Ubelaker (1992) favors a more conservative estimate of approximately 1.2 million people for North America prior to the arrival of Europeans to the continent. These data suggest a 50 to 95 percent decline in native population for various areas.

9. California Indian people generally lived in relatively small groups referred

to by anthropologists as "tribelets" (Kroeber 1962). Thus, there were hundreds if not thousands of tribelets within California, and these communities often identified themselves by a name that referred to the area in which they lived. Given this diversity, anthropologists generally consider California native groups by linguistic affiliation and that practice is also used here, unless otherwise noted.

10. "Historical anthropology" is more commonly considered "ethnohistory" when dealing specifically with colonial encounters.

2. MULTIPLE PERSPECTIVES ON A CRITICAL TIME

1. In Bunnell's (1990) account, the name of "old sachem" is spelled "Ten-ie-ya." The spelling used for Chief Tenaya here follows current practice, codified in part by USGS topographic map designations for hydrologic features named after the venerable leader.

2. Although referring to an exchange between Maj. James Savage and Tenaya, Bunnell (1990:9) readily acknowledged his practice of summarizing, rather than presenting full translations of, native interviews and orations in his text. He noted that "the Indian speeches here quoted are like all others of their kind, really but poor imitations. The Indian is very figurative in his language. If a literal translation were attempted his speeches would seem so disjointed and inverted in their method of expression that their significance could scarcely be understood; hence only the substance is here given."

3. Although Bunnell's account was originally published in 1880, it is unclear when it was actually written and to what extent Bunnell relied on memory rather than notes or journals to create his narrative. Mazel (2000) noted several literary conventions and choices of the author that suggest at least some passages were written or embellished from an earlier article (Bunnell 1859) closer to the time of publication than to when the events occurred. Similarly, Solnit (1994:231) concluded that the delay between the events and publication—and the potential for "embellishment" of conversations described therein—is an indication that the text "is valuable as myth as well as anecdote," especially with respect to Bunnell's role as the "first appreciator" of Yosemite Valley. Finally, Bunnell's reference to the ethnological work of the Smithsonian Institution, which only took on this responsibility with the establishment of the Bureau of Ethnology in 1879, also argues for authorship of at least some portions of the manuscript closer to the date of publication than at the time of the actual events.

4. Bunnell penned more brief accounts as early as 1859, focusing primarily on the "discovery" of Yosemite Valley rather than the reasons for the expedition or detail of the native people he encountered and customs he observed during the military expedition (Bunnell 1859). The impetus for writing the initial account seems to have been to refute erroneous information regarding the "discovery" and naming of Yosemite Valley disseminated by other authors who were not part of the corps (e.g., Hutchings 1856). Likewise, Bunnell's full account seems to have been an attempt at a final word on these subjects (see Mazel 2000:100), despite masquerading as a history of the Mariposa Battalion (Bunnell 1990:16). Solnit (1994:222) perceives no "humanity" in Bun-

nell's literary treatment of Yosemite Indians, despite his numerous references to the injustices perpetrated on these people by their forced removal from their homeland.

5. Although eighteen treaties were negotiated between 1851 and 1852 by U.S. Indian commissioners with California native groups—including some resident in the central and southern Sierra and foothills—none of these agreements was ever ratified by the Senate.

6. Originally published as *Vie et aventures d'un enfant de l'Ardenne* (Lamar 1985:xvi), Perlot's memoir was translated into English by Helen Harding Bretnor (Perlot 1985), and this study relies upon that translation.

7. Following the practice established by John Wesley Powell in his work as director of the Bureau of Ethnology (later Bureau of American Ethnology), Powers discussed native peoples and cultures within broad language groups (see Conn 2004). While *Miwok* is the term used by anthropologists to refer to the language spoken by his informants as well as to all people speaking languages within this family, *Me'-wuk* is used herein when referring to Sierra Nevada people, as this spelling is favored by several contemporary tribal groups in the greater Yosemite area. This usage also follows Merriam's (1907:338) distinction between Sierra (Me'-wuk) and other (Mew'-ko) Miwok speakers.

8. Although Gifford and Barrett both identified many of their informants as either Northern or Central Sierra Me'-wuk, Bates (1993) notes that this was often based on where individuals were living at the time ethnographic fieldwork was conducted rather than their place of birth or family heritage. Thus, some of the observations made by these ethnographers may actually have been obtained from Southern Sierra Me'-wuk individuals.

9. As Dunnell (1991:571) has noted, ethnographers were effectively amassing a list of traits that may or may not have had any direct relation to the "cultural systems" of native people prior to the impacts of nonnative people and disease. For Dunnell (1991) this represents a fundamental problem, since continuity in traits across the disease divide does not necessarily ensure continuity in the entirety of culture (e.g., the context and meaning of practices may have changed). Implicit in this observation, however, is the notion that native cultures did not change prior to European influence and, therefore, that colonial-era culture change *as a process* is somehow different than change in the more distant past. That is, Dunnell has assumed cultural discontinuity with the advent of colonialism, just as he has accused other archaeologists of assuming cultural continuity in the ethnographic record. In fact, it is incumbent upon archaeologists to demonstrate rather than assume either of these outcomes through a contextual, rather than trait-based, approach to archaeology.

3. COLONIAL ENCOUNTERS IN YOSEMITE VALLEY

1. Farquhar (1965:79) notes that the name *Boling* also appears as *Bowling* in various other historical documents.

2. Spelling of native names varies in different sources for the region (e.g., Barrett 1908; Bates and Lee 1990; Bunnell 1990; Clark 1907; Kroeber 1921, 1925; Levy 1978; Merriam 1917).

3. Boling's account of these incidents, reported in a letter to Major Savage at the time (see Russell 1992:38–39), differs somewhat from Bunnell's memory. It may be, however, that Boling was less than forthcoming about the true nature of these killings in his official report.

4. Johnston (1995; see also Russell 1992) discusses an alternate story of Tenaya's death recalled by Mario Lebrado, but he concludes that the factual errors in this story render it unbelievable.

5. Bates and Lee (1990:27) suggest, however, that other Yosemite Indians who were living at Bull Creek during the winter of 1851 were signatories to the Treaty of Camp Fremont signed on March 19, 1851.

6. This spelling follows that used by Bates and Lee (1990).

7. Ethnographic data for California (Kroeber 1925; see also Perlot 1985: 220–223) suggest that such conflicts were more likely skirmishes or periodic attacks by small groups of individuals rather than dedicated armed conflict by the entire male populace or prolonged combat with numerous fatalities more consistent with our modern concept of "war."

8. Milliken's (1995) study of mission records from the San Francisco Bay area has documented the extent of such recruitment and also has helped define the approximate location of traditional territories of some Costanoan (Ohlone), Miwok, and Yokuts tribelets in Central California during the late 1700s and early 1800s.

4. THE PEOPLE OF AWAHNEE

1. All archaeological determinations of cultural affiliation may be criticized somewhat for their reliance on ethnographic information and adherence to the direct historical approach. It is also possible that the archaeological record of Yosemite National Park represents sites associated with people of different ethnic affinity (e.g., seasonal use by Paiute, Washo, Me'-wuk, Yokuts, and others), so the tendency to lump all sites of a period together as one or another of these ethnolinguistic peoples may be unwarranted. On the other hand, the similarity between the archaeological record of the Late Prehistoric 3 period and the traits observed by Bunnell (1990) and Perlot (1985) is readily apparent.

2. Various scholars (e.g., Grayson 1994) have discussed problems with glottochronology and other techniques employed by historical linguists in reconstructions of this kind. Similarly, Hughes (1992) has admonished California archaeologists against relying on such information when assessing ancient migrations, population movements, or cultural affiliation, especially given the often undertheorized equivalences between material culture and cultural groups. In particular, Hughes is critical of both how ethnolinguistic identity is established by archaeologists and the appropriate scale for such identification (i.e., language stock, language family, or tribelet). Other linguistic and ethnohistoric evidence provides confidence in Me'-wuk affiliation for the Awahnichi and Awahnichi occupation of Yosemite Valley prior to the influx of nonnative disease, however, regardless of the specific estimates of Miwok language divergence summarized here.

3. Based on a cross-cultural study of Yokuts, Monache, and Southern Sierra Me'-wuk ethnography, Dick-Bissonnette (1998) concluded that the office of "chief" was a postcontact phenomenon that arose from the need to effectively negotiate and interact with nonnative people. Tenaya's identification of his father as a "chief" contradicts this with respect to the Awahnichi, although it is unclear what authority was either implied or entailed by this interpretation of Tenaya's words.

4. Dick-Bissonnette (1998) has argued that patrilocality and, by extension, patriarchy were traditions that evolved among the Yokuts, Monache, and Southern Sierra Me'-wuk after the Gold Rush rather than existing before nonnative incursion into the southern Sierra Nevada. Her argument is largely based on the importance of acorns in the diet and the fact that native women reported that acorn-gathering areas were passed down through the mother's line. While Dick-Bissonnette questions ethnographers' conclusions regarding patrilocality and patriarchy, she does not question whether matrilineal gathering areas were also the result of postcontact pressures, including the development of large villages. Given that movement and territories were much more constrained during and after the Gold Rush, we might equally interrogate this aspect of the ethnographic record. On the other hand, her contention that ethnographers and other observers of native people in the late 1800s may have had gender bias based on contemporary American social practices is certainly well taken.

5. Spelled as "Nang-Oua" in Perlot (1985:229).

5. PEOPLING THE PAST

1. Regional ethnohistoric and ethnographic information (e.g., Dick-Bissonnette 1998; Perlot 1985) suggest that the number of fatalities in native "war" were likely relatively small, as such conflicts entailed brief skirmishes, threats, and intimidation as much, if not more, than substantial armed conflict.

2. Seminal studies in this vein include Cameron (1990), Casselberry (1974), Casteel (1974), LeBlanc (1971), McMichael (1960), Read (1978), Sumner (1979), Turner and Lofgren (1966), and Wiessner (1974); see also Cook (1972), Hassan (1981), and Howell (1986).

3. *Village* as used here with respect to subsites refers to both camps and villages and is not limited to the large village settlements such as those observed by ethnographers (e.g., Gifford 1926b).

4. Obsidian debitage frequency was positively correlated with debitage weight (Hull 2002: figure 10), and this indicated that frequency was a useful gauge of material consumption.

5. These figures represent the archaeological sites known at the time this research was undertaken. Ongoing archaeological investigations, particularly related to monitoring of construction, have revealed a few additional deposits that lack surface evidence.

6. The one exception was CA-MRP-310, where excavation within the 1-by-1-meter unit was terminated at 150 centimeters in depth due to Occupational Safety and Health Administration regulations, despite the fact that the base of the deposit had not yet been reached.

7. Studies considering the influence of temperature on hydration rates include Friedman and Smith (1960), Leach and Hamel (1984), and Mazer et al. (1991). Other studies have examined the effects of relative humidity (e.g., Friedman et al. 1994; Mazer et al. 1991; Stevenson, Knaus et al. 1993) and intrinsic water (Stevenson, Sheppard et al. 1996; Stevenson, Mazer et al. 1998).

8. Primary data were collected by Mundy (1993), while temperature regressions were presented by Bevill and colleagues (2005).

9. For the purposes of the current analysis, dates for each face that did not fall within two standard deviations of one another based on variance around the hydration mean for each face were considered as two separate dates. This protocol differs somewhat from that used by Hull (2002, 2005) in the original data analysis, resulting in a slightly different total sample size. In addition, a minor adjustment to the calculation of effective hydration temperature (EHT) was made for the current analysis.

10. For the purposes of analysis, all "no visible hydration" measurements deriving from pieces recovered below 50 centimeters in depth were excluded.

11. There were, however, some very thin rims that fell in this range (i.e., they were not part of the extrapolated data), and these dates were included in the analysis.

12. As discussed by Hull (2005:368), even this large sample may be insufficient to accurately depict some cycles of population change that appear in the data prior to circa A.D. 550. This observation also pertains to exact reconstruction of demographic change in the centuries leading up to and including the colonial era. For the debitage proxy, sample sizes within many of the 50-year increments dating to this span should be approximately twice that available to ensure faithful reproduction of small-scale population signals within 50- to 100-year cycles; an even greater sample size would be required for the subsite proxy. The substantial sample is likely sufficient, however, to reveal overall population trends through time.

13. For the population proxy based on debitage, the data for the subsite from which only a 5 percent sample was examined were counted twice in order to approximate a 10 percent sample. Patterns in relative population trends using this method were consistent with those visible when the sample from this subsite was not doubled (see Hull 2002); that is, the doubling of these data did not alter the general trends in population growth and decline.

14. Following Bayham and Hull (1996), use of three-point averaging reduced noise in the data, and this allowed general trends to be recognized more easily.

15. The logarithmic formula is $y = 0.158 + 2.622 \ln(x)$, where x is the debitage frequency and y is the subsite frequency. Similarly, the power-function formula is $y = 1.133 x^{0.597}$. These formulas differ slightly from those derived by Hull (2002), since sampling protocols and EHT calculations employed in the current analysis are slightly different, as noted above.

16. Given trends that were apparent when data were examined at different temporal increments (see Hull 2002:247), the logarithmic, rather than power-function, calibration derived in the current analysis was selected for use.

17. As discussed by Hull (2002), such differences between the debitage and

subsite population proxies can also be due in part to difference in duration of site occupation, particularly if long intervals of time are used to analyze the data.

6. A TRADITION OF SURVIVAL

1. Changes in the generational length have relatively little impact on the dynamic between fertility and mortality for the low-growth populations considered herein.

2. These calculations exclude the anomalously high growth rates in the last 600 years likely facilitated, in part, by immigration.

3. Warfare might also have consequences for fertility of the remaining population, as regional ethnohistory suggests that adult women were frequently captured by the victors, and thus their reproductive potential would no longer have been available to their original group.

4. See also Bunnell (1990:261) on the apparent propensity of Yosemite Indians to engage in sexual relations during the spring, which would result in pregnancies coming to term in the winter. Perlot (1985:234) also notes winter and spring births.

5. Preston (1996, 1997, 2002) and others (Erlandson and Bartoy 1995) have argued that nonnative disease may have infiltrated California from sporadic contacts on the coast or spread from New Spain during the 1500s and 1600s. While introduction of Old World diseases into the Sierra Nevada seems unlikely via either of these routes at such an early date, earlier nonnative disease exposure cannot be completely discounted as a possible explanation for low population in Yosemite Valley circa A.D. 1450, given the data-averaging methods employed (i.e., the actual nadir might be somewhat later and thus within the period of initial European exploration along the California coast). On the other hand, the fact that this was a population nadir following a relatively steady demographic decline that spanned more than 900 years suggests that European disease probably played no part in this chapter of Yosemite Indian demographic history.

7. DAILY PRACTICES IN A CHANGING WORLD

1. Cusick (1998a) provides a useful summary of the history of such research.

2. This approach is discussed at length by Lightfoot (1995:205) and Lightfoot and colleagues (1998:201); see also Hendon (1996) and Tringham (1991).

3. See Lightfoot (1995:208–209), Lightfoot and colleagues (1998:217), and Hendon (1996:48) for discussion of this approach.

4. Although immunological analysis techniques continue to be the subject of ongoing research and debate (see Flint 1995), the most severe critiques have focused on methods other than CIEP (e.g., Eisele 1994). In addition, critics have questioned preservation with age (cf. Kooyman et al. 1992; Newman et al. 1996, 1997), although this issue was not as critical in the Yosemite Indian case given the relatively recent deposition of the artifacts under study. Positive

results from previous regional studies also provide confidence in the technique (see Hull, Roper et al. 1999:213), and background sampling for the current study addressed some of these methodological concerns.

5. Detailed discussion of the lithic analysis methods used in this study is available in Hull (2002:386–392).

6. These aspects of lithic technology are discussed at length by Andrefsky (1998), Callahan (1979), and Whittaker (1987, 1994), among others.

8. HOL'-LOW AND HE-LE'-JAH

1. This village is also referred to as Lah-koo'-hah (to appear, to emerge); the archaeological site designation is CA-MRP-57 (Hull and Kelly 1995).

2. The archaeological site designation is CA-MRP-62 (Hull and Kelly 1995).

3. Merriam (1917) does not provide a translation for this village name. Hull and Kelly (1995: appendix B) and Hull (2002) misattribute the pumice handstone from this site to Hol'-low.

4. The latter were collected by Bennyhoff (1956) and were part of the collections at the Phoebe A. Hearst Museum of Anthropology at the University of California, Berkeley (Hull 2002:440).

5. Classification of glass beads follows Karklins (1985).

6. Classification of shell beads follows Bennyhoff and Hughes (1987).

7. Merriam (1917) does not provide translations for the names of these three villages, We'-sum-meh', Kom'-pom-pa'-sah, and Koom-i-ne.

8. These figures accord well with Bunnell's (1990:73–75) notation of one major village, three camps, and additional residential locales in 1851.

9. Obsidian hydration studies are planned for CA-MRP-55/H (Elena Nilsson, personal communication 2006) but have not yet been undertaken.

10. Archaeological evidence at Sap-pah'-sam-mah is limited to a bedrock mortar, suggesting that it was a task-specific site rather than a village. Conversely, Merriam's (1917) study indicates it served as a camp or village.

11. Gassaway (2005) concluded that fire frequency in the western portion of Yosemite Valley increased substantially after A.D. 1800 relative to earlier times, but her analysis did not take into account the greater sample of trees postdating A.D. 1760. Only sixteen of the trees she sampled were present prior to A.D. 1650, and only six of these were present prior to A.D. 1600. Therefore, any conclusion regarding fire frequency prior to circa A.D. 1760 is tenuous. Reanalysis of the data focusing only on the thirty-three trees present throughout the span from A.D. 1700 to 1880 generally supports Gassaway's contention, with these data indicating an increase in fire return intervals after A.D. 1780.

12. Gassaway (2005:112) concluded that Hull's (2002) demographic reconstruction was in error because she believed that subsites in the western portion of Yosemite Valley were omitted from the sample. This conclusion is incorrect for two reasons. First, Gassaway failed to recognize that the demographic reconstruction was not based on existing archaeological data, which were biased toward the eastern end of Yosemite Valley. Rather, the demographic reconstruction was based on a random sample of deposits from throughout the

valley. Thus, the sample was both temporally and spatially representative—the paucity of sites in the western end of the valley relates to site occurrence not sampling. Second, contrary to Gassaway's assertion, deposits south of the Merced River—including one (CA-MRP-70/H) even farther west than one of her study areas—were included in the demographic sample.

9. THE COLONIAL EXPERIENCE

1. Warrick (2003:263) cites Trigger (1985:237) regarding the infiltration of disease near present-day Quebec City in 1535.

2. The location of Fort Nassau proved unsatisfactory due to flooding and it was abandoned by the Dutch in 1618. It was subsequently replaced by Fort Orange, which was constructed in 1624 and remained in use by the Dutch until the mid-1650s.

3. In addition to the Five Nations (later Six, with the addition of the Tuscarora), the League of the Iroquois is also known as the Haudenosaunee (People of the Longhouse) or the Iroquois Confederacy.

4. Except in one case, in which the site is known only from historical records, since no known archaeological deposit still exists at the well-defined location due to subsequent development (Snow 1996: table 1).

5. Snow's (1995, 1996) sample and chronological methods allowed him to significantly improve upon Ramenofsky's (1987) earlier attempt to examine colonial population decline among the Five Nations. In fact, this latter study has been criticized by other archaeologists on such methodological grounds (e.g., Warrick 2003:265; see also Henige 1998)

6. Although two villages existed at that time, only one of these sites endured throughout this fifty-five-year period. The other village changed locations twice during this span, and it was this latter village that witnessed significant population growth (Snow 1996: table 1).

7. To the south, W.C. Johnson (2001) has also noted the "disappearance" of the Monongahela around A.D. 1635, perhaps not coincidentally with the smallpox epidemic that devastated northern Iroquoian tribes. In this case, however, W.C. Johnson (2001:76) suggested that demise of the Monongahela may have been due to the Seneca's desire to reestablish access to marine shell from the Chesapeake by eliminating Monongahela middlemen. Due to hypothesized Seneca aggression, the Monongahelans may have joined the Susquehannock population to the east and later emerged as traders and raiders on the Chesapeake (W.C. Johnson 2001:82).

8. Dates for the Woodland period—which denotes a time in which agriculture replaced reliance on hunting and gathering for subsistence but prior to the introduction of civic-ceremonial mound construction (associated with the so-called Mississippian culture)—vary through the eastern United States based on when this cultural manifestation prevailed. In the Mid-Atlantic Piedmont, construction of large ceremonial mounds never occurred, so the Woodland period persisted until contact with Europeans.

9. As discussed by Blitz (1999:578) citing D.G. Anderson (1996:232), paramount chiefdoms are a particular form of complex chiefdom, as paramount

chiefs maintained control over other complex chiefdoms in addition to their own.

10. The *encomienda* system was a feudal system transplanted with the Spaniards from the Old World, in which overlords working for their own prosperity or that of the crown extracted labor and tribute from Indians, primarily in the form of agricultural products or ores. As discussed by Simpson (1950), Spaniards found that this system functioned best in areas where native people had an existing tradition of exerting such effort in the service of central authority, such as in the state-level societies of Central and South America ravaged by the conquistadores in the 1500s.

11. Galloway (1995) argues for use of the original, rather than a translated version of, historical accounts to clarify the issue of chiefdom complexity in specific cases.

12. See also Galloway (1995: table 3.2), which clearly shows the greater complexity and organization of Coosa relative to many other chiefdoms based on historical accounts of the Soto expedition.

13. Smith (2002:4) appears to have tempered his view somewhat since his initial consideration of this subject, as he recognized that there may have been multiple factors prompting relocation of settlements—including political factionalism, trade with European colonists, warfare, the slave trade, and environmental opportunism as nearby choice areas were abandoned or vacated due to disease or one or more of these factors.

14. Unless, of course, disease was spread via the numerous swine accompanying the Soto expedition (Ramenofsky and Galloway 1997).

15. A few survivors remained in Texas until A.D. 1534, although they resided farther south along the coast at an undetermined location.

16. Perttula (1992:85) arrives at an estimated population range of 8,500 to 12,675 based on multipliers of population decline proposed by Thornton (1987:30).

17. Henige (1998) was especially critical of Campbell's (1990) study, and asserted that her own data contradicted her conclusions. But he based this argument on one error in fact, numerous misunderstandings of archaeological argument and data, and several misrepresentations of Campbell's own discussion. In the latter case, Henige (1998:158, 160) implied that statements made by Campbell regarding the bone and feature indices—about which Campbell was quite explicit in her reservations—applied to the component, site, and shell indices. This was clearly not the case. And Henige (1998: table 3) sought to bolster his critique by then attempting to present some of Campbell's raw data. Unfortunately, the figures he cites as "volume of shell and bone" are, in fact, estimates of the total volume of sediment for the number of components dating to each fifty-year interval. That is, his table does not present the data it purports to depict. Campbell (1990: tables 6.6, 6.7, and 6.8) provided these volumetric estimates in order to calculate the accumulation rates for shell and bone—the volume of excavated sediment clearly has no relation to population size. Henige's misunderstanding of archaeological data is also evident elsewhere, as he concluded that Campbell intended to use ceramics to date components (Henige 1998:157, 158)—Campbell was instead referring

to Ramenofsky's (1987) study, since prehistoric ceramics were not used by the Indians of the Columbia Plateau—and that site types discussed by Campbell reflect size (Henige 1998:158) rather than function (Campbell 1990:189). Henige (1998:156, 159) also misrepresented some of Campbell's (1990:79, 181) statements by adding parenthetical words that distort or controvert her intent—and he even acknowledged one such misrepresentation, although only doing so in an endnote (Henige 1998:365).

10. CULTURE, HISTORY, AND COLONIALISM

1. Silliman (2005) has argued that it is impossible to state when and if colonialism has ended from the perspective of Native Americans, but one could also argue that it is difficult to know when colonialism began. This is particularly true if we take a broad view and include introduced disease as part of the colonial enterprise, albeit unintentional. This underscores the importance of the unintentional rather than simply the intentional—which is Silliman's focus—in studies of colonialism.

References

Alchon, Suzanne Austin
    2003 *A Pest in the Land: New World Epidemics in Global Perspective.* Albuquerque: University of New Mexico Press.

Alexander, Rani T.
    1998 Afterword: Toward an Archaeological Theory of Culture Contact. In *Studies in Culture Contact: Interaction, Culture Change, and Archaeology,* edited by James G. Cusick, pp. 476–495. Center for Archaeological Investigations Occasional Paper No. 25. Carbondale: Southern Illinois University.

Ames, Kenneth M., Don E. Dumond, Jerry R. Galm, and Rick Minor
    1998 Prehistory of the Southern Plateau. In *Plateau,* edited by Deward E. Walker Jr., pp. 103–119. Handbook of North American Indians, vol. 12, William C. Sturtevant, general editor. Washington, D.C.: Smithsonian Institution Press

Anderson, David G.
    1996 Fluctuations between Simple and Complex Chiefdoms: Cycling in the Late Prehistoric Southeast. In *Political Structure and Change in the Prehistoric Southeastern United States,* edited by J.F. Scarry, pp., 231–252. Gainesville: University Press of Florida.

Anderson, M. Kat
    1993 Native Californians as Ancient and Contemporary Cultivators. In *Before the Wilderness: Environmental Management by Native Californians,* edited by Thomas C. Blackburn and M. Kat Anderson, pp. 151–154. Menlo Park: Ballena Press Publications.

    2005 *Tending the Wild: Native American Knowledge and the Management of California's Natural Resources.* Berkeley: University of California Press.

Anderson, R. Scott, and Scott L. Carpenter
    1991 Vegetation Change in Yosemite Valley, Yosemite National Park, California, during the Protohistoric Period. *Madrono* 38(1):1–13.

Andrefsky, William, Jr.
    1998 *Lithics: Macroscopic Approaches to Analysis.* Cambridge: Cambridge University Press.

Anyon, Roger, T. J. Ferguson, Loretta Jackson, and Lillie Lane
    1996 Native American Oral Traditions and Archaeology. *Society for American Archaeology Bulletin* 14(2):14–16.

Arkush, Brooke
    1993 Yokuts Trade Networks and Native Culture Change in Central and Eastern California. *Ethnohistory* 40(4):619–640.

    1995 *The Archaeology of CA-Mno-2122: A Study of Pre-Contact and Post-Contact Lifeways Among the Mono Basin Paiute.* University of California Anthropological Records 31. Berkeley: University of California Press.

Baker, Brenda J., and Lisa Kealhofer
    1996 Assessing the Impact of European Contact on Aboriginal Populations. In *Bioarchaeology of Native American Adaptation in the Spanish Borderlands,* edited by Brenda J. Baker and Lisa Kealhofer, pp. 1–13. Gainesville: University Press of Florida.

Baker, Brenda J., and Lisa Kealhofer (editors)
    1996 *Bioarchaeology of Native American Adaptation in the Spanish Borderlands.* Gainesville: University Press of Florida.

Bamforth, Douglas
    1993 Stone Tools, Steel Tools: Contact Period Household Technology at Helo'. In *Ethnohistory and Archaeology: Approaches to Post Contact Change in the Americas,* edited by J. Daniel Rogers and Samuel M. Wilson, pp. 49–72. New York: Plenum Press.

Barrett, Samuel A.
    1908 The Geography and Dialects of the Miwok Indians. *University of California Publications in American Archaeology and Ethnology* 6(2):333–368.

    1919 Myths of the Southern Sierra Miwok. *University of California Publications in American Archaeology and Ethnology* 16(1):1–28.

Barrett, Samuel A., and Edward W. Gifford
    1933 Miwok Material Culture. *Bulletin of the Milwaukee Public Museum* 2(4):119–377. Reprinted by the Yosemite Natural History Association Inc., Yosemite National Park.

Basgall, Mark E.
    1989 Obsidian Acquisition and Use in Prehistoric Central Eastern California: A Preliminary Assessment. In *Current Directions in California Obsidian Studies,* edited by Richard E. Hughes, pp. 111–126. Contribu-

References

tions of the University of California Archaeological Research Facility 48. Berkeley.

Bates, Craig D.
1978 *The Reflexed Sinew-Backed Bow of the Sierra Miwok*. San Diego Museum of Man Ethnic Technology Notes 16. San Diego.
1993 Scholars and Collectors Among the Sierra Miwok, 1900–1920: What Did They Really Find? *Museum Anthropology* 17(2):7–19.

Bates, Craig D., and Martha J. Lee
1990 *Tradition and Innovation: A Basket History of the Indians of the Yosemite-Mono Lake Region*. Yosemite: Yosemite Association.

Bates, Craig D., and Karen P. Wells
1981 *Late Aboriginal and Early Anglo Occupation of El Portal, Yosemite National Park, California*. USDI National Park Service, Western Archeological and Conservation Center. Tucson.

Bayham, Frank E., and Kathleen L. Hull
1996 Diachronic Population Reconstruction Using Calibrated Obsidian Hydration Rim Frequencies. Paper presented at the Sixty-first Annual Meeting of the Society for American Archaeology, New Orleans.

Bennyhoff, James A.
1956 *An Appraisal of the Archaeological Resources of Yosemite National Park*. University of California Archaeological Survey Reports 34. Berkeley.

Bennyhoff, James A., and Richard E. Hughes
1987 Shell Bead and Ornament Exchange Networks Between California and the Great Basin. *Anthropological Papers of the American Museum of Natural History* 64(2):80–175.

Bettinger, Robert
1982 Aboriginal Exchange and Territoriality in Owens Valley, California. In *Contexts for Prehistoric Exchange*, edited by Jonathon E. Ericson, and Timothy K. Earle, pp. 103–127. New York: Academic Press.

Bevill, Russell, Elena Nilsson, and Kathleen L. Hull
2005 *Archeological Data Recovery Investigations at CA-Mrp-240/303/H, CA-Mrp-749, CA-Mrp- 1606/H, and CA-Mrp-1607/H, Yosemite National Park, California*. USDI National Park Service, Yosemite Research Center Publications in Anthropology 27. Yosemite National Park.

Bianchine, Peter J., and Thomas A. Russo
1995 The Role of Epidemic Infectious Diseases in the Discovery of America. In *Columbus and the New World: Medical Implications*, edited by Guy A. Settipane, pp. 11–18. Providence, RI: Oceanside Publications.

Bibby, Brian
1994 *An Ethnographic Evaluation of Yosemite Valley: The Native American Cultural Landscape*. Submitted to USDI National Park Service. Yosemite National Park.

2005 *Deeper Then Gold: A Guide to Indian Life in the Sierra Foothills.* Berkeley: Heyday Books.

Biersack, Aletta
1991 Introduction: History and Theory in Anthropology. In *Clio in Oceania: Toward a Historical Anthropology,* edited by Aletta Biersack, pp. 1–36. Washington, D.C.: Smithsonian Institution Press.

Binford, Lewis R.
1978 Dimensional Analysis of Behavior and Site Structure: Learning From an Eskimo Hunting Stand. *American Antiquity* 43(3):330–361.
1979 Organization and Formation Processes: Looking at Curated Technologies. *Journal of Anthropological Research* 35(3):255–273.
1980 Willow Smoke and Dogs' Tails: Hunter-Gatherer Settlement Systems and Archaeological Site Formation. *American Antiquity* 45(1):4–20.
1982 The Archaeology of Place. *Journal of Anthropological Archaeology* 1(1):5–31.

Birk, Douglas A., and Elden Johnson
1992 The Mdewakanton Dakota and Initial French Contact. In *Calumet and Fleur-de-Lys: Archaeology of Indian and French Contact in the Midcontinent,* edited by John A. Walthall and Thomas E. Emerson, pp. 203–240. Washington, D.C.: Smithsonian Institution Press.

Blitz, John H.
1999 Mississippian Chiefdoms and the Fission-Fusion Process. *American Antiquity* 64(4):577–592.

Blurton Jones, Nicholas G., Lars C. Smith, James F. O'Connell, Kristen Hawkes, and C. C. Kamuzora
1992 Demography of the Hadza, an Increasing and High Density Population of Savanna Foragers. *American Journal of Physical Anthropology* 89(2):159–181.

Boling [Bowling], John
1851 Major Savage's Battalion. *Daily Alta California,* June 12, 1851.

Bourdieu, Pierre
1977 *Outline of a Theory of Practice.* Cambridge: Cambridge University Press.

Boyd, Robert T.
1998 Demographic History Until 1900. In *Plateau,* edited by Deward E. Walker Jr., pp. 467–483. Handbook of North American Indians, vol. 12, William C. Sturtevant, general editor. Washington, D.C.: Smithsonian Institution Press.

Bradley, James W.
2001 Change and Survival Among the Onondaga Iroquois Since 1500. In *Societies in Eclipse: Archaeology the Eastern Woodlands Indians,* A.D. *1400–1700,* edited by David S. Brose, C. Wesley Cowan, and Robert Mainfort, pp. 27–36. Washington, D.C.: Smithsonian Institution Press.

References

Brady, Ryan T.
2006 Obsidian Source Distribution and Prehistoric Settlement Patterns at Mono Lake, Eastern California. Paper presented at the Fortieth Annual Meeting of the Society for California Archaeology, Ventura.

Brain, Jeffrey P.
1978 Late Prehistoric Settlement Patterning in the Yazoo Basin and Natchez Bluffs Regions of the Lower Mississippi Valley. In *Mississippian Settlement Patterns,* edited by Bruce D. Smith, pp. 331–368. New York: Academic Press.

Branstner, Susan M.
1992 Tionontate Huron Occupation at the Marquette Mission. In *Calumet and Fleur-de-Lys: Archaeology of Indian and French Contact in the Midcontinent,* edited by John A. Walthall and Thomas E. Emerson, pp. 177–202. Washington, D.C.: Smithsonian Institution Press.

Broadbent, Sylvia M.
1964 *The Southern Sierra Miwok Language.* University of California Publications in Linguistics 38. Berkeley: University of California Press.

Brose, David S.
2001 Introduction to Eastern North America at the Dawn of European Colonization. In *Societies in Eclipse: Archaeology the Eastern Woodlands Indians,* A.D. *1400–1700,* edited by David S. Brose, C. Wesley Cowan, and Robert Mainfort, pp. 1–8. Washington, D.C.: Smithsonian Institution Press.

Brose, David S., C. Wesley Cowan, and Robert Mainfort (editors)
2001 *Societies in Eclipse: Archaeology the Eastern Woodlands Indians,* A.D. *1400–1700.* Washington, D.C.: Smithsonian Institution Press.

Brown, James A., and Robert F. Sasso
2001 Prelude to History on the Eastern Prairies. In *Societies in Eclipse: Archaeology the Eastern Woodlands Indians,* A.D. *1400–1700,* edited by David S. Brose, C. Wesley Cowan, and Robert Mainfort, pp. 205–228. Washington, D.C.: Smithsonian Institution Press.

Bunnell, Lafayette Houghton
1859 How the Yo-semite Valley Was Discovered and Named. *Hutchings' California Magazine* 35:498–504.

1880 *Discovery of the Yosemite, and the Indian War of 1851 Which Led to That Event.* Chicago: Fleming H. Revell.

1990 *Discovery of the Yosemite and the Indian War of 1851 Which Led to That Event.* Yosemite: Yosemite Association. Reprint of 4th edition, originally published 1911, G. W. Gerlicher, Los Angeles.

Burton, John W.
1988 Shadows at Twilight: A Note on History and the Ethnographic Present. *Proceedings of the American Philosophical Society* 132(4):420–433.

Callahan, Errett
1979 The Basics of Biface Knapping in the Eastern Fluted Point Tradition: A

Manual for Flintknappers and Lithic Analysts. *Archaeology of Eastern North America* 7(1):1–180.

Cameron, Catherine M.
1990 The Effect of Varying Estimates of Pit Structure Use-Life on Prehistoric Population Estimates in the American Southwest. *Kiva* 55(2):155–166.

Campbell, Sarah K.
1990 *Postcolumbian Culture History in the Northern Columbia Plateau, A.D. 1500–1900.* New York: Garland Publishing Inc.

Casselberry, Samuel E.
1974 Further Refinement of Formulae for Determining Population from Floor Area. *World Archaeology* 6:118–122.

Casteel, Richard W.
1979 Relationships Between Surface Area and Population Size: A Cautionary Note. *American Antiquity* 44(4):803–807.

Castillo, Edward D.
1978 The Impact of Euro-American Exploration and Settlement. In *California,* edited by Robert F. Heizer, pp. 99–127. Handbook of North American Indians, vol. 8, William C. Sturtevant, general editor. Washington, D.C.: Smithsonian Institution.

1989 The Native Response to the Colonization of Alta California. In *Columbian Consequences,* vol. 1, *Archaeological and Historical Perspectives on the Spanish Borderlands West,* edited by David Hurst Thomas, pp. 377–394. Washington, D.C.: Smithsonian Institution.

Chatters, James C.
1995 Population Growth, Climatic Cooling, and the Development of Collector Strategies on the Southern Plateau, Western North America. *Journal of World Prehistory* 9(3):341–400.

Clark, Galen
1894 Letter to the Board of Commissioners of the Yosemite Valley and Mariposa Big Tree Grove. August 30. Yosemite Research Library, Yosemite National Park.

1902 Field journal. Library of Congress, Washington, D.C.

1907 *Indians of the Yosemite Valley and Vicinity.* Yosemite Valley: Galen Clark. Reprinted 1987, Diablo Books, Walnut Creek, CA.

Coale, Ansley J., and Paul Demeny
1966 *Regional Model Life Tables and Stable Populations.* Princeton, NJ: Princeton University Press.

Conn, Steven
2004 *History's Shadow: Americans and Historical Consciousness in the Nineteenth Century.* Chicago: University of Chicago Press.

Cook, Noble David, and W. George Lovell (editors)
1991 *Secret Judgments of God: Old World Disease in Colonial Spanish America.* Norman: University of Oklahoma Press.

Cook, Sherburne F.
   1939 Smallpox in Spanish and Mexican California. *Bulletin of the History of Medicine* 7(2):153–191.
   1955 The Epidemic of 1830–1833 in California and Oregon. *University of California Publications in American Archaeology and Ethnology* 43(3):303–326.
   1972 *Prehistoric Demography.* Modules in Anthropology No. 16. Reading, MA: Addison-Wesley.
   1976 *The Conflict Between the California Indians and White Civilization.* Berkeley: University of California Press.
   1978 Historical Demography. In *California,* edited by Robert F. Heizer, pp. 91–98. Handbook of North American Indians, vol. 8, William C. Sturtevant, general editor. Washington, D.C.: Smithsonian Institution.

Cordell, Linda S.
   1989 Durango to Durango: An Overview of the Southwest Heartland. In *Columbian Consequences,* vol. 1, *Archaeological and Historical Perspectives on the Spanish Borderlands West,* edited by David Hurst Thomas, pp. 17–40. Washington, D.C.: Smithsonian Institution.
   1997 *Archaeology of the Southwest.* New York: Academic Press.

Costello, Julia G.
   1989 Variability Among the Alta California Missions: The Economics of Agricultural Production. In *Columbian Consequences,* vol. 1, *Archaeological and Historical Perspectives on the Spanish Borderlands West,* edited by David Hurst Thomas, pp. 435–450. Washington, D.C.: Smithsonian Institution.

Costello, Julia G., and David Hornbeck
   1989 Alta California: An Overview. In *Columbian Consequences,* vol. 1, *Archaeological and Historical Perspectives on the Spanish Borderlands West,* edited by David Hurst Thomas, pp. 303–331. Washington, D.C.: Smithsonian Institution.

Crampton, C. Gregory (editor)
   1957 *Mariposa Indian War 1850–1851: Diaries of Robert Eccleston.* Salt Lake City: University of Utah Press.

Crosby, Alfred W.
   1986 *Ecological Imperialism: The Biological Expansion of Europe, 900–1900.* Cambridge: Cambridge University Press.

Cusick, James G.
   1998a Historiography of Acculturation: An Evaluation of Concepts and Their Application in Archaeology. In *Studies in Culture Contact: Interaction, Culture Change, and Archaeology,* edited by James G. Cusick, pp. 126–145. Center for Archaeological Investigations Occasional Paper No. 25. Carbondale: Southern Illinois University.
   1998b Introduction. In *Studies in Culture Contact: Interaction, Culture Change, and Archaeology,* edited by James G. Cusick, pp. 1–22. Center

for Archaeological Investigations Occasional Paper No. 25. Carbondale Southern Illinois University.

Cutter, Donald C.
1957 *The Diary of Ensign Gabriel Moraga's Expedition of Discovery in the Sacramento Valley, 1808.* Los Angeles: G. Dawson.

Davis, James T.
1961 *Trade Routes and Economic Exchange among the Indians of California.* University of California Archaeological Survey Reports 54. Berkeley.

Deagan, Kathleen A.
1983 *Spanish St. Augustine: The Archaeology of a Colonial Creole Community.* New York: Academic Press.
1995 *Puerto Real: The Archaeology of a Sixteenth-Century Spanish Town in Hispaniola.* Gainesville: University of Florida Press.

Deagan, Kathleen A., and Michael Scardaville
1985 Archaeology and History on Historic Hispanic Sites: Impediments and Solutions. *Historical Archaeology* 19(1):32–37.

Dean, Jeffrey S., William H. Doelle, and Janet Orcutt
1994 Adaptive Stress, Environment, and Demography. In *Themes in Southwest Prehistory,* edited by George J. Gumerman, pp. 53–86. Santa Fe: School of American Research Press.

Deetz, James F.
1963 Archaeological Investigations at La Purisima Mission. In *University of California Archaeology Survey Annual Report 1963–1964,* pp. 165–191. Los Angeles.

Denevan, William M.
1992 The Pristine Myth: The Landscape of the Americas in 1492. *Annals of the Association of American Geographers* 82(3):369–385.

Diamond, Jared
1997 *Guns, Germs, and Steel: The Fates of Human Societies.* New York: W. W. Norton.

Dibbie, Brian W.
1982 *The Vanishing American: White Attitudes and U.S. Indian Policy.* Lawrence: University Press of Kansas.

Dick-Bissonnette, Linda E.
1998 Gender and Authority among the Yokoch, Mono, and Miwok of Central California. *Journal of Anthropological Research* 54(1):49–72.

Dobyns, Henry F.
1966 An Appraisal of Techniques for Estimating Aboriginal Population With a New Hemispheric Estimate. *Current Anthropology* 7(4): 395–415.
1983 *Their Number Become Thinned: Native American Population Dynamics in Eastern North America.* Knoxville: University of Tennessee Press.

1991 New Native World: Links Between Demographic and Cultural Changes. In *Columbian Consequences,* vol. 3, *The Spanish Borderlands in Pan-American Perspective,* edited by David Hurst Thomas, pp. 541–560. Washington, D.C.: Smithsonian Institution Press.

Dunnell, Robert C.
1991 Methodological Impacts of Catastrophic Depopulation on American Archaeology and Ethnology. In *Columbian Consequences,* vol. 3, *The Spanish Borderlands in Pan-American Perspective,* edited by David Hurst Thomas, pp. 561–580. Washington, D.C.: Smithsonian Institution Press.

Echo-Hawk, Roger C.
2000 Ancient History in the New World: Integrating Oral Traditions and the Archaeological Record in Deep Time. *American Antiquity* 65(2):267–290.

Eerkens, Jelmer, Hector Neff, and Michael D. Glascock
1999 Early Pottery from Sunga'va and Implications for the Development of Ceramic Technology in Owens Valley, California. *Journal of California and Great Basin Anthropology* 21(1): 275–285.

Eisele, Judith
1994 *Survival and Detection of Blood Residues on Stone Tools.* University of Nevada Reno Department of Anthropology Technical Report 94-1. Reno.

Elliott, Wallace W., and Co.
1882 *History of Fresno County, California.* San Francisco: W.W. Elliott & Co.

Emerson, Thomas E., and James A. Brown
1992 The Late Prehistory and Protohistory of Illinois. In *Calumet and Fleur-de-Lys: Archaeology of Indian and French Contact in the Midcontinent,* edited by John A. Walthall and Thomas E. Emerson, pp. 77–128. Washington, D.C.: Smithsonian Institution Press.

Engstrand, Iris H.W.
1997 Seekers of the "Northern Mystery:" European Exploration of California and the Pacific. In *Contested Eden: California Before the Gold Rush,* edited by Ramon A. Gutierrez and Richard J. Orsi, pp. 78–110. Berkeley: University of California Press.

Ericson, Jonathon E.
1981 *Exchange and Production Systems in California Prehistory: The Results of Hydration Dating and Chemical Characterization of Obsidian Sources.* British Archaeological Reports International Series 110. Oxford.

Erlandson, Jon M., and Kevin Bartoy
1995 Cabrillo, the Chumash, and Old World Diseases. *Journal of California and Great Basin Anthropology* 17(2):153–173.

Farnsworth, Paul
  1989 The Economics of Acculturation in the Spanish Missions of Alta California. In *Research in Economic Anthropology,* vol. 11, edited by Barry Isaac, pp. 217–249. Greenwich, CT: JAI Press.
  1992 Missions, Indians, and Culture Contact. *Historical Archaeology* 26(1): 22–36.

Farquhar, Francis P.
  1965 *History of the Sierra Nevada.* Berkeley: University of California Press.

Fitzgerald, William R.
  2001 Contact, Neutral Iroquoian Transformation, and the Little Ice Age. In *Societies in Eclipse: Archaeology the Eastern Woodlands Indians, A.D. 1400–1700,* edited by David S. Brose, C. Wesley Cowan, and Robert Mainfort, pp. 37–48. Washington, D.C.: Smithsonian Institution Press.

Fitzhugh, William W. (editor)
  1985 *Cultures in Contact: The Impact of European Contacts on Native American Cultural Institutions, A.D. 1000–1800.* Washington, D.C.: Smithsonian Institution Press.

Fitzwater, Robert J.
  1962 Final Report on Two Seasons of Excavations at El Portal, Mariposa County, California. In *University of California Archaeological Survey Annual Report 1961–1962,* pp. 234–285. Los Angeles.

Flint, Sandra S.
  1995 Examining the Validity of Blood Residue Analysis by Cross-over Immuno-electrophoresis. Master's thesis, Department of Anthropology, California State University, Chico.

Foster, George M.
  1960 Edward Winslow Gifford 1887–1959. *American Anthropologist* 62(2): 327–329.

Freeland, L. S., and Sylvia M. Broadbent
  1960 *Central Sierra Miwok Dictionary with Texts.* University of California Publications in Linguistics 23. Berkeley: University of California Press.

Friedman, Irving, and Robert L. Smith
  1960 A New Dating Method Using Obsidian: Part 1, the Development of the Method. *American Antiquity* 25(4):476–522.

Friedman, Irving, Fred W. Trembour, Franklin L. Smith, and George I. Smith
  1994 Is Obsidian Hydration Dating Affected by Relative Humidity? *Quaternary Research* 41:185–190.

Frink, Lisa L.
  2007 Storage and Status in Precolonial and Colonial Coastal Western Alaska. *Current Anthropology* 48(3):349–374.

Gallivan, Martin D.
  2004 Reconnecting the Contact Period and Late Prehistory: Household and Community Dynamics in the James River Basin. In *Indian and Euro-*

pean Contact in Context: The Mid-Atlantic Region, edited by Dennis B. Blanton and Julia A. King, pp. 22–46. Gainesville: University Press of Florida.

Galloway, Patricia

1991 The Archaeology of Ethno historical Narrative. In *Columbian Consequences*. vol. 3, *The Spanish Borderlands in Pan-American Perspective*, edited by David Hurst Thomas, pp. 453–469. Washington, D.C.: Smithsonian Institution Press.

1994 Prehistoric Population of Mississippi: A First Approximation. *Mississippi Archaeology* 29:44–71.

1995 *Choctaw Genesis 1500–1700*. Lincoln: University of Nebraska Press.

2002 Colonial Period Transformations in the Mississippi Valley: Disintegration, Alliance, Confederation, Playoff. In *The Transformation of the Southeastern Indians, 1540–1760*, edited by Robbie Ethridge and Charles Hudson, pp. 225–247. Jackson: University Press of Mississippi.

2006 *Practicing Ethnohistory: Mining Archives, Hearing Testimony, Constructing Narrative*. Lincoln: University of Nebraska Press.

Gassaway, Linn

2005 Hujpu-st: Spatial and Temporal Patterns of Anthropogenic Fire in Yosemite Valley. Master's thesis, Department of Anthropology, San Francisco State University, San Francisco.

Gifford, Edward Winslow

1926a Miwok Cults. *University of California Publications in American Archaeology and Ethnology* 18(3):391–408.

1926b Miwok Lineages and the Political Unit in Aboriginal California. *American Anthropologist* 28(2):389–401.

1944 Miwok Lineages. *American Anthropologist* 46:376–381.

1955 Central Miwok Ceremonies. *University of California Anthropological Records* 14(4):261–318.

Goldberg, Susan K., and Elizabeth J. Skinner

1990 *Cultural Resources of the Crane Valley Hydroelectric Project Area, Madera County, California*. Vol. 4. Bass Lake Erosion Control Project, Limited Archaeological Site Data Recovery at CA-MAD-223, -244, and -392. Infotec Research Inc. Submitted to Pacific Gas and Electric Company. San Francisco.

Gordon-Cumming, Constance F.

1886 *Granite Crags of California*. London: William Blackwood and Sons.

Gosden, Chris

2004 *Archaeology and Colonialism: Cultural Contact from 5000 BC to the Present*. Cambridge: Cambridge University Press.

Grayson, Donald K.

1994 Chronology, Glottochronology, and Numic Expansion. In *Across the West: Human Population Movement and the Expansion of the Numa*, edited by David B. Madsen and David Rhode, pp. 20–23. Salt Lake City: University of Utah Press.

Green, William
1993 Examining Protohistoric Depopulation in the Upper Midwest. *The Wisconsin Archeologist* 74(1–4):290–323.

Greene, Linda Wedel
1987 *Yosemite: The Park and Its Resources.* USDI National Park Service, Denver Service Center. Denver.

Haines, Michael R.
2000 The White Population of the United States, 1790–1920. In *A Population History of North America,* edited by Michael R. Haines and Richard H. Steckel, pp. 305–370. Cambridge: Cambridge University Press.

Hammel, Eugene A., and Nancy Howell
1987 Research in Population and Culture: An Evolutionary Framework. *Current Anthropology* 28(2):141–160.

Haney, Jefferson W.
1992 Acorn Exploitation in the Eastern Sierra Nevada. *Journal of California and Great Basin Anthropology* 14(1):94–109.

Hantman, Jeffrey L.
2001 Monacan Archaeology of the Virginia Interior, A.D. 1400–1700. In *Societies in Eclipse: Archaeology the Eastern Woodlands Indians, A.D. 1400–1700,* edited by David S. Brose, C. Wesley Cowan, and Robert Mainfort, pp. 107–124. Washington, D.C.: Smithsonian Institution Press.

Hassan, Fekri A.
1981 *Demographic Archaeology.* New York: Academic Press.

Hastrup, Kirsten
1990 The Ethnographic Present: A Reinvention. *Cultural Anthropology* 5(1):45–61.

Heizer, Robert F.
1941 The Direct-Historical Approach in California Archaeology. *American Antiquity* 7(2):98–122.

1976 Editor's Introduction. In *Tribes of California,* by Stephen Powers, pp. 1–5. Berkeley: University of California Press.

Heizer, Robert F., and Mary Anne Whipple
1971 *The California Indians: A Source Book.* 2nd edition. Berkeley: University of California Press.

Hendon, Julia A.
1996 Archaeological Approaches to the Organization of Domestic Labor: Household Practice and Domestic Relations. *Annual Review of Anthropology* 25:45–61.

Henige, David
1998 *Numbers for Nowhere: The American Indian Contact Population Debate.* Norman: University of Oklahoma Press.

Hickerson, Daniel A.
 1997 Historical Processes, Epidemic Disease, and the Formation of the Hasinai Confederacy. *Ethnohistory* 44(1):31–52.

Hill, Jonathan D.
 1996 Introduction: Ethnogenesis in the Americas, 1492–1992. In *History Power, and Identity: Ethnogenesis in the Americas, 1492–1992*, edited by Jonathan D. Hill, pp. 1–19. Iowa City: University of Iowa Press.

Hill, Kim, and A. Magdalena Hurtado
 1996 *Ache Life History: The Ecology and Demography of a Foraging People*. New York: Aldine De Guynter.

Hodder, Ian
 1991 *Reading the Past*. 2nd edition. Cambridge: Cambridge University Press.

 2000 Agency and Individuals in Long-term Processes. In *Agency in Archaeology*, edited by Marcia-Anne Dobres and John E. Robb, pp. 21–33. London: Routledge.

Hoffman, Charles Frederick
 1868 Notes on Hetch-Hetchy Valley. *Proceedings of the California Academy of Sciences* 3(5):368–370.

Howell, Nancy
 1973 An Empirical Perspective on Simulation Models of Human Population. In *Computer Simulation in Human Population Studies*, edited by Bennett Dyke and Jean Walters MacCluer, pp. 43–57. New York: Academic Press.

 1979 *Demography of the Dobe !Kung*. New York: Academic Press.

 1986 Demographic Anthropology. *Annual Review of Anthropology* 15:219–246.

Hudson, Charles M., Chester B. DePratter, and Marvin T. Smith
 1989 Hernando de Soto's Expedition through the Southern United States. In *First Encounters: Spanish Explorations in the Caribbean and the United States, 1492–1570*, edited by J.T. Milanich and Susan Milbrath, pp. 119–134. Gainesville: University Press of Florida.

Hudson, Charles M., Marvin T. Smith, and Chester B. DePratter
 1990 The Hernando de Soto Expedition: From Mabila to the Mississippi. In *Towns and Temples along the Mississippi*, edited by David Dye and Cheryl Cox, pp. 181–207. Tuscaloosa: University of Alabama Press.

Hudson, Charles, Marvin T. Smith, D. Hally, Richard Polhemus, and Chester DePratter
 1985 Coosa: A Chiefdom in the Sixteenth-Century Southeastern United States. *American Antiquity* 50(4):723–754.

Hughes, Richard E.
 1989 A New Look at Mono Basin Obsidians. In *Current Directions in California Obsidian Studies*, edited by Richard E. Hughes, pp. 1–12.

Contributions of the University of California Archaeological Research Facility 48. Berkeley.

1992 California Archaeology and Linguistic Prehistory. *Journal of Anthropological Research* 48:317–338.

1994 Intrasource Chemical Variability of Artefact-Quality Obsidians from the Casa Diablo Area, California. *Journal of Archaeological Science* 21:263–271.

Hull, Kathleen L

2000 A Survey of Glass Trade Bead Distribution in Yosemite National Park. *Society for California Archaeology Newsletter* 34(4):32–33.

2001a A Diachronic Perspective on Use of Desert Side-Notched Projectile Points in the Central Sierra Nevada. Paper presented at the Northern California Data Sharing Meetings, Society for California Archaeology, Chico, California.

2001b Reasserting the Utility of Obsidian Hydration Dating: A Temperature-Dependent Empirical Approach to Practical Temporal Resolution with Archaeological Obsidians. *Journal of Archaeological Science* 28(10):1025–1040.

2002 *Culture Contact in Context: A Multiscalar View of Catastrophic Depopulation and Culture Change in Yosemite Valley, California.* Ph.D. dissertation, Department of Anthropology, University of California, Berkeley.

2004 Emergent Cultural Traditions in the Central Sierra Nevada Foothills. *Society for California Archaeology Proceedings* 17:113–118.

2005 Process, Perception, and Practice: Time Perspectivism in Yosemite Native Demography. *Journal of Anthropological Archaeology* 24(4): 354–377.

2007 The Sierra Nevada: Archaeology in the Range of Light. In *California Prehistory: Colonization, Culture, and Complexity*, edited by Terry L. Jones and Kathryn A. Klar, pp. 177–190. Lanham, MD: AltaMira Press.

Hull, Kathleen L., Russell W. Bevill, and Michael S. Kelly

1995 *Report of Selected Subsurface Archaeological Investigations in Yosemite Valley, 1986- 1991, Yosemite National Park, California.* USDI National Park Service, Yosemite Research Center Publications in Anthropology 14. Yosemite National Park.

Hull, Kathleen L., Russell W. Bevill, W. Geoffrey Spaulding, and Mark R. Hale

1995 *Archeological Site Subsurface Survey, Test Excavations, and Data Recovery Excavation for the Tuolumne Sewer Replacement Project in Tuolumne Meadows, Yosemite National Park, California.* USDI National Park Service, Yosemite Research Center Publications in Anthropology 16. Yosemite National Park.

Hull, Kathleen L., Mark R. Hale, Russell W. Bevill, and W. Geoffrey Spaulding
   1998 *Report of Archeological Subsurface Survey and Test Excavations at Yosemite Lodge, Yosemite Valley, Yosemite National Park, California.* USDI National Park Service, Yosemite Research Center Publications in Anthropology 20. Yosemite National Park.

Hull, Kathleen L., and Michael S. Kelly
   1995 *An Archaeological Survey of Yosemite Valley.* USDI National Park Service, Yosemite Research Center Publications in Anthropology 15. Yosemite National Park.

Hull, Kathleen L., and Michael J. Moratto, with contributions by Helen McCarthy, C. Kristina Roper, W. Geoffrey Spaulding, Mark R. Hale, and Elena Nilsson
   1999 *Archeological Synthesis and Research Design, Yosemite National Park, California.* USDI National Park Service, Yosemite Research Center Publications in Anthropology 21. Yosemite National Park.

Hull, Kathleen L., and C. Kristina Roper
   1999 Obsidian Studies. In *Archeological Synthesis and Research Design, Yosemite National Park, California,* by Kathleen L. Hull and Michael J. Moratto, pp. 297–355. USDI National Park Service Yosemite Research Center Publications in Anthropology 21. Yosemite National Park.

Hull, Kathleen L., C. Kristina Roper, and Michael J. Moratto
   1999 Prehistoric Economic Systems. In *Archeological Synthesis and Research Design, Yosemite National Park, California,* by Kathleen L. Hull and Michael J. Moratto, pp. 205–258. USDI National Park Service, Yosemite Research Center Publications in Anthropology 21. Yosemite National Park.

Humphreys, Kristin H.
   1994 Description and Analysis of the Glen Aulin and Pate Valley Obsidian Biface Caches. Maser's thesis, Department of Anthropology, California State University, Sacramento.

Hurtado, Albert L.
   1988 *Indian Survival on the California Frontier.* New Haven, CT: Yale University Press.

Hutchings, James M.
   1856 The Yo-ham-i-te Valley, and its Water-falls. *Hutchings' California Magazine* 1(1):2–7.
   1888 *In the Heart of the Sierras.* Oakland: Pacific Press Publishing House.

Ingold, Tim
   1993 The Temporality of the Landscape. *World Archaeology* 25(2): 152–172.

Jackson, Robert H., and Edward Castillo
   1995 *Indians, Franciscans, and Spanish Colonization: The Impact of the*

Mission System on California Indians. Albuquerque: University of New Mexico Press.

Jackson, Thomas L.
1974 The Economics of Obsidian in Central California Prehistory: Applications of X-ray Fluorescence Spectrography in Archaeology. Master's thesis, Department of Anthropology, San Francisco State University, San Francisco.

Jackson, Thomas L., and Jonathon E. Ericson
1994 Prehistoric Exchange Systems in California. In *Prehistoric Exchange Systems in North America,* edited by Timothy G. Baugh and Jonathon E. Ericson, pp. 385–415. New York: Plenum Press.

Jackson, Thomas L., and John Holson
1984 *Archaeological Data Recovery Excavations at CA-Fre-1211.* Archaeological Consulting and Research Services. Submitted to Southern California Edison Company. Rosemead.

Jennings, Francis
1976 *The Invasion of American: Indians, Colonialism, and the Cant of Conquest.* New York: W. W. Norton.

Jeter, Marvin D.
2002 From Prehistory through Protohistory to Ethnohistory in and near the Northern Lower Mississippi Valley. In *The Transformation of the Southeastern Indians, 1540–1760,* edited by Robbie Ethridge and Charles Hudson, pp. 177–223. Jackson: University Press of Mississippi.

Johnson, Jay K.
2000 The Chicksaws. In *Indians of the Greater Southeast: Historical Archaeology and Ethnohistory,* edited by Bonnie G. McEwan, pp. 85–121. Gainesville: University of Florida Press.

Johnson, Jay K., and Geoffrey R. Lehmann
1996 Sociopolitical Devolution in Northeast Mississippi and the Timing of the De Soto Entrada. In *Bioarchaeology of Native Habitation in the Spanish Borderlands,* edited by Brenda J. Baker and Lisa Kealhofer, pp. 38–55. Gainesville: University Press of Florida.

Johnson, William C.
2001 The Protohistoric Monongahela and the Case for an Iroquois Connection. In *Societies in Eclipse: Archaeology the Eastern Woodlands Indians, A.D. 1400–1700,* edited by David S. Brose, C. Wesley Cowan, and Robert Mainfort, pp. 67–82. Washington, D.C.: Smithsonian Institution Press.

Johnston, Hank
1990 Preface. In *Discovery of the Yosemite and the Indian War of 1851 Which Led to That Event,* by Lafayette Houghton Bunnell. Yosemite: Yosemite Association.

1995 *The Yosemite Grant, 1864–1906: A Pictorial History.* Yosemite: Yosemite Association.

References

Jordan, Kurt
    2006 Entangled Autonomy: Re-evaluating Indigenous "Freedom" in Settings of Cultural Entanglement. Paper presented at the Society for Historical Archaeology Annual Meeting, Sacramento.

Kardulias, Nick
    1990 Fur Production as a Specialized Activity in a World System. *American Indian Culture and Research Journal* 14(1):25–60.

Karklins, Karlis
    1985 *Glass Beads: The 19th Century Levin Catalogue and Venetian Bead Book and Guide to Description of Glass Beads.* Studies in Archaeology, Architecture and History. Ottawa: Environment Canada, National Historic Parks and Sites Branch.

Kelly, Howard A.
    1921 Lafayette Houghton Bunnell, M.D., Discoverer of the Yosemite. *Annals of Medical History* 3:2.

Kelly, Robert L.
    1988 The Three Sides of a Biface. *American Antiquity* 53(4):717–734.
    1995 *The Foraging Spectrum: Diversity in Hunter-gatherer Lifeways.* Washington, D.C.: Smithsonian Institution Press.

King, Adam
    2006 Historic Period Transformation of Mississippian Societies. In *Light on the Path: The Anthropology and History of the Southeastern Indians,* edited by Thomas J. Pluckhahn and Robbie Ethridge, pp. 179–195. Tuscaloosa: University of Alabama Press.

Kirch, Patrick V., and Roger Green
    2001 *Hawaiki, Ancestral Polynesia: An Essay in Historical Anthropology.* New York: Cambridge University Press.

Kooyman, Brian, Howard Ceri, and Margaret E. Newman
    1992 Verifying the Reliability of Blood Residue Analysis on Archaeological Tools. *Journal of Archaeological Science* 19(3):265–269.

Krause, Richard A.
    2001 Plains Village Tradition: Coalescent. In *Plains,* edited by Raymond J. DeMallie, pp. 196–206. Handbook of North American Indians, vol. 13, part 1, William C. Sturtevant, general editor. Washington, D.C.: Smithsonian Institution Press.

Kroeber, Alfred L.
    1907 Myths of South Central California. *University of California Publications in American Archaeology and Ethnology* 4(4):167–250.
    1921 Indians of Yosemite. In *Handbook of Yosemite National Park: A Compendium of Articles on the Yosemite Region,* edited by Ansel F. Hall, pp. 51–73. New York: G.P. Putnam's Sons.
    1925 *Handbook of the Indians of California.* Bureau of American Ethnology Bulletin 78. Washington, D.C. Reprinted 1976, Dover Publications, New York.

1934 Native American Population. *American Anthropologist* 36(1):1–25.

1939 *Cultural and Natural Areas of Native North America*. University of California Publications in American Archaeology and Ethnology 38. Berkeley.

1955 C. Hart Merriam as Anthropologist. In *Studies of California Indians*, by C. Hart Merriam, pp. vii–xiv. Berkeley: University of California Press.

1962 The Nature of Land-holding Groups in Aboriginal California. In *Two Papers on the Aboriginal Ethnography of California*, edited by Dell H. Hymes and Robert F. Heizer, pp. 19–58. University of California Archaeological Survey Reports 56. Berkeley.

Kulisheck, Jeremy
2005 The Archaeology of Pueblo Population Change on the Jemez Plateau, A.D. 1200 to 1700: The Effects of Spanish Contact and Conquest. Ph.D. dissertation, Department of Anthropology, Southern Methodist University, Dallas.

Kuykendall, Ralph S.
1921 History of the Yosemite Region. In *Handbook of Yosemite National Park: A Compendium of Articles on the Yosemite Region*, edited by Ansel F. Hall, pp. 3–47. New York: G. P. Putnam's Sons.

Lamar, Howard R.
1985 Introduction. In *Gold Seeker: Adventures of a Belgian Argonaut during the Gold Rush Years*, by Jean-Nicolas Perlot, pp. xv–xxxii. New Haven, CT: Yale University Press.

Larsen, Clark Spencer
1991 *Native American Demography in the Spanish Borderlands*. New York: Garland Publishing.

Larsen, Clark Spencer, and George R. Milner (editors)
1994 *In the Wake of Contact: Biological Responses to Conquest*. New York: Wiley-Liss.

Laslett, Peter
1984 The Family as a Knot of Individual Interests. In *Households: Comparative and Historical Studies of the Domestic Group*, edited by Robert McC. Netting, Richard R. Wilk, and Eric J. Arnould, pp. 353–379. Berkeley: University of California Press.

Latta, Frank F.
1999 *California Indian Folklore*. Salinas, CA: Brewer's Historical Press.

Leach, B. F., and G. E. Hamel
1984 The Influence of Archaeological Soil Temperatures on Obsidian Dating in New Zealand. *New Zealand Journal of Science* 27:399–408.

LeBlanc, Steven
1971 An Addition to Naroll's Suggested Floor Area and Settlement Population Relationship. *American Antiquity* 36:210–211.

References

Leonard, Zenas
  1978 *Narrative of the Adventures of Zenas Leonard.* Lincoln: University of Nebraska Press. Originally published 1839, D. W. Moore, Clearfield, Pennsylvania.

Levy, Richard
  1978 Eastern Miwok. In *California,* edited by Robert F. Heizer, pp. 398–413. Handbook of North American Indians, vol. 8, William C. Sturtevant, general editor. Washington, D.C.: Smithsonian Institution

Lightfoot, Kent G.
  1995 Culture Contact Studies: Redefining the Relationship Between Prehistoric and Historical Archaeology. *American Antiquity* 60(2):199–217.
  2005 The Archaeology of Colonization: California in Cross-Cultural Perspective. In *Archaeology of Colonial Encounters: Comparative Perspectives,* edited by Gil. J. Stein, pp. 207–235. Santa Fe: School of American Research Press.

Lightfoot, Kent G., and Antionette Martinez
  1995 Frontiers and Boundaries in Archaeological Perspective. *Annual Review of Anthropology* 24:471–492.

Lightfoot, Kent G., Antionette Martinez, and Ann M. Schiff
  1998 Daily Practice and Material Culture in Pluralistic Social Settings: An Archaeological Study of Culture Change and Persistence from Fort Ross, California. *American Antiquity* 63(2):199–222.

Livi-Bacci, Massimo
  1997 *A Concise History of World Population.* 2nd edition. Oxford: Blackwell.

Lorenz, Karl G.
  2000 The Natchez of Southwest Mississippi. In *Indians of the Greater Southeast: Historical Archaeology and Ethnohistory,* edited by Bonnie G. McEwan, pp. 142–177. Gainesville: University of Florida Press.

Mainfort, Robert C.
  2001 The Late Prehistoric and Protohistoric Periods in the Central Mississippi Valley. In *Societies in Eclipse: Archaeology the Eastern Woodlands Indians,* A.D. *1400–1700,* edited by David S. Brose, C. Wesley Cowan, and Robert Mainfort, pp. 173–190. Washington, D.C.: Smithsonian Institution Press

Mann, Charles C.
  2005 *1491: New Revelations of the Americas Before Columbus.* New York: Alfred A. Knopf.

Mason, Ronald J.
  2000 Archaeology and Native North American Oral Traditions. *American Antiquity* 65(2):239–266.
  2006 *Inconstant Companions: Archaeology and North American Indian Oral Tradition.* Tuscaloosa: University of Alabama Press.

Mayr, Ernst
 1942 *Systematics and the Origin of Species.* New York: Columbia University Press.

Mazel, David
 2000 *American Literary Environmentalism.* Athens: University of Georgia Press.

Mazer, J. J., C. M. Stevenson, W. L. Ebert, and J. K. Bates
 1991 The Experimental Hydration of Obsidian as a Function of Relative Humidity and Temperature. *American Antiquity* 56(3):504–513.

McMichael, Edward V.
 1960 Towards the Estimation of Prehistoric Population. *Indiana Academy of Sciences Proceedings* 69:76–82.

McNeill, William H.
 1976 *Plagues and Peoples.* Garden City, NY: Anchor Press/Doubleday.

Merriam, C. Hart
 n.d. Reel 21, Ethnography. C. Hart Merriam Papers, BANC Film 1022. Bancroft Library, University of California, Berkeley.
 1899–1902 Journal, 1899–1902. Papers of C. Hart Merriam, 1873–1942. Library of Congress, Washington, D.C.
 1907 Distribution and Classification of the Mewan Stock of California. *American Anthropologist* 9:338–357.
 1910 *The Dawn of the World: Myths and Weird Tales Told by the Mewan Indians of California.* Cleveland: Arthur H. Clark Company.
 1917 Indian Villages and Camp Sites in Yosemite Valley. *Sierra Club Bulletin* 10(2):202–209. Reprinted 1976 in *A Collection of Ethnographical Articles on the California Indians,* edited by Robert F. Heizer, pp. 47–53. Publications in Archaeology, Ethnology and History No. 7. Ramona, CA: Ballena Press.

Miller, Jay
 1998 Middle Columbia River Salishans. In *Plateau,* edited by Deward E. Walker Jr., pp. 253–270. Handbook of North American Indians, vol. 12, William C. Sturtevant, general editor. Washington, D.C.: Smithsonian Institution Press.

Milliken, Randall
 1995 *A Time of Little Choice: The Disintegration of Tribal Culture in the San Francisco Bay Area, 1769–1810.* Anthropological Papers No. 43. Menlo Park, CA: Ballena Press.

Milner, George R., David G. Anderson, and Marvin T. Smith
 2001 The Distribution of Eastern Woodlands Peoples at the Prehistoric and Historic Interface. In *Societies in Eclipse: Archaeology the Eastern Woodlands Indians, A.D. 1400–1700,* edited by David S. Brose, C. Wesley Cowan, and Robert Mainfort, pp. 9–18. Washington, D.C.: Smithsonian Institution Press.

Montague, Suzanna T.
  1994 *Report of Data Recovery Excavations of CA-Mrp-902/H, Yosemite Valley, Mariposa County, California.* Draft. USDI National Park Service. Yosemite National Park.
  1996 *Report of Test Excavations and Monitoring at CA-MRP-56 and -301, Yosemite Valley, Mariposa County, California.* USDI National Park Service, Yosemite Research Center Publications in Anthropology 18. Yosemite National Park.

Moore, John H.
  2001 Ethnogenetic Patterns in Native North America. In *Archaeology, Language, and History: Essays on Culture and Ethnicity*, edited by John Edward Terrell, pp, 31–56. Westport, CT: Bergin and Gonvey.

Moratto, Michael J.
  1972 A Study of Prehistory in the Southern Sierra Nevada Foothills, California. Ph.D. dissertation, Department of Anthropology, University of Oregon, Eugene.
  1984 *California Archaeology.* New York: Academic Press.
  1999 Cultural Chronology 2: The Yosemite Data. In *Archeological Synthesis and Research Design, Yosemite National Park, California*, by Kathleen L. Hull and Michael J. Moratto, pp. 121–204. USDI National Park Service, Yosemite Research Center Publications in Anthropology 21. Yosemite National Park.

Morgan, Kenneth
  1974 Computer Simulation of Incest Prohibition and Clan Proscription Rules in Closed, Finite Populations. In *Computer Simulation in Human Population Studies*, edited by Bennett Dyke and Jean W. MacCluer, pp. 15–42. New York: Academic Press.

Muir, John
  1894 *The Mountains of California.* New York: The Century Company.
  1911 *My First Summer in the Sierra.* Boston: Houghton Mifflin Company.
  1912 *The Yosemite.* New York: The Century Company.

Mundy, W. Joseph
  1992 *The Eastern Tioga Road Archeological Survey, Yosemite National Park, California.* USDI National Park Service, Yosemite Research Center Publications in Anthropology 17. Yosemite National Park.
  1993 Elevation-related Variables and Obsidian Hydration: A Diffusion Cell Study in Yosemite. Paper presented at the Twenty-seventh Annual Meeting of the Society for California Archaeology, Asilomar.

Mundy, W. Joseph, and Kathleen L. Hull
  1988 *The 1984 and 1985 Yosemite Valley Archeological Testing Projects.* USDI National Park Service, Yosemite Research Center Publications in Anthropology 5. Yosemite National Park.

Nabokov, Peter
   1996 Native Views of History. In *The Cambridge History of the Native Peoples of the Americas, Volume 1, North American, Part 1*, edited by Bruce G. Trigger and Wilcomb E. Washburn, pp. 1–59. Cambridge: Cambridge University Press.

Nassaney, Michael S.
   2004 Native American Gender Politics and Material Culture in Seventeenth-century Southeastern New England. *Journal of Social Archaeology* 4(3): 334–367.

Neel, James V., and Kenneth M. Weiss
   1975 The Genetic Structure of a Tribal Population, the Yanomama Indians. *American Journal of Physical Anthropology* 42(1):25–52.

Netting, Robert McC., Richard R. Wilk, and Eric J. Arnould
   1984 Introduction. In *Households: Comparative and Historical Studies of the Domestic Group*, edited by Robert McC. Netting, Richard R. Wilk, and Eric J. Arnould, pp. xiii–xxxviii. Berkeley: University of California Press.

Newman, Margaret E., Howard Ceri, and Brian Kooyman
   1996 Use of Immunological Techniques in the Analysis of Archaeological Materials: A Response to Eisele with Report of Studies at Head-Smashed-In Buffalo Jump. *Antiquity* 70(269):677–682.

Newman, Margaret E., Robert M. Yohe, and Brian Kooyman
   1997 "Blood" from Stones? Probably: A Response to Fiedel. *Journal of Archaeological Science* 24(11):1023–1027.

Newson, Linda A.
   1993 Highland-lowland Contrasts in the Impact of Old World Diseases in Early Colonial Ecuador. *Social Science and Medicine* 36(9):1187–1195,

Nilsson, Elena, Mark R. Hale, Kathleen L. Hull, and C. Kristina Roper
   1999 Other Technical Studies. In *Archeological Synthesis and Research Design, Yosemite National Park, California*, by Kathleen L. Hull and Michael J. Moratto, pp. 357–410. USDI National Park Service, Yosemite Research Center Publications in Anthropology 21. Yosemite National Park.

Ohnuki-Tierney, Emiko
   1990 Introduction: The Historicization of Anthropology. In *Culture through Time Anthropological Approaches*, edited by E. Ohnuki-Tierney, pp. 1–25. Stanford, CA: Stanford University Press.

Ortiz, Bev
   1988 It Will Live Forever: Yosemite Indian Acorn Preparation. *News from Native California* 2(4):24–28.

   1991 *It Will Live Forever: Traditional Yosemite Indian Acorn Preparation*. Berkeley: Heyday Books.

Ortner, Sherry B.
   1984 Theory in Anthropology Since the Sixties. *Comparative Studies in Society and History* 26(1):126–166.

Owsley, Douglas W.
　1992 Demography of Prehistoric and Early Historic Northern Plains Populations. In *Disease and Demography in the Americas,* edited by John W. Verano and Douglas H. Ubelaker, pp. 75–86. Washington, D.C.: Smithsonian Institution Press.

Palkovich, Ann M.
　1996 Historic Depopulation in the American Southwest: Issues of Interpretation and Context-Embedded Analyses. In *Bioarchaeology of Native American Adaptation in the Spanish Borderlands,* edited by Brenda J. Baker and Lisa Kealhofer, pp. 179–197. Gainesville: University Press of Florida.

Parks, Douglas R.
　2001 Arikara. In *Plains,* edited by Raymond J. DeMallie, pp. 365–390. Handbook of North American Indians, vol. 13, part 1, William C. Sturtevant, general editor. Washington, D.C.: Smithsonian Institution Press.

Pennington, Renee
　2001 Hunter-Gatherer Demography. In *Hunter-Gatherers: An Interdisciplinary Perspective,* edited by Catherine Panter-Brick, Robert H. Layton, and Peter Rowley-Conwy, pp. 170–204. Cambridge: Cambridge University Press.

Perlot, Jean-Nicolas
　1985 *Gold Seeker: Adventures of a Belgian Argonaut during the Gold Rush Years.* Translated by Helen Harding Bretnor. New Haven, CT: Yale University Press.

Perttula, Timothy K.
　1991 European Contact and Its Effects on Aboriginal Caddoan Populations Between A.D. 1520 and A.D. 1680. In *Columbian Consequences, Volume 3: The Spanish Borderlands in Pan-American Perspective,* edited by David Hurst Thomas, pp. 501–518. Washington, D.C.: Smithsonian Institution Press.
　1992 *The Caddo Nation: Archaeological and Ethnohistoric Perspectives.* Austin: University of Texas Press.
　1993 Kee-Oh-Na-Wah'-Wah: The Effects of European Contact on the Caddoan Indians of Texas, Louisiana, Arkansas, and Oklahoma. In *Ethnohistory and Archaeology: Approaches to Postcontact Change in the Americas,* edited by J. Daniel Rogers and Samuel M. Wilson, pp. 89–110. New York: Plenum Press.
　2002a Caddoan Area Protohistory and Archaeology. In *Between Contacts and Colonies: Archaeological Perspectives on the Protohistoric Southeast,* edited by Cameron B. Wesson and Mark A. Reed, pp. 49–66. Tuscaloosa: University of Alabama Press.
　2002b Social Changes Among the Caddo Indians in the Sixteenth and Seventeenth Centuries. In *The Transformation of the Southeastern Indians,*

1540–1760, edited by Robbie Ethridge and Charles Hudson, pp. 249–269. Jackson: University of Mississippi Press.

Petersen, William
  1975 A Demographer's View of Prehistoric Demography. *Current Anthropology* 16(2):227–269.

Phillips, George Harwood
  1993 *Indians and Intruders in Central California, 1769–1849.* Norman: University of Oklahoma Press.

Phillips, P., James A. Ford, and James B. Griffen
  1951 *Archaeological Survey in the Lower Mississippi Alluvial Valley, 1940–1947.* Peabody Museum of Archaeology and Ethnology Papers 25. Cambridge, MA: Harvard University.

Plog, Stephen, and Jeffrey L. Hantman
  1990 Chronology Construction and the Study of Prehistoric Culture Change. *Journal of Field Archaeology* 17(4):439–456.

Powers, Stephen
  1976 *Tribes of California.* Berkeley: University of California Press. Originally published 1877, Contributions to North American Ethnology 3, Department of the Interior, U.S. Government Printing Office, Washington, D.C.

Preston, William L.
  1996 Serpent in Eden: Dispersal of Foreign Diseases Into Pre-Mission California. *Journal of California and Great Basin Anthropology* 18(1):2–37.

  1997 Serpent in the Garden: Environmental Change in Colonial California. In *Contested Eden: California Before the Gold Rush,* edited by Ramon A. Gutierrez and Richard J. Orsi, pp. 260–298. Berkeley: University of California Press.

  2002 Portents of Plague from California's Protohistoric Period. *Ethnohistory* 49(1):69–121.

Ramenofsky, Ann F.
  1987 *Vectors of Death.* Albuquerque: University of New Mexico Press.

  1990 Loss of Innocence: Explanations of Differential Persistence in the Sixteenth-Century Southeast. In *Columbian Consequences,* vol. 2, *Archaeological and Historical Perspectives on the Spanish Borderlands East,* edited by David Hurst Thomas, pp. 31–48. Washington, D.C.: Smithsonian Institution Press.

  1991 Beyond Disciplinary Bias: Future Directions in Contact Period Studies. In *Columbian Consequences,* vol. 3, *The Spanish Borderlands in Pan-American Perspective,* edited by David Hurst Thomas, pp. 431–436. Washington, D.C.: Smithsonian Institution Press.

  1993 Diseases of the Americas, 1492–1700. *The Cambridge World History of Human Disease,* edited by Kenneth F. Kiple, pp. 317–327. Cambridge: Cambridge University Press.

1996 The Problem of Introduced Infectious Diseases in New Mexico: A.D. 1540–1680. *Journal of Anthropological Research* 52:161–184.

Ramenofsky, Ann F., and Patricia Galloway
1997 Disease and the Soto Entrada. In *The Hernando de Soto Expedition: History, Historiography, and "Discovery" in the Southeast,* edited by Patricia Galloway, pp. 259–279. Lincoln: University of Nebraska Press.

Ramenofsky, Ann F., Alicia K. Wilbur, and Anne C. Stone
2003 Native American Disease History: Past, Present and Future Directions. *World Archaeology* 35(3):241–257.

Read, Dwight W.
1978 Toward a Formal Theory of Population Size and Area of Habitation. *Current Anthropology* 19(2):312–317.

Reff, Daniel T.
1992 Contact Shock in Northwestern New Spain, 1518–1764. In *Disease and Demography in the Americas,* edited by John W. Verano and Douglas H. Ubelaker, pp. 265–276. Washington, D.C.: Smithsonian Institution Press.

Reynolds, Richard Dwan
1959 Effect of Natural Fires and Aboriginal Burning upon the Forests of the Central Sierra Nevada. Master's thesis, Department of Geography, University of California, Berkeley.

Rice, Prudence M.
1998 Contexts of Contact and Change: Peripheries, Frontiers, and Boundaries. In *Studies in Culture Contact: Interaction, Culture Change, and Archaeology,* edited by James G. Cusick, pp. 44–66. Center for Archaeological Investigations Occasional Paper No. 25. Carbondale: Southern Illinois University.

Rogers, Alexander K.
2006 Induced Hydration of Obsidian: A Simulation Study of Accuracy Requirements. *Journal of Archaeological Science* 33(12):1696–1705.

Rubertone, Patricia E.
2000 The Historical Archaeology of Native Americans. *Annual Review of Anthropology* 29:425–446.

Russell, Carl Parcher
1992 *One Hundred Years in Yosemite.* Yosemite: Yosemite Association.

Sahlins, Marshall
1981 *Historical Metaphors and Mythical Realities: Structure in Early History of the Sandwich Islands Kingdom.* Association for Social Anthropology in Oceania Special Publications 1. Ann Arbor: University of Michigan Press.

Scarry, John F. (editor)
1996 *Political Structure and Change in the Prehistoric Southeastern United States.* Gainesville: University Press of Florida.

Schacht, Robert M.
   1981 Estimating Past Population Trends. *Annual Review of Anthropology* 10:119–140.

Schiffer, Michael B.
   1976 *Behavioral Archaeology.* New York: Academic Press.

Schortman, Edward M., and Patricia A. Urban
   1998 Culture Contact Structure and Process. In *Studies in Culture Contact: Interaction, Culture Change, and Archaeology,* edited by James G. Cusick, pp. 102–125. Center for Archaeological Investigations Occasional Paper No. 25. Carbondale: Southern Illinois University.

Shackley, M. Steven
   2000 The Stone Tool Technology of Ishi and the Yana of North Central California: Inferences for Hunter-Gatherer Cultural Identity in Historic California. *American Anthropologist* 102(4):693–712.

Shennan, Stephen
   1993 After Social Evolution: A New Archaeological Agenda? In *Archaeological Theory: Who Sets the Agenda?* edited by Norman Yoffee and Andrew Sherratt, pp. 53–59. Cambridge: Cambridge University Press.

Shimkin, Dimitri B.
   1986 Introduction of the Horse. In *Great Basin,* edited by Warren L. D'Azevedo, pp. 517–524. Handbook of North American Indians, vol. 11, William C. Sturtevant, general editor. Washington, D.C.: Smithsonian Institution.

Shipley, William F.
   1978 Native Languages of California. In *California,* edited by Robert F. Heizer, pp. 80–90. Handbook of North American Indians, vol. 8, William C. Sturtevant, general editor. Washington, D.C.: Smithsonian Institution.

Sieh, Kerry, and Marcus Bursik
   1986 Most Recent Eruption of the Mono Craters, Eastern Central California. *Journal of Geophysical Research* 91(B12):12539–12571.

Silliman, Stephen W.
   2001 Agency, Practical Politics and the Archaeology of Culture Contact. *Journal of Social Archaeology* 1(2):190–209.

   2004 *Lost Laborers in Colonial California: Native Americans and the Archaeology of Rancho Petaluma.* Tucson: University of Arizona Press.

   2005 Culture Contact or Colonialism: Challenges in the Archaeology of Native North America. *American Antiquity* 70(1):55–74.

Simpson, Lesley Byrd
   1950 *The Encomienda in New Spain: The Beginning of Spanish Mexico.* Berkeley: University of California Press.

Sinclair, Anthony
   2000 Constellations of Knowledge: Human Agency and Material Affor-

dance in Lithic Technology. In *Agency in Archaeology,* edited by Marcia-Anne Dobres and John E. Robb, pp. 196–212. London: Routledge.

Skinner, Elizabeth
  1986 Appendix A.3: Lithics Analyses: Conclusions and Recommendations. In *Cultural Resources of the Crane Valley Hydroelectric Project Area,* vol. 3, *Archaeological Testing, Resource Evaluation, Impact Assessment, and Management Planning,* part 2, by Susan K. Goldberg, Sally S. Salzman, Elizabeth J. Skinner, Jeffrey Burton, Margaret E. Scully, John J. Holson, and Michael J. Moratto, pp. 579–594. INFOTEC Research Inc. Submitted to Pacific Gas and Electric Company. San Francisco.

Smith, Marvin T.
  1987 *Archaeology of Aboriginal Culture Change in the Interior Southeast: Depopulation during the Early Historic Period.* Gainesville: University of Florida Press.

  2001 The Rise and Fall of Coosa, A.S. 1350–1700. In *Societies in Eclipse: Archaeology the Eastern Woodlands Indians, A.D. 1400–1700,* edited by David S. Brose, C. Wesley Cowan, and Robert Mainfort, pp. 143–156. Washington, D.C.: Smithsonian Institution Press.

  2002 Aboriginal Population Movements in the Postcontact Southeast. In *The Transformation of the Southeastern Indians, 1540–1760,* edited by Robbie Ethridge and Charles Hudson, pp. 3–20. Jackson: University of Mississippi Press.

Snow, Dean R.
  1995 Microchronology and Demographic Evidence Relating to the Size of Pre-Columbian North American Indian Population. *Science* 268:1601 1604.

  1996 Mohawk Demography and the Effects of Exogenous Epidemics on American Indian Populations. *Journal of Anthropological Archaeology* 15:160–182.

  2001 Evolution of the Mohawk Iroquois. In *Societies in Eclipse: Archaeology the Eastern Woodlands Indians, A.D. 1400–1700,* edited by David S. Brose, C. Wesley Cowan, and Robert Mainfort, pp. 19–26. Washington, D.C.: Smithsonian Institution Press.

Snow, Dean R., and Kim M. Lanphear
  1988 European Contact and Indian Depopulating in the Northeast: The Timing of the First Epidemics. *Ethnohistory* 35(1):15–33.

Solnit, Rebecca
  1994 *Savage Dreams: A Journey into the Hidden Wars of the American West.* San Francisco: Sierra Club Books.

Stannard, David E.
  1991 Consequences of Contact: Toward an Interdisciplinary Theory of Native Responses to Biological and Cultural Invasion. In *Columbian Consequences,* vol. 3, *The Spanish Borderlands in Pan-American Per-*

spective, edited by David Hurst Thomas, pp. 431–436. Washington, D.C.: Smithsonian Institution Press.

Starna, William A., and José António Brandao
2004 From the Mohawk-Mahican War to the Beaver Wars: Questioning the Pattern. *Ethnohistory* 51(4):725–750.

Stearn, E. Wagner, and Allen E. Stearn
1945 *The Effect of Smallpox on the Destiny of the Amerindian.* Boston: Bruce Humphries.

Stein, Gil J.
2005 Introduction: The Comparative Archaeology of Colonial Encounters. In *Archaeology of Colonial Encounters: Comparative Perspectives,* edited by Gil. J. Stein, pp. 3–32. Santa Fe: School of American Research Press.

Stein, Gil J. (editor)
2005 *Archaeology of Colonial Encounters: Comparative Perspectives.* Santa Fe: School of American Research Press.

Stevenson, C. M., E. Knaus, J. J. Mazer, and J. K. Bates
1993 Homogeneity of Water Content in Obsidian from the Coso Volcanic Field: Implications for Obsidian Hydration Dating. *Geoarchaeology* 8:371–384.

Stevenson, C. M., J. J. Mazer, and B. E. Scheetz
1998 Laboratory Obsidian Hydration Rates: Theory, Method, and Application. In *Archaeological Obsidian Studies: Method and Theory,* edited by M. Steven Shackley, pp. 181–204. New York: Plenum Press.

Stevenson, C. M., P. J. Sheppard, D. G. Sutton, and W. Ambrose
1996 Advances in the Hydration Dating of New Zealand Obsidian. *Journal of Archaeological Science* 23:233–242.

Steward, Julian
1933 Ethnography of the Owens Valley Paiute. *University of California Publications in American Archaeology and Ethnology* 33(3).

Stewart, Frank Henderson
2001 Hidatsa. In *Plains,* edited by Raymond J. DeMallie, pp. 329–348. Handbook of North American Indians, vol. 13, part 1, William C. Sturtevant, general editor. Washington, D.C.: Smithsonian Institution Press.

Sumner, William M.
1979 Estimating Population by Analogy: An Example. In *Ethnoarchaeology: Implications of Ethnography for Archaeology,* edited by Carol Kramer, pp. 164–174. New York: Columbia University Press.

Sundstrom, Linea
1997 Smallpox Used Them Up: References to Epidemic Disease in Northern Plains Winter Counts, 1714–1920. *Ethnohistory* 44(2):305–343.

Swagerty, William R.
2001 History of the United States Plains Until 1850. In *Plains,* edited by

Raymond J. DeMallie, pp. 256–279. Handbook of North American Indians, vol. 13, part 1, William C. Sturtevant, general editor. Washington, D.C.: Smithsonian Institution Press.

Taylor, Rose Schuster
   1932 *The Last Survivor*. San Francisco: Johnck & Seeger.

Thomas, David Hurst (editor)
   1989 *Columbian Consequences, Volume 1: Archaeological and Historical Perspectives on the Spanish Borderlands West*. Washington, D.C.: Smithsonian Institution Press.

   1990 *Columbian Consequences*, vol. 2, *Archaeological and Historical Perspectives on the Spanish Borderlands East*. Washington, D.C.: Smithsonian Institution Press.

   1991 *Columbian Consequences, Volume 3: The Spanish Borderlands in Pan-American Perspective*. Washington, D.C.: Smithsonian Institution Press.

Thomas, Julian
   1993 The Hermeneutics of Megalithic Space. In *Interpretative Archaeology*, edited by Christopher Tilley, pp. 73–97. Oxford: Berg.

Thornton, Russell
   1987 *American Indian Holocaust and Survival: A Population History Since 1492*. Norman: University of Oklahoma Press.

   1997 Aboriginal North American Population and Rates of Decline, ca. A.D. 1500–1900. *Current Anthropology* 38(2):310–315.

   2000 Population History of Native North Americans. In *A Population History of North America*, edited by Michael R. Haines and Richard H. Steckel, pp. 9–50. Cambridge: Cambridge University Press.

Thornton, Russell, Tim Miller, and Jonathan Warren
   1991 American Indian Population Recovery Following Smallpox Epidemics. *American Anthropologist* 93(1):28–45.

Tilley, Christopher
   1994 *Phenomenology of Landscape*. Oxford: Berg.

Trigger, Bruce G.
   1966 Comments on Estimating Aboriginal American Population. *Current Anthropology* 7(4):439–440.

   1985 *Natives and Newcomers: Canada's "Heroic Age" Reconsidered*. Montreal: McGill-Queen's University Press.

   1989 *A History of Archaeological Thought*. Cambridge: Cambridge University Press.

Tringham, Ruth
   1991 Households with Faces: The Challenge of Gender in Prehistoric Architectural Remains. In *Engendering Archaeology: Women and Prehistory*, edited by Joan W. Gero and Margaret M. Conkey, pp. 93–131. Oxford: Basil Blackwell.

Tuck, James A.
　1971 *Onondaga Iroquois Prehistory: A Study in Settlement Pattern Archaeology.* Syracuse, NY: Syracuse University Press.

Turner, Christy G., and Laurel Lofgren
　1966 Household Size of Prehistoric Western Pueblo Indians. *Southwestern Journal of Anthropology* 22(2):117–132.

Ubelaker, Douglas H.
　1992 North American Indian Population Size: Changing Perspectives. In *Disease and Demography in the Americas,* edited by John W. Verano and Douglas H. Ubelaker, pp. 169–176. Washington, D.C.: Smithsonian Institution Press.

　2000 Patterns of Disease in Early North American Populations. In *A Population History of North America,* edited by Michael R. Haines and Richard H. Steckel, pp. 51–97. Cambridge: Cambridge University Press.

Upham, Steadman
　1986 Smallpox and Climate in the American Southwest. *American Anthropologist* 88(1):115–127.

　1992 Population and Spanish Contact in the Southwest. In *Disease and Demography in the Americas,* edited by John W. Verano and Douglas H. Ubelaker, pp. 223–236. Washington, D.C.: Smithsonian Institution Press.

Upham, Steadman, and Lori Stephens Reed
　1989 Regional Systems in the Central and Northern Southwest: Demography, Economy, and Sociopolitics Preceding Contact. In *Columbian Consequences,* vol. 1, *Archaeological and Historical Perspectives on the Spanish Borderlands,* edited by David Hurst Thomas, pp. 57–76. Washington, D.C.: Smithsonian Institution Press.

Van Bueren, Thad M.
　1983 Archaeological Perspectives on Central Miwok Cultural Change during the Historic Period. Master's thesis, Department of Anthropology, San Francisco State University, San Francisco.

Vansina, Jan
　1985 *Oral Tradition as History.* Madison: University of Wisconsin Press.

Verano, John W., and Douglas H. Ubelaker (editors)
　1992 *Disease and Demography in the Americas.* Washington, D.C.: Smithsonian Institution Press.

Voss, Barbara L.
　2002 The Archaeology of El Presidio de San Francisco: Culture Contact, Gender, and Ethnicity in a Spanish-Colonial Military Community. Ph.D. dissertation, Department of Anthropology, University of California, Berkeley.

Walker, Deward E., Jr.
　1998 Introduction. In *Plateau,* edited by Deward E. Walker, Jr., pp. 1–7. Handbook of North American Indians, vol. 12, William C. Sturtevant, general editor. Washington, D.C.: Smithsonian Institution Press.

Walker, Phillip L., and John R. Johnson
  1992 Effects of Contact on the Chumash Indians. In *Disease and Demography in the Americas,* edited by John W. Verano and Douglas H. Ubelaker, pp. 127–140. Washington, D.C.: Smithsonian Institution Press.
  2003 For Everything There Is a Season: Chumash Indian Births, Marriages, and Deaths at the Alta California Missions. In *Human Biologists in the Archives: Demography, Health, Nutrition and Genetics in Historical Populations,* edited by D. Ann Herring and Alan C. Swedlund, pp. 53–77. Cambridge: Cambridge University Press.

Walker, Phillip L., Patricia Lambert, and Michael J. DeNiro
  1989 The Effects of European Contact on the Health of Alta California Indians. In *Columbian Consequences,* vol. 1, *Archaeological Perspectives on the Spanish Borderlands West,* edited by David Hurst Thomas, pp. 349–364. Washington, D.C.: Smithsonian Institution Press.

Wall, Robert D.
  2004 The Chesapeake Hinterlands: Contact-Period Archaeology in the Upper Potomac Valley. In *Indian and European Contact in Context: The Mid-Atlantic Region,* edited by Dennis B. Blanton and Julia A. King, pp. 74–97. Gainesville: University Press of Florida.

Wallace, William J.
  1970 *Archaeological Investigations at Hidden Reservoir, Madera County, California.* Contributions to California Archaeology 7. Los Angeles.

Ward, H. Trawick, and R. P. Stephen Davis, Jr.
  2001 Tribes and Traders on the North Carolina Piedmont, A.D. 1000–1710. In *Societies in Eclipse: Archaeology the Eastern Woodlands Indians, A.D. 1400–1700,* edited by David S. Brose, C. Wesley Cowan, and Robert Mainfort, pp. 125–142. Washington, D.C.: Smithsonian Institution Press.

Warrick, Gary
  2003 European Infectious Disease and Depopulation of the Wendat-Tionontate (Huron-Petch). *World Archaeology* 35(2):258–275.

Waselkov, Gregory A., and Marvin T. Smith
  2000 Upper Creek Archaeology. In *Indians of the Greater Southeast: Historical Archaeology and Ethnohistory,* edited by Bonnie G. McEwan, pp. 242–264. Gainesville: University of Florida Press.

Washburn, Wilcomb E., and Bruce G. Trigger
  1996 Native Peoples in Euro-American Historiography. In *The Cambridge History of the Native Peoples of the Americas,* vol. 1, *North American, Part 1,* edited by Bruce G. Trigger and Wilcomb E. Washburn, pp. 61–124. Cambridge: Cambridge University Press.

Weaver, Richard A.
  1986 Notes on the Production, Use, and Distribution of Pottery in East-Central California. In *Pottery of the Great Basin and Adjacent Areas,*

edited by Suzanne Griset, pp. 75–82. University of Utah Anthropological Papers 111. Salt Lake City.

Wesson, Cameron B.
2001 Creek and Pre-Creek Revisited. In *The Archaeology of Traditions: Agency and History Before and After Columbus,* edited by Timothy R. Pauketat, pp. 94–106. Gainesville: University Press of Florida.

2002 Prestige Goods, Symbolic Capital, and Social Power in the Protohistoric Southeast. In *Between Contacts and Colonies: Archaeological Perspectives on the Protohistoric Southeast,* edited by Cameron B. Wesson and Mark A. Rees, pp. 110–125. Tuscaloosa: University of Alabama Press.

Wesson, Cameron B., and Mark A. Rees
2002 Protohistory and Archaeology: An Overview. In *Between Contacts and Colonies: Archaeological Perspectives on the Protohistoric Southeast,* edited by Cameron B. Wesson and Mark A. Rees, pp. 1–11. Tuscaloosa: University of Alabama Press.

Whitney, Joseph
1869 *The Yosemite Guide-book.* Sacramento: Geological Survey of California.

Whittaker, John C.
1987 Making Arrowpoints in a Prehistoric Pueblo. *Lithic Technology* 16(1): 1–12.

1994 *Flintknapping: Making and Understanding Stone Tools.* Austin: University of Texas Press.

Wiessner, Polly
1974 A Functional Estimator of Population from Floor Area. *American Antiquity* 39(2):343–350.

Wolf, Eric R.
1982 *Europe and the People without History.* Berkeley: University of California Press.

Wood, W. Raymond
2001 Plains Village Tradition: Middle Missouri. In *Plains,* edited by Raymond J. DeMallie, pp. 186–206. Handbook of North American Indians, vol. 13, part 1, William C. Sturtevant, general editor. Washington, D.C.: Smithsonian Institution Press.

Wood, W. Raymond, and Lee Irwin
2001 Mandan. In *Plains,* edited by Raymond J. DeMallie, pp. 349–364. Handbook of North American Indians, vol. 13, part 1, William C. Sturtevant, general editor. Washington, D.C.: Smithsonian Institution Press.

Worth, John E.
2000 The Lower Creeks: Origins and Early History. In *Indians of the Greater Southeast: Historical Archaeology and Ethnohistory,* edited by Bonnie G. McEwan, pp. 265–298. Gainesville: University of Florida Press.

Index

Italicized page numbers refer to figures, maps, and tables.

Abihka, 239
accident vs. choice, 28, 167, 169, 171–72, 179, 197, 201, 217, 287. *See also* choices; stochastic processes
accommodation, 72, 221, 238, 248, 260, 274, 291, 293, 295, 300
acculturation studies, 25, 171, 207, 221, 316n1
Ache, 140, 144
Acoma, 276
acorns/acorn caches: and Awahnichi cultural affiliation, 85–88, 90, 93; and colonial encounters, 33, 53, 56–57, 60, 73, 77, 154; and daily life/culture, 100, 107–8, 112, 314n4; and Hol'-low/He-le'jah sites, 181–83
agency, native, 23, 25, 28, 171, 295
aggregation, 9, 21, 88, 119, 290–91; and changes in daily practice, 157–63, 166, 171–72, 176, 179; and demographic archaeological study, 130–31; and Eastern Prairie communities, 223, 266; and interior Southeast societies, 237, 240, 242–43, 256, 258–59; and Iroquoian tribes, 228, 230; and middle Missouri River peoples, 267; and occupational history of villages, 209, 212; and Puebloan peoples, 276–77; and Salishan-speaking peoples, 273; and Siouan peoples, 234

aggression, 10–11, 21, 23, 30, 76; Bunnell's account of, 32–35, 53–60, 73, 311–12n4, 313n3; and Eastern Prairie communities, 262; and interior Southeast societies, 242–44, 247–48, 319n13; and Iroquoian tribes, 224–26, 228–31, 236, 262, 318n7; Perlot's account of, 36, 38. *See also* violence; warfare
agriculture, 5, 11, 22, 71, 109, 144, 147, 158, 281; and Eastern Prairie communities, 262–65; and interior Southeast societies, 236–37, 243, 246–47, 256, 259, 293, 319n10; and Iroquoian tribes, 226–27, 229, 293; and middle Missouri River peoples, 266, 268, 270; and Puebloan peoples, 275, 279; and Siouan peoples, 232, 234, 318n8
Agta, 144
Ah-wah'-ne village, 210–13
Ajacan (Spanish mission), 233
Alabamas, 239, 242
Alchon, Suzanne Austin, 310n5
Alexander, Rani T., 287–88, 294, 296
Algonquian-speaking people, 224–25, 261–62, 264
alliances, 77, 95, 226, 229, 242, 247, 267
Alvarado, Juan, 71
ancestral lands, 2, 15, 20, 61, 69; and Awahnichi cultural affiliation, 79, 86,

353

ancestral lands *(continued)*
92–93; and changes in daily practice, 158–60, 166 and cross-cultural comparisons, 254, 292–93. *See also* connection to place
Anderson, David G., 318–19n9
anthropological analyses, 3, 6–8, 12, 19, 21–27, 29, 81–82, 219, 282–83, 297–99, 310–11n9; and changes in daily practice, 172; and cross-cultural comparisons, 220, 281, 294, 297; and historical narratives, 36, 38, 40–41, 312n7; and memory culture, 42–46, 50–51, 312nn8,9. *See also* historical anthropology
antler tools. *See* bone and antler objects
Apalachee mission, 242, 244, 247
arbor shades *(sal'-lah)*, 100
archaeological evidence, 2–4, 6, 8–15, 19–26, 31, 280–83, 285–86, 289, 291, 293, 296–99, 310nn4,8, 312n9; and Awahnichi cultural affiliations, 27, 80, 83–91, *84, 85, 87,* 313nn1,2; and Caddo (interior Southeast), 254–60; and changes in daily practice, 28, 156–57, 159–60, 163–80, 316–17nn2–4; and Choctaws (interior Southeast), 245–46, 248–49; and daily life/culture, 27, 96, 99, 102, 112–13; and demographic archaeological study, 27–28, 117–34, 314nn3–6; and Eastern Prairie communities, 261–62, 264; and Hol'-low/He-le'jah sites, 29, 181, 183–209, *184, 185, 187, 190–91, 194,* 202, 216, 219, 317nn1,2; and Iroquoian tribes, 224–26, 228–31, 318nn4,5; and methodology for, 46–52; and middle Missouri River peoples, 268–70; and Natchez (interior Southeast), 250–53; and occupational history of villages, 209–16, *211,* 317–18nn1–12; and Puebloan peoples, 275–80; and Salishan-speaking peoples, 271–72, 274, 319–20n17; and significance of colonial-era depopulation, 135–36, 139–42, 145–51, 154–55; and Siouan peoples, 232–35; and Upper Creeks (interior Southeast), 239, 241–45
architecture, 14, 35, 48, 83, 117–18, 213, 218, 287, 291; and Eastern Prairie communities, 264; and interior Southeast societies, 237, 243, 256; and Iroquoian tribes, 226, 228–29, 264; and Puebloan peoples, 275; and Siouan peoples, 234–35. *See also* dwellings
Arikara, 266–68

Arkush, Brooke, 176, 189, 202, 205, 207
artifact assemblages, 188–89; and archaeological methodology, 46–49, 51–52; and Awahnichi cultural affiliation, 83–91, *85;* and changes in daily practice, 165, 168–70, 173–79, 316–17n4; and cross-cultural comparisons, 264, 291; and demographic archaeological study, 118, 121–31; and Hol'-low/He-le'jah sites, 183–89, *184, 185, 187,* 192–207, *194, 195, 196,* 202, 217–18, 317n4; nonnative, 13, 29, 52, 113–14, 124, 165, 169, 171, 176, 178–79. *See also names of specific artifacts*
artifact reuse, 83, 118–19, 127, 176, 200–201, 206. *See also* scavenging
artists, nonnative, 39–40, 81, 266
assembly house *(hange'-e),* 95, 100, 103, 113, 122, 179
atlatl, 85, 131
Awahnee, 60–65, 67, 69, 94, 98, 115–16. *See also* Yosemite Valley
Awahnichi, 181, 284–85, 287–89, 298–99; as ancestors of Yosemite Indians, 60–65, 67–69, 76, 93–94, 112, 313n6; and cross-cultural comparisons, 220–22, 224, 289–93; cultural affiliation of, 79–94, *84, 85, 87,* 313nn1,2; and demographic archaeological study, 115–18; and Hol'-low/He-le'jah sites, 181–82, 188–89, 198, 203, 208, 218; and language groups, 92–94, 313n2; and occupational history of villages, 209, 215; renaming of, 62, 69, 73. *See also* Yosemite Indians
awls. *See* bone and antler objects
Aw'-o-koi-e village, 211, 213
Ayres, T. M., 81

bands, 5, 22, 54, 69, 82, 281. *See also* hunter-gatherers
bark house, conical *(o'-chum),* 100–102, *101*
Barrett, Samuel A., 44–45, 101, 103, 109, 111–12, 312n8
basalt, 84, *185*
Basketmaker tradition, 275
basketry, 48, 56, 64, 74, 78; and Awahnichi cultural affiliation, 80, 93; burden, 106, 108, 110–11; and changes in daily practice, 178; coiled, 110; and daily life/culture, 102, 106, 108–13; and Hol'-low/He-le'jah sites, 181–82, 207; and occupational history of villages, 213; and Salishan-speaking peoples, 272; winnowing trays, 110

Index

Bates, Craig D., 74, 102, 313nn5,6
Bautista, 57
Bayham, Frank E., 315n14
Bay Miwok language group, 65
beads: brass, 13; *Haliotis* shell, 85, 208; stone, 177, 182, 194
bear, 69, 73, 89, 97, 106, 111, 189, 192
bedrock mortars, 77, 86–87, 90, 100, 107, 108, 112, 188, 208, 317n10
Belleborne, Jean Nicolet de, 261
Bennyhoff, James A., 90–91, 317n4
biases, 14, 24, 26, 49–51, 124, 131, 257, 314n4
Bienville (French trapper), 267
Bierstadt, Albert, 81
biface production, 83–85, 88–89, 121–22, 160, 184–87, *184, 185,* 199–200, 286; chevron flaking, 199–200, 203; collateral flaking, 198–200; and Hol'-low/He-le'jah sites, 183–87, *184, 185,* 198–201; notching flakes, 175, 199; oblique flaking, 199–200; transverse parallel pressure flakes, 198–201
bighorn sheep, 105–6
bioarchaeological analyses, 230, 235, 269–70
bioturbation, 49, 83, 173
bipolar reduction, 83, 85, 89, 175, *185,* 201, 206
birds, 106, *191,* 192
bison hunting, 256, 263, 266, 268
black sickness, 61–69, 76–77, 82, 91, 113, 115, 145, 150, 177, 221, 285
Blitz, John H., 318–19n9
Bodie Hills obsidian source, 87, 89, 204, 205
Boling, John, 53, 57–58, 60, 62, 98, 104, 288, 312n1, 313n3
bone and antler objects, 110, 194, 272, 319–20n17; antler tools, 109, 111; awlss, 186; bird bill/claw ornaments, 109
bows and arrows, 80, 85–88, 106, 111–12, 122–23, 131, 181
Bradley, James W., 229–31
Brain, Jeffrey P., 250, 252
Branstner, Susan M., 231
breast-feeding, 139, 285
breccia mortar, 203, 208
Bretnor, Helen Harding, 312n6
British colonists, 225–26, 230–33, 235, 239, 242–43, 247–49
Brown, James A., 264–65
brownware ceramics, 189
brush shelters, 102
Bunnell, Lafayette Houghton, 31–36, 39, 46, 60–65, 67–70, 73–74, 77, 81–82,
311–12nn1–4, 313n1, 316n4; and native daily life/culture, 94–95, 98–103, 105, 108–11, 113; and occupational history of villages, 216, 317n8; views on language, 32–33, 36, 62, 81, 92, 164, 310–11n9, 311n2
Bureau of Ethnology (Smithsonian Institution), 311n3, 312n7
burial practices/records: and archaeological methodology, 46; and cross-cultural comparisons, 228, 233, 235, 240–41, 246, 254–58; and demographic archaeological study, 118, 124. *See also* funeral rites; mortuary customs/populations
burning practices, 64, 88, 109, 126, 128; and occupational history of villages, 212, 214–16, *215,* 317–18nn11,12

Caddo, 158, 238, 254–61, *255,* 268, 280–81, 295, 319n16
California, annexation of, 16
California Academy of Sciences (San Francisco), 44
Campbell, Sarah K., 272–75, 319–20n17
camps, 39, 121, 160, 182, 273, 317nn8,10; and Awahnichi cultural affiliation, 81, 86; and colonial encounters, 54–60, 73, 76; and daily life/culture, 98–100, 102–3, 107
CA-MRP-190/191 (no ethnographic name), 213
CA-MRP-310 (no ethnographic name), 211
CA-MRP-55/H (no ethnographic name), 213, 317n9
CA-MRP-70/H (no ethnographic name), 317–18n12
CA-MRP-902/H (no ethnographic name), 213
canids, 89, 189–92, *190–91. See also* coyote; dog
Cartier, Jacques, 224
Casa Diablo obsidian source, 48, 89, 125–26, 204–7, *205*
Castillo, Diego del, 258
catastrophic depopulation, 8–11, 14, 21, 25, 77, 116, 283–84, 287, 289, 310n8; and changes in daily practice, 28, 156, 171, 179; and Hol'-low/He-le'jah sites, 219; and interior Southeast societies, 247–48, 251, 253–54, 259; and Iroquoian tribes, 230, 292; and middle Missouri River peoples, 267, 270; and Puebloan peoples, 278–79; significance of in colonial era, 138–39, 145–46, 152, 155

Catawba, 232
Catlin, George, 266
Cayuga, 227
cedar-bark slabs, 100–102, *101*, 111, 207
cemeteries, 118, 147, 233–34, 239, 256–58. *See also* burial practices/records
census data, 116–17, 121, 134, 147, 277, 279
Central Sierra Me'wuk groups, 90–92, 96–97, 103, 202
Central Valley, 19, 65, 68–71, 89, 131; as area of origin of Me'wuk language group, 92–94; and Hol'-low/He-le'jah sites, 203, 207–8
ceramic artifacts, 13, 110, 207, 291, 319–20n17; brownware ceramics, 189; and Eastern Prairie communities, 262–64; and interior Southeast societies, 236, 243, 251–52, 256; and Iroquoian tribes, 226, 228; and middle Missouri River peoples, 269; and Puebloan peoples, 275–76; and Siouan peoples, 234–35
ceramic seriation, 228, 252, 256, 269, 276
ceremonial life, 103–5, 168, 170, 173, 318n8. *See also* civic-ceremonial centers
charcoal frequencies, 88, 193
charismatic leaders, 221, 282, 288–89, 292, 297
Chatters, James C., 274
Chelan, 271
Cherokee, 242
chert, 84, 111, 181, *185*
Chickasaws, 244, 247, 249, 251
chiefdoms, 5, 10, 22, 281; and Choctaws (interior Southeast), 245–49, 290; and interior Southeast societies, 236–51, 262, 290, 318–19nn9–12; and Natchez (interior Southeast), 250–51; and Siouan peoples, 233; and Upper Creeks (interior Southeast), 239–45, 319n12
chiefs, 5; and daily life/culture, 95–96, 98; and interior Southeast societies, 237–39, 241, 245, 250–51, 256. *See also* chiefdoms; José, Chief; Tenaya, Chief
childbearing. *See* fertility rates
Chippewa, 33
Choctaws, 238, 240, 244, 245–49, 290–91, 293–94, 319nn14,15
choices, 20, 23, 30, 135, 286–87, 295; and changes in daily practice, 156–58, 161, 167, 169, 171–72, 179; and Hol'-low/He-le'jah sites, 197, 200–201, 217. *See also* decision-making processes
Christianity, 105
chronological control, 13, 298–99; and archaeological methodology, 46–49, 51–52; and demographic archaeological study, 119, 124–27; and Eastern Prairie communities, 265; and interior Southeast societies, 241, 252–53, 256–57, 260; and Iroquoian tribes, 228, 318n5; and middle Missouri River peoples, 269; and Puebloan peoples, 277–78; and Salishan-speaking peoples, 272–73
chronological sequences, 83–84, *84*. *See also names of periods*
Chumascado, Francisco Sanchez, 277
Chumash language group, 18
CIEP. *See* crossover immuno-electrophoresis
civic-ceremonial centers, 5, 236–37, 239–40, 251, 255, 257, 262–63
Clark, Galen, 40–42, 45, 74, 81, 93, 101, 145
Clark, William, 266, 271, 274
climate change, 227, 237, 263, 265, 268, 277
clothing, 74, 111, 113
Coale, Ansley J., 148
Coast Miwok Indians, 65
cobble choppers/pestles, 85–87, 108
colonial era, 4–30, 17, 50–78, 280–99, 309–10n1; and archaeological methodology, 46–49; and Caddo (interior Southeast), 256–61; and changes in daily practice, 156–57, 159, 162–63, 165–66, 168–69, 171, 176, 179–80; and Choctaws (interior Southeast), 245–49; and daily life/culture, 96–97, 113; and demographic archaeological study, 116–17, 124, 127, 133–34, 315n12; and Eastern Prairie communities, 261–66; historical narratives of, 31–42, 37, 49, 51, 81–82, 116, 311–12nn1–4,6; and Hol'-low/He-le'jah sites, 182–84, 188–89, 197, 201–3, 208, 216, 219; and Iroquoian tribes, 224–30, 318n5; and lag time of infectious diseases in, 77, 180, 244, 280–81, 289, 292, 295; and memory culture, 42–46, 82, 312nn8,9; and middle Missouri River peoples, 269–71; and Natchez (interior Southeast), 250–54; native fertility/mortality rates during, 135, 138–40, 142–50, 143, 153, 316nn1–4; and occupational history of villages, 209–13, 219; and Puebloan peoples,

Index 357

277–79; and Salishan-speaking peoples, 273–74; significance of depopulation in, 135–55, *137, 138, 143,* 316nn1–5; simulation studies of depopulation in, 147–51, 154, 158–59, 260; and Siouan peoples, 231–36; and survival, biological/cultural, 139, 151–54; and Upper Creeks (interior Southeast), 239–42, 244–45, 319n13
colonialism, 2–4, 11–13, 15–16, 19–21, 23, 25, 171, 288, 298–99, 309–10n1, 312n9, 320n1; and cross-cultural comparisons, 221–22, 224, 228, 238, 245–46, 281–82, 289, 291, 294, 296–97. *See also* colonial era
colonization vs. cultural entanglement, 288–89, 294, 296
Columbian landfall, 2–3, 7, 222, 227, 246, 259, 262, 265, 275, 281, 283, 296, 309–10nn1,3
Columbia Plateau, 223, *223,* 271–75, 280, 319–20n17
computer simulation, demographic, 147–51, 154, 158–59, 260
Condor *(mo'llok),* 93
confederacies, 158, 227, 239, 242–44, 246, 256, 274, 290–91, 294
connection to place, 2, 76–77, 93–94, 97, 159, 166, 177, 292–93, 299; and occupational history of villages, 209, 211–12, 216, 218
consumption of resources, 107, 120, 122–24, 130–33, 173–74; and Hol'-low/He-le'jah sites, 189, 192, 194, 197
contact, 8–13, 18–19, 25, 27, 33, 35, 51, 74–75, 77–78, 280, 288–89, 296–99, 309–10nn1,8; and changes in daily practice, 157, 161, 171–72; and daily life/culture, 96, 98, 102, 113; and Eastern Prairie communities, 261; and interior Southeast societies, 237–39, 245, 247, 249, 252–53, 256, 260; and lag time of depopulation, 77, 180, 244, 280–81, 289, 292, 295; and memory culture, 45–46; and middle Missouri River peoples, 266–68, 270; and Salishan-speaking peoples, 274; and significance of colonial-era depopulation, 154–55; and Siouan peoples, 233, 281
Cook, Sherburne, 8–9, 67
Cooper, James Fennimore, 34
Coosa, 239–45, 257, 290–91, 319n12
copper, 13, 235–36, 256
core reduction, 83–85, 88–89, 121–22, 160, 184, *185,* 201
Coronado, Francisco Vásquez de, 277

cosmology, 92
Costanoan language group, 18, 65, 313n8
Cottonwood Triangular projectile points, *85,* 87, 200, 202
coyote, 97, 111, 189, *190*
Coyote *(ahē'li),* 93
Creek Confederacy, 242–44, 291
Creeks. *See* Lower Creeks; Upper Creeks of interior Southeast
cremation, 104
cremation area *(yu'lah),* 100
Creoles, 16
creolization, 157, 159, 161–65, 167, 170–71, 173, 178–79, 291; and Hol'-low/He-le'jah sites, 187–88; and occupational history of villages, 216
cross-cultural comparisons, 5, 117–18, 220–82, 223, 289–97, 314n2, 316n1; Caddo (interior Southeast), 158, 238, 254–61, *255,* 268, 280–81, 295, 319n16; and changes in daily practice, 157–58, 172; Choctaws (interior Southeast), 238, 240, 244, 245–49, 290–91, 293–94, 319nn14,15; Eastern Prairie communities, 223, *223,* 261–66, *263;* of hunter-gatherers, 140–45, *143,* 147, 153; interior Southeast societies, 222–23, 223, 236–61, 276, 293, 318–19nn9–11; Iroquoian tribes of interior Northeast, 158, 223, *223,* 224–31, *225,* 236, 262, 264, 290–93, 318nn1–7; middle Missouri River peoples, 223, *223,* 266–71, *267,* 280–81; Natchez (interior Southeast), 238, 240, 248, 249–54, 290, 292; Puebloan peoples, 223, *223,* 275–80, 276; Salishan-speaking peoples, 223, *223,* 271–75, 280, 319–20n17; Siouan peoples, 223, *223,* 231–36, *232,* 261, *263,* 268, 291–93, 318n8; Upper Creeks (interior Southeast), 158, 238, 239–45, 240, 249, 291, 294
crossover immuno-electrophoresis (CIEP), 174–75, 316–17n4
cultural consequences of depopulation, 3, 10–15, 20–29, 77, 114, 117, 155, 220–23, 282, 284–89, 292, 295–99; and changes in daily practice, 156–80, 316–17nn1–4; and Eastern Prairie communities, 262, 264–66; and historical anthropology, 49, 51; and historical narratives, 36, 45; and Hol'-low/He-le'jah sites, 183, 216, 218–19; and interior Southeast societies, 237–38, 241–42, 244, 248–49, 256–61; and middle Missouri River peoples, 268;

cultural consequences *(continued)*
    and Salishan-speaking peoples, 274;
    and Siouan peoples, 234, 236
cultural continuity/persistence, 23, 25,
    27–30, 51–52, 80, 112, 118, 156, 218–19, 286, 312n9; and cross-cultural
    comparisons, 223, 226, 234, 243–44,
    254, 265, 279, 281, 291–95
cultural diversity, decreasing, 157, 167–69, 171, 178–79
cultural entanglement, 287–88, 294, 296
cultural flexibility, 22, 72, 74–76, 78,
    159, 163; and cross-cultural comparisons, 220–21, 260, 268, 279, 282,
    288, 293, 295
cultural identity, 15, 20–22, 25, 76–77,
    79–80, 112; and changes in daily practice, 159, 161–64, 172, 174–76; and
    cross-cultural comparisons, 243, 248,
    294–95; and Hol'-low/He-le'jah sites,
    183, 198, 203, 217; and occupational
    history of villages, 216
cultural memory, 20–23
culture-contact research, 172, 299, 316n1
Cypriano, 58, 60

daily life and culture, 96–114, *101, 107,*
    314nn3–5; and Hol'-low/He-le'jah
    sites, 183–92, *184, 185, 187,* 216–18.
    See also daily practice changes/
    continuity
daily practice changes/continuity, 2, 6,
    21, 23, 29, 156–80, 286–88, 295,
    298; and aggregation, 157–63, 166,
    171–72, 176, 179; and creolization/
    ethnogenesis, 157, 159, 161–65, 167,
    170–71, 173, 178–79, 187–88; and
    cross-cultural comparisons, 226,
    234, 239, 246, 248, 257, 271; and
    despecialization/simplification, 157,
    169–70, 173, 178–79, 186–87; and
    external relations/regional interaction,
    165–67, 171–72, 176–79, 188; and
    founder effect in decreasing diversity,
    167–69; historical narratives of, 33,
    35–36, 38–40, 81–82; for individuals/
    households/groups, 170–79, 316–17nn1–4. *See also* daily life and
    culture
darts, 84–86, 122, 131
Davis, R. P. Stephen, Jr., 233
deadfall traps, 106
debitage, 83, 89, 175, 177; and Hol'-low/
    He-le'jah sites, 181, 183–88, *184, 185,
    187,* 193, 197–206, *205;* and occupational history of villages, 210. *See also*
    debitage proxy

debitage proxy: and demographic archaeological study, 119–25, 127–32, *132,
    302–7,* 314n4, 315nn12,13, 316n17;
    and occupational history of villages,
    209; and significance of colonial-era
    depopulation, 136–42, *137, 138,*
    145–46
decision-making processes, 1, 23, 32,
    69, 100, 102, 287; and changes in
    daily practice, 156, 160–61, 170–71,
    173, 177–78; and cross-cultural comparisons, 220–21, 248, 259, 281–82,
    290–93, 295, 297; and Hol'-low/
    He-le'jah sites, 182, 200–201; and
    occupational history of villages, 213,
    218; and significance of colonial-era
    depopulation, 28, 134–35, 147,
    151–54
deer, 89, 103, 106–7, 111, 189–92, *190–91, 196*
deerskin trade, 166, 235, 244, 248, 280
Del Campo de los Franceses (French
    Camp), 71
Delgado, Marcos, 247
Demeny, Paul, 148
demographic change, 21–23, 26, 30, 51,
    68–69, 77, 281, 284–91, 295–300,
    310nn5,8; and Awahnichi cultural
    affiliation, 84, 88, 112; and Caddo
    (interior Southeast), 256–60, 319n16;
    and changes in daily practice, 156–58,
    162, 165–67, 169, 177–80; and Choctaws (interior Southeast), 245–49; and
    daily life/culture, 96–99; and demographic archaeological study, 28, 115–34, *132, 136–42, 137, 138,* 314nn1–6,
    315nn12–16, 316n17; and Eastern
    Prairie communities, 223, 261–62,
    264–65; and fertility/mortality rates
    in colonial era, 135, 138–40, 142–50,
    143, 153, 316nn1–4; in historical narratives, 34–35; and Hol'-low/He-le'jah
    sites, 181–82, 188, 203, 205, 208, 219;
    and Iroquoian tribes, 227–31, 318n6;
    and middle Missouri River peoples,
    268–70; and Natchez (interior Southeast), 251–54; and occupational history of villages, 210, 213–14, 216, 317–18n12; and Puebloan peoples, 275–80;
    and Salishan-speaking peoples, 271–75;
    and significance of colonial-era depopulation, 135–36, 139–42, 145–51, 154–55; and simulation studies of depopulation, 147–51, 154, 158–59, 260; and
    Siouan peoples, 233–34; and survival,
    biological/cultural, 139, 151–54; temporal scale in, 127–30, 315nn9–14; and

Index

three scenarios for depopulation, 10–13, 135, 154–55, 223, 284–85, 288; and Upper Creeks (interior Southeast), 240–44
dendrochronology, 27, 51, 63–64, 68, 77, 115, 136, 193, 212, 214–15, *215*, 276, 285
dental increment analyses, 192, 197
Department of Agriculture, U.S., 43
depopulation, 3–4, 8–15, 21–22, 24–26, 114, 280–81, 283–86, 288–90, 292–97, 310nn4,8; and Awahnichi cultural affiliation, 79–80; and black sickness, 65, 76–77, 113; and Caddo (interior Southeast), 256–60; and changes in daily practice, 28, 156–61, 165–80; Chief Tenaya's account of, 32, 36; and Choctaws (interior Southeast), 245–49; and demographic archaeological study, 27–28, 115–17, 127, 133; and Eastern Prairie communities, 262, 264–66; and fertility/mortality rates in colonial era, 135, 138–40, 142–50, *143*, 153, 316nn1–4; and Hol'-low/He-le'jah sites, 183–84, 188, 192, 197–98, 200–201, 203, 205–6, 208–9, 216–19; and Iroquoian tribes, 226, 230–31; and lag time of contact, 77, 180, 244, 280–81, 289, 292, 295; and middle Missouri River peoples, 269–70; and Natchez (interior Southeast), 252–54; and occupational history of villages, 202, 207, 209–14, 216, 218; and Puebloan peoples, 278–80; and Salishan-speaking peoples, 271–75; significance of in colonial era, 28, 135–55, *137*, *138*, *143*, 316nn1–5; simulation studies of, 147–51, 154, 158–59, 260; and Siouan peoples, 233–35; and survival, biological/cultural, 139, 151–54; three scenarios for, 10–13, 135, 154–55, 223, 284–85, 288; and Upper Creeks (interior Southeast), 240–42, 244–45
deserted villages, 56, 59, 73, *75*, 76
Desert Side-Notched projectile points, 87–88, 199–203, *202*, 208
despecialization, 157, 169–71, 173, 178–79, 186–87
diachronic trends, 38, 177; and archaeological methodology, 47–48; and cross-cultural comparisons, 254, 264, 276; and demographic archaeological study, 122, 124, 127, 134; and Hol'-low/He-le'jah sites, 203, 209, 217; and significance of colonial-era depopulation, 136–39, *137*, *138*

359

Dick-Bissonnette, Linda E., 314nn3,4
diet, 5, 48, 71; and Awahnichi cultural affiliation, 80, 83, 85, 88–90; and changes in daily practice, 162, 173–74; and cross-cultural comparisons, 232, 234, 263, 271, 275; and daily life/culture, 105–9, 113; and Hol'-low/He-le'jah sites, 189–92, *190–91*, 217. *See also* subsistence practices
digging sticks, 106
Dill, William, 53
diphtheria, 68
direct historical approach, 25, 313n1
diseases. *See* infectious disease; *names of diseases*
disease vectors, 65, 242, 253, 260
disposal areas, 194–95, 197
Dobe !Kung. *See* !Kung
Dobyns, Henry, 8–10, 77, 161–62, 165, 167–70, 241, 273, 287, 310n8
documentary records. *See* historical records
dog, 101, 106; as food, 89, 189, *190*
drills, 183, *184*, 186, 196
droughts, 93, 152, 259
Dunnell, Robert C., 312n9
Dutch colonists, 224, 226, 230, 318n2
dwellings, 145; and changes in daily practice, 173–74; and colonial encounters, 56, 99; and cross-cultural comparisons, 227, 234, 264, 266, 268, 271–72, 275, 277; and daily life/culture, 100–102, *101*; and Hol'-low/He-le'jah sites, 188, 192–94, 216–17; and occupational history of villages, 211, 213, 216–18. *See also* architecture; *names of specific types of dwellings*

Early Prehistoric period (Yosemite), 84–85, *84*, 121
earthlodges, 264, 266, 268
Eastern Miwok languages, 91–92
Eastern Muskogean-speaking peoples, 239
Eastern Prairie communities, 223, *223*, 261–66, *263*
Eastern Pueblos, 276, 278. *See also* Puebloan peoples
Eccleston, Robert, 63
ecofacts, 173, 175, 178
edge-modified flakes (EMFs), 183, *184*, 186–88, 192, 194–96, *195*, 200; rounding on, 186–87, *187*, 194; step flaking on, 186, *187*, 194
El Capitan (Tutankanula), 93
elder informants, 10, 42–43, 45
elk, 89–90, 106, *190*

Elko Corner-Notched projectile points, 85, *85*
Emerson, Thomas E., 264
emigration. *See* migration/emigration/immigration
empty land *(terra nullius)*, 13, 30
encomienda system, 239, 319n10
endogenous factors, 264–65
Eno people, 232
environmental factors, 7, 310n4; and Awahnichi cultural affiliation, 83, 86–87; and changes in daily practice, 159, 162; and cross-cultural comparisons, 237, 259, 265, 268, 270, 279–80, 319n13; and demographic archaeological study, 120, 126–27; and Hol'-low/He-le'jah sites, 206
epidemics, 3, 7–9, 11, 19, 22, 30, 51, 77, 280–81, 310nn2,3,8; and black sickness, 61–63, 65, 67–69; and changes in daily practice, 161, 165–66; and interior Southeast societies, 241, 244, 246, 257, 260; and Iroquoian tribes, 229, 318n7; and middle Missouri River peoples, 267; and Puebloan peoples, 278; and Salishan-speaking peoples, 272–74; and significance of colonial-era depopulation, 137–39, 141, 145–47, 149–50, 154; and Siouan peoples, 234–35. *See also* infectious diseases
epidemiological studies, 7–10, 20–21, 222, 278, 310n4
Espejo, Antonio de, 277
Esselen language group, 18
ethnoarchaeological studies, 117, 175, 314n2
ethnogenesis, 157, 161–63, 170, 291
ethnographic present, 42–43, 82, 113
ethnographic studies, 24, 26, 31, 50, 283, 286–87, 299, 313n7; and Awahnichi cultural affiliation, 79, 83, 88, 90, 313n1; and changes in daily practice, 164, 175, 178, 180; and cross-cultural comparisons, 250, 256, 271, 274; and daily life/culture, 27, 80, 94, 96, 99–100, 112–13, 314n4; and demographic archaeological study, 115, 117–19, 121–22, 131, 314nn1,3; and historical narratives, 35–36, 38, 82; and Hol'-low/He-le'jah sites, 29, 188, 216; and memory culture, 42–46, 51, 82, 312nn8,9; and significance of colonial-era depopulation, 139–40, 145–46, 150, 153
ethnohistorical sources, 8–10, 14, 22, 24–25, 46, 50–51, 77, 283, 285–86, 288–89, 291, 298–99, 310n8, 311n10; of Awahnichi cultural affiliation, 68, 80, 82, 313n2; and changes in daily practice, 157, 159–60, 172, 180; and daily life/culture, 27, 94–96, 100, 102, 111–13; and demographic archaeological study, 115, 117, 136, 314n1; and Eastern Prairie communities, 264; and Hol'-low/He-le'jah sites, 29, 216; and interior Southeast societies, 239, 245, 250, 253; and middle Missouri River peoples, 268–70; and Salishan-speaking peoples, 272, 274; and significance of colonial-era depopulation, 139, 145, 153–54, 316n3; and Siouan peoples, 235
ethnolinguistic groups, 66, 287, 310–11n9, 312n7; and Awahnichi cultural affiliation, 82, 90–91, 313nn1,2; and changes in daily practice, 163–64; and cross-cultural comparisons, 224, 232, 250; and significance of colonial-era depopulation, 139. *See also names of specific groups*
ethnology, 36, 40, 42–44, 50, 82, 311n3
event-centered approach, 23–26
excavations, 125, 314n6; and archaeological methodology, 47–49; and changes in daily practice, 173–75, 178–80, 316n3; and Hol'-low/He-le'jah sites, 183, 193–97; and occupational history of villages, 212
exchange, 5, 7, 27, 286; and archaeological methodology, 47; and Awahnichi cultural affiliation, 80, 83, 85–86; and changes in daily practice, 164–66, 171, 176–79; and daily life/culture, 95, 114; and demographic archaeological study, 122, 124, 130–31; and Eastern Prairie communities, 262; and Hol'-low/He-le'jah sites, 181–82, 187, 206–9, 218; and interior Southeast societies, 241, 249, 251–52, 256, 259; and Puebloan peoples, 275–76; and Salishan-speaking peoples, 274; and Siouan peoples, 233. *See also* trade relations
exogamous marriage, 97, 113, 116, 119, 147, 150–51, 154, 164, 286–87
expedient tools, 85, 87–88, 123, 183–84, 187, 198
explorers, 4, 70, 116; and Caddo (interior Southeast), 258; and Choctaws (interior Southeast), 245, 247, 249, 319nn14,15; and Eastern Prairie communities, 261; and Natchez (interior Southeast), 250–51, 253–54; and Puebloan peoples, 277–78; and Siouan peoples, 232–33; and Upper Creeks (interior Southeast), 239–44. *See also names of explorers*

Index

external relations, 286; and changes in daily practice, 157–58, 165–67, 171–72, 176–79; and cross-cultural comparisons, 254, 291; and Hol'-low/He-le'jah sites, 188, 203–9, 205. *See also* exchange; trade relations

"extinctions," 147–51

eyewitness accounts, 33, 36, 50. *See also* historical narratives

face painting, 111
factionalism, 161–62, 173, 319n13
Falcon *(we'kwek)*, 93
Farquhar, Francis P., 312n1
faunal and floral assemblages, 83, 89–90, 174, 291; and Hol'-low/He-le'jah sites, 189–92, *190–91*, 194–97, *195*, *196*, 217
feathers, 109–11
fertility rates: and changes in daily practice, 157–58; and cross-cultural comparisons, 229, 270; and demographic archaeological study, 28, 116, 120, 133; and significance of colonial-era depopulation, 135, 138–39, 142–50, *143*, 153, 316nn1–4
festivals, 95, 234, 292
field houses, 279
firearms, 226
fire history, 64, 88, 109, 126, 128; and occupational history of villages, 212, 214–16, *215*, 317–18nn11,12
fish/fishing, 5, 18; and colonial encounters, 74, 78; and cross-cultural comparisons, 224, 271, 273; and daily life/culture, 94, 105–7, 113; and Hol'-low/He-le'jah sites, *191*, 192
fish spears, 106–7
Fiske, George, 81
Five Nations people, 227–30, 262, 293, 318nn3,5
flaked stone artifacts, 175, 286, 291; and archaeological methodology, 47–48, 52; and Awahnichi cultural affiliation, 83, 85, 87–89; bifaces, 184–87, *184*, *185*, 198–200, 203; chevron flaking, 199–200, 203; collateral flaking, 198–200; Cottonwood Triangular projectile points, *85*, 87, 200, 202; and daily life/culture, 100, 111; debitage, 83, 89, 175, 177; and demographic archaeological study, 122, 125–26, 128, 131; Desert Side-Notched projectile points, 87–88, 199–203, *202*, 208; drills, 183, *184*, 186, 196; edge-modified flakes (EMFs), 183, *184*, 186–88, *187*, 192, 194–96, *194*, *195*, 200; Elko Corner-Notched projectile points, 85, *85*; flake scars, 198–201; gravers, 183, *184*, 186; and Hol'-low/He-le'jah sites, 181, 183–88, *184*, *185*, 187, 192–205, *194*, *195*, *196*, 202, 217; oblique flaking, 199–200; overshot flakes, 199–200; rounding on edge-modified flakes, 186–87, *187*, *194*; serrated projectile points, 201–3, *202*, 206, 208; Sierra Concave Base projectile points, 85–86, *85*, 89; step flaking on edge-modified flakes, 186, *187*, *194*; Stockton Serrate projectile points, 202–3; transverse parallel pressure flakes, 198–201
flintknappers, 198–201, 204
floral assemblages. *See* faunal and floral assemblages; vegetal materials
food-preparation areas, 173–74, 179; and Hol'-low/He-le'jah sites, 181–82, 188–89, 192. *See also* hearths; milling features/tools; mortars
Foote, W. W., 42
foragers, 222, 273, 289, 293, 297. *See also* hunter-gatherers
founder effect, 167–69
Fremont, John C., 71
French missionaries, 231, 250, 261
French trappers/explorers/settlements, 68, 71; and Caddo (interior Southeast), 254–57, 259–61; and Choctaws (interior Southeast), 245–49; and Eastern Prairie communities, 264, 266; and Iroquoian tribes, 224, 226–31; and middle Missouri River peoples, 266–67; and Natchez (interior Southeast), 250–51, 253–54, 292
Fresno River reservation, 36, 54–55, 57–59, 78, 98
Friend, Washington F., 81
funeral rites, 97, 104, 113. *See also* burial practices; mortuary customs
fur trade, 16, 68, 70–71, 224, 226, 256, 266–67, 269, 280

Galloway, Patricia, 50, 238, 242, 244–49, 254, 284, 292, 319nn11,12
Gassaway, Linn, 214–15, 317–18nn11,12
gender roles, 97–98, 168, 173–75, 178, 188, 294
genealogical information, 27, 62–64, 68, 136
genetic diversity, 7, 167, 310n3
genocide, 11, 285
geochemical source analyses, 83, 88–89, 123, 125–26, 189, 203–5
geographic scope, 13, 19, 22, 31, 40, 44; and Awahnichi cultural affiliation, 87–

geographic scope *(continued)*
  90; and changes in daily practice, 158–60, 166; and cross-cultural comparisons, 29, 221, 227–28, 254, 265, 277; and demographic archaeological study, 116, 118, 125, 128, 153; and Hol'-low/He-le'jah sites, 202, 205; and language groups, 91–94; and occupational history of villages, 209–10, 213
geomorphological factors, 121, 234
Gifford, Edward W., 44–45, 94, 96–97, 99, 101, 103–4, 109, 111–13, 312n8
glass artifacts, 13, 286; and changes in daily practice, 166, 169; and cross-cultural comparisons, 228, 253; and daily life/culture, 110–11, 114; and Hol'-low/He-le'jah sites, 194, 196, 202, 207–8, 218, 317n5; and occupational history of villages, 212–13
Gold Rush era, 16, 20, 71–73, 75, 77–78, 153, 166, 217, 286–87; and daily life/culture, 95–96, 102, 104, 112–13, 314n4; and memory culture, 45–46; narratives of, 26, 32–38, 39, 82, 311–12n4; and subsistence practices, 53, 71, 106, 108
Gordon-Cumming, Constance, 39–40, 81, 102
Gosden, Chris, 12
granaries *(chuk-a)*, 108–9, 122. *See also* storage facilities
granite, 55, 111, 184, 193
gravers, 183, 184, 186
Great Spirit *(Nang-wa)*, 105, 154, 314n5
Green, William, 264–65
grizzly bear, 69, 73, 97. *See also* bear
group structure. *See* household/group structure
"Guardian of the Valley," 40–41
guardian spirits, 104
Gulnac, William, 71

habitation site frequency, 118–22
Hadza, 140–41, 144
Hale, Mark R., 210
Half Dome *(Tis-sa'ack)*, 93
hammerstones, 111, 184
handstones, 84–85, 188–89, 206, 317n3
Hantman, Jeffrey L., 233
Harriman, E. H., 43
Hastrup, Kirsten, 43
Haw-kaw-koo'-e-tah village, 210
hearths, 49, 56, 83; and changes in daily practice, 179; and daily life/culture, 100–102; and Hol'-low/He-le'jah sites, 181–83, 193–97, 194, 195, 196, 204, 209, 217; and Iroquoian tribes, 228

heirlooms, 13, 207
He-le'-jah site, 178–80, 182–219, 317n2; daily life and culture of, 183–92, 184, 185, 187, 190–91; and external relations/regional interaction, 203–9, 205; and hearths, 182–83, 193–97, 194, 196, 204, 209, 217; and occupational history of villages, 213, 216; and specialist production of flaked stone tools, 197–203, 202
Henige, David, 116, 273, 319–20n17
hibernation, 192
Hidatsa, 266–68, 291, 293
hierarchical societies, 5, 22, 169–70, 240, 246, 255–56, 262, 290
Hill, Thomas, 81
historical anthropology, 23–26, 29, 45–46, 49–52, 282, 311n10
historical demography, 28, 116
historical narratives, 24, 31–42, 81–82, 116; biases in, 49, 51; of Bunnell, 31–36, 311–12nn1–4; of Chief Tenaya, 31–36, 115, 209, 311nn1,2; of Perlot, 36–38, 312n6; secondary, 38–42
historical records, 280, 282, 294; and archaeological methodology, 47–48; and Awahnichi cultural affiliation, 27, 80–82; biases in, 50–51; of colonial encounters, 6–8, 13, 15, 19, 22, 67, 76–77; and demographic change, 116, 127; and Hol'-low/He-le'jah sites, 219; and interior Southeast societies, 238–39, 241–44, 246, 249–51, 254; and Iroquoian tribes, 228–30; and middle Missouri River peoples, 269–70; and Puebloan peoples, 277–79; and Siouan peoples, 234. *See also* visual records
history, 2, 4, 14–16, 19–23, 26–30, 36, 38, 42, 283, 297. *See also* oral traditions; *entries beginning with* historical
Hitchiti speakers, 243
Hodder, Ian, 297
Hohokam, 275
Hol'-low site, 178–219, 317n1; daily life and culture of, 183–92, 184, 185, 187, 190–91, 317n3; and external relations/regional interaction, 203–9, 205; and hearths, 181–83, 193–97, 194, 195, 204, 209, 217; and occupational history of villages, 213; old Indian woman found at, 56–57, 63, 213; and specialist production of flaked stone tools, 197–203
Ho-low village, 213
homesteading, 73
Hopi, 276
horses, 54–55, 61, 69; and cross-cultural

Index

comparisons, 256, 266–69, 271, 273–74, 280; as food, 71, 106, *190*, 192; and Hol'-low/He-le'jah sites, *190*, 192, 207–8. *See also* horse thievery
horse thievery, 53, 59, 71, 73, 77–78, 207
horticultural tradition. *See* agriculture
hotels, 39, 74
household/group structure: and daily life/culture, 94–98, 314nn3,4; and changes in daily practice, 158, 162, 170–79, 316–17nn2–4; and Hol'-low/He-le'jah sites, 182–83, 188–89, 217; and significance of colonial-era depopulation, 145, 150
Howell, Nancy, 140, 143–44
Hudson, Charles M., 250
Hughes, Richard E., 313n2
Hull, Kathleen L., 210, 315nn9,12–16, 316n17, 317–18nn3,12
hunter-gatherers, 5–6, 10–11, 18, 20, 22, 287; and changes in daily practice, 158, 160, 162, 168 and cross-cultural comparisons, 140–45, *143*, 147, 153, 227, 267, 269, 275, 279, 281, 318n8; and daily life/culture, 105–9
hunting: and changes in daily practice, 160, 174; and colonial encounters, 16, 18, 72, 74, 78; and daily life/culture, 94–95, 98, 103, 106–7; and demographic archaeological study, 122–23, 131; and Eastern Prairie communities, 263; and Hol'-low/He-le'jah sites, 187, 189–92, *190–91*; and interior Southeast societies, 236, 256, 259; and Iroquoian tribes, 227; and middle Missouri River peoples, 266, 268; and Siouan peoples, 234. *See also* hunter-gatherers
hunting/fishing trespasses, 94
Hutchings, James, 39, 62–63, 74, 81, 97–98
Hutchings' California Magazine, 39

Iberville, Pierre Le Moyne d', 248
immigration. *See* migration/emigration/immigration
immunity, lack of, 6–7, 10, 65, 230, 234
incest prohibition, 150–51
Indian commissioners, U.S., 54, 57–58, 312n5
Indian languages, of Yosemite region, 44, 50; and Awahnichi cultural affiliation, 79, 82, 91–94; Bunnell's account of, 32–33, 36, 62, 81, 92, 164, 310–11n9, 311n2; and Chief Tenaya, 62, 69, 92, 164; and geography, 91–94
Indians of the Yosemite Valley and Vicinity (Clark), 41–42
Indian trails, 39, 73, 100
Indian women, 36, 49–50, 54, 74, 116, 213, 226; and aged woman found in rockshelter, 56–57, 63, 213; and changes in daily practice, 164, 168, 175, 178; and cross-cultural comparisons, 228–30, 243, 254, 267; and gender roles, 97–98, 168, 173–75, 178, 188, 294; and group/household structure, 94, 97–98, 100, 314n4; and Hol'-low/He-le'jah sites, 181, 188; and significance of colonial-era depopulation, 142–46, *143*, 150, 153, 316n3; and spiritual life/ceremonies, 104; tools of, 106, 110–11, 188. *See also* marriage practices
individuals, 22, 30, 32, 82; and burial practices, 235, 258; and changes in daily practice, 157–58, 161–63, 168–79, 316n1; and creolization, 161–63; decisions made by, 23, 28, 135, 297; and demographic archaeological study, 117–19, 129, 133; and Hol'-low/He-le'jah sites, 197–203, 217; and hunting, 107; and significance of colonial-era depopulation, 135, 139, 153; and spiritual life, 105. *See also* charismatic leaders; traditional leaders
infectious disease, 2–3, 280–83, 287–96, 309–10nn1–3,6–8, 320n1; and Awahnichi cultural affiliation, 27, 79–80, 313n2; black sickness as, 61–69, 76–77, 82, 91, 113, 115, 145, 150, 177, 221, 285; and changes in daily practice, 28, 156–61, 164–65, 167–68, 171–72, 176–77, 180; Chief Tenaya's account of, 32, 36, 61, 177; and colonial encounters, 6–10, 18 25, 30, 32, 36, 51–52, 61, 76; and daily life/culture, 94, 96, 113–14; and demographic archaeological study, 28, 115–16, 133, 136–38; and Eastern Prairie communities, 261–62, 264–66; exposure to, 3, 8, 10, 67, 76–77, 116, 259, 270–71; and Hol'-low/He-le'jah sites, 29, 182–83, 188–89, 192, 197, 205, 216, 219; and immunity, lack of, 6–7, 10, 65, 230, 234; and interior Southeast societies, 236–48, 251, 253–54, 256–60, 319n13; and Iroquoian tribes, 224–27, 229–31, 262, 318n1; lag time of, 77, 180, 244, 280–81, 289, 292, 295; and memory culture, 45–46, 312n9; and middle Missouri River peoples, 267, 269–71; mosaic spread

infectious disease *(continued)*
  of, 254, 259, 270, 280, 295; and occupational history of villages, 209, 211, 218; and Puebloan peoples, 278–80; and Salishan-speaking peoples, 271–75; and significance of colonial-era depopulation, 28, 136–39, 145–46, 149, 152–55, 316n5; and Siouan peoples, 233–36; and three scenarios for depopulation, 10–13, 135, 154–55, 223, 284–85. *See also* names of specific diseases
influenza, 7, 310nn6,7
innkeepers, 26–27, 39, 81
Inspiration Point, 55, 56
interior Southeast societies, 222–23, 223, 236–61, 276, 293, 318–19nn9–11; Caddo, 158, 238, 254–61, 255, 268, 280–81, 295, 319n16; Choctaws, 238, 240, 244, 245–49, 290–91, 293–94, 319nn14,15; Natchez and Yazoo Basin neighbors, 238, 240, 248, 249–54, 290, 292; Upper Creeks, 158, 238, 239–45, 240, 249, 291, 294
intermarriage, 51, 69, 95, 152; and changes in daily practice, 161–62, 165, 67, 169, 172, 175, 177–78; and cross-cultural comparisons, 248, 289; and demographic archaeological study, 123–24; and Hol'-low/He-le'jah sites, 182, 187–89, 203, 206, 217–18
Intermediate Prehistoric periods (Yosemite), 84, *84*, 121
intersite analyses, 170, 172, 175, 178–79. *See also* site-specific data
intrasite analyses, 129, 165, 171–72, 175, 177–80, 204, 269
Iroquoian tribes of interior Northeast, 158, 223, 223, 224–31, 225, 236, 262, 264, 290–93, 318nn1–7
irrigation systems, 158, 170
isopleth maps, 173, 178, 193, *195*, *196*

Jamestown settlement, 234–35
Jemenez Plateau, 276, 279
Jesuit missionaries, 224, 229
Jeter, Marvin D., 250, 252, 254
Johnson, W. C., 318n7
Johnston, Hank, 70, 313n4
Jolliet, Louis, 261
Jordan, Kurt, 228
Jorgensen, Chris, 81
José, Chief, 95, 105
journalists, 26, 39–40
juvenile mortality, 230, 234, 241, 246

Kashaya Pomo, 16
Keith, William, 81
Kelly, Michael S., 317n3
kin-based political structure, 5, 96, 99, 116, 155, 161–62, 164, 254
King site, 241
Kom'-pom-pa'-sah village, 210–11, 317n7
Koom-i-ne village, 211, 213, 317n7
Krause, Richard A., 268
Kroeber, Alfred, 8, 40, 44, 94, 288
Kulisheck, Jeremy, 279
!Kung, 140–41, 143–45
Kuykendall, John J., 53, 288
Kuzedika (Mono Paiute), 163. *See also* Mono Paiute

labor, native, 4, 16, 18, 70–74, 78, 100, 170, 213, 239, 284, 293–94, 319n10
lactation amenorrhea, 138–39
La Florida, 237, 241, 244, 246, 249, 253
land use, patterns of, 83, 120–21, 160–61, 212, 216
language groups. *See* ethnolinguistic groups
La Salle, René-Robert Cavelier, 250–51
Last of the Mohicans, The (Cooper), 34
Late Archaic period (Mono Basin), 189
Late Prehistoric periods: Columbia Plateau, 272; Yosemite, 83–84, *84*, 86–91, 121–22, 313n1
Late Woodland period, 234, 236
La Verendrye, Pierre Gaultier de Varennes, 267
League of the Iroquois, 227–30, 262, 293, 318nn3,5
Lebrado, Mario, 313n4
Lee, Martha J., 74, 313nn5,6
Laguna pueblo, 276
Le Moyne d'Iberville, Pierre, 248
Leonard, Zenas, 70
Levy, Richard, 94, 104
Lewis, Meriwether, 266, 271, 274
lexicostatistical techniques, 92, 313n2
Library of Congress, 44
life expectancy, 63, 133, 143–46, *143*
lifetables, 147–48
lightning strikes, 214
lineages, 5, 94, 97–98, 248–49
linguistic data. *See* ethnolinguistic groups
lithic technology, 83–89, 121–25, 128, 130–31, 175, 204, 317nn5,6; manufacturing errors, 175, 199–201, 217; notching flakes, 175, 199; overshot flakes, 199–200
Little Ice Age, 227, 237, 263, 265
"little routines," 173, 177, 183, 284
Livi-Bacci, Massimo, 144

Index   365

Loi-ah village, 213
longhouse architecture, 226, 228, 264, 272, 291
Lookout Mountain subsource, 89, 204
López, Nicolás, Fray, 258
Lower Creeks, 239, 243–45
Luna, Tristán de, 241, 244–45

macroscale analyses, 171, 179–80, 216
magnitude of depopulation, 3, 10, 15, 24–25, 27, 29, 49, 283; and cross-cultural comparisons, 223, 292, 295; and demographic archaeological study, 115, 117, 133; and significance of colonial-era depopulation, 146, 155
maize, 5, 293; and Eastern Prairie communities, 262–63, 265; and interior Southeast societies, 236–37, 246, 256, 259; and Iroquoian tribes, 226–27; and middle Missouri River peoples, 268; and Puebloan peoples, 275; and Siouan peoples, 232, 234
malaria, 68
mammals, 189–92, 190–91, 207; marine, 5, 16
Mandan, 266–68, 291, 293
manifest destiny, 38
manufacturing debris, 83, 85, 100, 286; and archaeological methodology, 47–49; and changes in daily practice, 162, 166, 169–70, 173–75, 179; and demographic archaeological study, 120–26; and Hol'-low/He-le'jah sites, 181, 183–89, 184, 185, 187, 193–203, 194, 195, 196, 217–18
manufacturing errors, 175, 199–201, 217
manzanita berries, 112
marine shell trade, 225, 236, 256, 318n7
Mariposa Battalion, 32–36, 37, 39, 53–58, 60, 62–63, 67, 69–70, 72–73, 78, 81, 96, 99, 108, 189, 213, 215, 288, 311–12n4
Mariposa Grove of Big Trees, 41, 81
"Mariposa Indian War," 34, 95. See also Mariposa Battalion
Marquette, Jacques, 261
marriage practices, 3, 285–87; and aggregation, 158–59, 172; and changes in daily practice, 158–59, 161–62, 164–65, 167, 169, 172, 175, 177–78; and creolization/ethnogenesis, 161–62, 178; and cross-cultural comparisons, 248, 289; and daily life/culture, 95, 97–100, 113; and Hol'-low/He-le'jah sites, 182, 187–89, 203, 206, 217–18; and significance of colonial-era depopulation, 138, 146–48, 150–51, 154

Martín, Hernando, 258
mass burials, 235, 240–41
material culture, 10–11, 13–14, 24–25, 29, 35, 39; and archaeological methodology, 48–49; and Awahnichi cultural affiliation, 81–91, 85, 313n2; and changes in daily practice, 161, 168–70, 173–75; and cross-cultural comparisons, 228–29, 231, 235, 256, 264, 272; and daily life/culture, 109–13; and Hol'-low/He-le'jah sites, 186–87, 217
material shortages, lithic, 201, 206, 218
matrilineal social organization, 226, 228–30, 314n4
Mazel, David, 311–12nn3,4
McDougal, John, 53
measles, 7, 61, 65, 67, 104, 116, 137, 310nn2,7
medicinal plants, 104–5
medicine men, 61–62, 69, 105, 164, 288
memory culture, 42–46, 50–51, 82, 113, 299, 312nn8,9
Mendoza, Juan Domínguez de, 258
menstrual huts, 100
Merced River, 37, 41, 54–60, 70, 72–73, 76, 88, 93, 95–97, 100, 317–18n12
Merced River canyon, 38, 56, 58–59, 81, 84, 102
Merced River watershed, 43, 86–87, 89–92, 96
Merriam, C. Hart, 43–45, 76, 91, 99–100, 103, 145, 317nn3,7,10
Mesoamerica, 239, 245
metal objects, 13, 166, 187–88, 207, 217, 253, 269, 286
Mew'-ko peoples, 91
Me'-wuk language groups, 44, 312nn7,8; and Awahnichi cultural affiliation, 86–87, 90–93, 313nn1,2; changes in daily practice of, 163–64, 176; diet of, 105–9, 107; group/household structure of, 94–98, 145, 150, 163–64, 314nn3,4; immigration of, 139, 145, 210; material culture of, 105–9; and projectile-point serration, 202; spiritual life and ceremonies of, 103–5; village life of, 98–103, 101
Me'-wuk legends, 92–93
Mexican government, 71–72
Mexicans, 19, 69, 71, 96
microscale observations, 175–76, 178–80, 216–17
middle Missouri River peoples, 223, 223, 266–71, 267, 280–81
migration/emigration/immigration, 28, 86, 286, 288–92; and aggregation, 157–

migration *(continued)*
63, 179; and changes in daily practice, 157–65, 167, 170–71, 179; and Choctaws (interior Southeast), 246–49; and creolization/ethnogenesis, 161–64; and demographic archaeological study, 117, 120; and Eastern Prairie communities, 223, 262, 264–65; and Hol'-low/He-le'jah sites, 182, 198, 203, 209, 217; and Iroquoian tribes, 226–29, 231; and middle Missouri River peoples, 268; and Natchez (interior Southeast), 250, 252, 254, 292; and Salishan-speaking peoples, 273; and significance of colonial-era depopulation, 135, 139–40, 142, 145, 152–53, 155; and Siouan peoples, 234–36; and Upper Creeks (interior Southeast), 240–44

militias, 20, 32, 53. *See also* Mariposa Battalion

Milliken, Randall, 67, 313n8

milling features/tools: and archaeological methodology, 47; and Awahnichi cultural affiliation, 84–87, 90; and daily life/culture, 108, 111; and demographic archaeological study, 121, 124, 130; and Hol'-low/He-le'jah sites, 188–89, 206, 216–17; and occupational history of villages, 212

miners/mining, 26, 115, 287; and changes in daily practice, 180, 183; Clark as, 41; and colonial encounters, 53–54, 59, 70, 72–73; and daily life/culture, 27, 81, 95, 100, 106, 111; and "Mariposa Indian War," 34, 95; Perlot as, 36–37, 60

missionaries. *See* French missionaries; Jesuit missionaries; Spanish missions

mission neophytes, 19, 65, 70, 202

Mission San Francisco, 67–68

Mission Santa Clara, 67–68

Mississippian culture, 237, 242, 246, 248, 251–53, 262, 290, 318n8

"Mississippian Decline," 242

Miwokan language, 91, 164

Miwok language group, 16, 18, 40, 43–45, 69, 312n7, 313n8; and Awahnichi cultural affiliation, 82, 90–92, 94, 112, 313n2; and changes in daily practice, 163–64. *See also names of specific Miwok language groups*

Mohawk, 225–31, 291, 318nn4–6

moieties, 97, 99, 113, 116, 150, 248

Monacans, 232, 235–36

Monache, 164, 314nn3,4

Mono Basin, 160, 163–64, 176, 182, 189, 202, 205–6, 215

Mono Craters obsidian source, 87, 88, 189, 204–6, 205

Mono Glass Mountain obsidian source, 89, 204

Mono Lake, 59, 61, 111, 160

Monongahela, 318n7

Mono Paiute: Bunnell's account of, 35; and colonial encounters, 59, 61, 69, 78; and daily life/culture, 96, 102, 108, 112, 291; and changes in daily practice, 163–64; and Hol'-low/He-le'jah sites, 176, 188–89, 217; and occupational history of villages, 215

Monterey Presidio District, 18

Moore, Tredwell, 59, 99

Moraga, Gabriel, 70

Moratto, Michael J., 84, 86, 91

morbidity rates, 7–8, 310n3

Morgan, Kenneth, 148–51

mortality rates, 7–8, 28, 77, 310nn2,3; and changes in daily practice, 157–58; and demographic archaeological study, 115–16, 120, 136–37, *137*; and interior Southeast societies, 240–41, 248, 257; and Iroquoian tribes, 229–30, 292; and middle Missouri River peoples, 270; and significance of colonial-era depopulation, 135, 139–40, 142–50, *143*, 153, 316nn1–4; and Siouan peoples, 234–35

mortars: and Awahnichi cultural affiliation, 86–87, 90; Bunnell's account of, 77; and daily life/culture, 100, *107*, 108, 112; and Hol'-low/He-le'jah sites, 181–84, 188, 203, 208; and Sap-pah'-sam-mah village, 317n10

mortuary customs/populations, 118, 142, 147; and cross-cultural comparisons, 231, 232–33, 246, 248, 257. *See also* burial practices/records; cemeteries; funeral rites

Moscoso, Luis de, 254

mound construction, 236, 239, 292; and Caddo (interior Southeast), 255, 257–58; and Choctaws (interior Southeast), 246; and Eastern Prairie communities, 263; and Natchez (interior Southeast), 250–52; and Siouan peoples, 235, 318n8; and Upper Creeks (interior Southeast), 239–41, 243

Moundville culture, 242, 246–47, 249, 290, 293

Mount Hicks obsidian source, 89, 204, 205

mourning ceremonies, 104, 113–14

Muir, John, 39, 100

mules, 53, 106

Index

multiethnic households/groups: and Awahnichi cultural affiliations, 92; and changes in daily practice, 162–64, 172, 178; and Eastern Prairie communities, 264; and Hol'-low/He-le'jah sites, 182, 188–89, 217
multifamily residential units, 271–72, 277
musical instruments, 109
Muskogean-speaking people, 238–39, 247
Muybridge, Eadweard, 81
myths, 32, 40, 44, 82, 90, 92–93, 105, 110, 112, 114

nadir population size, 136–38, 149, 272–73, 316n5
Narváez, Pánfilo de, 245, 258, 319n15
Nassau, Fort, 224, 318n2
Natchez people and Yazoo Basin neighbors, 238, 240, 248, 249–54, 290, 292
National Park Service, 46–47, 214
Nation du Neutre (Neutral Iroquois), 227
natural disasters, 12, 21, 152
natural history literature, 39, 41
naturalists, 26, 39, 76
natural resources, 284; and changes in daily practice, 162, 165–66, 174, 177; and cross-cultural comparisons, 224, 226, 273, 275; and daily life/culture, 95
Navajo, 150
nena. See patrilineal joint families
Nevada Fall (Yo-wy-we-ack), 93
Newson, Linda A., 310n4
Nilsson, Elena, 213, 317n9
Niza, Marcos de, Fray, 277
"noble savage," 34–35, 38, 42
nonnative goods, 13, 29, 52, 286, 291; and changes in daily practice, 165, 169, 171, 176, 178–79; and daily life/culture, 113–14; and Eastern Prairie communities, 262, 264, 266; and Hol'-low/He-le'jah sites, 187–88, 198, 203, 206–7, 217–18; and interior Southeast societies, 236–37, 241, 251–53, 256–58; and middle Missouri River peoples, 269; and Puebloan peoples, 275; and Salishan-speaking peoples, 272
Northern Sierra Me'-wuk groups, 91–92, 96
notching flakes, 175, 199
Nutchu, 57–58, 73, 78, 96, 102

obsidian hydration dating: and archaeological methodology, 48–49, 51–52; and Awahnichi cultural affiliation, 83,

367

89; and changes in daily practice, 176–77; and demographic archaeological study, 118, 125–29, 132, 315nn7–14; and Hol'-low/He-le'jah sites, 205; and "no visible hydration" data, 126–28, 137–38, 141; and occupational history of villages, 209–13, 211, 317n9; and significance of colonial-era depopulation, 137–38, 141; temperature influence on, 126–27, 315nn7–9
obsidian quarry sources, 87, 88–89, 120–21, 123–26, 204–6, 205
obsidian tools: and Awahnichi cultural affiliation, 84–89; and changes in daily practice, 166–67, 176–77, 179; and daily life/culture, 110–12; and demographic archaeological study, 120–32, 314n4; and Hol'-low/He-le'jah sites, 181–82, 185, 199–200, 203–7, 205, 217–18
Occaneechi, 232, 234, 236
occupational histories, 26, 29, 49, 84; and changes in daily practice, 159–60; and cross-cultural comparisons, 226, 262, 264; and demographic archaeological study, 119–23, 130, 316n17; and Hol'-low/He-le'jah sites, 206; of villages, 209–16, 211, 217nn1–10, 218. *See also* settlement patterns
Ohlone (Costanoan) language group, 65, 313n8
Okfuskee, 239
Olivella shell beads, 85, 87, 207–8
Oñate, Juan de, 277
Oneida, 227, 229
Oneota culture, 262–63
Onondaga, 227, 230–31, 281, 291–92, 294
oral traditions, 2–3, 6, 12–13, 15, 19–20, 22–28, 50–51, 56, 283, 287, 298; and Awahnichi cultural affiliation, 79–80, 82, 152; and black sickness, 67, 76–77; and changes in daily practice, 175, 180; of Chief Tenaya, 31–32, 311nn1,2; and cross-cultural comparisons, 220–22, 243, 245–47, 249–51, 268, 274, 280–82, 289, 295; and daily life/culture, 95, 114; and demographic archaeological study, 117; and Hol'-low/He-le'jah sites, 206; and memory culture, 46
Orange, Fort, 318n2
organic material, paucity of, 48, 118, 175; and Awahnichi cultural affiliation, 80, 83, 89–90; and Hol'-low/He-le'jah sites, 183, 189, 192, 196, 216
origin myths, 92–93
ornamental objects, 13, 286; and Awahn

ornamental objects *(continued)*
  ichi cultural affiliation, 85–87; and changes in daily practice, 166, 169, 177; and cross-cultural comparisons, 228, 253; and daily life/culture, 109–12; and Hol'-low/He-le'jah sites, 182, 194, 195, 198, 207–9, 218; and occupational history of villages, 212–13
osteological data, 270, 278
Ouachita River valley, 257, 260
Overland Monthly, 40
overshot flakes, 199–200
Owsley, Douglas W., 270

"Pafalaya" people, 247
Paiute, 59, 61, 69, 88, 90, 95, 98, 163–64, 189, 313n1. *See also* Mono Paiute
paleodemographic studies, 118, 144
palisades, 232–33, 241, 265–66, 268
Palkovich, Ann M., 278–80
pandemics, 8–9, 30, 68, 135, 241, 270, 280, 295, 310n8. *See also* epidemics; infectious diseases
Panoche de San Juan y de los Carrisolitos, 71
Panum Dome, 205
paramount chiefdoms, 236, 239, 281, 318–19n9
Pardo, Juan, 238, 241, 244
pathogens, 7–12, 21, 27, 77, 116, 157, 310nn3,7,8; and black sickness, 64–65, 67–68; and cross-cultural comparisons, 220, 231, 234, 260, 272, 278–79, 295; and significance of colonial-era depopulation, 135, 146, 149. *See also* infectious diseases
patrilineal joint families *(nena)*, 94–98, 104, 113, 314nn3,4
patrilocality, 98, 164, 188, 217, 314n4
Patwin, 65
Penutian language stock, 91
Perlot, Jean-Nicolas, 46, 60, 73–74, 154, 313n1, 314n5; personal memoirs of, 36–38, 81–82, 287, 312n6; views on native daily life/culture, 95–97, 99, 102, 105–6, 113
personal memoirs, 31–32, 38, 51; of Bunnell, 34, 67, 82; of Perlot, 36–38, 82, 287, 312n6
Perttula, Timothy K., 256–60, 319n16
photographers, 40–41, 81
photographs, historical, 100–103, 113, 127. *See also* visual records
pictographs, 88, 181, 269. *See also* rock-art production
Pima, 159
Pineda, Alonso Álvarez de, 245, 251, 258

pinyon pine nuts, 108
pithouses, 271, 275
Plains Miwok language group, 65, 90–92, 202
Plaquemine culture, 251–52, 254, 290
pneumonia, 68, 104, 137, 310n2
Pohonichi, 54, 57, 92, 94, 96
pollen stratigraphic studies, 88
polygyny, 97–100, 145
Ponwatchee, 54, 58, 78
population biology, 133
population collapse. *See* catastrophic depopulation; depopulation
population proxies: and cross-cultural comparisons, 253, 269, 272–74, 279, 319–20n17; and demographic archaeological study, 117, 119, 122, 130, 302–7. *See also* debitage proxy; proxy measures; subsite proxy
population rebound, 3, 9–11, 21, 28, 51, 116, 180, 289; and cross-cultural comparisons, 223, 231, 251, 253–54, 260, 264, 270, 273–74, 281, 295; and significance of colonial-era depopulation, 135–36, 138–40, 142, 149, 151–53
population size. *See* demographic change; *entries beginning with* population
porcupine, 189, 190
postdepopulation sites, 178–80. *See also* He-le'-jah site
pottery production, 243, 252, 268
Powell, John Wesley, 312n7
Powers, Stephen, 40–41, 75–76, 96–97, 102, 312n7
Powhatan, 233, 235
precontact times, 9, 13, 15–16, 23, 28, 30, 45, 48, 77, 221, 223, 223, 296, 310n8; and changes in daily practice, 171, 176; and daily life/culture, 102, 113; and Eastern Prairie communities, 261–62, 264–66; and historical narratives, 35, 40, 82; and interior Southeast societies, 241, 246, 250, 253, 258; and memory culture, 42–43, 46; and middle Missouri River peoples, 268–70; and Puebloan peoples, 275–79; and Salishan-speaking peoples, 271–75; in scenario for depopulation, 10–11, 135, 154–55, 284
predepopulation sites, 178–80. *See also* Hol'-low site
prehistoric periods, 83–91, 84, 121–22, 144, 252–53, 260, 272
"prehistory," 23, 82, 297
presidios, 18, 64–65, 260
Preston, William L., 67, 316n5
processing activities: and Awahnichi cul-

tural affiliation, 86–87; and changes in daily practice, 173–74; and daily life/culture, 107; and Hol'-low/He-le'jah sites, 184, 186–89, 192–94, 196–97, 217
processual archaeology, 47
procurement activities, 16, 78, 111, 173; and demographic archaeological study, 123, 126; and Hol'-low/He-le'jah sites, 181, 187, 189, 192–93. *See also* exchange; hunting; trade relations
profane ceremonies, 103–4. *See also* ceremonial life
projectile points, 286; and Awahnichi cultural affiliation, 84–90, 112; Cottonwood Triangular, *85*, 87, 200, 202; and cross-cultural comparisons, 256, 272; and demographic archaeological study, 122–23; Desert Side-Notched, 87–88, 199–203, 202, 206, 208; Elko Corner-Notched, 85, *85*; and Hol'-low/He-le'jah sites, 182–87, *184*, *185*, 189, *195*, *196*, 198–203, 202, 205–6, 208; serrated, 201–3, 202, 206, 208; serrate Desert Side-Notched, 201–3, 202, 206; Sierra Concave Base, 85–86, *85*, 89; Stockton Serrate, 202–3
Prospect Ridge subsource, 204
protohistoric period, 176, 189, 253–54, 309–10n1
Protohistoric period (A.D. 1500–1683), 256–60
Protohistoric period (A.D. 1800–1847), 84, 113
proxy measures: causes of covariation in, 129–33, *132*, 315nn15,16, 316n17; and cross-cultural comparisons, 272–74, 279, 319–20n17; and demographic archaeological study, 117–33, 285, 302–7, 315nn12,13; sampling strategies for, 118–21, 124–29, 131–32, 315nn12,13; and significance of colonial-era depopulation, 136–41, *137*, *138*, 145–46; temporal scale of, 118–19, 123–24, 127–29, 315nn9–14
Puebloan peoples, 223, *223*, 275–80, 276
Pueblo Revolt (A.D. 1680), 277, 279
pueblos, 18, 65, 277
pumice, 109, 111, 188–89, 206, 317n3

Queen (Truman Meadows) obsidian source, 89, 204, *205*
Quigualtam, 250–51
Quizquiz, 250

rabbit, 106, 109, 111, 189–92, *190–91*, 196

radiocarbon dating, 13, 118, 127, 193, 298; and archaeological methodology, 46, 48, 51; and cross-cultural comparisons, 228, 252, 264–65, 269, 272, 274, 276
Ramenofsky, Ann F., 252–54, 269, 278–79, 310nn4,6–8, 318n5, 319–20n17
ranchos, 12, 71–72, 74, 296
Red River area, 258
Reff, Daniel T., 278–79
regional perspective, 20, 42, 281; and archaeological methodology, 47–49, 52; and Awahnichi people, 83, 90–91, 112; and Caddo (interior Southeast), 258–59; and changes in daily practice, 157, 159–61, 163, 165–67, 170–71, 175–80, 316–17n4; and demographic archaeological study, 116, 118–19, 121–25, 130–33; and Eastern Prairie communities, 264–66; and Hol'-low/He-le'jah sites, 203–9, *205*, 217–18; and middle Missouri River peoples, 268–69; and Natchez (interior Southeast), 252–54; and occupational history of villages, 209–16, 211, 218; and Puebloan peoples, 275–78; and Salishan-speaking peoples, 272–75; and significance of colonial-era depopulation, 30, 146; and Siouan peoples, 235–36; and Upper Creeks (interior Southeast), 239, 241, 243, 245
Reilly, J. J., 81
reiterative use of sites, 161, 172–73, 176, 179, 209–10
remarriage, 97, 150–51
residential mobility, 4, 10, 22, 84, 86, 121, 130–31, 269, 273, 293
residential patterns. *See* occupational histories; settlement patterns
Reynolds, Richard Dwan, 214
rituals, 10, 103–5, 230. *See also* ceremonial life
Roanoke Island colony, 233
roasting pits, 234
rock-art production, 88, 90, 181
rock-cairn burials, 235
rockshelters, 182–83, 188, 192–94; and occupational history of villages, 211, 213, 216–18; old Indian woman found in, 56–57, 63, 213
rodent activity, 49, 83, 173
Rodriquez, Augustín, 277
romanticism, 34–35, 42
room counts, 118, 277–78
Rose Spring Corner-Notched projectile points, 86–88
Ross, Colony, 16, 17, 18

round house. *See* assembly house (*hange'-e*)
Rubertone, Patricia E., 299
Russian mercantile colonies, 16, 17, 18–19

sacred ceremonies, 103. *See also* ceremonial life
Salinan language group, 18
Salishan-speaking peoples, 223, 223, 271–75, 280, 319–20n17
salt production, 109, 111, 256, 259
sampling strategies, 177, 289; and cross-cultural comparisons, 222, 253, 257, 264–65, 269, 318n5; and demographic archaeological study, 118–21, 124–29, 131–32, 137, 315nn12,13; and Hol'-low/He-le'jah sites, 197, 203, 216; and occupational history of villages, 210, 212, 214, 216, 317–18n12
Sap-pah'-sam-mah village, 213, 317n10
Sasso, Robert F., 264–65
Savage, James D., 26, 53–55, 57, 59, 62, 69, 72–73, 96, 164, 311n2, 313n3
Sawmill Ridge subsource, 204
scaffolds, drying (*he-wa'-ah*), 100
scarlet fever, 7, 68, 310n7
scavenging, 49; and Awahnichi cultural affiliations, 83, 89; and demographic archaeological study, 120, 122, 124, 126–28; and Hol'-low/He-le'jah sites, 184, 206–7
Scipiano, 60, 95, 108, 154
seasonal environments: and cross-cultural comparisons, 264–65, 269; and daily life/culture, 99–102; and demographic archaeological study, 121, 123–24, 130; and Hol'-low/He-le'jah sites, 181–82, 188, 192, 197, 206, 213, 216–18; and occupational history of villages, 213, 215–16, 218; and Salishan-speaking peoples, 271–72
second waves of disease, 65, 251, 259
sedentary groups, 118, 130, 268, 275, 281
seed beaters, 106, 110
Seneca, 225, 227, 318n7
Sentinel Rock (Loya), 93
serrated projectile points, 201–3, 202, 206, 208
Sessapahaw, 232
settlement patterns, 3, 5, 9–10, 14, 27, 30, 51, 286–87, 291, 293; and archaeological methodology, 47; and Awahnichi cultural affiliation, 80, 83–84, 86, 88, 90; and Caddo (interior Southeast), 255–56, 258–60; and changes in daily practice, 158–61, 163, 171–72, 176–79; and Choctaws (interior Southeast), 246, 290; and daily life/culture, 94, 98–99, 112–13; and demographic archaeological study, 115, 118–24, 130–32; and Eastern Prairie communities, 262, 264–66; and Iroquoian tribes, 226–27, 229–31, 243; and middle Missouri River peoples, 268–70; and Natchez (interior Southeast), 252; and Puebloan peoples, 275–77, 280; of reoccupied villages, 183, 209–16, 211, 217nn1–10, 218; and Salishan-speaking peoples, 271, 273–74; and Siouan peoples, 232–35; and Upper Creeks (interior Southeast), 240–41, 243, 319n13
shaft burials, 255, 258. *See also* burial practices
shamanism, 104–5, 113
sheep, 89, 105–6
shell beads and ornaments: and Awahnichi cultural affiliations, 85–87; and changes in daily practice, 166, 169, 177; and daily life/culture, 109–12; and Hol'-low/He-le'jah sites, 182, 194, 207–9, 317n6; and Salishan-speaking peoples, 272, 319–20n17
Sierra Concave Base projectile points, 85–86, 85, 89
Sierra Miwok language groups, 82, 88, 90–92, 96–97, 103, 105, 314nn3,4
Silliman, Stephen W., 320n1
simplification of social structure, 157, 169–70, 173, 179, 246, 276
Simpson, Lesley Byrd, 319n10
simulation studies, demographic, 147–51, 154, 158–59, 260
Sinclair, Anthony, 174–75
Sinkayuse, 271
Siouan peoples, 223, 223, 231–36, 232, 261, 263, 268, 291–93, 318n8
site counts, 253
site-specific data, 29; and changes in daily practice, 170–71, 179; and demographic archaeological study, 118, 123–24, 132; and Hol'-low/He-le'jah sites, 203; and occupational history of villages, 209–12; and significance of colonial-era depopulation, 141
slave raids/trade, 235, 242, 244, 247–49, 280, 293–94, 319n13
smallpox, 7, 61, 65, 67–68, 116, 137, 149–50, 310nn2,7; and cross-cultural comparisons, 229, 257, 267, 272–74, 318n7
Smith, Jedediah, 70
Smith, Marvin T., 240–41, 244, 257, 319n13

Index

Smithsonian Institution, 36, 311n3
Snow, Dean R., 227–29, 318nn4,5
soapstone. *See* steatite objects
social structure, 5, 10, 295; and changes in daily practice, 157, 169–73, 175, 178; despecialization/simplification of, 157, 169–71, 173, 179, 246. *See also* household/group structure
Solnit, Rebecca, 38, 311–12nn3,4
Soo-sem'-moo-lah village, 189, 317n3
Sosa, Gaspar Castaño de, 277
Soto, Hernando de, 238–39, 254. *See also* Soto *entrada*
Soto *entrada*, 241–45, 247, 249–51, 253–56, 258, 319nn12,14
Soule, J. P., 81
Southern Sierra Me'-wuk groups, 90–92, 97, 139, 202, 314nn3,4
Spanish colonists/explorers, 4, 17, 18–20; and Caddo (interior Southeast), 257–59; and changes in daily practice, 166; and Chief Tenaya, 61–62, 69; and Choctaws (interior Southeast), 245, 247, 249; and colonial encounters, 61–62, 69–72, 77, 79; and daily life/culture, 96, 106, 108; and Hol'-low/He-le'jah sites, 29, 203, 207; and Natchez (interior Southeast), 250, 253; and Puebloan peoples, 277–79; and Salishan-speaking peoples, 274; and Siouan peoples, 231; and Upper Creeks, 239–42, 244. *See also* colonial era; Spanish missions
Spanish missions, 4, 12, 16, 17, 18–19, 296; and Awahnichi cultural affiliation, 92; and black sickness, 62, 64–65, 67–69; and colonial encounters, 62, 72, 313n8; and cross-cultural comparisons, 221, 233, 237, 242, 244–45, 253, 260, 277; and demographic archaeological study, 117; and Hol'-low/He-le'jah sites, 207; and native spiritual life/ceremonies, 105; neophytes fleeing from, 19, 65, 70, 202; secularization of (1834), 18–19, 51, 71. *See also names of missions*
spatulate utensil, 186
specialist production, 5, 286–87; and changes in daily practice, 165, 168–70, 175, 178; and daily life/culture, 111; and demographic archaeological study, 122–23, 131; and Hol'-low/He-le'jah sites, 183, 186–87, 197–203, 217–18; and interior Southeast societies, 246. *See also* despecialization
spiritual life, 103–5, 314n5
squirrel, 106, 190, 192

steatite objects, 87, 110–12, 181, 194, 195, 198, 218
stochastic processes, 14, 28, 148–49, 151, 169, 171, 179, 201
Stockton Serrate projectile points, 202–3
stone tools, 286; and archaeological methodology, 47–49, 52; and Awahnichi cultural affiliations, 83–85, 87–91; and changes in daily practice, 166–67, 175, 179; and daily life/culture, 100, 110–11; and demographic archaeological study, 120–32; and Hol'-low/He-le'jah sites, 181–89, *184, 185, 187,* 192–207, *194, 195, 196, 202,* 217–18
storage facilities, 100–101, 108–10, 122, 130, 183, 207, 234
strategic marriage, 95
stratigraphic excavations, 47–48
subsistence practices, 5, 27, 73, 291, 293; and archaeological methodology, 47; and Awahnichi cultural affiliations, 80, 83, 89–90; and changes in daily practice, 158, 160–61, 163, 166, 174–75; and daily life/culture, 105–9; and demographic archaeological study, 120–23; and Eastern Prairie communities, 264–65; and Hol'-low/He-le'jah sites, 189–92, *190–91;* and interior Southeast societies, 246, 248, 252, 254, 290; and Iroquoian tribes, 227, 229, 231; and Puebloan peoples, 275; and Salishan-speaking peoples, 271, 274; and significance of colonial-era depopulation, 146, 153–54; and Siouan peoples, 233–34, 318n8
subsite proxy: and demographic archaeological study, 119–22, 124–25, 127–32, *132,* 302–7, 314n3, 315nn12,13, 316n17; and occupational history of villages, 209–13, *211,* 317–18n12; and significance of colonial-era depopulation, 137, 141
Sundstrom, Linea, 269–70
survival, biological/cultural, 1–2, 4, 12, 30; and changes in daily practice, 156–58, 165, 167–71; of colonial encounters, 20–23, 32, 60–62, 65, 69, 72, 78–79; and cross-cultural comparisons, 220, 233–34, 251, 267, 282, 291, 293; and Hol'-low/He-le'jah sites, 182; and significance of colonial-era depopulation, 139, 151–54
Susquehannock, 225, 318n7
Sutter's Fort, 71
sweathouses *(chap-poo'),* 100, 103, 113
swine, 242, 319n14

Taber, Isaiah West, 81
Takic language group, 18
Talisi, 243–44
Tallapoosa, 239
talwa (town group), 239
Tascaloosa, 244
task-specific logistical sites, 86, 100, 121–22
tattoos, 111
-tcī suffix, 92, 112
technologies, 1, 286; and archaeological methodology, 47; and Awahnichi cultural affiliation, 27, 80, 83–89; and changes in daily practice, 160, 169–70, 174–75, 177; and cross-cultural comparisons, 231, 234, 265, 291; and daily life/culture, 106–13; and demographic archaeological study, 121–25, 128, 130; and Hol'-low/He-le'jah sites, 183–88, *184, 185, 187,* 197–206. *See also* weapons technology
temporal scale, 26, 50–52, 298–99; and Awahnichi cultural affiliations, 82–84, *84;* and changes in daily practice, 168–69, 171, 176, 177–80; and cross-cultural comparisons, 222, 269, 272, 275, 297; and demographic archaeological study, 118–19, 123–24, 127–30, 315nn9–14, 316n17; and Hol'-low/He-le'jah sites, 205; and occupational history of villages, 209–11, *211. See also* chronological control
Tenaya, Chief, 26, 54–55, 57–64, 67–70, 77–78, 104, 149–50; age of, 62–64; and changes in daily practice, 160–61, 163–64, 177; as charismatic leader, 288–89; death of, 35, 59, 313n4; and group/household structure, 95–96, 98–99, 145, 314n3; historical narrative of, 31–36, 115, 311nn1,2; as linguist, 62, 69, 92, 164; and occupational history of villages, 209, 215–16
textiles, 187–88, 217
thermoluminescence dates, 264, 277
Thornton, Russell, 149–50, 319n16
timing of depopulation, 3, 8–10, 14–15, 283, 298–99; and colonial encounters, 19–20, 24–25, 27, 49, 76–77; and cross-cultural comparisons, 29, 223, 235–36, 247, 256–57, 264–65, 271, 273; and demographic archaeological study, 115, 133. *See also* chronological control; diachronic trends; temporal scale
Tionontate (Petun), 227–28, 230–31, 281, 293
Tis-sa'ack, 110, 152
tobacco, 109

tool sharing, 130–31
total fertility rate (TFR), 143–46, *143.* *See also* fertility rates
To-too-yah. *See* Ydrte, Maria Lebrado
tourism, 41, 73–74, 76, 78, 110, 287
trade relations, 3–4, 8, 19, 65, 67, 286, 293–94; archaeological evidence of, 83, 85–86, *87,* 88; and Caddo (interior Southeast), 256, 258–60; and changes in daily practice, 166, 177; and Choctaws (interior Southeast), 245, 247; and daily life/culture, 111–12, 114, 116; and Eastern Prairie communities, 261, 265; and Hol'-low/He-le'jah sites, 181–82, 207–9, 218; and Iroquoian tribes, 224–26, 228–30; and middle Missouri River peoples, 266, 269–70; and Natchez (interior Southeast), 250, 253; and Puebloan peoples, 275, 278; and Salishan-speaking peoples, 272; and Siouan peoples, 233, 235; and Upper Creeks (interior Southeast), 241–45, 319n13. *See also* exchange
trading posts, 12, 33, 53–54, 72–73, 111; and cross-cultural comparisons, 225, 233, 247, 249, 260–61, 296
traditional knowledge, 10, 20–22, 30, 61, 74–76, 78, 286; and changes in daily practice, 167–68, 172–75, 177; and cross-cultural comparisons, 220; and memory culture, 42–43, 46
traditional leaders, 22, 26, 31–32, 61, 288–89; and cross-cultural comparisons, 221, 282, 292, 297. *See also* Tenaya, Chief
travelers, 27, 39–41, 81
travel literature, 39, 41, 49
treaties, 36, 54, 60, 312n5, 313n5
Treaty of Camp Fremont (March 19, 1851), 313n5
tree-ring data. *See* dendrochronology
tribelets, 66, 310–11n9, 313n8; and changes in daily practice, 159, 170, 101. *See also names of tribelets*
tribes, 5, 22, 166, 233, 237, 239–40, 245–47, 263. *See also names of tribes*
Tribes of California (Powers), 40
tuberculosis, 9
Tunican speakers, 250, 252
Tuolumne Meadows, 85, 100
Tuolumne Me'-wuk people, 96
Tuolumne River, 70, 88, 95, 100
Tuolumne River watershed, 87, 90–91, 95
turquoise, 256
Tuscarora, 318n3
typhus, 7, 68, 310n2

Ubelaker, Douglas H., 310n8
uncleanliness, perceived, 49
University of California, Berkeley, 44, 46
Upham, Steadman, 278–79
Upper Creeks of interior Southeast, 158, 238, 239–45, 240, 249, 291, 294
urn burial, 246
Ursua, Julian, 71
use-life, 118, 175
use-wear, 186–87, 187, 194
Utian language stock, 91

Vanishing American trope, 34–36, 38, 42, 50
vegetal materials, 80, 85, 87, 109–11, 188–89, 196, 234. See also faunal and floral assemblages
venereal disease, 9, 104
Vernal Fall (Yan-o-pah), 93
villages, 5, 73, 76, 86, 141, 286, 291, 293–94; and changes in daily practice, 158, 160, 163, 176, 179; and daily life/culture, 96–103, 113; and demographic archaeological study, 115, 119–23, 314n3; and Eastern Prairie communities, 262, 265; and interior Southeast societies, 237, 243–44, 247; and Iroquoian tribes, 226, 228–29, 318n6; and middle Missouri River peoples, 266–70; occupational histories of, 189, 210–13, 317n3, 317nn1–3,7–10; and Salishan-speaking peoples, 271; and Siouan peoples, 233–35. See also He-le'-jah site; Hol'-low site
violence, 23, 34–35, 53–54, 59, 72–73, 86, 115, 166, 287; and cross-cultural comparisons, 244, 247, 268–71, 277, 290, 293; and daily life/culture, 94–95, 113; and significance of colonial-era depopulation, 135, 138, 144, 149. See also aggression; warfare
"virgin soil" epidemics, 9, 137, 149, 241
vision quests, 104
visual records, 24–25, 31, 39–40, 74, 81, 100–103, 113, 127, 266
volcanic activity, 205–6

Walker, Joseph, 70, 72
Ward, H. Trawick, 233
warfare: and black sickness, 61–62, 313n7; and colonial encounters, 11, 34, 41, 54, 60, 76–78, 316n3; and changes in daily practice, 158, 165–66; and daily life/culture, 94–95, 104; and demographic archaeological study, 115, 314n1; and interior Southeast societies, 242–43, 319n13; and Iroquoian tribes, 224–30; and middle Missouri River peoples, 271; and Puebloan peoples, 279; and Salishan-speaking peoples, 274. See also aggression; violence
Warrick, Gary, 228
Watkins, Carleton, 81
Wawona basin, 41, 47, 54, 73–74, 102
weapons technology, 22, 84–91, 85, 187
Weber, Charles, 71
Weed, C. L., 81
Wenatchee, 271
Wendat (Huron), 224, 227–29
Western Miwok language group, 91–92
Western Mono, 69, 88
Western Pueblos, 276, 278. See also Puebloan peoples
We'-sum-meh' village, 210, 317n7
Whitney, Joseph, 39, 94
whooping cough, 7
Woodland period, 232, 234, 236, 268, 318n8

X-ray fluorescence analysis, 177, 203–4

Yanamamo, 144
Yazoo Basin, 238, 240, 246, 249–54
Ydrte, Maria Lebrado (To-too-yah), 62, 97
Yelland, Raymond Dabb, 81
Yokuts, 65, 69, 86, 92, 207, 313nn1,8, 314nn3,4
Yosemite Indians, 25–30, 283, 288, 299–300; anthropological perspectives on, 42–46, 50–51, 82; and archaeological methodology, 46–49; as Awahnichi descendants, 27, 60–65, 67–69, 73, 76, 79–80, 93–94, 112, 313n6; and changes in daily practice, 156–57, 160, 162–63, 166, 169–77, 180, 316–17n4; colonial encounters of, 2–4, 20–25, 31–42, 54–60, 77–79, 82; and cross-cultural comparisons, 140–45, 143, 221–24, 271, 280–81, 293–95, 297, 316n1; daily life and culture of, 96–114, 101, 107, 314nn3–5; and demographic archaeological study, 115–34; diet of, 105–9, 107; group/household structure of, 94–98, 314n3; in historical narratives, 31–42, 49–50; and Hol'-low/He-le'jah sites, 182–83, 188–89, 197–98, 218–19; material culture of, 109–12; naming of, 62, 69, 73; and occupational history of villages, 209–16, 211, 218; origin myths of, 92–93; and significance of colonial-era depopulation, 135–55, 137, 138, 143, 316nn1–5; and simulation studies of

Yosemite Indians *(continued)*
depopulation, 147–51, 154, 158–59; spiritual life and ceremonies of, 103–5; village life of, 98–103, *101*. *See also* Awahnichi

Yosemite National Park, 47, 313n1

Yosemite Valley, *17*, *20*, 25–26, 29, 51, 286–87, 298–99; and Awahnichi cultural affiliation, 80–91, *84*, *87*, 313n2; black sickness in, 60–69, 76–77, 82, 91, 113, 115, 145, 150, 177, 221; changes in daily practice in, 157, 160–61, 163–66, 168–70, 173–80; colonial encounters in, 53–60, 56, 69–73, 77–78; daily life and culture in, 96–114, *101*, *107*, 314nn3–5; and demographic archaeological study, 115, 118–33, 137; exile from, 51, 63, 69, 105, 136, 149, 151–53, 160–61, 163, 166, 177, 182, 208–9, 215–16, 285, 287, 293; in Gold Rush era, 73–76; historical narratives of, 31, 33–35, 37, 39, 76, 311–12n4; and language groups, 91–94, 163–64; reoccupation of, 115, 119, 136, 161, 182, 209–13, 218, 286, 288, 293, 317n8; significance of colonial-era depopulation in, 137, 140–42, 149–54, 316n5; as state reserve (1864), 41. *See also* He-le'-jah site; Hol'-low site

Yuman-speaking peoples, 18

Zuni, 276–77

Text:	10/13 Sabon
Display:	Sabon
Cartographer:	Bill Nelson
Compositor:	BookMatters, Berkeley
Indexer:	Sharon Sweeney
Printer and binder:	Thomson-Shore, Inc.